GROUP PROCESSES

To *Amy, Jon, Kirsten* and *Lyn,*

Living testament to the fact that though
a group may change, its emotional significance
to its members can remain undiminished

GROUP PROCESSES

Dynamics within and between groups

SECOND EDITION

Rupert Brown
University of Kent

BLACKWELL
Publishers

Copyright © Rupert Brown 1988, 2000

The right of Rupert Brown to be identified as author of this work
has been asserted in accordance with the Copyright, Designs and
Patents Act 1988.

First published 1988
Reprinted 1989, 1990, 1992, 1993 (twice), 1994, 1995, 1996, 1997, 1998
Second edition published 2000

2 4 6 8 10 9 7 5 3 1

Blackwell Publishers Ltd
108 Cowley Road
Oxford OX4 1JF
UK

Blackwell Publishers Inc.
350 Main Street
Malden, Massachusetts 02148
USA

British Library Cataloguing in Publication Data

A CIP catalogue record for this book is available from the
British Library.

Library of Congress Cataloging-in-Publication Data

Brown, Rupert, 1950–
Group processes: dynamics within and between groups / Rupert
Brown. — 2nd ed.
p.   cm.
Includes bibliographical references and index.
ISBN 0–631–21852–1 (alk. paper). — ISBN 0–631–18496–1 (alk. paper)
1. Social groups.   2. Interpersonal relations.   3. Intergroup
relations.   I. Title.
HM131.B726   2000
302.3—dc21   99–37854
                                              CIP

Typeset in 10½ on 13 pt Palatino
by Graphicraft Limited, Hong Kong
Printed in Great Britain by MPG Books Ltd, Bodmin, Cornwall

This book is printed on acid-free paper

CONTENTS

FIGURES

TABLES

PREFACE

For some years now, at least in the industrialized West, groups have received rather a bad press. Football hooliganism, inner-city riots and protest demonstrations are frequently attributed to 'mob rule'; governments proclaim the virtues of individual enterprise and choice, and denigrate policies aimed at promoting social welfare and collective responsibility; newspaper editorials regularly blame industrial unrest on small groups of 'militants' coercing ordinary workers to take action against their wishes; collective bargaining is being replaced by private contract between employer and employee; the owner of a small business, battling against government bureaucracy, is championed, while a group of workers occupying a factory due for closure is ridiculed.

Within social psychology the picture is not much different. Even the most cursory survey of currently popular textbooks and the main scientific journals reveals that group processes receive very short shrift indeed compared to phenomena associated with dyadic or interpersonal relationships and – increasingly in recent years – individual cognitive processes (Steiner, 1986). Where group behaviour is discussed, considerable emphasis is often given to its negative or socially undesirable aspects – deindividuation, prejudice, social loafing and 'groupthink' – rather than the more positive aspects of team spirit, intergroup cooperation, group productivity and collective problem solving. Indeed, such is the concentration on the allegedly antisocial nature of groups that one commentator has been moved to suggest, only half-jokingly, that 'Humans would do better without groups' (Buys, 1978).

One of my intentions in writing – and rewriting – this book is to contribute to a reversal of this cultural and scientific bias against groups. This correction is necessary, I believe, both scientifically and politically, first because, as I hope will become evident, groups are an inescapable part of human existence. Like them or not, they simply are not going to go away. People grow up in groups, sometimes called families; they work in groups, as engine crews, design teams or hunting parties; they learn in groups; they play in groups, in a multitude of team games; they make decisions in groups, whether these be government committees, village councils or courtroom juries; and, of course, they also fight in groups, as street gangs, revolutionary cadres and national armies. In short, human beings are group beings. Thus, a social psychology that ignores or neglects the study of groups is unlikely to be of much assistance in helping to understand many important areas of human endeavour.

The second reason follows from the first. It seems to me that many of today's most pressing social problems involve groups of various kinds. The control of environmental pollution demands not only nationally agreed policies on waste disposal and gas emissions but international collaboration as well; the protection of children from abuse or neglect requires the collective diagnostic skills of medical and social work professionals as well as sensitive intervention work with the families concerned; the growing threat of racism may well need a greater awareness among different ethnic minorities of their common oppression and the development by them of political strategies to bring about long overdue social change; and, above all, the persistence of international conflicts around the world in an age of nuclear weaponry urgently necessitates better methods of resolving or avoiding such conflicts and underlies the importance of finding ways to abandon the arms race. In all these examples we are concerned with people's behaviour as group members, towards both those in their own group and those belonging to other groups. It follows, then, that if social psychology is to make even the smallest contribution to the resolution of these problems it will come not from the insights derived from a psychology of the isolated individual but from the informed application of our knowledge of group processes.

Now a few words on how I have chosen to present this book. Let me straight away warn any readers looking for the exposition of a single conceptual framework that they will be disappointed. I have been deliberately eclectic in the theoretical approaches I have espoused. This is for both intellectual and pedagogic reasons – intellectual because I have come to the conclusion, after more than twenty years of researching into and teaching group processes, that there is no one theory that can do justice to the complexities of intra- and intergroup behaviour. To be sure, some theories are more useful than others – and in this book I have not hesitated to point up the weaknesses of those perspectives that seem theoretically ill conceived or empirically unfounded – but ultimately it seems to me that for a half-decent explanation of most group phenomena of interest we need to draw on the strengths of two or three *different* theoretical models. This implies that for teaching purposes it is equally inappropriate to present everything from just one point of view. For while there are obvious gains in theoretical continuity and coherence from such a monopolist strategy, these are, to my mind, outweighed by the value of exposing students to a variety of competing explanations. A pluralist approach like this is more likely to encourage them to make critical choices of their own, which, I believe, is a fundamental objective of the educative process.

If I have been eclectic in my choice of theories, I have been equally catholic in the range of empirical sources I have drawn on. In these pages will be found quantitative results from tightly controlled laboratory experiments and large-scale surveys, qualitative material from field interviews and participant observations, anecdotes from contemporary life and even the occasional literary allusion. Again, the pluralism is deliberate and is much influenced by the views of three of the founders of modern group psychology, Kurt Lewin, Muzafer Sherif and Henri Tajfel. Lewin was the originator of the phrase 'action research', a conception of scholarship in which theory and practice are inextricably linked. Theory, for Lewin, only had validity to the extent that it was effective in promoting social change: 'research which produces nothing but books will not suffice' (Lewin, 1948, p. 203). Sherif, too, was acutely conscious of the need to bridge the gap between academic research and social reality. As the creator of group psychology's most artificial – and yet deeply significant – laboratory experiment (Sherif, 1936; see chapter 2), and as the inspiration behind some of its classic naturalistic studies (Sherif, 1966; see chapter 6), he remains the most successful exponent of the coordinated use of field and laboratory methods. Tajfel had slightly different concerns. Ever impatient with methodological orthodoxy (he once remarked to me that an over concern with methodology was like packing your bags for a journey you never make), he was particularly keen to stress the importance of locating individuals, and the research findings they produce, in their social and cultural context. Theory and research that did not take account of the social system in which people lived were, for Tajfel, 'experiments [conducted] in a vacuum' (Tajfel, 1972). It was these dialectical views of theory and practice, laboratory experiment and field study, and social research and social context that dictated my choice of the kind of empirical work to feature most prominently in this book.

The fact that I have chosen to eschew theoretical and methodological singularity does not mean that there are no unifying themes running through the book. The most general of these is an assumption that dynamics *within* groups and dynamics *between* groups are closely related. For three decades after the War the study of 'group dynamics' was synonymous with the analysis of the inner workings of the small group. In the past two decades there has been a growing recognition of the significance of relations *between* groups in shaping people's behaviour (e.g. Turner and Giles, 1981; Worchel and Austin, 1986). However, as yet, there have been few concerted attempts to integrate these two areas of study (notable exceptions are the classic text by Sherif and Sherif (1969), the text by Turner et al. (1987) and Hogg and Abrams' (1988) treatment of group processes from a social identity perspective. Another of my aims, therefore, has been to demonstrate the connections between intra- and intergroup processes. Although in any one chapter there will be more emphasis on one aspect than the other, the close link between them is the dominant message of the book.

Subsumed within this general argument are three other recurring themes. The first is the idea that *groups are a source of social identity* for people. It has long been recognized that our group memberships contribute in a major way to our sense of who we are and of our place in the world. Indeed, this idea was central to the thinking of some of the earliest social psychologists (e.g. Mead, 1934). However, despite its early prominence, the concept of identity featured only sporadically in the work of those interested in groups (e.g. Lewin, 1948) and only recently has it been restored to its proper place at the heart of the study of group processes (Tajfel, 1978, 1982a; Turner et al., 1987). Most of these developments have been concerned with the implications of identity processes for intergroup behaviour in analyses of social conflict and prejudice. However, as I hope to show, several traditional topics in the study of group dynamics – e.g. deindividuation, group structure, social influence – may also be illuminated by an understanding of the role of social identification in group behaviour.

The second theme is the *distinction between task and socio-emotional orientations*. This is a widely held distinction between those aspects of group life that have to do with task performance and the achievement of group goals, and those that concern people's relationships with one another. The distinction originated in the pioneering work of Bales (1950), who believed that these two orientations were fundamental and opposed facets of all group processes. According to Bales, people in groups are basically concerned with achieving some task; to do this successfully they need to be sensitive to other group members' needs and motives; such interpersonal concern detracts from getting on with the job at hand and so there is a resurgence of task activity; and so it goes on. As we shall see, this basic distinction crops up in various different guises in the study of leadership, social influence and group productivity. It is thus a useful second theme with which to integrate research on groups.

The third theme is the *importance of social comparison processes*. Dominating the literature on small groups after the War was Festinger's (1954) theory of social comparisons. In this theory it was proposed that other people serve as vital reference points for the evaluation of our abilities and the validation of our opinions. This simple idea has been used extensively to analyse and understand a wide range of phenomena – for example, group formation and cohesion, status relations within groups, and conformity and polarization in group decision making. In recent years the importance of comparisons at the *inter*group level has also come to be recognized, particularly in relation to the causes of relative deprivation and the maintenance of social identity (Runciman, 1966; Tajfel and Turner, 1986). Thus, the idea of social comparison is one of the crucial links in demonstrating the relatedness of intra- and intergroup behaviour.

In chapter 1, I begin with the concept of the 'group' as it has developed in social psychology, and go on to establish the importance of groups as an aspect of identity and analyse behaviour in the crowd, one of the most basic forms of group. In chapter 2 some elementary group processes are considered. The most central of these is the tension between task and socio-emotional orientations. Other processes considered in this chapter are the consequences of joining a group, the effects of different forms of interdependence, group cohesion, and the acquisition and development of group norms. These group processes take place within an organized framework or group structure. The nature of that structure and its implications for group members are examined in chapter 3. Groups can be structured around roles, communication channels and, above all, status. The existence of status differences and their origin in and maintenance through social comparisons occupy most of the chapter. High status is sometimes formalized into positions of leadership, and that topic is also treated in chapter 3. In chapter 4, the discussion turns to processes of social influence in groups – the means by which uniformity in the group is attained or, alternatively, changes in group norms are brought about. Both majority and minority influences are examined. In chapter 5, I consider the age-old question of whether it is better to work alone or with others. Several areas of individual versus group productivity are reviewed, and the adequacy of current theories of group performance is assessed. A closely related topic, also considered in chapter 5, is group decision making.

In these five chapters the spotlight is mainly on the interior of the group, although intergroup factors are never completely absent. In chapter 6 the emphasis shifts towards people's behaviour towards members of groups other than their own when the situational determinants of intergroup conflict and cooperation are discussed. One of the more prominent individualistic accounts of prejudice – frustration–aggression theory – is criticized. An alternative explanation for social discontent in terms of relative deprivation is put forward as a preferred alternative. Then a more general approach, one that stresses the importance of objective relationships between groups, is discussed. The effects of such positive and negative interdependencies on intergroup attitudes are described. In chapter 7 I analyse the cognitive underpinnings of intergroup behaviour, particularly those that stem from social categorization, the foundation stone of intergroup relations. Associated with social categorization is a raft of judgmental biases, behavioural preferences and – importantly for the course of intergroup relationships – stereotyping processes. In the final chapter the focus remains on intergroup behaviour as I consider research suggesting that simply belonging to a group is enough to cause intergroup discrimination. One explanation for this finding is in terms of social identity processes. A central idea here is the importance for individuals of being able to see their group as positively distinct from other groups. The chapter concludes with a discussion of the implications of social identity processes for the reduction of intergroup discrimination and the establishment of genuinely pluralistic societies.

ACKNOWLEDGEMENTS

This book carries my name only on its cover but, like most intellectual creations, it is really a collective product. I would like here to acknowledge the help of those who have contributed to its completion, especially: Derek Rutter, who painstakingly read the whole first edition in draft form and who was a vital and constant source of encouragement from the start of the project all those years ago, and who has been a supportive colleague ever since; all my other colleagues, who shared with me the excitement, frustration and fun of conducting the collaborative research which finds its way into these pages – most notably, Dominic Abrams, Sabina Aharpour, Dora Capozza, Gabi Haeger, Karen Gardham, Miles Hewstone, Steve Hinkle, Lorella Lepore, Pam Maras, Jorg Middendorf, Bernd Simon, Ana Torres, Jim Vivian and Mia Yee. Finally, I realize it is rather unfashionable in an age of desktops, laptops and palmtops to admit to a preference to writing by hand. However, I take some comfort from the fact that I am at least in good company. I recently discovered that such wonderful writers as Roger Brown and Iris Murdoch also eschewed mechanical writing aids. Doubtless they, like me, had the assistance of superb secretarial support. In my case, I am indebted to Trudy Ellis and Tamsin Harris, who assisted immeasurably in the preparation of the manuscript.

Department of Psychology, University of Kent, May 1999

The author and publisher wish to thank the following for permission to reproduce copyright material:

Figure 2.2, from R.F. Bales, *Interaction Process Analysis* (1950), copyright © University of Chicago Press; figure 3.3, from F.E. Fiedler, 'A contingency model of leadership effectiveness', in L. Berkowitz (ed.), *Advances in Experimental Social Psychology*, vol. 1 (1965), with the permission of Academic Press; figure 5.1, from A.G. Ingham, G. Levinger, J. Graves and V. Peckham, 'The Ringelmann effect: studies of group size and group performance', *Journal of Experimental Social Psychology*, 10 (1974), 371–84, with the permission of Academic Press; figure 5.3, from S. Worchel, H. Rothgerber, E.A. Day, D. Hart and J. Butemeyer, 'Social identity and individual productivity within groups', *British Journal of Social Psychology*, 37 (1998), 389–413, © The British Psychological Society; figure 5.5, from E.B. Ebbesen and R.J. Bowers, 'Proportion of risky to conservative arguments in a group discussion and choice shifts', *Journal of Personality and Social Psychology*, 29 (1974), 316–27, copyright © 1974 by the American Psychological Association; figure 6.1, from M.D. Foster and K. Matheson, 'Double relative deprivation: combining the personal and political', *Personality and Social Psychology Bulletin*, 21 (1995), 1167–77, reprinted by permission of Sage Publications; figure 6.2, from M. Sherif, *Group Conflict and Cooperation* (1966), copyright © 1966 by Houghton Mifflin Company, Boston; table 7.1, from S.L. Gaertner, J. Mann, A. Murrell and J.F. Dovidio, 'Reducing intergroup bias: the benefits of recategorization', *Journal of Personality and Social Psychology*, 57 (1989), 239–49, copyright © 1989 by the APA; table 7.2, from L.F. Pendry and N. Macrae, 'What the disinterested perceiver overlooks: goal-directed social categorization', *Personality and Social Psychology Bulletin*, 22 (1996), 249–56, reprinted by permission of Sage Publications; figure 7.4, from J.W. Howard and M. Rothbart, 'Social categorization and memory for ingroup and outgroup behaviour', *Journal of Personality and Social Psychology*, 38 (1980), 301–10, copyright © 1980 by the APA; table 7.4, from D.L. Hamilton and T.L. Rose, 'Illusory correlation and the maintenance of stereotypic beliefs', *Journal of Personality and Social Psychology*, 39 (1980), 832–45; figure 7.5, from M. Chen and J.A. Bargh, 'Nonconscious behavioral confirmation processes; the self-fulfilling consequences of automatic stereotype activation', *Journal of Experimental Social Psycho-*

logy, 33 (1997), 541–60, with the permission of Academic Press; figure 8.3, from N. Ellemers, H. Wilke and A. van Knippenburg, 'Effects of the legitimacy of the low group or individual status as individual and collective status-enhancement strategies', *Journal of Personality and Social Psychology*, 64 (1993), 766–78, copyright © 1993 by the APA.

Every effort has been made to trace all the copyright holders, but if any have been inadvertently overlooked, the publisher will be pleased to make the necessary arrangements at the first opportunity.

1

THE REALITY OF GROUPS

1

In this book's title and in its preface the existence of human groups is taken for granted: I have assumed both the reality of groups and some agreement over what we mean when we use the word 'group'. But, in fact, both of these assumptions have been the subject of considerable controversy in the history of social psychology. Since the turn of the century, there have been heated debates not just about what groups are but about whether, indeed, groups exist at all. This chapter returns to those debates in order to clarify some of the issues that will recur throughout the book. I begin, conventionally enough, with a definition of the group, which, while admittedly imprecise, will at least provide us with a few signposts to guide us through the terrain ahead. The discussion then turns to the question of the relationship between the individual and the group: is the latter reducible to the former or can they both be considered as real and interrelated entities? My answer to this question stresses the importance of making a distinction between behaviour in interpersonal settings and behaviour in group settings, and I outline some of the social psychological processes that may underlie this distinction. A key concept here, as indeed it will be throughout the book, is that of *social identity* – a person's sense of who he or she is. Finally, by way of illustration of these issues, I examine social behaviour in that most rudimentary of all groups – the crowd.

Definition

Even the most superficial survey of textbooks on group dynamics quickly reveals a wide diversity of meanings associated with the word 'group' (see Cartwright and Zander, 1969). For some theorists, it is the experience of *common fate* which is the critical factor (e.g. Lewin, 1948; Campbell, 1958; Rabbie and Horwitz, 1988). Thus, we can say that the Jews in Nazi Europe constituted a group because of their common (and tragic) fate of stigmatization, imprisonment and extermination. For other thinkers, the existence of some formal or implicit *social structure*, usually in the form of status and role relationships, is the key (e.g. Sherif and Sherif, 1969). The family is a good example here: we can regard the family as a group because its members have very well-defined relationships with one another (as parent, child, sibling etc.) and these relationships usually carry with them clear power and status differences. However, a third school of thought suggests that these structural relations come about because of a still more elementary feature of groups – the fact that they consist of people in *face-to-face interaction* with one another (e.g. Bales, 1950). And, of course, this is a characteristic of most of the groups to which we belong – our family, our work group and a host of others.

The second and third types of definition only really seem applicable to small groups (say, of twenty members or less) and would seem to exclude large-scale social categories such as ethnic groups (as in the example of the Jews cited above), social class or nationality. And yet, as we shall see in later chapters, these category memberships can influence people's behaviour just as surely as the most cohesive face-to-face group. This problem has led some writers to propose a more subjective definition of the group in terms of people's *self-categorizations* (Tajfel, 1981; Turner, 1982). According to this view, a group exists when

two or more individuals . . . perceive themselves to be members of the same social category. (Turner, 1982, p. 15)

Thus, to return to our first example, Jews constitute a group because a significant number of people say to themselves 'I am a Jew'. The value of this characterization is its simplicity and its inclusiveness. It is difficult to imagine a group in which its members did not at some stage mentally classify themselves as actually belonging to it.

Despite its attractive parsimony, Turner's definition is perhaps rather *too* subjectivist; it seems not to capture an important feature of groups – that their existence is typically known to others (Merton, 1957). After all, as social scientists we probably would not be much interested in studying two people who secretly decided that they would define themselves as a group, but whose existence remained hidden to everyone else. A central theme of this book is that we need to consider groups not just as systems in their own right but *in relation to* other groups. For this reason, I extend Turner's (1982) definition and propose that *a group exists when two or more people define themselves as members of it and when its existence is recognized by at least one other*.[1] The 'other' in this context is some person or group of people who do not so define themselves. This could be, for example, the experimenter in a laboratory study or, more generally, others (or other groups) in the social environment.

In summary, a great many groups can be characterized as a collection of people bound together by some common experience or purpose, or who are interrelated in a micro-social structure, or who interact with one another. All these may be sufficient conditions to say that a group exists. But perhaps the crucial necessary condition is that those same people also share some conception of themselves as belonging to the same social unit.

The Individual–Group Relationship

Before we can begin investigating the properties of groups and their effects, there is an important issue that must be discussed first.[2] This concerns the nature of the relationship of the individual to the group – what Allport (1962) described as social psychology's 'master problem'. To put it at its simplest, the question is this: is there more to groups than the sum of the individuals that comprise them?

Allport himself was in no doubt about the answer to this question. In one of the earliest social psychology texts he wrote:

There is no psychology of groups which is not essentially and entirely a psychology of individuals. (Allport, 1924, p. 6)

The thrust of this often-quoted remark was aimed at some of his contemporaries, who held that groups had some mental properties over and above the consciousness of the individuals who make them up. Thus, Le Bon (1896) and McDougall (1920) both talked of a crowd possessing a 'group mind' which led it to perform deeds that would be considered unthinkable by the individual crowd members on their own. We shall return to this theory of crowd behaviour later in the chapter but for the moment let us consider Allport's argument against this 'group mind' thesis. Allport's main point was that a term like the 'group mind' could not be independently verified; it was not possible to touch or observe this entity, which was supposed to possess consciousness, *apart from the individuals that comprised it*.

4

In this he was surely right: to talk of a group having a 'mind of its own' does seem to be an unfortunate lapse into metaphysics. However, in rejecting the idea of a 'group mind', Allport wanted to go further and dispose of the concept of the group altogether. Although in his later writings (e.g. Allport, 1962) he appeared to modify his position somewhat, at heart he was still an individualist, believing that group phenomena could ultimately be reduced to individual psychological processes. One consequence of this has been that much subsequent theory and research on group dynamics has followed his lead and has attempted to show that such phenomena as prejudice and conflict are little more than interpersonal behaviour on a larger scale.

This reductionist view has not gone completely unchallenged, however. Others have argued that a rejection of the 'group mind' fallacy does not imply that we should abandon the study of group processes in their own right. Beginning with Mead (1934), and followed by Sherif (1936), Asch (1952) and Lewin (1952), these thinkers have insisted on the reality and distinctiveness of social groups, believing them to have unique properties that emerge out of the network of relations between the individual members. This idea was nicely expressed by Asch (1952) with a chemical analogy. A substance like water, he argued, is made up of the elements hydrogen and oxygen and yet has very different properties from either constituent. Furthermore, these same molecular constituents when differently organized or structured produce substances with quite different characteristics (e.g. ice, water, steam). Thus, in a real sense the compound H_2O is *not* the simple aggregate of its constituents but is crucially affected by their arrangement. So, too, with human compounds, or groups:

We need a way of understanding group process that retains the prime reality of individual *and* group, the two permanent poles of all social processes. We need to see group forces arising out of the actions of individuals and individuals whose actions are a function of the group forces that they themselves (or others) have brought into existence. (Asch, 1952, p. 251)

For both Asch and Sherif the reality of groups emerges out of people's common perceptions of themselves as members of the same social unit and in various relations to one another within that unit.

5

Associated with these perceptions are various group products such as slogans, norms and values, and these, too, can become internalized and hence serve to guide people's behaviour. For these reasons it is possible to accept Allport's critique of the 'group mind' and yet disagree with his conclusion that the concept of 'group' has no place in a rigorous social psychology. Endorsing the words of Sherif, that pioneer of group psychology, the view taken in this book is:

We cannot do justice to events by extrapolating uncritically from man's [sic] feelings, attitudes, and behaviour when he is in a state of isolation to his behaviour when acting as a member of a group. Being a member of a group and behaving as a member of a group have psychological consequences. There are consequences even when the other members are not immediately present. (Sherif, 1966, pp. 8–9)

The Interpersonal–Group Continuum

What does it mean to say a person is 'acting as a member of a group'? Tajfel (1978), an important theorist of group processes, also stressed the need to distinguish interpersonal behaviour from behaviour in group settings. He suggested three criteria that help us to make the distinction. The first, and most crucial, is the presence or absence of at least two clearly identifiable social categories, e.g. a black and a white person, man and woman, worker and employer. The second is whether there is low or high variability between persons within each group in their attitudes or behaviour. Group behaviour is typically homogeneous or uniform, while interpersonal behaviour shows the normal range of individual differences. The singing and dancing of jubilant Parisians following France's 1998 World Cup triumph provide a graphic illustration of such behavioural uniformity. Those same Parisians, the day before or after, went their multitudinous individual ways. The third is whether there is low or high variability in one person's attitudes and behaviour towards other group members. Does the same person react similarly to a wide range of different others (as in group stereotyping – see chapter 7), or does he or she show a differentiated response to them? In brief, Tajfel saw all social behaviour as lying on a continuum where at one end the interaction is seen as being determined by the membership of various groups and relations between them, while at the other it is more decided by personal characteristics and interpersonal relationships (see Tajfel, 1978; Brown and Turner, 1981).

This distinction is beautifully caught in a scene from Ken Loach's (1995) film about the Spanish Civil War, *Land and Freedom*. In it, the English hero of the story, a Communist Party member from Liverpool, has been making love with a Spanish comrade in arms whom he met while fighting for POUM, one of the several groups aligned against Franco's fascists. Just after their moments of intimacy he reveals that he is leaving POUM to join the communist-led International Brigade. Instantly, her attitude towards him changes and she leaves with hardly another word. The discovery that he was abandoning POUM for another party, a group she saw as opposed to the cause she was struggling for, transformed their interpersonal relationship as two lovers into an intergroup one as members of rival political factions.

What underlies this sudden 'switching' process? Turner (1982) has suggested that it is governed by changes in self-concept functioning – changes in the way people view themselves. Turner views the self-concept as comprising two components: personal identity and social identity. Personal identity, in his view, refers to self-descriptions in terms of personalistic or idiosyncratic characteristics; for example, 'I am a friendly sort of person' or 'I am a lover of blues music'. Social identity, on the other hand, denotes definitions in terms of category memberships; for example, 'I am a man' or 'I am a Liverpool supporter'. This idea that belonging to a group forms part of people's identity is, as we shall see, a central aspect of the study of group processes. It helps us to make sense of much of people's behaviour towards other groups (see chapter 8), as well as helping us to understand why it is that group members so often show such uniformity in their attitudes and behaviour (see chapters 2 and 4). The reason behind this uniformity, suggests Turner, is that in defining themselves as a member of a particular group people also typically associate themselves with the various common attributes and norms that they see as being part and parcel of that group. So, not only do individuals see members of *other* groups in stereotyped ways, they also see *themselves* as being relatively interchangeable with others in their own group. Hence their attitudes and actions take on the uniformity that is so characteristic of group settings.

7

As illustrations of this interpersonal–group distinction, let us consider the findings from two experiments. The first comes from a study by Doise, Deschamps and Meyer (1978). Here, children were asked to look at a series of photographs of boys followed by a similar set of pictures of girls (or vice versa). For each picture they had to check off various trait adjectives which they thought applied to the boy or girl in question. In the 'experimental' condition the children were made aware of the two sets of photographs from the onset. In other words, we might assume that for the 'control' children the second set of pictures arrived somewhat as a surprise and hence presumably gender was less salient for them while they were making their initial judgements. We could, therefore, classify this second condition as being somewhat more 'interpersonal' in nature as compared to the former, more group-orientated condition. The judgements made by the children seemed to be consistent with this assumption. In the 'experimental' condition the judgements were clearly patterned along gender lines: the male and female photographs received few traits in common, and *within* each set there were more identical traits checked. In the 'control' condition, in contrast, the children seemed to pay more attention to the idiosyncratic features of each picture: there was much less perceived differentiation between the boys and girls and less perceived similarity within each category.

The second comes from Deutsch and Gerard's (1955) study of conformity. This was modelled on Asch's (1951) classic demonstration that people may be influenced to give incorrect answers to a straightforward physical judgement by the presence of a unanimous but incorrect majority (see chapter 4). Deutsch and Gerard showed how this conformity could be dramatically increased simply by defining the collection of subjects taking part in the experiment as a group with a clear-cut goal. In our terms, the introduction of this 'grouping' cue shifted the situation towards the 'group' pole of the behavioural continuum with a corresponding increase in uniformity of behaviour *between* individuals.

Before we leave this issue, there are three further points to be made. The first is that what distinguishes interpersonal and group behaviour is not primarily the number of people involved. Thus, where police and strikers face each other across a picket line, what locates that interaction towards the 'group' pole is not necessarily the fact that many people are involved or that they belong to different groups. What indicates it as an instance of group behaviour is the uniformity of their behaviour, which suggests that the participants appear to be interacting *in terms of* their group memberships rather than their distinctive personal characteristics. This is important because social encounters are frequently rather ambiguous to define. Take, for instance, an interaction between just two people who happen to belong to different social categories (e.g. a man and a woman). Is this encounter an interpersonal one because just two people are involved or is it a group-based interaction because of the category difference? From the barest description I have just given it is not possible to say; what would be needed before we could characterize this situation would be a close study of the content of the interaction between them. If it appeared by word and gesture that the participants were orientating towards each other in a relatively predictable and sex-stereotypic fashion then this would indicate an instance of group behaviour. In the absence of this, the idiosyncratic nature of the interaction would suggest a more interpersonal encounter.

This raises the second point: that the interpersonal–group distinction is based on a continuous dimension and is not an either/or dichotomy. Most social situations will contain elements of both interpersonal and group behaviours. After all, people enter even the most group-based interaction with a unique prehistory and set of personal dispositions, and even the most intimate exchange between two lovers will contain some group-stereotypic features. While this necessarily complicates a complete analysis of any particular situation, since both sorts of processes will be at work, it does not obviate the need for a clear understanding of the difference between these sorts of processes and how they both interact.

The third and most important point is that if we accept this difference then it follows that we may need rather different kinds of theories to understand group process than we typically use to explain interpersonal behaviour.[3] Theories about interpersonal behaviour typically invoke either or both of two kinds of process. One is the operation of some factor within the individual – for instance, the person's personality make-up, cognitive style or emotional state. The other is the nature of the relationship between individuals – for instance, relations of attitude similarity. In other words, variations in people's behaviour are explained either by differences between the people themselves or by differences in the personal relations between them. But once we are dealing with group situations such explanations are less useful because two of the key characteristics of group situations have to do with *uniformities* between individuals rather than their differences. One football fan may taunt another, particularly if they are wearing different coloured scarves, in ignorance of, or in spite of, many similarities of attitude, socio-economic status, physical appearance and personality. And if there are a thousand such supporters together, the multiplicity of personality types and the complexity of interpersonal relations both within each group and between the groups become enormous, and *yet* their behaviour is often strikingly uniform. The conclusion must be, therefore, as we wrote elsewhere:

that the direct extrapolation of theories about interpersonal behaviour to group contexts is inherently fraught with difficulties and thus that alternative theories, relating specifically to group behaviour, are necessary. (Brown and Turner, 1981, p. 46)

One of the purposes of this book is to examine those other theories and assess their utility and relevance for understanding ourselves and our society.

The Emergence of Collective Behaviour: The Crowd as a Group

On a spring afternoon in 1980 a working-class area in the centre of Bristol, with little previous history of unrest, suddenly erupted into violence.[4] This 'riot', as it was later dubbed by media commentators, was occasioned by a police raid on a local cafe, ostensibly to investigate allegations of illegal substance use. Initially the raid provoked little reaction, but within an hour the police began to be pelted with bricks from onlookers. Police reinforcements – around thirty or forty officers – were summoned to the scene but by now the situation had escalated and a large crowd of several hundred people had gathered. Further attempts by still more police to disperse this crowd and to rescue their abandoned vehicles and colleagues were unsuccessful, and later that evening police cars and other vehicles were set on fire and some shop and bank windows were smashed. For much of that night the neighbourhood became a 'no-go' area to the police, although by the next day the crowd had dispersed and the incident was over.

By the standards of what was to happen the following year – most notably the riots in Liverpool and London in the summer of 1981 – or, much later, in Los Angeles after the 1992 acquittal of some white police officers from the charge of assaulting an innocent black passer-by, this was an insignificant enough event. However, as an example of crowd behaviour with which to begin our discussion it will serve our purposes well – the more so since the events in question have been studied by a social psychologist who was living in Bristol at the time and who has provided a penetrating analysis of the episode (Reicher, 1984a). We will return to Reicher's work later in the chapter but before doing so four further points about this so-called 'riot' must be mentioned. The first is that the violence was not random or uncontrolled but seemed to be aimed at very specific targets. Foremost of these, of course, were the police and their vehicles. Some property was also damaged (e.g. a bank and a pub), but the majority of local shops and private houses were untouched. The second is that the crowd consisted almost entirely of people who lived in the immediate neighbourhood and who were known to one another. Third, the violence was geographically contained. There was no attempt to spread it outside a very well-defined area, which constituted the centre of the local community. Finally, spontaneous comments made by crowd participants reflected a strong identification with and pride in that community, a feeling of acting to defend themselves against 'outsiders'. By the same token, the police clearly regarded the 'rioters' as a group, albeit one that had 'taken the law into its own hands'. This last point is particularly important because it satisfies us that we are, indeed, dealing with an instance of group behaviour (see above).

Deindividuation and behaviour in groups

How, then, are we to understand these events in Bristol and others like them? Why do crowds behave as they do? An early attempt to answer these questions suggested that in crowd settings people regressed to a primitive or instinctive mode of behaviour (Le Bon, 1896). According to Le Bon, the anonymity, contagion and suggestibility that he saw as being endemic to crowds caused people to lose their rationality and identity, creating instead a 'group mind'. Under the influence of this collective mentality, and freed from normal social constraints, people's destructive instincts are released, resulting in wanton violence and irrational behaviour. For Le Bon, then, the Bristol 'riot' would be a classic instance of this 'decline into barbarity' similar to those which he claimed to have observed at the time of the Paris Commune in the nineteenth century.

Although, as we have seen, Le Bon's hypothesis of a 'group mind' has since largely been rejected, his speculations about the effects of anonymity in the crowd have proved influential for subsequent attempts to explain collective behaviour. Foremost of these has been Zimbardo's (1969) theory of deindividuation. Zimbardo has taken up many of Le Bon's ideas and formalized them into a model involving a number of input variables, some intervening psychological changes and the resulting behaviour. For our purposes, the three most important 'inputs' are anonymity, diffused responsibility and the size of the group. According to Zimbardo, being in a large group provides people with a cloak of anonymity and diffuses personal responsibility for the consequences of one's actions. This is thought to lead to a loss of identity and a reduced concern for social evaluation. This is what Zimbardo terms the psychological state of deindividuation. The resulting 'output' behaviour is then 'impulsive', 'irrational' and 'regressive' because it is not under the 'usual' social and personal controls. Although Zimbardo does allow that this disinhibited behaviour might take prosocial forms (e.g. Zimbardo, 1969, p. 300), the main thrust of his theory is to suggest that people's behaviour will degenerate in crowd settings. The violent behaviour of the crowd in Bristol on that April afternoon would, for Zimbardo, represent an example of this. The example would be strengthened still further by the fact that the violence escalated over the evening as darkness fell, thus increasing the anonymity of the crowd members.

To substantiate his theory, Zimbardo (1969) conducted a number of experiments in which groups of participants, under the pretext of a 'learning experiment', were given the opportunity of administering mild, but apparently real, electric shocks to the putative 'learner' in the experiment.[5] In some conditions these participants were deindividuated by being asked to wear a large, shapeless coat and a hood over the head with holes cut out for their eyes and mouth. In other conditions, they retained their individual identity and were given large name tags to reinforce this. In the first experiment, involving students, the results were largely supportive of the theory: the mean duration of 'shock' administered was nearly twice as long in the deindividuated condition as it was in the individuated one. However, in a subsequent experiment, using a very similar procedure with Belgian soldiers, an exactly opposite result was obtained: those in the anonymous conditions delivered consistently *shorter* length 'shocks' than those who were identifiable. In a rather circular explanation for this unexpected finding, Zimbardo suggested that the soldiers, because they were already in uniform, were deindividuated before the experiment began. The effect of donning the coats and hoods for the deindividuation condition of the experiment was, he argued, to reindividuate them (Zimbardo, 1969, p. 276)!

Other studies have reported findings consistent with Zimbardo's theory. For instance, Watson (1973), in an archival study of ethnographic records, found a clear correlation between cultures that indulged in highly aggressive practices towards their enemies (e.g. torture or mutilation) and those that also regularly changed their appearance before battle (e.g. by face or body painting or the wearing of masks). Of the 23 cultures studied, 13 were judged to be highly aggressive and, of these, 12 engaged in various rituals to disguise their appearance before battle. On the other hand, of the 10 less aggressive societies only 3 had similar rituals. Although deindividuation is only one of a number of possible interpretations of this correlation, Zimbardo's theory has also received support from a more controlled experimental study by Jaffe and Yinon (1979), where they simply compared the mean intensity of 'shock' administered by individuals with that administered by groups of three. As predicted, those participating in groups consistently gave much stronger 'shocks' than those acting on their own. This difference was even evident on the first trial before there had been any discussion in the group.

Some have suggested that a contemporary illustration of deindividuated behaviour is provided by the current vogue for computer-mediated communication – electronic mail, computer conferencing and the like (Siegel et al., 1986). In these various modes of communication one typically interacts with others – and there may be only a few or literally thousands – via a computer terminal in the privacy of the office or home. Somewhat paradoxically, argue Siegel et al. (1986), such an individualized method of relating to others may generate precisely the experience of deindividuation hypothesized by Zimbardo, giving rise to the phenomenon of 'flaming', where the emotional (and often negative) tone of the messages quickly degenerates well below conventional levels of cordiality. A possible reason for this is that participants in such electronic 'conversations' may feel somewhat anonymous, thinking – usually mistakenly – that their identity is masked by the technology they are using. Moreover, they are also deprived of normal non-verbal and paralinguistic cues, which would allow them to detect and to 'smooth over' rough edges in the interaction (Rutter, 1987). Siegel et al. (1986) recorded the exchanges between groups of three people discussing some choice-dilemma scenarios, either face-to-face or anonymously via a computer network. They found that the 'electronic groups' made fewer remarks to one another but these did contain a rather higher incidence of 'uninhibited' comments such as swearing, name-calling and insults.

Despite this supportive evidence, it is becoming increasingly clear that Zimbardo's one-sided emphasis on the negative consequences of group membership (e.g. identity loss and antisocial behaviour) is misplaced. As we have seen from his own experiment with Belgian soldiers, anonymity sometimes *reduces* aggression. Similarly, Diener (1976) found that anonymity had no effect on aggressive behaviour and that group membership actually decreased it. It is also the case that the circumstances that are alleged to cause deindividuation may give rise to other forms of behaviour, apart from aggression. In another experiment, Diener (1979) showed that a prior experience of activities designed to create group cohesion (e.g. adoption of a group name, group singing and dancing) subsequently led individuals to engage in more unusual and uninhibited behaviours (e.g. playing with mud, finger painting with their nose, sucking liquids from baby bottles) than those who had had an initial experience which made them feel rather self-aware. Finally, and perhaps most convincing of all, Johnson and Downing (1979), using a very simple modification of Zimbardo's procedure, found that an increase in *pro*social behaviour can result from deindividuation. Like Zimbardo, they compared anonymous and individuating conditions. Although all participants had to wear

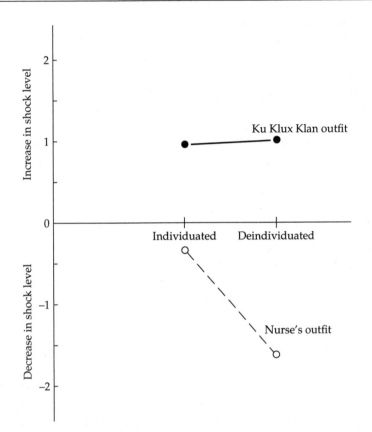

Figure 1.1 Aggression as a consequence of deindividuation and situational norms (adapted from Johnson and Downing, 1979, table 1)

special clothing, in the individuating conditions the participants' names were attached to their costumes and other people's responses could be identified. However, Johnson and Downing also varied the situational norms prevailing in the experiment. In half the conditions, the costume consisted of a robe resembling a Ku Klux Klan outfit, a point remarked on by the experimenter. In the remaining conditions, the participants were asked to wear an equally anonymous looking robe but one which was alleged to have been a nurse's gown borrowed from a hospital recovery room. In the subsequent 'learning' experiment those wearing the nurse's uniform chose to *reduce* the level of 'shocks' administered, and especially in the deindividuated conditions (see figure 1.1).

15

In fact, deindividuation by itself failed to increase aggression significantly, even for those wearing the Ku Klux Klan outfit.

The importance of these findings is that they show quite conclusively that being in a group does not necessarily lead people to act in a wantonly destructive fashion, as Zimbardo seems to imply. Quite how they will behave depends very much on which norms are salient in each particular situation (Turner and Killian, 1957). This is the conclusion reached by Diener (1980). He argues that the key factor in crowd behaviour is a loss of self-awareness. Drawing on Duval and Wicklund's (1972) 'theory of objective self-awareness', Diener suggests that factors present in some crowd situations – for example, anonymity, enhanced arousal, cohesion – lead people to direct their attention outwards and correspondingly less on themselves and on private standards. The result, according to Diener, is that people's behaviour becomes *less* self-regulated (i.e. determined by pre-existing values and mores) and *more* controlled by immediate cues and norms in the environment. These, of course, will not always dictate violent action but will vary from situation to situation. Diener's explanation of the events in Bristol, then, would be that as the crowd grew in size and in excitement people became less self-aware and hence more easily affected by cues in the environment – others throwing rocks, for example.

That increased crowd size may be associated with less self-attentive behaviour is suggested by Mullen's (1986) analysis of newspaper reports of lynch mobs. Mullen argued that people in larger mobs – and in the reports he studied they were typically over 1000 strong – would be likely to be less self-attentive and, given the normative context provided by a lynching, would be more prone to acts of atrocity. This research certainly supported this hypothesis: there was a significant correlation between the size of the crowd at a lynching and the gruesomeness of their assaults on the victim (ranging from 'mere' hanging to dismemberment and mutilation).

Collective behaviour from an intergroup perspective

The advantage of Diener's explanation in terms of self-awareness is that it can account for a wide variety of behaviours – prosocial as well as antisocial. However, it shares with Zimbardo's theory an emphasis on behaviour becoming deregulated in collective situations. For Diener, as for Zimbardo, being in a crowd still generally implies a loss of identity[6] and hence a loss of self-control. But do people always lose themselves in a crowd and get out of control? Let us return to that Bristol 'riot' with which we began this discussion. There are a number of features of that event that do not fit easily with such a point of view. Recall, first, that the crowd's behaviour, despite its violent character, was actually rather controlled. It was aimed at specific targets (e.g. the police) and avoided others (e.g. local shops and houses). Furthermore, it was geographically confined. If people had been responding simply to stimulus cues, why did they not chase the police far beyond the immediate neighbourhood and spread the violence elsewhere? Second, it is important to note that in that event in Bristol, as in other disturbances, the rioters and the police behaved differently. And yet the police constituted a crowd also! If people simply lose self-awareness in a crowd and respond to immediate stimuli we need to know why the police attend to different stimuli from the rioters. Third, it cannot really be said that the crowd was anonymous in that instance. As we have already noted, many of the participants were known to each other. Finally, those taking part in the 'riot', far from losing their identities, seemed quite unanimous in a new sense of pride in their community engendered by their activities.

These points have all been made by Reicher (1984a). Reicher begins by noting two features of many crowd situations. First, they nearly always involve more than one group. In the Bristol example we have the local inhabitants and the police. In other cases it may be rival groups of football supporters (as in the Heysel stadium tragedy in Brussels in 1985), or strikers and strike breakers (as in the British coal dispute of 1984–5). The fact that crowd behaviour is so often *intergroup* behaviour has been virtually ignored in all previous theories of the crowd (Reicher and Potter, 1985). This is important for Reicher's second point, which is that people often take on a new identity in a crowd rather than become anonymous. This follows from Turner's (1982) suggestion about the different components of the self-concept – the personal and the social. In a crowd, people may indeed lose some sense of their personal identity but at the same time they will often adopt a stronger sense of their *social* identity as a member of a particular group – hence the positive comments about their neighbourhood made by the Bristol 'rioters' (Reicher, 1984a), and similar remarks made several years earlier by a participant in the Watts riot in the USA (quoted in Milgram and Toch, 1969, p. 576). According to Reicher, therefore, crowd behaviour involves a *change* rather than a loss of identity. Alongside this change are changes in what are seen as the appropriate or normative standards of behaviour. These now become determined by the group rather than by private, idiosyncratic or environmental factors. This helps to explain why the behaviour of rioters and police can be so different. Although exposed to the same environmental stimuli, in adopting their respective identities they become influenced by very different goals and social norms (see also Reicher, 1984b).

Subsequent research has lent support to these ideas. As we have seen, a recurring theme in the deindividuation literature has been the importance of (in)visibility. Earlier in the chapter I discussed some research investigating the hypothesis that computer-mediated communication, by virtue of its relative anonymity, could lead to deindividuation and negative consequences for social relations (Siegel et al., 1986). However, Spears, Lea and Lee (1990) have argued that the effects of such electronic networks are more complex than this and depend crucially on the extent to which a single group identity is salient among the members of the network. They arranged for groups of three psychology students to discuss a series of topical issues among themselves using an interactive computer network. In one condition the participants were seated at their terminals in the same room so they could see each other; in the other, 'deindividuated', condition they were in separate rooms and never met. For half the groups their group identity as psychology students was particularly stressed; in the remainder they were only ever referred to as individuals. Analysis of the participants' positions on the various discussion topics revealed that deindividuation had the effect of making them more extreme in the direction of the (psychology) group norm, but *only* when their identity as psychologists was salient. In the other condition they actually moved in the opposite direction. Importantly, and in contrast to the findings of Siegel et al. (1986), they found no evidence of more negative interpersonal evaluations or increases in uninhibited remarks as a result of deindividuation (Lea and Spears, 1991). Thus, the 'flaming' that some observers have associated with computer-mediated communication seems not to be a general phenomenon after all.

In conclusion, we can note three important points. The first is that Zimbardo's pessimism about groups, like that of Le Bon before him, seems unwarranted. Depending on what norms are salient in the situation, both pro- and antisocial behaviour can become more probable in group settings. Where Zimbardo may be right is to suggest that people's behaviour in such situations may become more extreme. (This polarization, which is so typical of groups, is dealt with more fully in chapter 6.) The second and related point is that people's behaviour in crowds does not always undergo degradation. Both Zimbardo and Diener suggest that in groups people suffer a loss of identity and a loss of control. However, research with both laboratory and natural groups suggests that this is mistaken. These studies have shown that people's behaviour is still regulated, albeit by different psychological processes. In particular, it seems that groups often have specific goals in mind in acting as they do, and also that their actions are often motivated by identification with a group. Third, these goal- and identity-directed aspects of collective behaviour are particularly evident when viewed from an intergroup perspective. In nearly every instance of collective behaviour it is possible to identify an outgroup, which plays a determining role in the proceedings. This third point is particularly important. As we shall see throughout this book, a group rarely exists in isolation, and its relationships with other groups are critical for understanding what goes on within that group itself.

Summary

1 A group has variously been defined as two or more people experiencing some common fate *or* coexisting within some social structure *or* interacting on a face-to-face basis. The simpler and more comprehensive definition adopted here is two or more people possessing a common social identification and whose existence as a group is recognized by a third party.

2 Some have argued that groups can be reduced to the simple aggregate of the members that comprise them. However, just as chemical compounds may differ radically from their constituent

elements so, too, people in groups may act very differently from how they behave when they are in isolation.

3   It is possible to conceive of all social behaviour as lying on a continuum from interpersonal settings to group settings. The key features of the latter are that two or more social categories can be identified, behaviour of group members is typically rather uniform and individuals' treatment of others becomes stereotyped. Underlying this continuum is a transition of psychological functioning from personal to social-identity processes. These different processes may require us to adopt different group-based theories for the study of groups.

4   The crowd can be considered as an elementary form of group. Some have suggested that in crowds people become deindividuated and, as a result, act in an antisocial, unreasoning and uncontrolled fashion. However, a careful study of crowd and crowd-like situations reveals that people's behaviour can sometimes become more prosocial and is often aimed at specific targets (suggesting some goal-directedness).

5   Most instances of collective behaviour involve more than one group. Once this intergroup aspect is recognized, it is possible to see behaviour in groups as becoming more and not less regulated, involving a change rather than a loss of identity. People's *social* identities as group members become more important, their *personal* identities as unique individuals less so.

Notes

1   It has been pointed out to me that, strictly speaking, this definition would exclude 'secret societies' which, by definition, are *not* known to others. Of course, I do not deny the existence of such groups nor that they may occasionally have exerted some covert and hence unrecognized influence on social events. However, I suspect that such organizations are numerically rather rare and, ironically enough, their ability to maintain their continued 'secrecy' is probably inversely related to the amount of their actual impact on the world around them. For these reasons we can probably safely overlook them as potential counterexamples to our definition.

2   For a more detailed discussion of the issues covered in this and the following section, see Brown and Turner (1981) and Brewer and Brown (1998).

3   Note that in suggesting that we may need other kinds of theories I am not proposing here that these need to be pitched at a different level of explanation. Indeed, with Allport, I believe that a social psychology of group processes should be concerned with the behaviour of individuals. The difference is that I am concerned with individuals as group members and not with individuals as individuals.

4   I am indebted to my colleague Stephen Reicher for this example and also for much of the analysis that follows.

5   In fact, of course, no shocks were actually administered.

6   Actually, Diener is somewhat ambiguous on this question of loss of identity since he does allow that groups can occasionally provide people with a social identity (see Diener, 1980, pp. 234–5). This is much closer to the position taken here.

Further Reading

Asch, S.E. (1952) *Social Psychology*, ch. 9. Englewood Cliffs, NJ: Prentice Hall.

Brown, R.J. and Turner, J.C. (1981) Interpersonal and intergroup behaviour, in Turner, J.C. and Giles, H. (eds) *Intergroup Behaviour*. Oxford: Blackwell.

Prentice-Dunn, S. and Rogers, R.W. (1989) Deindividuation and the self regulation of behaviour, pp. 87–110 in Paulus, P. (ed.) *The Psychology of Group Influence*, 2nd edn. Hillsdale, NJ: Lawrence Erlbaum.

Reicher, S.D. (1982) The determination of collective behaviour, in Tajfel, H. (ed.) *Social Identity and Intergroup Relations*. Cambridge: Cambridge University Press.

2

ELEMENTARY PROCESSES IN GROUPS

In this chapter and the next, I consider some of the fundamental characteristics of life in groups. For convenience of exposition, the emphasis in this chapter is on process while in chapter 3 it will shift to more structural aspects, but the distinction between them is not very clear cut. Some of the issues covered here could have been dealt with in later chapters and vice versa.

Five major topics are discussed. I first consider what happens when we become members of a group. Under this heading, I look at such issues as how people reconnoitre groups they envisage joining, the consequences of group membership for the self-concept, and what may lie behind the rituals of entry which typify the attainment of group membership. The second section deals with interdependence in groups – how we are linked to others in terms of outcomes and the effects of different kinds of linkages. An important conclusion that emerges here is the significance of the group's goal or task in determining its behaviour. The third topic – the distinction between task behaviours and socio-emotional behaviours – is a key one not just in this chapter but for the book as a whole. Running through the whole field of group dynamics we find again and again the polarity between 'getting on with the job' and 'getting on with others'. Appropriately enough, it is the work of R.F. Bales, to whom the credit for first clarifying the distinction should go, which dominates this third section. Fourth, I examine group cohesiveness – its nature, its origins and some of its effects. In the fifth and final section, the wheel turns full circle as I return to the question of entry into the group, this time in relation to the acquisition and development of social norms. As I shall show, the group's prevailing customs and traditions exert a profound influence in regulating behaviour, not just in the immediate situation but also when the individual is alone or has left the group some time previously.

Becoming a Member of a Group

The process of becoming part of a group often provokes anxiety. Whether it be a child going to a new school or an adult changing jobs, the experience of entry into the group, while often exciting, may involve a degree of stress. Why should this be? It is tempting, perhaps,

24

simply to label these reactions as 'fear of the unknown' and leave it at that. Indeed, as we shall see later in the chapter, the process of new group members acquiring norms may well be motivated by attempts to reduce uncertainty in a novel situation. But a more detailed study of what happens when people join groups reveals that there are other processes at work too. These have been discussed in some detail by Levine and Moreland (1994), who have proposed a temporal model of group socialization covering the whole sequence from people's initial investigation of the group and recruitment to it to their eventual exit. An important feature of their model is its emphasis on the reciprocity of the individual and the group: it is not just the individual who experiences changes as a result of entering the group; the group also has to accommodate its new members. In this section I deal with three of the many phenomena discussed by Levine and Moreland: reconnaissance of prospective groups, changes in people's self-concepts as they join a group and the process of initiation into the group.

Reconnoitring groups

There is an important stage in becoming a group member that occurs *before* entering the group. This is the reconnaissance process, the whole business of investigating – and then deciding between – the various potential groups we might join. Of course, for some of the groups we belong to such decisions are made for us. We do not get to choose which gender we are assigned to, nor into which culture or class we are born. Such 'ascribed' group memberships, as they are sometimes termed, are undeniably important influences on us, as will become clear in subsequent chapters. Nevertheless, throughout our lives there are many other groups that we can (and do) choose to belong to, or not. Children can choose which clubs to join at school; on entering college students are confronted with a bewildering array of societies aiming to sign them up; some people still get to decide which jobs to do, even if in these times of economic recession it is a luxury permitted to a fortunate few; and to cater for people's needs for diversion, spiritual enlightenment or political involvement there are any number of hobby groups, churches and political organizations to join (Zander, 1972). What factors govern our choice to seek out and then to attempt to join voluntary associations such as these?

25

Levine and Moreland (1994) suggest one answer: people look to join groups that will be maximally rewarding to them and minimally costly. This proposition stems from an old idea in social psychology, social exchange theory (e.g. Homans, 1950), which broadly conceives of people's social relations in terms of profit maximization, where investments and outcomes can take psychological as well as material forms. The obvious inference from this approach is that people's reconnaissance activities will be mainly concerned with sizing up what groups can do for them, and what they will expect in return. (Parenthetically, we can note that exactly the same analysis would apply to groups' efforts to investigate and recruit new members – see, for example, Cini et al., 1993).

But what affects people's perceptions of rewards and costs? Pavelchak et al. (1986) reasoned that an important source of information in this regard is people's prior experiences with other groups. If these have been favourable, they will be more likely to seek out membership in groups that they anticipate will furnish them with similar kinds of rewards. When Pavelchak et al. (1986) surveyed a large number of new students to a university they found some evidence in support of this. They asked their respondents various questions about groups they had belonged to at school, and how pleasant and important they now rated those memberships. These ratings were significantly, though weakly, related to the students' efforts to identify and join university societies. In addition, these same students' evaluations of their prospective groups showed a clear bias towards perceiving more rewards associated with the groups than costs (the number of rewards outnumbered the costs by about two to one). Interestingly, those who had belonged to a similar organization at school noted both more rewards *and* more costs, indicating the realistic informational value of that prior experience.

The fact that prospective group members anticipate more rewards than costs implies something of an optimistic outlook on their part. Brinthaupt et al. (1991) discovered that this optimism has an ego-enhancing aspect to it. In another survey of new university students they asked respondents to list both the rewards and costs that they believed they themselves would encounter in their chosen campus organization, and also those that others would experience. The results showed that the students saw more rewards and fewer costs for

26

themselves than for others. In attempting to track down the source of this over-optimism, Brinthaupt et al. (1991) found that it was related neither to the groups' recruitment efforts (e.g. painting an overly rosy picture of group life), nor to the level of visible prior investment in finding out about the group, a potentially important factor in arousing feelings of cognitive dissonance (Festinger, 1957). However, there was one exception to this latter finding: those looking to join sororities and fraternities *did* show a significant relationship between their expressed optimism and the extent of psychological investment in joining. The reasons for this will become apparent in the section after next.

In concluding this discussion, there are two issues that merit our consideration, one practical and one theoretical. On the practical side, the research suggests that anyone contemplating joining a group would do well to gather as much information as possible about that group to build up a realistic picture of what membership in it will entail. This seems to be especially important in view of people's tendency to have a slightly inflated view of a group's attractions prior to entry. Similarly, on the other side, those doing the recruiting to the group might want to avoid painting the group too rosily to prospective members. The risk of doing so is that those new recruits may display something of a 'rebound' effect in their commitment to the group once they experience the full array of both positive and negative aspects of group life. Indeed, there is some evidence that employers who provide realistic job previews in their personnel selection procedures do better at retaining staff than those who do not (Wanous, 1977).

A theoretical issue that would repay further investigation is whether the social exchange model which Levine and Moreland (1994) propose tells the whole story of group reconnaissance. Although, as we have seen, perceived rewards and costs clearly enter into people's calculations about group joining, some of the observed correlations were quite weak (though statistically reliable). Hogg (1992) has suggested that another important factor guiding people's attraction to different groups is the extent to which they perceive themselves as corresponding to the prototypical member of each group. In effect, he argues, people's social identities, whether derived from prior group memberships or more generally from socio-cultural socialization, need to be well matched to that likely to be provided by the new group. Evidence for this process was provided by Niedenthal et al. (1985),

27

who asked students for their preferences for different types of accommodation (e.g. apartments, dormitories, fraternities, sororities). In addition, they also obtained measures from the students of their self-concepts (on a large number of trait adjectives) and of the typical person belonging to each of the different housing types (on the same list of traits). As expected, there was a clear inverse correlation between choice of residence and the discrepancy between self-concept and the housing prototype: the smaller the discrepancy, the greater the preference.

Changes in self-concept

As we have just seen, our social identity – our sense of who we are and what we are worth – is intimately bound up with our group memberships. Thus, one of the major consequences of becoming a member of a group is a change in the way we see ourselves. Joining a group often requires us to redefine who we are, which in turn may have implications for our self-esteem. This process of redefinition was nicely illustrated during interviews I once conducted with shop stewards in a large aircraft engineering factory (Brown, 1978). One of the questions in the interview asked the respondents what they felt about belonging to their particular section and what they would feel about moving elsewhere. The majority of those interviewed expressed a strong desire to remain where they were and many of them went on to explain why that particular group membership was important to them. As one of them put it:

I went into the army. I had no visions of any regiment to go in or different kind of preference for tank or artillery. But once I was in the artillery, to me that was the finest regiment. Even now it is and I've left the army twenty years ... I think it's the same as when you come into a factory. You get an allegiance to a department and you breed that. And you say, 'fair enough I'm a Development worker', and you hate to think of going into Production ... Once someone gets in a department you've got that allegiance to it. (Brown, 1978, p. 426)

This change in self-definition so graphically described by that shop steward is a very common consequence of joining a group. Kuhn and McPartland (1954) devised a simple instrument to explore these self-definitions. Respondents were simply asked to pose themselves the question 'Who am I?' and to provide up to twenty answers to it. Kuhn and McPartland found that all but a small handful of their respondents gave at least one 'consensual' or group reference (e.g. 'I am a student', 'I am a Baptist'), and over half gave ten such responses or more. The instrument's validity was supported by the finding that self-professed members of religious groups were much more likely to give religious group references in their answers than were those who did not belong to a religion.

An experimental study by Moreland (1985) provided good evidence that new members do go through a process of self-redefinition and that this may also have behavioural consequences. Moreland (1985) suggested that people joining a group often categorize themselves – and doubtless are categorized by others in the group – as 'new' members in contrast to existing or 'old' members. In his experiment Moreland led two members of a discussion group to believe that they were new to the group, alleging that the remaining three members had actually met together twice previously. (In fact, all five members of the group were novices, so that the remaining three, who were given no misleading information, acted as 'control' participants.) Moreland found that initially these 'new' members were more anxious than the 'control' participants, and anticipated that they would enjoy the forthcoming sessions less. Furthermore, it was clear that the categorization of their world into 'old' and 'new' members reliably affected their behaviour: analysis of their verbal utterances revealed that they talked more to their fellow 'novices' and expressed more agreement with them than with those whom they believed had already acquired fully fledged membership status. This behavioural discrimination between 'new' and 'old' members declined over time as the group met together for further sessions, and was paralleled by a gradual increase in the favourability of the novices' attitudes towards the group as a whole.

So far I have discussed changes in self-concept consequent on group membership simply as changes in the way we define or describe ourselves. But becoming a member of a group may also have consequences for our evaluation of ourselves, for our self-esteem. If we internalize our group memberships as part of our self-concept it follows that any prestige or value associated with those groups will have implications for our feelings of self-worth. This was shown by Zander et al. (1960), who studied the psychological consequences of belonging to cohesive and non-cohesive laboratory groups that then experienced success or failure. Cohesive groups were created by maximizing cues for 'groupness': members were seated close to one another, encouraged to think up a name for their group, and attention was drawn to the members' interpersonal similarities. By contrast, in the non-cohesive groups – although it is doubtful whether the word 'group' is really appropriate here – members were allowed to sit anywhere, the group was assigned a number rather than being allowed to generate a name, and the participants were never openly referred to as a group. The groups were set a fashion design task at which half were deemed to have done well relative to other groups, while the remainder were alleged to have done poorly. In measures of self-esteem this group outcome only affected members of cohesive groups, the group's success or failure being reflected in raised or depressed levels of self-esteem (see also Hogg and Sunderland, 1991). For the other groups the outcome of the group task was immaterial. Furthermore, the cohesive group members' anticipation of *personal* competence to carry out some future (and unrelated) task on their own was also reliably affected by their group's perceived achievement.

Although, as we shall see later in the chapter (and elsewhere in the book – see chapter 8), the effects of group success and failure can sometimes be more complex than this, this early experiment does underline how the positivity of our self-concept can be influenced by the social evaluation of the groups to which we belong.

Initiation into the group

In the previous section we concentrated on changes in individuals as they become group members. How does the rest of the group respond to these newcomers? Moreland and Levine (1982) note that entry into the group is often marked by some ceremony or ritual. This is especially true of established or formal groups and organizations, although somewhat less typical of informal friendship and peer groups. These initiation ceremonies can take different forms, ranging from a warm welcome to a distinctly unpleasant (not to say painful) experience in which the newcomer is mocked, embarrassed or even physically assaulted. Examples of the former type include the fringe benefits and privileges that some organizations bestow on their new employees and the celebrations that accompany the achievement of full membership of some religions (e.g. the Jewish bar mitzvah). Examples of negative entry experiences are numerous. Anthropologists have noted the prevalence of initiation ceremonies in a wide variety of cultures (e.g. van Gennep, 1960). These are used to mark transitions in status or role within a society – what van Gennep (1960) termed 'rites de passage' – and may involve the inflicting of pain or some act of bodily mutilation (e.g. circumcision rituals). Such entry proceedings are not restricted to non-industrialized societies. Joining military organizations frequently involves a series of humiliating experiences. Apparently, US marines have to undergo brutal initiations involving the driving of metal spikes into their bare chests (The *Observer*, 2 February 1997; see also Dornbusch, 1955). Some North American college fraternities still engage in practices of 'hazing' new members. These require initiates to perform some degrading or humiliating activities for the amusement of existing members of the fraternity. Similar phenomena can be observed at the workplace. Vaught and Smith (1980) have documented the ritual of 'making a miner' in a Kentucky coal mine, a process which apparently involves physical assault and occasional sexual debasement.

Why should groups go to these lengths to mark the entry of new members into their ranks? There are several possible reasons. The first is that they may serve a symbolic function both for the newcomer and for the group itself. For the newcomer it helps in the process of identity transition that we discussed earlier. After the initiation the individual can say, 'I am not what I used to be' (van Maanen, 1976, p. 101). The group, too, may need symbols to define its boundaries. If the initiation involves the acquisition of characteristic markings or the donning of new clothing, it helps to underline the group's distinctiveness from other groups, an important feature of intergroup relationships (van Gennep, 1960; Tajfel, 1978; see also chapter 8). Second, some entry procedures may serve as an apprenticeship for the individual, introducing him or her to the normative standards of the group and relevant skills needed for effective functioning in it. We shall return to this process of norm socialization later in the chapter.

A third function served by initiation rituals may be to attempt to elicit some loyalty from the new member. This applies particularly to initiations that involve favourable treatment or special dispensations for the novice. The gratitude and perhaps even guilt which these favours may induce in the newcomer may enhance his or her commitment to the group's goals and activities (Lewicki, 1981).

The widespread occurrence of initiations that involve negative experiences is more puzzling, however. Although these may still serve the symbolic functions just noted, intuitively they would seem to act as a deterrent for the would-be member rather than as an inducement to identify with the group. Aronson and Mills (1959) proposed a rather ingenious explanation to account for these unpleasant experiences. They suggested that for most people the experience of group life is rarely completely positive. Attracted though they may be to the group, there will still be some aspects that do not appeal. This, then, may lead to a weakening of the cohesion of the group. However, Aronson and Mills suggested that groups can counter these effects by having group members undergo a painful or discomforting initiation. This will happen, they argued, because people's awareness that they have undergone the unpleasant experience to gain entry to the group is inconsistent with their subsequent discovery that there are things about the group that are not as they had anticipated. Drawing on Festinger's (1957) famous *Theory of Cognitive Dissonance*, Aronson and Mills reasoned that this perception of inconsistency (or dissonance) is psychologically uncomfortable and that people will look for ways to reduce it. Since the initiation may be too vivid or painful to repress easily, one avenue to reduce dissonance is to enhance one's evaluation of the group: 'if I went through all that to become a member of this group, it must be really attractive for me'. This led Aronson and Mills to the non-obvious hypothesis that the more severe the initiation, the more attractive the group would appear.

They tested this hypothesis in a now classic experiment (Aronson and Mills, 1959). Women college students were recruited to take part in group discussions on the 'psychology of sex', which, they were led to believe, would involve them joining an ongoing discussion group. Before doing so, however, they were asked to take part in a 'screening pre-test'. This test (or initiation) involved the subjects reading aloud some sexually orientated material. The nature of this varied in the different experimental conditions. In the 'severe' initiation condition the women were asked to read aloud some lurid passages from sexually explicit novels. In the 'mild' condition, on the other hand, they simply had to read out five words that had some sexual connotation but were not obviously obscene. There was also a 'control' group who did not have to read anything. On some pretext, the subjects were actually prevented from joining in the expected group discussions, but they were permitted to listen in on a discussion that appeared to be already in progress. In fact, however, the discussion was pre-recorded and was identical for all subjects. And pretty dull it turned out to be. Far from the interesting discussion on the psychology of sex that had been promised, the excerpt that they heard was a tedious and stilted conversation about the secondary sexual behaviour of lower animals! Afterwards, the subjects were asked to rate both the discussion and the group on a number of scales. Despite the fact that they had all heard the same boring discussion, those who had experienced the 'severe' treatment rated both the discussion and its participants more favourably than those in the 'mild' or 'control' conditions.

Gerard and Mathewson (1966) subsequently confirmed this finding and showed that the results could not simply be attributed to, for example, the possibly greater sexual arousal in the 'severe' condition, or to feelings of 'relief' at discovering that the discussion group was not as embarrassing as the pre-test. They accomplished this by modifying the design of Aronson and Mills in a number of ways, the most crucial change being that real electric shocks ('mild' or 'severe') were used as the initiation procedure.[1] This was designed to circumvent the 'sexual arousal' alternative explanation. All subjects received these shocks, although in the control condition it was alleged that they were simply part of a 'psychological experiment', while in the experimental conditions they were clearly linked to a forthcoming group experience. This was to test whether it was the unpleasant experience itself (and subsequent 'relief' afterwards) that caused the effects, or the fact that it was an unpleasant *initiation*. The results were clear cut. Evaluations of the (boring) group discussion and its participants were in general more favourable when the electric shocks were seen as an initiation rather than as simply part of an experiment. The effects of altering the severity of the shock depended on

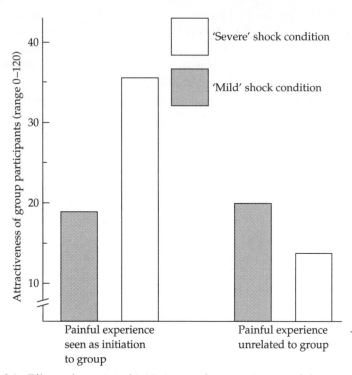

Figure 2.1 Effects of severity of initiation on the attractiveness of the group (from Gerard and Mathewson, 1966)

this factor also. Those people who believed that the shocks were really an initiation test gave higher ratings of the group when the shocks were 'severe' than when they were 'mild'. In the control condition, this result was reversed (see figure 2.1).

Whether the underlying psychological process here is really one of dissonance reduction or some other mechanism is still a matter of controversy (Alexander and Sagatun, 1973; Schlenker, 1975). However, there seems little doubt about the phenomenon itself: undergoing an unpleasant initiation experience does result in greater attraction to the group and hence may be used by groups as a device to bolster loyalty and cohesiveness. As such, it is but one of several factors implicated in the generation of group cohesion, as we shall see in a later section.

Interdependence and Group Process

We have already encountered quite a range of different groups in an equally wide variety of social settings. Crowds, industrial workgroups, military institutions, ethnic and gender categories, and the ubiquitous *ad hoc* laboratory group have all cropped up so far in the discussion. However, despite their diversity, there is one factor common to many, if not all, these groups. This is that their members are usually *inter-dependent*; one person's experiences, actions and outcomes are linked in some way to the experiences, actions and outcomes of the others in the group.

The importance of interdependence in the formation and functioning of groups was first noted by Lewin (1948), who had a profound effect on the thinking of a whole generation of group dynamics researchers (e.g. Cartwright, Deutsch, Festinger and Rabbie). Two of Lewin's ideas have proved to be especially important to an understanding of elementary group processes: interdependence of fate and task interdependence.

Interdependence of fate

Lewin believed that groups come into existence in a psychological sense not because their members necessarily are similar to one another (although they may be); rather, a group exists when the people in it realize that their fate depends on the fate of the group as a whole. Thus, a collection of passengers travelling in an aeroplane hardly constitutes a group since their degree of interdependence is minimal. However, the appearance of hijackers with grenades transforms them from 'passengers' into 'hostages', whose fate is now very much interconnected. Anecdotal evidence from survivors of such events confirms the power of this kind of interdependence to weld the participants into a cohesive group (Jacobson, 1973). Indeed, sometimes that cohesion extends even to the hijackers themselves, about whom hostages have been known to speak quite sympathetically, despite the fact that they were the ostensible cause of their ordeal.

The importance of interdependence of fate – or 'being in the same boat', as it is colloquially known – was demonstrated experimentally

35

by Rabbie and Horwitz (1969). They set out to establish what were the minimal conditions for the formation of a group. Dutch schoolchildren who were strangers to each other were first divided into small groups on a random basis. The groups were labelled 'green' and 'blue', allegedly for 'administrative reasons'. Then, depending on experimental condition, one of a number of things happened. Some of the children were told that one of the groups was to receive a reward (some new transistor radios) for helping with the research, while the other would not, apparently due to a shortage of resources. This common outcome of 'reward' or 'deprivation' was decided by the toss of a coin, by the experimenter in an arbitrary fashion, or by one of the two groups themselves. In Lewin's terms all of these groups experienced 'interdependence of fate', whether they obtained the radios or not. However, in the remaining control condition this experience was omitted; the group members thus had nothing more in common than their colour label. Finally, the participants were asked to rate each other privately on a number of sociometric scales. The question was: would these impressionistic ratings of what were more or less complete strangers be influenced by their respective group memberships and thus indicate that some primitive group had formed? The results showed that in the conditions in which some interdependence existed there did indeed seem to be some group influence on the ratings. Those in the child's own group were rated more favourably than those from the other group. This was true regardless of whether they had been 'rewarded' or 'deprived' and irrespective of how that fate had been decided. On the other hand, in the control condition the ratings of ingroup and outgroup members appeared not to differ. Rabbie and Horwitz (1969) concluded from these results that mere classification itself was not sufficient to form a group and influence people's judgements along group lines. What seemed to be necessary for group formation was some experience of interdependence.

Actually, as we shall see in chapter 7, that conclusion turned out to be premature. Under the right conditions, simply being arbitrarily categorized into one group rather than another does reliably generate forms of group behaviour. Indeed, Rabbie and Horwitz themselves found indications of this when, in a follow-up study, they increased the size of their control group. With the larger sample (and hence greater statistical power) some significant ingroup–outgroup differences were then visible, even in this most minimal of group situation (Horwitz and Rabbie, 1982). Nevertheless, these biases were still much weaker than those observed in the 'common fate' conditions, thus confirming Lewin's initial surmise about the importance of interdependence of fate.

Task interdependence

Common fate is the weakest form of interdependence. Much more important as far as group process is concerned, argued Lewin (1948), is some interdependence in the goals of group members: where the group's task is such that each member's achievements have implications for his or her fellow members' achievements. These implications may be positive or negative. In the former case one person's success either directly facilitates others' success or, in the strongest case, is actually necessary for those others to succeed also. Thus, in a sports team one player's brilliance (or ineptitude) has beneficial (or deleterious) consequences for the other players in the same team. In some kinds of teams there is a high degree of complementarity between the members, with each person playing a crucial role. A group of scientific researchers comprised of theoretical specialists, technical designers and computer analysts would be a case in point. In negative interdependence – known more usually as competition – one person's success is another's failure. The practice in some companies of providing financial incentives based on individual performance relative to other individuals is an example of negative interdependence.

What evidence is there for the importance of task interdependence in determining group process, and what exactly are the consequences? To begin with, we should note that for a great many groups the very rationale for their existence is explicitly defined in terms of some common goal or objective. In the written constitution of my trade union, for example, the first paragraph of substance spells out the 'objects of the Association', which are 'the advancement of University Education and Research, the regulation of relations between University Teachers and their employers, the promotion of common action by University Teachers and the safeguarding of the interests of the members' (Association of University Teachers, 1985). In a survey of some 300 voluntary associations, Zander (1972) observed how the public descriptions of their activities nearly always referred to the purposes (or objectives) of the group.

What effect does defining the group's task in different ways have on the subsequent process in the group? The first serious attempt to answer this question was made by Deutsch (1949a), who developed Lewin's ideas into a number of testable hypotheses. Deutsch argued that under positive interdependence people are motivated to cooperate with and help each other and will like each other, and the group as a whole will be propelled strongly towards its goal. On the other hand, in situations of negative interdependence they will be more motivated to compete with others and will like them less, and the overall group force in the direction of the goal will be lessened. Associated with these effects should be a greater amount of communication about the task and higher group productivity in the positively interdependent situations. Deutsch (1949b) tested these hypotheses using a small number of student groups attending a psychology course. Half the group members were informed that they would be evaluated according to the performance of their group. In fact, all members of the group would receive the same grade, this being determined by comparing their group's performance with other groups in the class. These people were therefore positively interdependent on each other. The remaining students were informed that they would receive individual grades according to how well they performed in the group, the best students receiving the best grades. Thus, these were negatively interdependent on one another. Over a period of five weeks, the groups worked on a series of human relations and logical problems and their discussions were monitored by observers. In addition, self-report measures of attitudes towards the task and fellow group members, and objective measures of performance were taken. As expected, the groups working under conditions of positive interdependence showed more cooperativeness towards one another, appeared to participate and communicate more in the discussion tasks, liked one another more, were less aggressive and on various indices were actually more productive than the groups working under negative task interdependence.

Later research has largely confirmed these findings. For example, Rosenbaum et al. (1980) examined both group performance and group process in a tower construction task where the degree of positive or

Table 2.1 Group performance and group process under different forms of interdependence

| | Type of interdependence | | | | |
	100% positive	80/20	50/50	20/80	100% negative
Productivity (no. of blocks)	110.5	84.5	88.4	75.6	69.0
Coordination (turn-taking)	0.8	0.7	0.7	0.7	0.5
Interpersonal attraction for other group members	27.2	26.1	22.4	24.5	23.2

Source: Rosenbaum et al. (1980), table 4. Copyright (1980) by the American Psychological Association. Reprinted by permission of the author

negative interdependence was carefully controlled. In groups of three, the object of the exercise was to build as high a tower as possible. Depending on which condition the group was in, they were financially rewarded in the following ways: as a function of the total number of blocks comprising the tower (maximum positive interdependence), according to who had contributed the most blocks to the construction, the winner receiving all the money (maximum negative interdependence), or according to some combination of these two allocation systems. As can be seen from table 2.1, as the degree of interdependence among the group members becomes more negative, the productivity drops off, the degree of coordination (indicated by turn-taking) declines and the amount of interpersonal attraction decreases. Just as Deutsch had found some thirty years earlier, where the group task links its members in a cooperative structure the result is greater cooperation, increased cohesion and enhanced performance.

This superiority of cooperative task structures on performance was confirmed by Johnson et al. (1981) in an extensive review of studies of group performance. Of the 109 studies that compared cooperative with competitive structures, they found that 65 showed a superiority of the cooperative structure, and only 8 the reverse.

The motivation and performance advantages conferred by cooperation have important implications in education (Sharan, 1990; Slavin, 1983). Evidence is accumulating that organizing students into cooperative learning groups produces consistently better student achievement. In such a system, one typically makes a whole group responsible for producing some single piece of work or for achieving a certain standard of performance among the individual group members. Ideally, one arranges the reward incentives (e.g. marks, teacher praise) to be allocated to the group as a whole. When this is done students usually respond by working harder and are motivated to assist their less able peers. Indeed, Slavin (1983) reports that over 80 per cent of intervention studies using such cooperative learning techniques produced noticeable gains in student learning. And, as we shall see (chapter 8), the advantages of cooperative learning groups are not solely academic; social relations and intergroup attitudes are also more positive when students are learning cooperatively (Johnson et al., 1984; Miller and Davidson-Podgorny, 1987; Slavin, 1983).

This apparently unassailable superiority of cooperation should cause us to question seriously the overwhelming emphasis on *competitive* arrangements in our educational institutions and workplaces. The evidence is that such arrangements are quite literally counterproductive.

Achieving the Task and Maintaining Relationships

Although Deutsch and other researchers in the Lewinian tradition convincingly demonstrated the importance of task goals for determining the subsequent group process in general terms, little of this work sheds much light on how the task was actually achieved. Even those Lewinians who specifically addressed questions of communication in the group tended to be more concerned with the quantity and direction of communications rather than with a detailed analysis of their content (e.g. Festinger, 1950; Schachter, 1951).[2] This gap was filled by another group of researchers working at the same time as, and indeed in close geographical proximity to, Deutsch and his colleagues. At the centre of this group was the figure of R.F. Bales, who, like Lewin, came to exert a considerable influence on post-War group psychology.[3]

Interaction process analysis

Bales's starting point was to assume that the *raison d'être* of any small group is the achievement of some task. Thus, for Bales, any activity in the group is seen as being ultimately directed towards this end.[4] From this basic standpoint, Bales went on to make a number of important observations.

The first and most fundamental is his distinction between task-related or 'instrumental' behaviour, and socio-emotional or 'expressive' behaviour. Ultimately, as we have just noted, Bales believes that people's actions in a group are geared towards the group goal. Thus, whether they be social workers in a case conference, jurors in a trial or engineers grappling with a design problem, what the participants say and do to one another will mainly revolve around the group's goal (recommend a course of action for a client, reach a verdict or solve the technical difficulty). However, in all this 'instrumental' activity certain problems may arise that threaten the stability of the group. People may disagree with one another over the way the group should tackle the task at hand, the discussion may expose conflicting value systems, or perhaps there is some urgency implied by an externally imposed timetable. These kinds of factors are likely to generate tensions that, suggests Bales, may impede the group's progress towards its goal. Accordingly, counteracting processes will come into play to deal with those tensions. Bales (1953) uses a cathartic metaphor to describe this; he suggests that the tensions in the group need to be 'bled off' by means of 'expressive' activities. These processes focus on interpersonal relationships and reveal themselves in behaviours that are directly expressive of the person's own emotions or that are concerned in some way with the feelings of others. They may take the form of outbursts of laughter or anger, or expressions of sympathy or rejection for another in the group. However, since these socio-emotional behaviours are essentially subservient to the task-related activities, they are more likely to take a positive (or reinforcing) form than to be negative or inhibitory.

A second key aspect to Bales's theorizing – one that follows directly from his functionalist perspective – is his assumption that groups have a natural tendency towards equilibrium (Bales, 1953). Any action is likely to produce a *reaction*. Questions will tend to elicit answers or attempted answers. 'Instrumental' activities need to be balanced by 'expressive' activities, and so on. This homeostatic principle is closely tied to Bales's conception of how groups go about the business of tackling their task. He proposed that this has three components: orientation, evaluation and control. The group must first orientate itself to the problem it faces and acquaint itself with all the relevant information. Typically, this will involve a high level of communication and exchange of opinions. These different ideas then need to be evaluated to enable the group to move towards some decision. As the decision time approaches, the members of the group will start to exert control over each other in order that the decision is successfully articulated and implemented. Typically, at this stage, there is also a need for an increase in socio-emotional activity to reduce any tensions aroused by the preceding stages.

On the basis of these ideas Bales (1950) devised a coding scheme for the observation and analysis of group interaction. In this scheme – called interaction process analysis (IPA) – the interaction in the group is broken down into a series of microscopic 'acts'. Exactly what constitutes an act is rather ambiguous in the coding system. For example, a sentence in a verbal utterance, some non-linguistic vocalization and non-verbal behaviours such as facial expressions, gestures or bodily attitude could all be regarded as acts in IPA. Essentially an act is the smallest meaningful and discriminable piece of behaviour that an observer can detect, and through training some consensus is reached between judges as to how fine the distinctions should be. Each act is classified by the observer(s) into one of the twelve mutually exclusive categories shown in figure 2.2, together with a note of the committer of the act and its intended recipient.

At the end of the period of observation it is possible to collate the observations in each category and provide an interaction profile of the group as a whole (in terms of the percentages of time spent engaged on the different categories of behaviour), of individuals in the group, or (the most complete picture of all) the proportion of time each person spent interacting with the others and in what manner. These profiles have many uses. They can be used as data for the testing of particular research hypotheses about the consequences of certain independent variables on group process, or they may be used in clinical and educational settings for analysing the recurrent interaction patterns

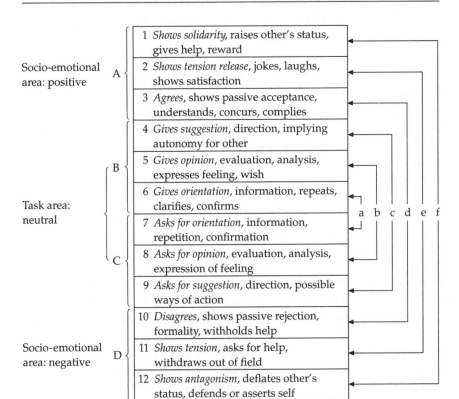

Figure 2.2 The coding categories in interaction process analysis and their major relations: (a) problems of communication; (b) problems of evaluation; (c) problems of control; (d) problems of decision; (e) problems of tension reduction; (f) problems of reintegration; (A) positive reactions; (B) attempted answers; (C) questions; (D) negative reactions (from Bales, 1950. Copyright © University of Chicago Press)

in, for example, a family or a seminar group. Examples of studies that have used IPA are reviewed in Hare (1976).

Just how reliable and valid is IPA? After three or four months' intensive training, observers are reported to be able to achieve reasonable reliability both in the sense of agreeing among themselves and being reasonably consistent over time when re-scoring the same material (Borgatta and Bales, 1953; Heinicke and Bales, 1953). Mann (1961) found that varying the group's activity between a relatively task-orientated problem with a clear-cut solution and a more socio-emotional issue involving value judgements and consensus did produce small but reliable differences in the amount of behaviour scored in several of the IPA categories, thus indicating that the system is responsive to presumed changes in the group's behaviour. Ultimately, however, the value of any methodological innovation lies less in these formal assessments of reliability and validity than in its ability to shed new light on the phenomena of interest. In this, IPA has been strikingly successful. Hare (1976) and McGrath (1984) have summarized some of the more important conclusions that have emerged from research with IPA: some group members consistently talk more than others; people who talk the most tend to receive the most attention from the group; the discrepancy between the leading initiator in the group and his or her peers increases with the size of the group – large groups are more likely to be dominated by a single individual; different people in the group often tend to predominate in particular coding categories, suggesting a degree of role specialization (see chapter 3); the interaction profile for a typical laboratory discussion group is quite stable and consists of nearly two-thirds task 'acts' (especially categories 4–6), one-quarter positive socio-emotional behaviours (categories 1–3) and the remainder negative socio-emotional behaviours, although other kinds of group reveal very different patterns; in problem-solving groups there are consistent changes over time in the preponderance of different kinds of activities – for example, the proportion of informational 'acts' declines as the discussion proceeds, while positive socio-emotional 'acts' typically increase, especially during the final decision phase.

All of these generalizations are based on the detailed objective observation of group behaviour that is the hallmark of IPA. Almost completely missing from all this work is the more subjective data from within the group itself. In his early work, Bales deliberately eschewed this source of information but subsequently he has rectified this omission by turning his attention to the nature of relationships within the group as perceived by the group members themselves (e.g. Bales, 1970; Bales and Cohen, 1979).

Group Cohesion

A recurring theme in several of the previous sections has been how various structural features of groups and different social processes that go on within them can contribute to the development and maintenance of group solidarity, commitment, morale, esprit de corps – call it what you will. It is this collection of terms, usually subsumed under the general heading of 'cohesion', which is the focus of this section. What exactly do we mean by cohesion? What gives rise to it? And what are its major consequences? These are the three questions I want to try to answer here.

What is cohesion?

In everyday language it is reasonably clear what we mean when we talk of a cohesive team or workgroup: it is a group that seems to stick together and in which the members want to remain. This common-sense definition of cohesion is reflected in one of the first definitions of the term:

the 'cement' binding together group members and maintaining their relationships to one another. (Schachter et al., 1951, p. 229)

The trouble with this early formulation is that it was rather vague as to what the 'cement' consisted of. As subsequent researchers grappled with the issue, a consensus emerged that cohesion should be regarded as the sum of the interpersonal attractions that existed among the group members (e.g. Lott and Lott, 1965). In other words, a cohesive group was one in which everyone liked one another and, moreover, the degree of cohesion could be measured by how much they did so. As we shall see, equating cohesiveness with friendship patterns in this way strongly influenced three decades of research into the origins of group cohesion.

Treating cohesion and positive interpersonal relations as equivalent had an attractive simplicity and certainly made life easier for the empirically orientated groups researcher. For now it seemed possible to obtain a quantitative measure quite straightforwardly from the collated sociometric preferences of the group members. Unfortunately, as Hogg (1992) has pointed out, such a conceptualization was an oversimplification. First, it reduced a quintessentially group phenomenon to the mere aggregate of some individual properties, implying that the group was no more (or no less) than the sum of its constituents

(Gross and Martin, 1952). As we saw in chapter 1, such a reductionist viewpoint is not without its problems. Second, it ran into problems at an empirical level since some measures of attraction to the group seemed unrelated to measures of sociometric preference (Eisman, 1959). Even more problematically, as we shall shortly discover, it is possible for a group to remain cohesive even when its members *dislike* each other! Third, conceiving of cohesion in terms of what are presumably face-to-face relationships excludes its use in connection with much larger groups, in which the majority of the members may not know each other at all. Such groups could include sports crowds or employees in a large corporation, about which it is still possible (and useful) to talk of cohesion.

Hogg's (1992) solution to these difficulties is to define cohesion in terms of group members' attraction to the *idea* of the group, its consensual prototypical image and how that is reflected in typical member characteristics and behaviour. That is, a group is cohesive to the extent that its members identify strongly with its key features and aspirations. This perspective stems from Turner et al.'s (1987) Self Categorization Theory, which proposes that assimilation (to the ingroup prototype) and contrast (from an outgroup prototype) are the basic processes determining all group behaviour (see chapter 4). Thus, for Hogg (1992), the group cohesiveness stems from 'social' attraction to one's fellow group members *as group members*, whatever they are like as individuals; this should be distinguished from the traditional perspective, which emphasizes 'interpersonal' attraction to other individuals who happen to be in the group and who happen to possess desirable personal characteristics. As we shall see in the next section, such a theoretical distinction generates some interesting implications although, in practice, the two kinds of attraction are often conflated: we may like the members of our team just because they are on our side, but we frequently like them for who they are too.

The origins of cohesion

Not surprisingly, given the initial definitions of cohesion in terms of mutual liking among group members, early work on the origins of cohesiveness tended to focus on factors that were associated with interpersonal attraction. The simplest of these is physical proximity, which usually leads to greater frequency of interaction and hence to liking, presumably through the discovery of similarity of tastes and attitudes. The classic demonstration of the effects of propinquity was a study of friendship networks in a student housing complex (Festinger et al., 1950). Festinger et al. (1950) showed how groups of friends tended to spring up within a particular apartment block and often within the same corridor within these blocks. The researchers were able to link this friendship formation quite precisely to the physical distance apart that people lived, a finding later confirmed by others (Ebbesen et al., 1976). Moreover, that these were genuine groups (as opposed to a series of personal friendships) was demonstrated by observing the operation of normative standards within each residence block (Festinger et al., 1950).

Such normative standards lead to greater uniformity of opinion within the group, which, over time, reinforces the mutual attraction. This was observed by Newcomb (1961) in a famous longitudinal study of acquaintanceship, also conducted in a college residence. The development of dyadic and triadic networks among a collection of students who were initially all strangers to one another was related to an increasing tendency for them to develop similar attitudes. Most laboratory studies of group cohesion capitalize on this link between similarity and attraction by employing experimental manipulations that lead the would-be group members to believe that they share similar views and hence will probably like one another (e.g. Zander et al., 1960).

However, similarity among members is not always an important determinant of cohesion. In task-focused groups the ease with which the group goal can be achieved may assume priority. This was shown by Anderson (1975), who created laboratory groups that were actually composed of people with similar or dissimilar values. Their goal was to design a new student dormitory. This goal was facilitated (or impeded) by providing the group members with similar (or different) briefing and training materials. Cohesion was measured by a simple question at the end of their discussion: would they wish to remain in the group for a further session? The results were clear: the majority (85 per cent) of those whose task interaction had been more straightforward said they wished to stay put while only 45 per cent of those in the 'impeded' condition so indicated. Importantly, value similarity had *no effect* on desire to remain in the group.

47

The fact that successful cooperation on a joint task increases cohesion should come as no surprise. In an earlier section I noted how positive task interdependence was an important ingredient of many groups and typically leads to better morale and performance. It is important to realize that it is not just interdependence within the group that affects cohesion; the nature of the *intergroup* relationship is also significant. Anyone who has ever participated in a team competition or been involved in any kind of intergroup dispute will testify how these lead to an increase in the solidarity within the ingroup. In 1996 university staff all over Britain staged an almost unprecedented one-day strike over pay. Despite (or perhaps because of) the novelty of this form of industrial action for most academics, it was remarkable how, in the days before and after the strike, previously unacquainted colleagues engaged in much supportive interaction with each other.

Many years ago the sociologist William Sumner, commenting on this phenomenon, suggested a direct and functional link between intergroup conflict and cohesion:

The relation of comradeship and peace in the we-group and that of hostility and war towards others-groups are correlative of each other. The exigencies of war with outsiders are what make peace inside, lest internal discord should weaken the we-group for war. (Sumner, 1906, p. 12)

This is, of course, exactly what Sherif and his colleagues observed in their famous 'summer camp' studies (Sherif, 1966; see chapter 6). As the competition between the groups intensified so each group became more tightly knit. This connection between conflict and cohesion was confirmed by Julian et al. (1966) when they compared army squads training under a competitive team regime and squads under less competitive conditions. On a number of measures they found that the competitive squads showed greater solidarity and morale than the control groups.

In intergroup competitions, there are winners and losers. What are the consequences of such outcomes for group cohesion? Common sense suggests that when the result is favourable for the ingroup, cohesion will increase; when the ingroup looks like losing there may be forces towards resentment and disintegration. A study by Myers (1962) lent support to this idea. He compared over a four-week period the changes in morale of army cadet rifle teams who took part in either a competitive league (against one another) or a non-competitive league (against some absolute standard). As usual, intergroup competition had the effect of increasing group morale, but this greater cohesion was strongly qualified by how well the teams did in the rifle shooting events. In general, those who succeeded (whether in competition or not) showed higher morale; those who did badly reported less satisfaction with one another (see also Worchel et al., 1975).

The conclusion from these studies seems clear: success breeds cohesion, failure lowers morale. But does defeat always result in such negative outcomes? Experience suggests not. Many years ago my son was playing for his school football team. They had a disastrous season, losing every match except one, sometimes by double-figure margins! And yet, despite this string of ignominious defeats, the team remained remarkably buoyant and pleased with itself, after each match finding solace in the reduced size of the deficit, the number of goals they had scored or how hard they had tried. A similar phenomenon was observed (somewhat more systematically) by Taylor et al. (1983) in their longitudinal case study of a college ice hockey team. Like my son's football side, this team did not have a very good year, winning only 3 of its 25 games and in one match going down by a full 16 goals! Nevertheless, Taylor et al., who were able to obtain ratings from team members after every game, report that the overall level of cohesiveness and team spirit stayed high throughout the season. While there were consistent positive correlations between each match's outcome and the team members' levels of cohesion, the latter seldom dipped below the midpoint of the satisfaction scale, even after that crushing 16-goal defeat.

There is also some evidence that a positive reaction to negative outcomes may be linked to developmental processes. In a study of children's intergroup comparisons we allocated 3-, 5-, 7- and 9-year-old children to an obviously 'fast' or 'slow' team for a forthcoming egg-and-spoon race (Yee and Brown, 1992). One of our dependent measures assessed cohesion ('how much would you like to stay in your team?'). Not surprisingly, a vast majority (86 per cent) of the 'fast' team members elected to stay, and this was true in all four age groups studied. Those in the 'slow' team generally showed the opposite reaction. With the exception of one age group, over 70 per cent now wanted to *leave* their group. The exceptions were the 5-year-olds, of

49

whom over two-thirds still felt sufficiently positive about their group to want to remain in it. It is possible that this strong attachment to the group in these children, even in the face of imminent loss of group status, is associated with a more generic collectivist orientation at that age which manifests itself as strong ethnic and gender identification and, not infrequently, in an ethnocentric outlook towards other groups (Aboud, 1988; see chapter 8).

How can this maintenance of cohesion in the face of repeated failure be explained? According to Turner et al. (1984), it may have to do with the group members' high level of identification with and commitment to the group, which have been fostered by them choosing to belong to the group in the first place. Resurrecting an idea from cognitive dissonance theory (Festinger, 1957), they argue that when people feel personally responsible for their behaviour – for example, when they have voluntarily chosen to join a group – then if that behaviour results in negative consequences for them (i.e. the group does badly) they will justify these negative consequences by increasing their identification with the group. Such reasoning might go as follows: 'I chose to enter this group because it seemed attractive to me. Nevertheless, the group failed in its objectives. Why, then, did I join this apparently not so good group? It must have been because it was even more important for me than I originally thought'. To test this hypothesis, Turner et al. designed an experiment in which schoolgirls took part in an intergroup problem-solving competition. The crucial variable manipulated was whether the girls believed they had chosen to belong to their group or, alternatively, whether it seemed to have been decided completely by the experimenters. The distinction was, in fact, illusory since nobody was really given any choice, but in half the groups it was made to seem that they were by giving them a form to sign, which stated that they agreed to stay in their present group. After the competition – which, of course, one group had to lose – various scales measuring self-esteem and cohesiveness were administered. For those who had had 'no choice' about their group membership, the usual pattern emerged: winning groups showed greater cohesiveness and reported higher levels of self-esteem than losers. However, for the voluntary 'choice' groups this pattern was completely reversed, as can be seen from figure 2.3; losing groups had more cohesion (and higher self-esteem) than winning groups.

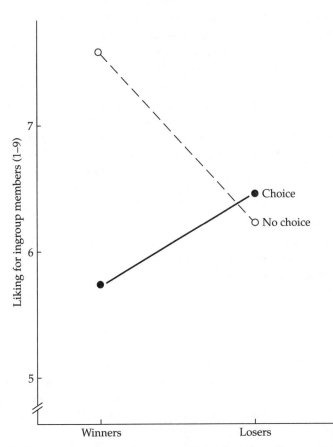

Figure 2.3   Group cohesiveness after victory and defeat (from Turner et al., 1984)

The emphasis on interpersonal similarity and the outcomes of interdependence in much of the work on cohesion has its roots in an essentially functionalist perspective of the group. People are attracted to a group in so far as it satisfies certain of their needs (e.g. of affiliation or of goal achievement). However, as we saw in discussing how to define cohesion, this is not an undisputed view. Hogg (1992), in particular, has argued that an elementary form – perhaps *the* elementary form – stems from categorization processes: the simple dichotomy of the world into ingroup and outgroup. As noted earlier, he terms this 'social attraction' and argues that it results from group members' desire to model themselves more closely on what they perceive to be the prototypical position of the ingroup. They are thereby attracted to those who resemble that prototype, whether or not they have much else in common with them personally.

Two interesting implications follow from this analysis. One is that it ought to be possible to distinguish this form of cohesion from the more traditional variety based on interpersonal attraction. They should be independent and have separate effects and antecedents. The second is that cohesion should be observable even in what are otherwise 'unattractive' groups (i.e. groups comprised of unlikeable individuals). The evidence for these two predictions is mixed. On the one hand, a series of studies conducted with both real groups (e.g. sports teams) and experimental groups have found that there is usually a stronger correlation between social attraction and prototypical group members than between personal attraction and those same people (Hogg et al., 1993; Hogg and Hardie, 1992; Hogg and Hains, 1996). Moreover, Hogg and Turner (1985) found that the experimentally varied likeableness of stimulus individuals in an impression-formation task strongly affected people's interpersonal liking for them and their perceived similarity to the person making the rating. More interestingly, though, was the effect of an experimentally induced categorization. In some conditions individuals were classified as belonging to the subject's own group or another group; in other conditions no such categorization occurred. The effect of this categorization variable was to make the groups more or less attractive (irrespective of how likeable the individual members of them were). This supports the idea that group-based cohesion effects seem to be driven by different factors than cohesion deriving from interpersonal attraction. Nevertheless, the two types of cohesion are not usually completely independent, as a strict interpretation of Hogg's (1992) model should suggest. Hogg and Hardie (1992) and Hogg et al. (1993) reported significant and sometimes sizeable correlations between measures of personal and social popularity – i.e. people's 'best friends' were often also 'good group members'. It is still too early to say whether these associations reflect the complexity and multiplicity of variables inherent in the naturalistic settings in which these studies were conducted, or some underlying common causation.

Consequences of cohesion

Group cohesion is a 'good thing' – or so common sense (and human resource management manuals) would have us believe. It is good because it means that group members like one another more, which should mean they are happier, and if they are happier they are likely to work harder. In fact, as is so often the case, the story is not quite so simple. First, the cohesion–performance relationship, while a reliable effect, is not very strong and seems to vary greatly across different group contexts. This was revealed by Mullen and Copper (1994) in a meta-analysis of 49 studies. They did observe a significant correlation between cohesion and performance across these studies but it was of modest size (averaging around 0.25). Some kinds of groups – particularly sports teams – showed a much stronger relationship; others – e.g. work and laboratory groups – showed a weaker correlation. Second, as Mullen and Copper (1994) also discovered, it seems that cohesion based on commitment to the group task is a more effective determinant of performance than cohesion based on interpersonal attraction. Thus, if increased cohesion has beneficial effects on group productivity, it does so because the members are more strongly identified with the group goals than because they necessarily like one another more. Third, and most problematic of all for the common-sense hypothesis, it seems that the causal direction that it proposes (from cohesion to performance) may be back to front. This was first suggested by Bakeman and Helmreich (1975) in a longitudinal study of ten deep-sea diving teams. These teams spent a long time under water (182 days) and their behaviour over this time was carefully monitored by trained observers. From these observations measures of cohesion (derived from conversational patterns among the team members) and performance (proportion of time spent on 'work' behaviours) were constructed at different points of the 'dive'. Overall, these two indices were well correlated. But a cross-lagged panel analysis[5] strongly suggested that it was performance causing the cohesion rather than the other way around: superior performance early on in a team's dive was correlated with subsequent cohesion, but initial cohesion was not reliably related to later performance. This pattern (of a stronger performance–cohesion than cohesion–performance link) was confirmed by Mullen and Copper (1994).

Perhaps the strongest argument of all against accepting a facile link between cohesion and performance was provided by the earliest experiments investigating the issue (Berkowitz, 1954; Schachter et al., 1951). These researchers reasoned that the primary effect of cohesion is to increase adherence to the prevailing norms in the group rather than to affect performance *per se*. If these norms favour greater productivity then cohesion should, indeed, enhance performance. On the other hand, if the norms inhibit productivity then increased cohesion should lead to *lowered* performance. In their experiment, Schachter et al. (1951) found evidence for the second but, ironically, not for the first of these predictions. They created high and low cohesion groups by informing the participants that prior testing had established that they would (or would not) get along with one another. The groups were then set to work on a task. Each group member was given a separate job to perform and was separated from fellow group members in cubicles. By this device the experiments could control the type of communication between the group members (written notes only). By intercepting the notes that the participants wrote to each other and substituting other messages, Schachter et al. were able to generate 'high' or 'low' performance norms in different experimental conditions (e.g. in the high norm condition a message might read, 'Time's running out, let's make a spurt'; in the low norm condition a typical message was, 'take it easy, I'm tired'). Schachter et al. found that performance in the low performance norm conditions was significantly impaired among the highly cohesive groups but not for the less cohesive groups. There was no corresponding effect in the opposite direction in the high norm conditions. However, a subsequent study, using a very similar procedure but a slightly stronger manipulation of cohesiveness, found significant decrements *and* increments in the low and high norm conditions, respectively, just as predicted (Berkowitz, 1954; see figure 2.4).

If cohesion has any effects on enhancing performance, then it seems that it does so via norms fostering higher productivity. In fact, this conclusion turns out to be a special case of a more general consequence of group cohesion: that of an increased adherence to the norms relevant to the particular context. This was first observed by Festinger et al. (1950) in their study of student residences described earlier. In one of the housing complexes they noticed a reliable negative correlation

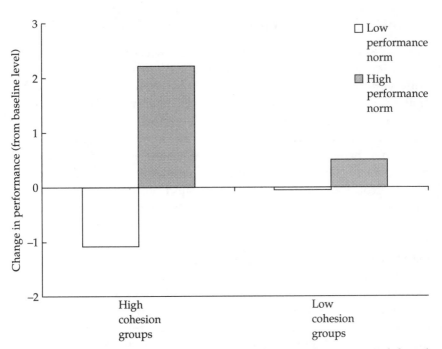

Figure 2.4 Group performance depends on both cohesion and group norms (adapted from Berkowitz, 1954, table 2)

between the cohesion of each block and the percentage of 'deviates' in that block: the more cohesive the group, the fewer people there were who 'stepped out of line', thus indicating greater conformity to the local norms. The link between cohesion and normative influence had not always been found, however. O'Reilly and Caldwell (1985) found very weak and inconsistent correlations between cohesiveness and the intensity of group norms in a business organization. Nor is it necessary for cohesion to be measured (or induced) through group member interaction or attraction (as it was in these studies) to observe greater conformity to group norms. Hogg and Hardie (1992) found that the mere mention of the word 'group' in the introductory instructions on an autokinetic experiment (see next section) was enough to cause significantly increased convergence in people's judgements. That the mere invocation of a category could have had such an effect is further evidence that cohesion can have origins other than interpersonal attraction (Hogg, 1992).

The Acquisition and Development of Group Norms

In previous sections much of the emphasis was on the regularities in the patterning of behaviour, which seemed fairly consistent across a wide variety of groups. In this section, by contrast, the key word is *idiosyncrasy* rather than communality. For, as even the most superficial observation confirms, groups have various ways of viewing the world; they hold different values and attitudes; and, in the last analysis, they behave quite uniquely. Underlying all this diversity are systems of norms, systems that are to be found in every imaginable human group – from the loosest knit collection of friends to the most structured of institutions. Because of the universality of such systems and because of their importance in governing people's behaviour, the factors involved in the acquisition and development of norms represent the last of our 'elementary group processes'.

Just what is a norm? Paraphrasing Sherif and Sherif (1969), we can say that a norm is a scale of values which defines a range of acceptable (and unacceptable) attitudes and behaviours for members of a social unit. Norms specify, more or less precisely, certain rules for how group members should behave and thus are the basis for mutual expectations among the group members. Examples of group norms in action would include the different styles of dress and appearance adopted by various subgroups in Britain, ranging from the colourful unorthodoxy of 'punks' to the bizarre traditionalism of the royal enclosure at Ascot. The varied lifestyles and mores of different sections of society (those favourite topics for Sunday newspaper exposés) also reflect the operation of different normative standards, as do, in a much wider context, the rich variety of cultural practices around the world, which have been documented by social anthropologists (e.g. Mead, 1935; van Gennep, 1960).

Earlier in this chapter we saw what happens when people join a group for the first time. I want now to return to this theme to illustrate how group norms come to be incorporated by the new members. One of the earliest attempts to document this process was Newcomb's study of an American college in the 1930s, the Bennington Study (Newcomb, 1961). Bennington College was a small, private college with a strong liberal political ethos. However, despite its progressive outlook it recruited mainly from very conservative upper middle class families. What Newcomb showed, by a careful longitudinal study of cohorts of students through the college, was that their initially conservative attitudes underwent a radical reversal during their college career. Just one example will suffice to illustrate this. During the study the 1936 US Presidential election occurred and within the college a mock election was also held. Newcomb was able to analyse the votes cast in this mock election. From the first-year students, who had only been at the college a month or two, there was a solid majority for the conservative Republican candidate over the more liberal Roosevelt (62 per cent versus 29 per cent). This was entirely consistent with their conservative family backgrounds. However, the third- and fourth-year students, whose families were no less reactionary, voted 54 per cent to 19 per cent in favour of Roosevelt, and fully 30 per cent of them even voted for the Communist/Socialist candidates! (Versus only 9 per cent of the first years.) The impact of Bennington's liberal norms on its students seems clear.

Of course, it could be objected to Newcomb's findings that the different year groups within the college may not have been strictly comparable. For instance, the senior students were also older. Perhaps what he had discovered was simply a maturational effect rather than any effect of group norms. That this is an unlikely explanation was shown by Siegel and Siegel (1957) in a rather similar study. In the college they studied there were two kinds of housing available to students. There were the traditional and rather conservative sorority-type residences and there were more liberal dormitories and halls of residence. Allocation to these different types of housing was essentially random, names being drawn out of a hat. Siegel and Siegel exploited this almost perfect natural experiment by measuring students' attitudes in these different residences at the beginning and end of their first year, using a measure of political conservatism. Because the groups had been formed randomly (as in a good laboratory experiment) they should have been very nearly equivalent at the start of the year. Their conservatism scores confirmed this: the mean score in the sorority group was 103 as against 102 in the other group. However, by the end of the year the effect of the different group norms prevailing in the two residences was plain: the mean conservatism in the liberal group had dropped by nearly 15 points, while in the more traditional sorority it had declined by a trivial 4 points.

In these two studies the impact of the group's norms on individuals' behaviour could only be indirectly inferred from changes in their attitudes, and the actual process of acquisition was studied in a rather gross fashion. However, detailed observational research on new entrants to children's groups has revealed how individuals come to incorporate pre-existing group standards into their own behaviour. For instance, McGrew (1972) studied the behaviour of young Scottish children (3–4 years) over the first few days in their nursery. He noticed how the new children tended not to join in the communal activities at first but spent most of their time in careful observation of the others at play. Similar findings were obtained in the USA by Feldbaum et al. (1980), who observed that some of the differences between the newcomers and their 'hosts' persisted for as long as four weeks after entry. It seems as if new members of children's groups spend some time trying to discover what the appropriate 'ground rules' are before joining in fully. Experience of my own children going to nursery and then to primary school confirms for me the reality of this 'probationary period'. Putallaz and Gottman (1981) analysed the behaviour of 'popular' and 'unpopular' children upon entry to the group and concluded that the 'popular' entrants were those who tended to join in the ongoing activities rather than try to impose new games on the others, supporting observations of Phillips et al. (1951) some years previously. More generally, there is increasing evidence that peer groups exert as strong, if not stronger, an influence over children's development, attitudes and behaviour than parents or family (Harris, 1995).

Individual and social functions of norms

There seems little doubt, then, that the group's norms, whether these be long-established traditions or merely informally evolved patterns of activity, have considerable significance for group members. What functions do these norms serve and why are they so fundamental to an understanding of group behaviour? We can answer this question in two ways: first by considering what functions they serve for the *individual*, and then by assessing their *social* significance from the perspective of the group itself.

For the individual, norms act as frames of reference through which the world is interpreted. They can be seen as construct systems with associated values, which bring order and predictability to a person's environment. Thus, the norms that my students and I evolve over the first few meetings of a seminar group about the extent of preparatory work that will be needed and about how the seminar discussions should proceed help me – and I hope them also – to function more effectively in the seminar. Norms are especially useful in novel or ambiguous situations, where they can act as pointers to how to behave. Hence the wariness of those nursery children in the studies discussed above: without a clear idea of what was socially appropriate, they hung back and watched.

The idea of norms as 'signposts' guiding the individual through unfamiliar territory was beautifully illustrated by Sherif (1936) in what is justly regarded as one of the single most significant experiments in the history of social psychology. In this experiment Sherif made use of an optical illusion known as the autokinetic effect. The illusion can be experienced by staring at a minute pinprick of light in a completely dark room. Very soon the light appears to move erratically even though the source itself remains stationary.[6] Sherif confronted individual participants with this illusion and asked them to estimate orally how far the light moved on each occasion. Over a hundred trials, Sherif found that each participant's estimates tended to stabilize around some idiosyncratic mean value. Sherif then ran exactly the same experiment in groups of two and three and made a remarkable discovery: the participants' estimates of movement rapidly converged until they were giving almost indistinguishable answers from one another. They had, in other words, developed a primitive group norm that served to constrain their judgements within quite narrow limits. Intriguingly, this norm continued to be influential even when they were retested on their own, their subsequent estimates deviating very little from the previously established value.

An obvious interpretation of these findings is that the judgements of the others took the place of the usual physical cues that aid visual perception (Gibson, 1966). The group norm served as a useful frame of reference in what was otherwise a completely unstructured and perhaps somewhat anxiety-provoking situation. And there is no question that this norm must be a genuinely social product. Objectively the light is fixed and so there can be no right or wrong judgements. Consequently, left to their own devices people report widely different amounts of movement. It is only when they are exposed to the influence of each other that they converge to a common point of view.

If norms are useful to individuals in helping them to construe and predict their world, they serve equally useful social functions also. First, they help to regulate social existence and hence help to coordinate group members' activities. To return to my seminar example, if we did not have those norms concerning the conduct of the seminar (e.g. that people should not all talk simultaneously), it is doubtful whether the group could really function as a learning unit at all. This social regulatory function is, of course, closely related to the predictability that norms contribute on an individual level. Second, norms will be closely tied to the goals of the group, which we have already seen as being of critical importance. Once a group develops a clearly defined goal inevitably norms encouraging goal-facilitative actions and discouraging inhibitory behaviours will emerge. An example of this was observed by Coch and French (1948) in their study of group productivity in a factory. A worker was transferred to a new department which had a well-established production norm of around 50 units per hour. After a few days the newcomer's productivity started to creep up to nearly 60 units per hour. This was regarded by the others in the group as contrary to the group's interests since it might be seen as giving management the chance to worsen their working conditions, and so they put strong pressure on the new member to come into line with the group norm. Finally, norms may serve to enhance or maintain the identity of the group. This is particularly true of norms concerning particular styles of dress or forms of linguistic or cultural expression. Unorthodox clothing, hairstyles or distinctive dialects, while not directly functional in themselves, help to demarcate members of the group from non-members and thus define that group's identity more clearly (see chapter 8).

Variations in norms

It should not be thought that norms always prescribe exactly how group members should behave. Depending on the domain to which they refer and the person's position in the group, the range of acceptable

behaviours – what Sherif and Sherif (1969) call the 'latitude of acceptance' – may be quite broad or very narrowly defined indeed. General
norms and norms that refer to peripheral aspects of group life will
have wide tolerance, while on issues that are central to the group's
existence, or that concern one's loyalty to the group, the bounds of
acceptable behaviour will be quite restrictive. Thus, while in many
communities there may be some latitude regarding such matters as
clothing, appearance and personal eccentricities, on such antisocial
behaviours as theft or physical assault which threaten the viability of
the group, the limits of acceptability are finely drawn. A person's
standing in the group will have a great influence on how closely
he or she must adhere to established norms. Typically, high-status
members will be able to deviate much further from norms than their
subordinates. However, once again, on key group activities and particularly activities relating to dealings with outgroups, a leader will
be expected to be a model group member and stick strictly to the 'party
line'. Witness the watchfulness displayed by many rank-and-file trade
unionists when their leaders conduct negotiations with employers on
their behalf.

Much of the evidence to support these conclusions was uncovered
by Sherif and Sherif (1964) in their study of adolescent gangs. Groups
of teenage boys in several different American cities were infiltrated
by participant observers, who made a detailed study of each group
over several months. These observers were able to identify clear norms
in all the groups over a number of issues. Most groups had given
themselves names and had adopted various insignia (e.g. tattoos).
Often these were associated with rivalry with neighbouring groups.
The type of clothing permitted in each group was often very rigidly
defined, which may seem surprising over such an apparently incon-
sequential matter. However, it is clear that for these particular subcultural groups, style of dress was a crucial marker distinguishing
one gang from another; hence the importance attached to clothing
norms (see also Sherif et al., 1973). Each group had its own well-
defined sexual mores and rigid codes of conduct for dealings with
'outsiders' (e.g. parents, police). As already noted, leaders in the groups
could get away with much more (for example, being able to commit
fouls in games which would not be permitted from lower-status members) except in certain critical areas. The Sherif and Sherif report how

one of the gang leaders was criticized by his fellow gang members for being picked up by the police in possession of an offensive weapon, an incident that threatened the existence of the group.

It is not just between members of the group that one can observe variations in norms. Norms may also change over time in response to the changing circumstances faced by the group. For instance, in the Coch and French (1948) study mentioned above the researchers witnessed a dramatic change in production norms in three workgroups following the implementation of a new management policy. Two of the groups were consulted by management before the change and were able to participate to some degree in the formulation of the policy. The third group was simply informed of the change that was to occur. In the days following the change the work rate of the two 'participative' groups rose steadily, while that for the 'non-participative' group fell. By the end of the evaluation period, the norms of the participative groups had diverged by nearly 50 per cent from that of the non-participative group. This is another example of how a change at the intergroup level (in management–worker relations) has effects at the intragroup level (in norms within the work group), underlining one of the central themes of this book, the interrelatedness of between and within group processes.

Of course, not all norms are subject to change. Many group practices and traditions are remarkably stable. Sherif and Sherif (1967) report a follow-up study of one of their adolescent groups through three generations. They were able to locate former members of the gang, then in their 20s and 30s, as well as the current group. They found that very little had changed. Although the individuals comprising the group had come and gone, the customs were very similar to those observed in the original study. The same rivalry with a nearby gang persisted. Interestingly, the erstwhile members of the gang still saw each other socially and still referred to each other by the special names they had used as teenagers. This lasting impact of adolescent group norms was confirmed by follow-up studies of Bennington College and its former graduates (Institute for Social Research, 1991–2; Newcomb et al., 1967). These managed to trace a substantial proportion of the students who had been studied so intensively decades previously. It was clear that many of the progressive values imparted by the college in the 1930s had stayed with the students. On a number of comparisons they were politically more liberal than a variety of groups of similar age and socio-economic status. And it was not just the individuals who showed stability; a careful analysis of the college itself revealed that it, too, had retained much of the radical ethos with which it had been founded all those years ago.

No discussion of the acquisition and development of group norms would be complete without considering the social processes whereby they are enforced. However, that discussion properly belongs under the heading of 'social influence' and so is deferred until chapter 4, where the impact of majorities and minorities in shaping and changing group members' normative judgements is investigated in detail.

Summary

1 Prior to joining a group both the prospective group members and the group they aim to join often engage in some mutual reconnaissance. A common motivation underlying this activity is an assessment of the rewards and costs associated with joining the group.

2 Becoming a member of a group has implications for the way we see ourselves. We are more likely to define ourselves in terms of that group membership, which may then have positive or negative consequences for our self-esteem, depending on the fortunes of the group.

3 Initiation into the group is often marked by some ritual, frequently involving embarrassment or pain. The function of the ritual may be symbolic – to delineate more clearly who belongs to the group and who does not. The associated discomfort may serve to increase the subsequent commitment to the group through processes of dissonance reduction.

4 One of the most elementary aspects of group formation may be the experience of common fate, the perception that one's outcomes are bound up with those of others.

5 An even stronger form of interdependence is that shaped by the task goals of the group. Where these bring people into a *positive* relationship with one another then cooperation, cohesion

and enhanced group performance are likely. *Negative* inter-dependence, on the other hand, leads to competition, reduced liking for others in the group and, usually, lower performance.

6 A fundamental distinction in group life is that between behaviours focused on achieving the group goal and behaviours concerned with feelings for others in the group. This task/socio-emotional dimension can be discerned by careful observation of interacting groups. One useful observation system is Bales' interaction process analysis (IPA).

7 The cohesion of a group has traditionally been defined in terms of aggregated inter-member attraction. However, a current model places more emphasis on cohesion as an attraction to the idea or prototype of the group rather than to specific individuals.

8 Cohesion has been observed to be associated with such factors as physical proximity, frequency of interaction, similarity among group members and, most importantly, a commitment to the group's goals. Intergroup conflict usually leads to increased cohesion within each of the competing groups, and especially for the 'successful' group. However, group failure does not always lead to lowered cohesion, particularly if initial membership in the group was voluntary.

9 Cohesion is often thought to lead to enhanced group performance. However, this relationship, while statistically reliable, is only of modest size. Moreover, there is stronger evidence that enhanced performance leads to cohesion rather than the reverse. A crucial moderating variable is the prevailing norm in the group – whether this encourages or inhibits productivity. In general, cohesion leads to increased adherence to group norms.

10 All groups evolve systems of norms that define the limits of acceptable and unacceptable behaviours. Norms help the individual to structure and predict his or her environment and they provide a means by which behaviour in the group can be regulated. They also facilitate the achievement of group goals and express aspects of the group's identity. Normative limits vary depending on the centrality of the issue for the group and the status of the group member. Norms may change with changing circumstances, but can also be stable over many years.

Notes

1   The authors do not reveal what voltage these shocks were and neither do they discuss the questionable ethics of this manipulation.

2   We shall come back to this work in chapter 4 in our discussions of social influence.

3   The Center for Group Dynamics – the base for Lewin and his colleagues – was at the Massachusetts Institute of Technology in the late 1940s. Bales himself was at Harvard, not many miles away. Although Bales actually worked at the Center, curiously he does not include a reference to Lewin in his first book (Bales, 1950), although several of Lewin's associates are mentioned, including Deutsch. In later publications he has made explicit the influence that Lewin's ideas had in the development of his work (Bales and Cohen, 1979; Bales, 1984).

4   In this he is clearly adopting a functionalist perspective, a point under-lined by his close association with Parsons, a leading figure in functional-ist sociology (e.g. Parsons et al., 1953).

5   Crossed-lagged panel analysis is a technique that permits some causal inference even from correlational research designs. Essentially, it compares the correlation between two variables (A, B) at two points in time (1, 2). If A *causes* B then the correlation between A at t_1 and B at t_2 (A_1B_2) ought to be stronger than the correlation of B at t_1 and A at t_2 (A_2B_1) (Campbell and Stanley, 1963; Kenny, 1975).

6   The illusion has long been known to astronomers and navigators used to observing stars at night. The experience of movement is compelling and persists even when one is fully aware that the light does not move. The subjects in the experiment, however, were not actually told that the move-ment was illusory, merely that 'after a short time the light will start to move' (Sherif, 1936, p. 95).

Further Reading

Cartwright, D. and Zander, A. (eds) (1969) *Group Dynamics*, 3rd edn, chs 31, 35. New York: Harper & Row.

Hogg, M. (1992) *The Social Psychology of Group Cohesiveness: From Attraction to Social Identity*. London: Harvester Wheatsheaf.

Levine, J.M. and Moreland, R.L. (1994) Group socialization: theory and re-search, pp. 305–36 in Stroebe, W. and Hewstone, M. (eds) *European Review of Social Psychology*, vol. 5. Chichester: Wiley.

Sherif, M. and Sherif, C.W. (1969) *Social Psychology*, chs 9–10. New York: Harper & Row.

3

STRUCTURAL ASPECTS
OF GROUPS

This book is concerned with various processes within and between groups that govern our social behaviour. 'Processes' signify movement and change over time and, to be sure, group relations are often in a state of flux. However, this should not blind us to the fact that there are facets of group life that show some stability. Most prominent of these are those that reflect the *structure* of the group – the framework within which the elementary processes discussed in chapter 2 take place. This chapter is concerned with those structural aspects.

Sherif and Sherif (1969, p. 150) defined group structure as 'an interdependent network of roles and hierarchical status' and, following their lead, the first two sections of the chapter deal with *role* and *status* differentiation. Both 'role' and 'status' refer to predictable patterns of behaviour associated not so much with *particular* individuals in the group but with the *positions* occupied by those individuals. They are, if you like, the parts and script of a play rather than the actors who perform in it. The main difference between role and status is one of value. The various roles in a group can be of equal worth whereas different status positions are, by definition, differentially valued.

The existence of status differences is closely related to a social process which constitutes the second of this book's three major themes – that of social comparison. As I shall show, social comparisons take place within – and, indeed, often give rise to – status hierarchies, and it is suggested that this strongly implicates self-evaluation as the motive underlying them. By locating ourselves in the group's status structure we gain insight into our abilities relative to our peers. One type of group member who possesses more status (and power) than most is the leader. It is natural, therefore, that the next major portion of this chapter is given to a discussion of leadership. Leadership is examined as a personal attribute, as an outcome of situational determinants, as an interaction of personality *and* situation, and finally – recalling some ideas from chapter 2 – as a *process* of negotiation between leaders and followers. The final section deals with communication structures and how these influence group performance and morale.

Role Differentiation

In chapter 2 we saw how important norms were in generating expectations about how group members should or should not behave. Mostly, the norms we considered were general rules applying more or less strictly to everyone in the group. Often, however, we find that different expectations are associated with particular people or positions within the group. This is what is meant by role differentiation, and it is an exceedingly common feature of group life.

Sometimes roles are formally prescribed. Thus, in a factory a worker may be paid to carry out certain specific functions within the production team (e.g. lathe operator, welder). Similarly, in institutions like schools there will usually be well-defined roles of head teacher, departmental head, class teacher, student and probably various designated positions within each class. In smaller units, such as a sports team or group of mountaineers, the various participants are also designated different jobs (e.g. mid-field player, medical support). Sherif et al. (1961) observed exactly such a differentiation of roles in groups of boys in a summer camp. After just two or three days of interaction the groups of strangers had developed a clear structure, with boys being allocated different tasks. However, in a great many groups such clear demarcation of roles is not immediately visible. Among friends or in informal discussion groups, for instance, it is rare for different role positions to be explicitly referred to. Nevertheless, it is possible to identify role differentiation as having occurred even in these apparently amorphous groupings.

One of the earliest studies to do so was by Slater (1955). Using Bales' Interaction Process Analysis (IPA) system, he observed twenty problem-solving groups over four consecutive sessions. In addition, he obtained subjective ratings from the participants themselves on who they regarded as having the best ideas in the group, who exerted the most guidance and who they liked the best. A number of interesting findings emerged. First, the person regarded by his peers as being the most influential was not usually the person who was liked the most; there was some positive correlation between the two attributes but not a very strong one, and it became progressively weaker over time. This suggested to Slater that Bales' primary distinction between instrumental and expressive behaviours (see chapter 2) might be reflected in two basic roles in a problem-solving group: the task specialist (the 'ideas' person) and the socio-emotional specialist (the person whom everyone liked). Sure enough, when he divided his sample into those ranked high on 'ideas' and those ranked high on 'liking', some clear behavioural differences were visible. 'Ideas' men were observed to spend more time than 'best-liked' men on task-related activities (IPA categories 4–9) but correspondingly less on positive socio-emotional behaviours (IPA categories 1–3).

Some of the clearest examples of role differentiation are to be found in that most important of all small groups, the family. Whether we consider the nuclear family typical of the industrialized West or the variety of other family arrangements around the world, it is nearly always possible to identify a number of formally ascribed positions (e.g. parent, child, caretaker), as well as some more socially functional roles (e.g. those associated with emotional support or with discipline). Scott and Scott (1981), in an analysis of nearly 300 primary groups of different types, found the family to be easily the most role (and status) differentiated. Zelditch (1956), in a cross-cultural analysis of ethnographic reports of fifty different societies, found that more than three-quarters of them showed some differentiation between task and socio-emotional roles within the family.

Parsons and Bales (1956) argued that Zelditch's finding implied that the family should be regarded merely as one particular kind of small group and, as such, it faced the usual problem of reconciling instrumental and expressive behaviours. Since they also believed that it was difficult for one person to carry out these functions simultan- eously (recall that task and socio-emotional orientations are usually assumed to be inversely related – see chapter 2), this suggested to them that the most effective and cohesive families would be those where there was a clear division of roles between different family members. They went on to argue that this role specialization would be universally effected by allocating the roles along gender lines, with fathers adopting the instrumental role and mothers fulfilling expressive functions. This suggestion was based on psychoanalytic theorizing about the assumed need for children to be able to achieve identification with the same sex parent. Zelditch's data appeared to support this idea since in both matrilineal and patrilineal societies the allocation of roles was predominantly by sex. Furthermore, there is a wealth of evidence – mainly, it is true, from Western sources – indic- ating a bias in personality style towards socio-emotional orientation in women and towards task orientation in men (Spence and Helmreich, 1978).

Although some differentiation of role in families undoubtedly does occur, the idea that this necessarily has to coincide in an invariant way with two principal parents, or indeed has to be allocated between different family members at all, is rather questionable. There are several reasons for saying this. First, as Slater (1961) pointed out, the Parsons–Bales theory of the family rested on the assumption that task and socio-emotional activities were always incompatible. Actually this is not the case, as Slater's (1955) study had shown. Although he had found some differentiation into task and socio-emotional specialists, the correlation between subjective ratings along these two dimensions was *positive*, although not strongly so. This suggests that the same individual can sometimes fulfil both roles, and Slater (1961) unearthed additional anthropological evidence to suggest that in several societies this is indeed what happens. Alternatively, role differentiation in the family may not fall *along* the task–socio-emotional dimension but orthogonal to it. For instance, both parents could be equally 'instrumental' in family affairs but perhaps in different domains (e.g. garden and kitchen). Nor is it clear that a high degree of differentiation is always associated with internal family solidarity. Although Scott and Scott (1981) did observe a general trend across all the types of groups they studied for role differentiation and solidarity to be positively correlated, within the subset of families the relationship was actually significantly *negative*. Perhaps too rigid a family role structure creates more problems than it solves (Minuchin, 1974).

There certainly is some evidence from task groups that a too inflexible pattern of role differentiation can become a serious handicap because it is liable to prevent the group from being able to adapt to new situations (Gersick and Hackman, 1990). Gersick and Hackman describe a tragic real-life example of this phenomenon: the crew of a passenger aircraft had adopted such a fixed pattern of role responsibilities in their pre-flight checks that they failed to notice a serious build up of ice on the aircraft's wings and thus omitted to activate the deicing devices that were available to deal with the problem. The result was the plane crashed shortly after take-off.

At the beginning of this section it was noted that role differentiation is a pervasive feature of group life. Why should this be? One obvious reason is that roles imply a division of labour among the group members, which can often facilitate the achievement of the group's goal, an important motivating factor as we saw in the last chapter. As we shall see later in our discussion of leadership, one of the problems faced by a group is to find ways to share the work and responsibility among the group members to prevent the leader(s) from becoming physically or cognitively overloaded. This is why so many committees, political groups and clubs find it useful to designate people to the roles of chair, secretary, treasurer etc., each with its own range of duties and functions. This also means that the adoption of roles may be situation-specific as the group goals change. A child at school might play a minor role in the academic setting of the classroom but emerge as a key figure in a school sports team.

Perhaps it is in recognition of the value of the coordination of different roles that health professionals now often operate in multi-disciplinary teams with nurses, health visitors, doctors, psychiatrists and social workers all joining forces to provide treatment for their patients (Berteotti and Seibold, 1994; West and Wallace, 1991). The point of such heterogeneous groups is that each professional could, in principle, contribute something important and possibly unique from his or her discipline's perspective. Of course, this is the ideal but, as Berteotti and Seibold (1994) observed in their study of a healthcare team in a hospice for the terminally ill, an over-attachment to one's disciplinary identity or an assumption of its superiority over others can sometimes impede the delivery of optimal care. Thus, role differentiation within the group can transform itself into an intergroup conflict situation unless some group superordinate goal predominates (see chapter 6).

A second function of roles is similar to that provided by normative systems: they help to bring order to the group's existence. Like norms, roles imply expectations about one's own and others' behaviour, and this means that group life becomes more predictable and hence more orderly. The emergence of task and socio-emotional roles, in so far as this occurs, is important in this respect since group members will quickly learn who to look and respond to at certain points in the group's existence or in particular situations.

Finally, roles also form part of our self-definition within the group, our sense of who we are. Having a clearly defined role undoubtedly contributes in important ways to our identity. This is revealed when a person's role becomes ambiguous, overloaded or in conflict with other roles. If any of these conditions becomes too acute, whether this happens in a large organization or in the micro-context of the family, problems may result both for the individual and for the group itself. These reveal themselves in various ways. For example, Rizzo et al. (1970) found that, among employees of a large manufacturing company, role ambiguity was consistently correlated with lowered job satisfaction, increased anxiety and general fatigue, and intentions to leave the company (see also Jackson and Schuler, 1985). There are also indications that role problems in families are associated with mental illness and family dysfunction (e.g. Minuchin, 1974). In sum, not knowing who you are or what is expected of you seems to be bad for you.

Status Differentiation

Not all roles taken on by different group members are equally valued, nor do they carry the same power to exert influence or control over others. Each member is respected or liked to a different degree. In a classroom, the teacher has more prestige than the pupils and usually has the power to dispense sanctions and rewards to them. Once in the playground some children may be faster, stronger or more popular than others and, as a result, may be deferred to in making decisions about choices of activities and so on. When they return home, these same children will again occupy a subordinate position, this time in relation to their parents or an older brother or sister. In other words, closely tied to the pattern of roles in a group is the existence of a status hierarchy (Scott and Scott, 1981).

How should status be defined? This question has long preoccupied social scientists, and from the wealth of different answers that have been put forward I want to pick out two recurring themes (see also Cartwright and Zander, 1969). One is that high status implies a *tendency to initiate ideas and activities* that are taken up by the rest of the group. This is the view taken by Bales, as we have seen, and by Sherif and Sherif (1964), whose work we touched on in chapter 2 and to which we will return shortly. The other important aspect of status is that it implies some *consensual prestige*, a positive evaluation or ranking by others in the group. This is the position of Homans (1950), among others. These two indicators of status are nearly always highly correlated with each other and are worth distinguishing only because sometimes one tends to rely on the first aspect, while in a questionnaire or interview schedule the second may be easier to elicit.

The prevalence of status hierarchies in informal groups was confirmed by Sherif and Sherif (1964) in their study of adolescent gangs. In addition to analysing the normative systems in these gangs (see chapter 2), the Sherifs were able to obtain quantitative data on the various group structures both from within the gang itself (from the participant observers and the group members) and from outside the group from independent observers. One of the measures involved ranking the members in terms of being able to take effective initiative in various group activities. In all of the groups this proved possible, indicating that hierarchical structures were indeed a common phenomenon – and a genuine one, as comparisons of the different rankings revealed. The rank orderings of the independent and participant observers correlated very highly with each other (around +0.9) and with the rank orders the group members themselves produced, suggesting that the measures were tapping something psychologically significant. Interestingly, the correlations between these status rankings and popularity were somewhat lower, echoing Slater's (1955) laboratory findings, which indicated a distinction between task effectiveness and liking.

The ease and regularity with which status differences may be observed in groups should not mislead us into thinking that the hierarchy will necessarily remain fixed. Sherif and Sherif (1964) noted changes in the positions in the group structure as members entered and left the group. Another source of instability is the changing intergroup context in which the group finds itself. For instance, one of the groups in the Sherifs' study developed an interest in basketball. In the ensuing contests with other groups it soon became apparent that the existing leader was not the best player and his high-status position was soon taken by a more athletic gang member. A similar change in group structure as a result of changed intergroup relations was found in one of the summer camp studies also undertaken by the Sherifs (Sherif et al., 1961; see chapter 6).

What are the origins of this widespread occurrence of status differentials in groups? One explanation is to be found in the by now familiar theme of the need for predictability and order. We saw in the previous section that role positions carry with them expectations of the *kind* of behaviour that the person occupying them will engage in. So it is with status positions, only here the expectations concern people's *competence* in various domains. We believe that different people in our group are better or worse than us at this activity or that, which then enables us to allocate people (and be allocated ourselves) to certain tasks in an appropriate manner. Ordering the group in this way may help to stabilize the group and allow it to concentrate more effectively on achieving its goals.

Sometimes this can generate self-fulfilling prophecies so that people conform to the level expected of them, even though their actual abilities may be higher or lower than this. Many years ago I taught in a secondary school which grouped its pupils by presumed ability in certain subjects after their first year. I well remember the experience of teaching fourth- and fifth-year students who had been designated as 'low ability'. Their actual level of competence was well below that of some of the 'low ability' first-year children who had not yet been so labelled. Even making allowances for their monumental lack of motivation, it was quite clear that, after three or four years' occupation of the 'bottom set' status position, they had actually internalized the official view that they were academically not very able, and performed accordingly.

That this anecdote is not a completely idiosyncratic experience is confirmed by a substantial body of theory and research. Perhaps the most systematic account of how status influences behaviour is given by Expectations States Theory (e.g. Berger and Zelditch, 1985). In this theory it is assumed that in most group task settings individuals will either already have or will quickly develop expectations as to the relative performance abilities of their fellow group members. These expectations serve as social psychological anchors for subsequent behaviour so that presumed higher status individuals will initiate – and be permitted to initiate – more ideas and activities than those of lower status, and hence be perceived as more influential. Moreover, other not strictly warranted inferences may be made about the capabilities of the higher status group members so that they come to be seen as more competent in other domains also. In this cyclical way the initial status differences are reinforced and magnified.

A good example of this process is provided by Whyte (1943) in his study of an Italian immigrant gang in an American city. He recorded how in the gang's various sporting activities the lower-status members always seemed to play badly, even though in other contexts they were actually better athletes. Here is his description of 'Frank', ranked seventh in the gang, at a baseball match:

In the basis of his record, Frank was considered the best player on either team, yet he made a miserable showing. He said to me: 'I can't seem to play ball when I'm playing with fellows I know ...' Accustomed to filling an inferior position, Frank was unable to star even in his favourite sport when he was competing against members of his own group. (Whyte, 1943, p. 19)

Several experimental studies have observed a similar phenomenon under more controlled conditions (e.g. Berger et al., 1972; Harvey, 1953; Kirchler and Davis, 1986).

Of course, status differences do not always emerge solely from within the group. Expectation States Theory also proposes that external markers like ethnicity and sex often act as diffuse status characteristics from which performance-related attributes are inferred. Because there are culturally based stereotypes associated with these kinds of social categories, a black person or a woman joining a task group may be perceived very differently from a white person or a man, resulting in different patterns of social interaction and consequently a different allocation to a position in the group's structure. Cohen (1972) observed groups of school students, each containing two black and two white boys, playing a board game in which the group as a whole was required to make various decisions as the game progressed. Careful study of these sessions revealed that in over 70 per cent of them, a white boy was the most active participant and in over two-thirds white boys were also the second most active participant. Moreover, the most active white participant had 95 per cent of his suggestions accepted by the group as compared to only 74 per cent of those made by the most active black boy. Lockheed (1985), reviewing 29 studies of mixed sex groups, found a similar asymmetry of influence between men and women: 70 per cent of these reported greater male influence, 17 per cent no sex difference and only 13 per cent found women to be higher status. However, there are some current indications that this traditional sex-linked status difference may be less marked than it once was. Carli (1989) carried out an observational analysis of 64 single-sex and 64 mixed-sex dyads engaged in a discussion task. According to Expectation States Theory, one should find greater evidence of sex differentiation in the latter type of group since there the diffuse status characteristic of sex is more likely to be salient. In fact, she found virtually no evidence of sex differences in task behaviours or influenceability in the mixed-sex dyads, and quite marked differences in the same-sex dyads (i.e. comparing all-male to all-female groups). This absence of status differentiation in mixed-sex groups was confirmed by Stiles et al. (1997) in an analysis of verbal behaviour in five very different types of groups (e.g. casual conversation between strangers, heterosexual couples making decisions). This suggests that, at long last, some of the traditional gender status differences may be beginning to dissipate.

Self-Evaluation through Social Comparison

In chapter 2 I described how social norms could serve both social and individual needs. So, too, can status differentials. Not only do they provide useful functions for the group as a whole, but by acting as a kind of social yardstick they also assist the individual in the crucial business of self-evaluation. If roles help us to know *who* we are, our status position helps us to know *how good* we are.

Social comparison theory

One of the first people to recognize the psychological importance of self-evaluation was Leon Festinger. Some forty years ago he proposed a theory to explain how self-evaluation may be achieved and what happens when it is. That theory, 'A theory of social comparison processes' (Festinger, 1954), can with some justice be regarded as one of the landmarks in the history of social psychology since its influence has spread far beyond its original concerns. The centrality of the notion of social comparison within social psychology generally is reflected in the study of group dynamics. Time and again in the chapters that follow we will find that social comparison processes provide a vital clue in understanding different facets of group behaviour.

77

Festinger (1954) begins by proposing that there is a universal human drive to evaluate our opinions and abilities.[1] The basis for this bold assumption is Festinger's belief that life would be difficult, if not impossible, unless we had a way of correctly appraising our abilities. As an illustration of the survival value of accurate self-evaluation, consider what would happen if we did not know how well we could drive a car. Not only our own life but that of others too would be in jeopardy if we took to the road without some inkling as to our competence in this sphere. Indeed, one of the tragedies of the influence of alcohol on driving ability is precisely that it can lead drivers to overestimate their competence to control their vehicle, all too often with fatal consequences. At a less life-threatening level, consider the decision of teenagers regarding a choice of career. Surely a critical component of that decision is their assessment of their particular abilities. Someone who regards him/herself as innumerate is unlikely to choose a career in accountancy, just as a person whose athletic prowess is in doubt will not seek trials for Liverpool Football Club.

How do we come by this self-knowledge? The most obvious and reliable method is to find some objective means of assessment. If I want to know how fast I can run, I can time myself over a known distance. However, often such objective measurements are not so readily available. Some years ago, I happened to be learning the guitar. For such an activity I did not have access to the musical equivalent of a tape measure and stopwatch to be able to know how well I could play. In situations like this Festinger suggests that we turn to others to obtain information about our abilities: by comparing myself to other guitarists I was able to get some sense of my own (lack of) musicality. Such social comparisons are important even if an objective evaluation is possible. Suppose, to return to my athletic example, I discover that I can run the 1500 metres in six minutes. Does this mean I am a fast or a slow runner? Without knowledge of how fast others can run such a question has little meaning. Similarly, intelligence tests, believed by some psychologists to be objective measures of cognitive ability, are in reality measures of an individual's performance *relative* to some population of other individuals. In other words, to quote Menander (343–292 BC), commenting 2000 years ago on the famous Delphic oracle:

In many ways the saying 'know yourself' is not well said. It were more practical to say 'know other people'. (quoted in Bartlett, 1962, p. 27)

Of course, not just any 'other people' will do. In order to make a realistic appraisal of our abilities we need to choose people who will provide the most – and the most reliable – information for us. To know how fast I can run does it make sense for me to compete against Linford Christie? Festinger suggested that a comparison like this between people so wildly different in competence is not very informative, and that typically we will choose others who are like ourselves. The achievements of others who are similar to us in ability act as a guide to our own likely achievements. This is why status differentiation in the group is so important. Since it provides group members with a rough rank ordering of ability on various attributes, it permits them to choose *comparable* others for purposes of self-evaluation.

This was illustrated by Radloff (1966), who examined the accuracy of self-evaluations among groups of sailors performing a pursuit rotor task. This task was said to be a good measure of eye–hand coordination, which would be useful to them in the operation of naval equipment. The sailors were thus highly motivated to know how good at this task they were. The experimenter artificially manipulated their apparent performance in practice trials so that in each group there were always two 'average', one 'above-average' and one 'below-average' performers. Following Festinger (1954), Radloff reasoned that those designated as 'average' would be capable of the most accurate self-evaluations since they had someone similar to compare themselves with. So it turned out. As a measure of accuracy, Radloff correlated everyone's estimated performance with their actual score and found that the allegedly 'average' members' correlations were markedly higher than the 'superior' or 'inferior' members' correlations taken together.

If Festinger's similarity hypothesis is examined carefully, it seems rather circular. The whole point of social comparison activity is to discover the ability of another person so that we may infer our own ability. But if we already know they are similar to us in ability, why do we need to make the comparison in the first place? Goethals and Darley (1977), noting this tautology, suggested that what we really do in seeking out 'similar others' for comparative purposes is to look for others who are similar to us on *attributes that are related to* the ability in question. As any parent or schoolteacher will confirm, a common preoccupation of young children is to know how good they are – how fast, how clever, how strong – compared to others *of their age.* They assume, quite reasonably, that many of these abilities are correlated with the attribute of age and hence disregard the superior performances of their older siblings or peers and concentrate on their immediate contemporaries (Smith et al., 1987).

This was shown very convincingly by Zanna et al. (1975), who asked college students which other group's average score on a cognitive ability test they would like to know, given a rough idea of their own score. They were given the option of choosing between students of the same or opposite sex, students taking the same or different degree subjects as their own, or non-students. Almost unanimously (97 per cent), they chose to learn the score of someone of their own sex. There was also a clear but less strong tendency to choose people taking the same degree, and virtually none opted to see the score of non-students. The students had clearly made the assumption that sex was related to cognitive ability and hence knowing the scores of same-sex students would give them some indication of their own ability. Very similar results were obtained by Wheeler et al. (1982), who used the related attribute 'amount of practice' at the experimental task. Those who had been told that practice was related to eventual performance were more likely to compare themselves with someone who had practised the same amount as them than those who were told that practice was irrelevant to performance. Following Goethals and Darley's (1977) argument, then, we can see that our status position in the group acts as a kind of general 'related attribute'. By observing the performance of others of similar status at some particular activity, we are able to infer our own competence in that same domain.

Such related attributes comparisons are not without their disadvantages, however, since they may mislead people as to the outcomes that they are entitled to. This was illustrated in some experimental studies by Major and her colleagues (Major, 1994). In one of these, men and women were randomly assigned to work on different types of task and were subsequently paid (always the same amount) for their work (Major and Forcey, 1985). Following this, they were asked which other people's pay they would like to know. The comparison choices open to them were: average female (or male) pay for same (or different) type of task, or average female and male pay combined for same (or different) type of task, making six possible choices in all. In this situation the only genuinely 'related attribute' was the type of task and so rationally everyone should have chosen the 'same task, averaged across male and female' option to establish if they had been appropriately paid. In fact, only 21 per cent chose to see this pay rate; the vast majority (63 per cent) selected the 'same task, same sex' comparator. In other words, the participants seemed to perceive gender as a related attribute when, according to the 'equal pay for equal worth' principle, it manifestly should not be (Treiman and Hartman, 1981). The practical implications of such an inappropriate perception are apparent in the real world of work, where some employers continue to pay women lower wages than men (Grubb and Wilson, 1992). Often they attempt to justify this inequality by merely labelling certain jobs differently for men and women in an effort to create an illusion of differential worth. Since male and female workers are thereby effectively segregated, they may restrict their wage comparisons to same-sex workers and overlook the discrepancies in pay between men and women (Crosby, 1982).

Whither to compare, up or down?

So far we have considered the social comparisons that people engage in as if they were affectively neutral behaviours from which people disinterestedly make inferences about their abilities. Naturally, things are not quite so simple. To begin with, any inference about our own abilities has consequences for our self-esteem – we feel better about ourselves if we have done well at something. Since high self-esteem is preferable to its absence, this might suggest that we would be motivated to avoid comparisons with those who are better than us since the outcome of those comparisons is likely to be invidious.

However, comparing with those of lower standing in the group is not without its problems either. To be sure, if we do better at some task it confirms our superiority, but only if we can assume that they were trying just as hard as us. If we cannot then the inference becomes unclear. Furthermore, there is always the risk that the outcome of

81

such a comparison might be unfavourable for us, which leads to a much more unambiguous inference of inferiority than from the same negative outcome *vis-à-vis* a high-status person. Finally, as Festinger (1954) pointed out in the original theory, in many Western cultures at least there is a value on better performance, which will motivate people to try to excel each other's achievements. Festinger called this a 'unidirectional drive upwards' and suggested that it would have two general effects on status relations in the group. First, it would introduce some instability as the group members jockeyed with one another for position. Second, people would tend to compare upwards rather than downwards in an attempt to improve their standing. Taking all these considerations together, the broad conclusion is that people will tend to choose others who are just slightly better than themselves for comparison purposes.

There is certainly evidence that this is what people do. Wheeler (1966) gave groups of students a fake personality test, leading them to believe that it would be used for selecting people for a new seminar course. Each person in the group was given an exact score and rank position although, unknown to them, they all received the same score and were led to believe that this was the median value (fourth in a group of seven). They were also given the approximate scores of the best and worst person and then asked which other person's score in the group they would like to know, given only their rank positions. As expected, there was a strong tendency to compare upwards rather than downwards and this preference was most pronounced for the person *just* above them. This preference for those 'slightly better' was confirmed by Nosanchuk and Erickson (1985). They asked bridge club members who they would like to discuss various hypothetical game situations with (e.g. a contract that just failed to make, a contract that was won against the odds etc.). In nearly every case they found that the players opted to seek advice (or consolation) from someone who was recognizably a better player than themselves.

Important though similarity is in determining comparison choice, there are occasions when it may be as useful to know the *range* of abilities in the group. This was shown by Wheeler et al. (1969), who investigated the effect of depriving people of this information. They gave groups of students a bogus personality scale, which was said to measure intellectual traits. Each person in the group was told what he had scored and that this had been the median value for the group. Half the participants were then given information as to the approximate scores of the highest and lowest performers in the group, while the others were not. As usual, the critical question concerned which other people's scores in the group they would like to know. The results were clear. Of those who did not know the range of scores in the group, 70 per cent asked for the score of the top-ranking member, as compared to only 24 per cent of those who already knew the range. Moreover, the second choice of comparison among those who did not know the range was predominantly for the *bottom*-ranked person. Thus, there are circumstances when Festinger's similarity hypothesis gives way to a preference to know about *dissimilar* others.

There may be other circumstances, too, when people prefer downward to upward comparisons. One is when their own situation is particularly aversive. Here it may be of some comfort to know that there are some even worse off than we are. This hypothesis has been actively promulgated by Wills (1991), who believes that the primary motive for such downward comparisons is to protect a threatened self-esteem. Some early evidence for this hypothesis was provided by Hakmiller (1966). He employed a variant of the 'rank order' paradigm used by Wheeler et al. (1966) above. Groups of participants in Hakmiller's experiment were first tested on a bogus personality test involving looking at some ambiguous pictures while their galvanic skin response was measured. They were told that the particular trait being assessed was hostility towards one's parents. Half of them had this described in extremely negative and threatening terms (e.g. that it was associated with various personality defects), while for the remainder it was presented more positively. Having been informed of their own score on this test (always the second lowest in the group), they were invited to choose one other person whose score they would like to know. Those in the high-threat condition were more likely to select the highest ranking individual than those in the low-threat condition, and since the score on this test represented a negative trait this was clear evidence of *downward* comparison: the threatened people wanted to know how different they were from the most undesirable other group member. Other experiments involving negative or failure feedback following ability testing have found similar preferences for seeking information about worse performers, although, as we shall see in a moment, the whole story is far from being unequivocal (Levine and Green, 1984; Pyszczynski et al., 1985).

Outside the laboratory there is also evidence that people in adverse situations sometimes turn to others even worse off than themselves for comparison purposes, although even here the picture is complicated. The clearest evidence for such downward comparisons under threat was provided by Wood et al. (1985) in their study of women with breast cancer. They found that over half of these women compared their lot with someone whose physical condition was worse than their own, and only a tiny fraction (4 per cent) made upward comparisons. The coping function played by such downward comparisons is well illustrated by one of their respondents:

I had just a comparatively small amount of surgery on the breast, and I was so miserable, because it was so painful. How awful it must be for women who have had a mastectomy . . . I just can't imagine it, it would seem to be so difficult. (Wood et al., 1985, p. 1178)

Although, as we have seen, downward comparisons are sometimes made in response to ego-threatening information, it is doubtful that they are quite as common as Wills (1991) supposes, or that they are always associated with enhancing or protecting self-esteem. For instance, Schulz and Decker (1985) found that only a quarter of their sample of people with physical disabilities said that they compared themselves with other disabled persons; 16 per cent specifically compared themselves with people without disabilities and over half to 'people in general'.

More important than making downward comparisons, a key variable in predicting these people's sense of well-being was their perceived control over various life circumstances. This same factor cropped up in a study by Buunk et al. (1990). Like Wood et al. (1985), they were interested in the experiences of cancer patients and, as in the earlier study, they found that downward comparisons were more common than upward comparisons. However, there was no straightforward relationship between the direction of these comparisons and the respondents' reports of positive or negative affect. True, downward comparisons were often associated with feeling good but they were also frequently connected to negative affect. Moreover, upward comparisons, when they were made, were more likely to be linked to positive than to negative feelings. Some other results from this study provided some important clues as to the significance of these different types of comparison. First of all, the objective prognosis of each patient (by an oncologist) was not related to the kinds of comparisons they made or how they felt about them. More important were two personal variables. First, those with high self-esteem reported feeling less negatively, whether after making upward or downward comparisons, than those with low self-esteem. Second, those who felt they had more control over their illness were less likely to report feeling negatively in response to worse-off others. The lack of an effect for the oncologist's prognosis and the direction of the relationship between self-esteem and affect are both inconsistent with Wills' (1991) theory on the process underlying downward comparisons.

One reason why people in threatening situations may still prefer to turn their attention upward instead of downward is suggested by Taylor and Lobel (1989). They argue that while downward comparisons can be superficially ego-enhancing for threatened people ('at least I'm not as badly off as them'), upward comparisons can offer the hope and prospect of self-improvement ('I too could be like them one day').

Social comparison and performance

One aspect of social comparison processes that we have not yet examined is their consequence for people's actual performance. Festinger (1954) made two predictions about this. One, which followed directly from the hypothesized drive upward, was that people would tend to try to improve their performance, especially in relation to those similar to or immediately above them. The other, rather less obviously, was that high-status members would be motivated either to attempt to improve the performance of those below them (by coaching or practice) or, failing that, might actually perform below their capability so as not to become too different from others in the group.

Compared to the plethora of studies investigating self-evaluation and comparison choices, these hypotheses have received comparatively little attention. Nevertheless, the available evidence certainly seems to support at least the first hypothesis. Köhler (1926, 1927), using a weight-lifting task, revealed that participants performing this task in dyads or triads were actually able to exceed the sum of their individual performances *provided that the members of these groups were not too discrepant in individual strength* (Witte, 1989). In fact, the group composition for optimal performance was where the weakest member was between 60 per cent and 80 per cent of the strongest member; if they were too similar or too discrepant then the group performance tended to decline.

Modern research has tended to bear out these early observations. Stroebe and Diehl (1996) replicated Köhler's findings and concluded that the increased group output was mainly attributable to enhanced performance of the weaker group members. Seta (1982) observed people's performance in a simple button-pressing task. When paired with a peer who was apparently slightly faster than them, participants speeded up. The same facilitation was not observed with an exactly similar or a clearly superior comparison person. Children, on the other hand, may be more sensitive to similarity per se. France-Kaatrude and Smith (1985) got 6- and 9-year-old children to perform a pursuit rotor task. Every so often they were given the opportunity to observe another child recorded on video undertaking the same task. This comparison child seemed to be much better, worse or similar in ability to the real participant. The children were much more likely to choose to watch the video when paired with a 'similar' other, and this was particularly evident among the younger age group. They also worked harder at the task in the 'similar' condition than in either of the other two, and this was true regardless of age.

A brief evaluation of social comparison theory

As we have seen, Festinger's (1954) theory provides a useful framework for understanding the causes and effects of status differentiation in groups. Nevertheless, despite its undoubted historical significance, a few cautionary notes are necessary before we leave it.

First, we may question his assumption that, in the absence of objective criteria, self-evaluation needs are only satisfied through *social* comparison processes. Albert (1977) proposed an addendum to Festinger's theory, in which *temporal* comparisons were argued to

86

play an important role – that is, comparing one's performance with some past or future performance. Albert suggested that these kinds of comparisons might assume greater importance for people if social comparisons yield unfavourable outcomes for the self. Moreover, in some circumstances people may elect to make comparisons with some abstract standard, what we have called an 'autonomous orientation' (Hinkle and Brown, 1990). Evidence is beginning to emerge documenting the existence of these various non-social means of evaluation. For example, Gibbons et al. (1994) found that incoming university students, when asked about how they evaluated their academic and athletic abilities, did report that they relied more on social than temporal comparisons but the latter were certainly in evidence. This was particularly so for the less able students, for whom social comparisons were less favourable.

The relative importance of social and temporal comparisons may also change with the life span (Suls and Mullen, 1982). Very early in life (say, 4–8 years) or very late (over 65 years), temporal and other social comparisons may be more significant for people than social comparisons. But throughout childhood, adolescence and the majority of adulthood social comparisons will predominate. There certainly seems to be some evidence for this idea. Frey and Ruble (1985) found that in their observational study of an American kindergarten and primary school, children took some time to display the classic Festinger-type ability comparisons.[2] Moving up the age range, Suls (1986) and Brown and Middendorf (1996) both observed that elderly respondents (>65 years) exhibited the most interest in temporal comparisons, as compared to their younger counterparts. Interestingly, in the latter study the importance of *social* comparisons did not vary much with age; it was the temporal comparisons which showed the changes (see figure 3.1).

Another issue neglected by Festinger is the possibility that comparisons may not be confined to within the group but may involve other groups also. In the original theory Festinger made it clear that he regarded such intergroup comparisons as unlikely:

Comparisons with members of a different status group, either higher or lower, may sometimes be made on a phantasy level, but very rarely in reality. (Festinger, 1954, p. 136)

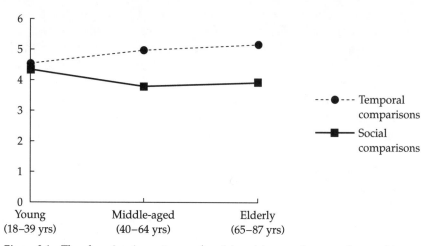

Figure 3.1 The changing importance of social and temporal comparisons with age (adapted from Brown and Middendorf, 1996, table 1)

In later chapters I shall be discussing a wealth of evidence which suggests that this phenomenon is by no means as rare as Festinger believed. For now, however, two examples will suffice. One is provided by Abeles (1976) in his study of black militancy in the USA. One of his surveys, conducted in 1968 at the height of civil rights activity, revealed that in answer to the question, 'what sorts of people are doing noticeably better than you or your family?', 31 per cent of his black respondents mentioned whites, 14 per cent Cubans and only 25 per cent mentioned (the same status) blacks. For a more contemporary example we can turn to a study we carried out in six European countries (Brown and Haeger, 1999). Respondents were asked, first of all, to write a few brief sentences about what came to mind when thinking of their country. Content analysis of these descriptions revealed a spontaneous use of comparative references by about a third of the sample, with social comparisons outnumbering temporal comparisons by about 2:1. Nevertheless, the use of temporal comparisons at all (by 11 per cent of the sample) is interesting and bears out my earlier comments about the importance of this neglected mode of evaluation. In a later part of the questionnaire we invited the respondents to choose another country with which they compared their own. The overwhelming trend in all but one of the six countries we sampled was to choose a higher status country for comparison purposes. For most, this upward comparison was of the 'similar but just superior' variety that, as we noted earlier, seems to be the rule for intragroup comparisons. However, at least two of the lower status countries opted for a very discrepant higher status group, and the one exception to the 'upward' trend was the highest status country, which made a marked downward comparison. It was also noteworthy that there was no sign of the 'downward comparisons under threat' that Wills (1991) has hypothesized. In all these cases, then, we have clear evidence that people can and do make between-group comparisons in reality, and not just 'in phantasy' as Festinger suggested. Some of the origins and consequences of those intergroup comparisons will be discussed in later chapters (see chapters 6–8).

A third issue concerns Festinger's unstated assumption that social comparison activity is generic, engaged in by everyone to a more or less equal degree. In fact, this is probably not the case. In recent years scales have been developed that measure people's habitual tendency to engage in social comparisons, whether these be at an intergroup or an interpersonal level (Brown et al., 1992; Gibbons and Buunk, 1999). Some people, it seems, are chronically more interested in obtaining social comparison information than others. Gibbons and Buunk (1999), for instance, found that high scorers on their comparison orientation scale spent more time investigating other people's scores after a bogus testing session than low scorers. Similarly, van der Zee et al. (1998) found that cancer patients who scored high on the same scale were more interested to discover information about other cancer patients than were low scorers.

Finally, we may question how deliberative social comparison processes are. Festinger assumed that people are typically quite strategic in their choice of comparators, consciously selecting those group members who are maximally informative for self-evaluation and ignoring those who are not so diagnostic. However, Gilbert et al. (1995) speculate that comparison activity may be rather less controlled than this. They suggest that we often make comparisons willy-nilly with whoever we happen to be confronted with, and only later 'undo' the comparison if it then proves to be inappropriate. To demonstrate this automatic quality of comparing, they presented their participants with an obviously inappropriate comparison target, a videotaped confederate

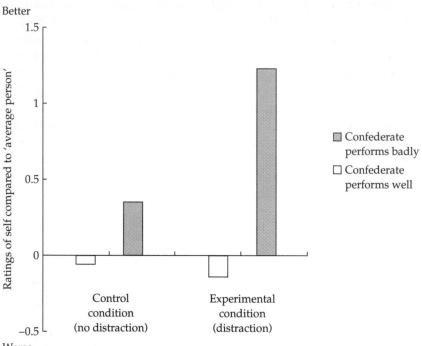

Figure 3.2 Effects of cognitive distraction on exposure to an inappropriate comparison person (from Gilbert et al., 1995, table 1)

who was seen to be singularly good (or bad) at a clinical diagnostic task, a task that the participants subsequently performed themselves, always receiving the same (bogus) feedback about how they had done. The inappropriateness of this confederate was achieved by revealing that either she had had substantial practice at the task (in the 'good' performance condition) or she had been deliberately misled about it (in the 'poor' performance condition). Since neither of these applied to the real participants, they should really have ignored the confederate's score when asked how good they were compared to the average person. Indeed, in the 'control' conditions this appeared to be what happened: people's self-perceived competence was unaffected by the confederate's performance (see figure 3.2, left half). However, in the experimental conditions participants had to perform an additional distracting task (rehearsing an eight-digit number) while they were undertaking the clinical task. Gilbert et al. reasoned that the extra cognitive load imposed by this activity would disrupt the normal process of 'undoing' an inappropriate comparison, and hence their self-ratings should now be affected by the confederate's performance. As can be seen from figure 3.2, this seemed to have happened. When the confederate's performance was poor, participants thought they were pretty good, but when the confederate had done well, they thought of themselves as only average. This implies, therefore, that we are sometimes obliged to make comparisons with others whether we like it or not, and regardless of how 'comparable' those others appear to be at first sight.

Leadership

In this section I want to focus on one aspect of status structure, those occupying high-status positions – otherwise known as leaders – and their interactions with the rest of the group, the leadership process. We have seen that a key characteristic of high-status group members is that they have a tendency to initiate ideas and activities in the group. In other words, they have some means of influencing others to change their behaviour. However, since social influence is always a reciprocal process (as we shall see in chapter 4), perhaps it would be more precise to say that what really characterizes leaders is that they can influence others in the group more than they themselves are influenced. In everyday language the word 'leader' has dozens of synonyms: shop steward, team captain, line manager and director are just some of the many terms in frequent use. Equally various are the methods by which leaders come to attain their position. Election, appointment, usurpation or 'spontaneous' emergence are some of the most common of these. As we shall see, each can have quite different consequences for the morale and effectiveness of the group.

Leaders: personality types or products of the situation?

14 February 1996 was a sad day for followers of Liverpool Football Club. It was the day that Bob Paisley, their most successful manager ever, died at the age of 77. In his nine years as manager, Liverpool won thirteen trophies, including six league championships and three

European Cups, a feat that no other British manager before or since has emulated. To many observers, one of the most surprising facts about Bob Paisley was that he achieved this amazing record despite a notable lack of flamboyance, extraversion, charisma or any of the other traits that people commonly associate with successful leaders. Alan Hansen, that doyen of Liverpool defenders during the Paisley era, summed him up thus:

He had little personality, no charisma, and he struggled to express himself. (The *Guardian*[3])

This example is instructive for social psychologists because it seems to run counter to much accepted wisdom about leadership. For example, a commonly held view about leaders is that they possess certain personality characteristics that distinguish them from 'ordinary' people. Thus, leaders around the world – past and present – are all thought to have traits in common that have enabled them to attain their positions of power and allowed them to exert a controlling influence over their peoples. Just what are the characteristics linking a Saddam Hussein with a Mother Teresa, or a Margaret Thatcher with a Nelson Mandela? Perhaps not surprisingly, in the face of this diversity, proponents of the 'great man' (or, more properly, 'great person') theory (as it is known) have found it hard to be precise, usually resorting to such vague terms as 'charisma' or 'genius' to explain the success of these 'heroes' (Carlyle, 1841). However, when examined more carefully, this personality explanation of leadership proves to be of only limited worth. Stogdill (1974), reviewing a large number of empirical investigations of leadership traits, could find few reliable correlates. In general, it seems, leaders tend to be slightly more intelligent, self-confident, dominant, sociable and achievement-orientated than their followers. But all these associations tend to be rather inconsistent across different studies (averaging out to correlations of less than 0.30). Although some recent commentators have tried to resurrect the personality theory of leadership, pointing to new leader traits that seem to be associated with improved group performance, it remains that none of these correlations is very strong (Hogan et al., 1994; Zaccaro et al., 1991).

In complete contrast to the personality theory is an explanation in terms of the functional demands of the situation. According to this view, expressed by Bales (1950) among others, the most effective leader in a given context is the person who is best equipped to assist the group to fulfil its objectives. In another time or another place someone else may emerge as leader. This was well illustrated by Sherif et al.'s (1961) summer camp studies alluded to briefly earlier. When competition with another group was heightened, one of the groups underwent a change in leadership, with a boy of greater physical prowess replacing the previous leader. The new situation had presented the group with different problems, requiring a new leader for their resolution. An experimental demonstration of the same point was made by Carter and Nixon (1949). They gave pairs of high school students three different tasks to perform, an intellectual task, a clerical task and a mechanical assembly task. Contrary to the 'great leader' hypothesis, they found little evidence of the same person emerging as leader in all three tasks. Those who took the lead in the first two situations seldom were the same people who dominated in the mechanical task.

If the idea of leadership as a product of the situation is more useful than simply regarding it as a characteristic possessed by some but not others, it is still not entirely satisfactory. It does not tell us very much about what leaders actually do, nor, crucially, does it tell us much about the process by which they emerge in a given situation. It is these omissions that provide the focus for the following sections.

The behaviour of leaders

It is not who you are that is important to leadership success, it is how you behave, or at least so argued Lippitt and White (1943) in one of the earliest and most influential studies of leadership. They believed that an important function of the leader was to create a 'social climate' in the group, and that the group's morale and effectiveness would be dependent on the nature of the climate engendered. Accordingly, they set up an experimental situation using young schoolboys engaged in after school clubs. The leaders of these clubs were confederates of the researchers and each was trained in the adoption of three quite different leadership styles. In the first, the leader acted *autocratically*, organizing the group's activities, telling the children what should be done at all times and generally remaining rather aloof from the

93

group. In the second, labelled the *democratic* style, the leader made a point of discussing all decisions and activities with the group and allowing the children to choose their own work partners. In general, the leader adopting this style attempted to become a 'regular group member'. Finally, there was a laissez-faire style in which the group was left to its own devices with minimal intervention by the leader. Each leader stayed with his group for seven weeks and for that period maintained a consistent style of leadership. The leaders then changed groups (twice) and at each change they also changed their behavioural style. This meant that any effects observed in the groups could be attributed to the leaders' behaviour rather than to their underlying personalities. And effects there were. The 'democratic' leaders were liked more than either of the other two types. The atmosphere in these groups tended to be friendly, group-centred and reasonably task-orientated while with the 'autocratic' leaders there was more aggression, a greater dependence on the leader and a more self-centred orientation. The laissez-faire leaders tended to elicit considerable demands for information and were reasonably well liked, but more of the children's time was spent in play rather than work. As far as measurable productivity was concerned, the autocratically led groups worked the hardest but only so long as their leader was actually present. When, on a pretext, the 'autocratic' leader left the room they more or less stopped work altogether. The democratically led groups, although a little less productive, were scarcely affected by the leader's absence. In the laissez-faire groups the productivity actually seemed to increase when the leader left the room. These results led Lippitt and White (1943) to a strong endorsement of the democratic leadership approach, both on grounds of group autonomy and morale, and for overall effectiveness.

At about the same time, Bales (1950) was developing his IPA system (see chapter 2) and, along with it, a theory of leadership. Earlier in this chapter I described how Bales identified the roles of task and socio-emotional specialist in the group (Slater, 1955). These, in Bales' theory, correspond to the leaders of the group. He placed most emphasis on the former role, arguing that the person most likely to emerge as the 'task specialist' was the one perceived to be best equipped to assist the group in the performance of its current task. Behaviourally, these kinds of people can usually be distinguished: they tend to be the biggest participators in the group's activities and their behaviour is concentrated in the task interaction categories, particularly those concerned with offering opinion and direction. On the other hand, the socio-emotional specialist spends more time paying attention to and responding to the feelings of other group members. Bales implies that these two roles are difficult for the same person to occupy simultaneously and suggests that most often they devolve onto separate people.

It is probably no coincidence that Bales' task versus socio-emotional dichotomy bears such a close resemblance to Lippitt's and White's autocratic versus democratic experimental distinction. Shorn of their ideological overtones, one of the key differences between these two leadership styles was a concern with directing the task as opposed to paying attention to the concerns of the group members. This same polarization recurs even more clearly in yet another research programme, the Ohio State leadership studies (e.g. Fleishman, 1973; Stogdill, 1974). These consisted of a large number of investigations among mainly military and industrial groups in which, through questionnaires to subordinates and other measures, the behaviour and effectiveness of group leaders were assessed. The first major finding from this work came from people's descriptions and ratings of their leader's behaviour, in which two main themes could be discerned: one was a concern for *initiating structure* and the other was a *consideration* for others. These, of course, are very close to Bales' two orientations just discussed. However, in one respect the two formulations are crucially different: in Bales' theory, it is assumed that the task and socio-emotional orientations are bipolar opposites whereas the Ohio State researchers concluded that they could be better regarded as independent dimensions. The main evidence for this is derived from factor analyses of questionnaire data in which the two factors emerged not as inversely related (as Bales would have expected), but as *orthogonal* to each other. This means that, in theory, one could have a leader who is high in both structure and consideration, or high in one and not the other, or high in neither.

This brings us to the second conclusion from these studies. This concerned leader effectiveness. The best leader, it seemed, was the person who was rated above average on both attributes: someone who could organize the group's activities while remaining responsive to their views and feelings (Stogdill, 1974). This was confirmed in a longitudinal experiment involving observations of twelve problem-solving groups (Sorrentino and Field, 1986). Those who were elected by their peers as group leaders at the end of the five-week testing programme were those who had been consistently observed to score highly in both the task and the socio-emotional category classes in Bales' system. However, the situation may not be quite as simple as this, as Fleishman (1973) has pointed out. For instance, it appears that consideration and structure do not have a straightforward association with group morale. At very high or very low levels on either dimension, the relationship seems to disappear, thus producing overall curvilinear relationships. Furthermore, the two attributes may not be symmetrically complementary. A high level of consideration by the leader may help to offset too little concern with structure, but the reverse may not be true. However concerned with structure one is, one cannot compensate for a complete absence of consideration.

A further complexity has emerged from cross-cultural research into leadership style (Smith et al., 1989). These researchers investigated how managers were perceived in a number of factories in Britain, the US, Japan and Hong Kong. Consistent with the Ohio State findings, they found that two general themes emerged in all four cultures: a concern for task performance and a concern for group maintenance. However, despite this cross-cultural similarity, the specific behaviours associated with these leadership styles varied considerably. In the US, for example, 'performance' supervisors were those who strongly emphasized task activities and maintained a formal relationship with subordinates while 'maintenance' supervisors were seen to be participative and consultative, and less likely to focus on work issues. In contrast, in Japan there was a less clear-cut distinction between the two general styles: 'performance' supervisors were seen to meet socially after work and also to talk to subordinates about personal difficulties, and 'maintenance' leaders were rated highly on concerns over teaching new job skills, talking about work problems and speaking about subordinates in their absence. Thus, effective leadership the world over does seem to combine both task and socio-emotional elements, but the way in which these are expressed and the relationship between them are culturally quite specific.

In recent years the search for the optimal leadership style has taken a new direction. Several theorists have sought to revive the concept of 'charisma' as an important component of successful leadership (Bass, 1985; Burns, 1978; House, 1997). In these 'new' theories of leadership, charisma is not regarded in its conventional sense as being a personality trait so much as being characteristic of a particular kind of a relationship between leader and followers. Although there are differences of emphasis in the various theories, there is some consensus that charismatic leadership involves the leader in providing some vision or inspiration to the rest of the group so that they become motivated to transcend their usual performance goals, 'to go the extra mile' in the service of the collective interest. Bass (1985) has labelled this style 'transformational', which he contrasts with 'transactional' leadership, in which the leader is much more reactive, only intervening when it is apparent that some problem exists.

Bass (1990) suggests that, in general, transformational leadership will elicit superior performance but particularly in crises or in situations undergoing change. When things are on a more even keel, transactional leadership can be as beneficial. The observed correlations between measures of transformational leadership and perceived effectiveness are respectably high (typically 0.7 to 0.8), and certainly much higher than for transactional leadership (Bryman, 1992). However, they are not in themselves conclusive evidence for the efficacy of transformational leadership. For one thing, they are bedevilled by the usual problem of inferring causality from correlational relationships. More seriously, they may simply reflect group members' naive theories about what successful leaders should be like. As I noted earlier, some common-sense wisdom holds that leadership is strongly associated with certain personality traits; the research tells a different story.

Nevertheless, there is some experimental and longitudinal research that is supportive of the utility of the charismatic and transformational leadership style. For example, Howell and Frost (1989) trained confederate leaders to adopt either charismatic, considerate or task structuring styles in managing students undertaking a relatively unstructured task (unfortunately, *combinations* of the three styles were not also examined). There was some evidence that the charismatic style elicited better group performance than the other two styles (although on only two of the four performance indices). Much more striking were the effects on member satisfaction and absence of role conflict: the charismatic style easily outscored the other two on these measures. Similar results were forthcoming from a field study of managers in a Canadian finance company (Howell and Avolio, 1993). These managers were assessed by their subordinates on a measure of charisma. One year later the managers' performance was measured by examining their achievement of various production targets. There were some reliable positive correlations between charisma and performance, and some negative associations for transactional leadership. Given the longitudinal design of this study, an inference of causality seems plausible: those leaders seen to be charismatic do actually deliver the goods.

The idea of charismatic leadership is an intuitively appealing one. We can all think of certain public figures who readily seem to fit the bill (or not, as the case may be). In recent British political history the contrast between the charismatic style of Tony Blair and the stolid persona adopted by John Major provides a vivid illustration. However, this 'new leadership' perspective is not without its drawbacks. Perhaps the foremost of these is a lack of specification of what exactly it is that contributes to charismatic leadership. Since most writers are clear that it is not primarily a personality characteristic but, instead, is a product of the leader–follower relationship there is a risk of some circularity here. House et al. (1991), despite being proponents of the 'new leadership' approach, put their finger on the problem:

If a man runs naked down the street proclaiming that he alone can save others from impending doom, and if he immediately wins a following, then he is a charismatic leader: a social relationship has come into being. If he does not win a following, he is simply a lunatic. (Wilson (1975), quoted in House et al., 1991, p. 366)

We shall return to the concept of charisma later, when we shall attempt to link it more closely to some features of the group's conception of itself and its relation to others. In the meantime we must turn our attention to another approach, one that does not focus exclusively on either leadership style or situational factors, but on how the two interact.

Interaction of leader style and situation

With the demise of the trait view of leadership, the leadership style approach seemed to command the field: what was needed for effective leadership, it seemed, was the right combination of task-centredness and consideration for others. Fiedler (1965) was one of the first to notice the shortcomings of this simple dictum. Drawing on data from a variety of different kinds of groups (e.g. basketball teams, aircraft crews), he observed that there was no straightforward relationship between the leader's predominant style and the effectiveness of the group. Sometimes very task-orientated leaders seemed to be effective; elsewhere, the socio-emotional leaders did best. Fiedler's resolution of these puzzling findings was to propose an interactionist model of leadership, in which effectiveness was seen as *contingent* upon the match of the leader's style with the kind of situation which he or she faced. In a nutshell, the type of leader attitude required for effective group performance depends on the degree to which the situation is favourable or unfavourable to the leader (Fiedler, 1965).

Fiedler accepts the basic distinction between task-orientated and socio-emotionally orientated leadership styles and, indeed, has developed a measuring instrument in an attempt to quantify the difference. This scale – called the least preferred co-worker (LPC) scale – simply asks would-be leaders to think of all the people they have ever known and then describe the one person with whom it has been most difficult to work. They do this by rating this individual on 18 bipolar scales (e.g. pleasant–unpleasant, boring–interesting, friendly–unfriendly etc.). High scorers (high LPC) on this scale (that is, those who evaluate their least preferred co-workers favourably) are thought to be those who habitually adopt a relationship-orientated or considerate leadership style, while low scorers (low LPC) are assumed to be more task-orientated kinds of people.[4] There are two important points to note here about Fiedler's distinction between high and low LPC leaders. The first is that he regards a person's LPC score as reflecting a relatively fixed personality characteristic, which is consistent across situations and over time. In a way, therefore, Fiedler is resurrecting part of the old trait theory of leadership. The second is that he does not view the high and low LPC categories as completely exclusive. Rather, the high and low scorers differ in the relative importance that they attach to person and task aspects of the group. In his terms, they have different 'motivational hierarchies': high LPC means that people are primary and the task is secondary, and the reverse is true for low LPC (Fiedler, 1978).

Having distinguished between two basic leader types, Fiedler then goes on to identify three elements which he believes determine the 'favourableness' of the situation for the leader. The first, and most important, is the atmosphere of the group, which Fiedler calls *leader–member relations*. A leader who enjoys the confidence, loyalty and affection of the group will find his or her work easier than one who does not. Second in importance is *task structure*: a group with clear instructions for achieving a well-defined goal is thought to be easier to manage than one whose job is less well formulated and which has a number of possible outcomes. The obvious contrast here is between a production workgroup on a factory assembly line and a design team attempting to discover a new process or product. In the former case the components of the job are usually specified in the most minute detail and the end product is known in advance. In the latter, by definition, the outcome is uncertain and often the means of achieving it are equally ambiguous. Finally, the leader may have attained – or may be invested with – more or less *power*. Leaders may have many rewards and sanctions at their disposal and be able to exercise considerable authority or, alternatively, their position may be weak and they may have little competence or few means to influence the group members.

Suppose, now, every leadership situation can be defined as 'high' or 'low' in each of these three factors. This produces eight possible combinations or degrees of 'favourableness', ranging from good leader–member relations, high task structure and high position power to the opposite of these three. Because Fiedler assumes leader–member relations to be most important followed by task structure and power, this suggests the order for the intermediate degrees of favourableness shown at the foot of figure 3.3. Fiedler's basic hypothesis is that low LPC leaders will be most effective in situations lying towards either end of this eight-level continuum, while high LPC leaders will excel in the situations falling in the middle. The rationale behind this prediction is complex: when the situation is very favourable for leaders (they are well liked by the group, the task is straightforward and their authority is unquestioned) they need waste no time in worrying about the morale of the group members and they have the means and the power to be wholly task directive. A similar style is called for at the opposite extreme, although for different reasons. Here, things are so unfavourable for the leaders (disliked by the group, an ambiguous task and little power) that they have little to lose by being fairly autocratic. Attempts to win over the group by a more considerate approach will probably fail anyway, resulting in lost time and hence lowered effectiveness. At the intermediate levels, on the other hand, the leader may, by adopting a suitably relationship-orientated style, be able to improve the leader–member relations sufficiently to compensate for an ill-defined task or a lack of authority. Taken together, these three lines of reasoning suggest that if one correlates the effectiveness of the group (according to some performance criteria) with the leader's LPC score, the sign and size of the correlation should vary across the eight situational combinations, being clearly negative at either end but positive in the middle. This predicted pattern of correlations is shown as the dashed curve in figure 3.3.

How well does this fit with observed correlations from leadership studies? In an early paper, Fiedler (1965) summarized the findings from a dozen published studies, which generated more than fifty separate correlations between LPC and effectiveness. These correlations were allocated to their appropriate situational classification and the median correlation for each of the eight situations was determined. These are shown as the solid line in figure 3.3, and the fit is apparently quite close. In a later review, Fiedler (1978) presented evidence from further experiments, which seemed largely to confirm the original picture except for octants II and VII, where, in both instances, he found a more positive median value than had been predicted.

Strube and Garcia (1981), in a meta-analysis of 178 empirical tests of the theory, concluded that there was substantial support for it, although their review did resurrect the doubts about the second and seventh octants which Fiedler (1978) had already identified. A more refined meta-analysis of a subset of the studies examined by Strube and Garcia came to a similar conclusion (Schriesheim et al., 1994). Given the very extensive range of studies on which these reviews are based, it does seem that Fiedler's theory provides a reasonably good model to explain leadership effectiveness, even if there remain some doubts as to its completeness.

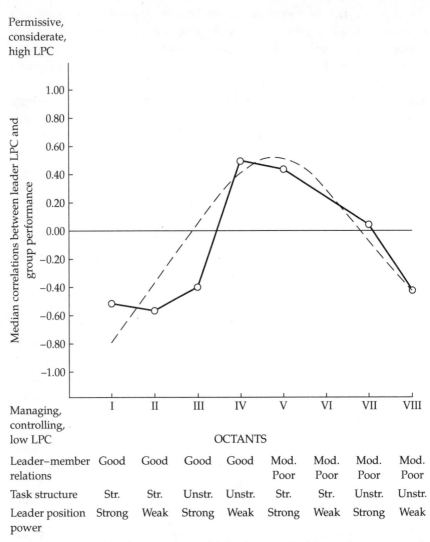

Permissive, considerate, high LPC

Managing, controlling, low LPC

Median correlations between leader LPC and group performance

OCTANTS

	I	II	III	IV	V	VI	VII	VIII
Leader–member relations	Good	Good	Good	Good	Mod. Poor	Mod. Poor	Mod. Poor	Mod. Poor
Task structure	Str.	Str.	Unstr.	Unstr.	Str.	Str.	Unstr.	Unstr.
Leader position power	Strong	Weak	Strong	Weak	Strong	Weak	Strong	Weak

Figure 3.3 Optimal leader attitudes and behaviour required by various group task situations. ---, pattern predicted by contingency theory; —, observed pattern of median correlations (from Fiedler, 1965)

In spite of supportive evidence like this, Fiedler's theory has excited considerable controversy over the years. A central issue in this debate has been the extent to which a leader's style should be considered a 'given', unaffected by circumstances. There are at least three grounds for doubting whether the leader's orientation is as immutable as Fiedler claims. First, the claim is based on a trait view of personality, which suggests that people will be consistent over time and across situations. But this conception of personality has attracted much criticism. For example, Mischel (1968) has convincingly shown that there is, in fact, very little temporal and cross-situational consistency in people's behaviour. This implies that personality traits may not be quite the fixed entities that Fiedler believes them to be. Indeed, if people's leadership style was so difficult to alter, how could Lippitt and White (1943) have so successfully trained their confederates to adopt different styles in the study described earlier? Further evidence of the instability of people's leadership orientation comes from attempts to establish the test–retest reliability of the LPC scale, which have produced correlations varying from 0.01 to 0.93 with a median of around 0.67 (Rice, 1978). While the latter figure is comparable with reliability co-efficients from other personality scales, it still implies that more than half the variance at the second time of testing is unaccounted for by the first set of scores. Rice points out that the lowest reliability figures were obtained in environments designed to bring about change (e.g. training courses), further suggesting that any traits underlying the LPC score are not completely unaffected by the situation.

A second question about Fiedler's theory concerns his assumption that the eight different situation types form an ordered continuum of favourableness, with each octant being equally distant from the next. There are two problems here. The first is that the order of importance attributed to the three situational factors was essentially arbitrary in the original formulation of the model (Fiedler, 1965). With a different ordering – for example, by assuming that task structure was more important than leader–member relations – the predicted pattern of LPC–effectiveness correlations would look very different. Although Fiedler (1978) was later able to offer some empirical support for his *a priori* ordering, he still assumed that the octants formed an approximately interval scale. However, Singh et al. (1979) have suggested that this assumption may also be problematic. They asked respondents to rate a number of situations, which varied systematically along each of Fiedler's three factors, for their favourableness to the leader. As expected, each factor did indeed prove to be an important determinant of perceived favourableness. Somewhat less expected, however, was the relative importance of the three factors. Leader–member relations proved to be the most important factor in only two out of the four studies. In all four, position power was a strong influence, the strongest in two of the studies. This is especially difficult for Fiedler's theory since this is conventionally assumed to be the *least* important factor of the three! Singh et al. (1979) further showed that if the octants were positioned according to how favourably they are actually perceived (rather than simply assumed to be equidistant from each other), a rather more regular pattern of LPC–effectiveness correlations results. Perhaps this might help to explain the equivocal findings in some of the octants (Schriesheim et al., 1994; Strube and Garcia, 1981).

A third limitation of Fiedler's theory is its presumption that all leaders and would-be leaders can be dichotomously categorized as high or low LPC. In accounts of the theory (e.g. Fiedler, 1965), or in derivations from it – for example, in the Leader Match training programme (e.g. Fiedler and Chemers, 1984) – people are conventionally classified as 'high' LPC if their score exceeds 64 and 'low' if it falls below 57. As Kennedy (1982) pointed out, that leaves a sizeable group of people – perhaps as large as 20 per cent (Fiedler, 1978) – unaccounted for, those scoring in the middle of the scale. Leaving aside the wisdom of excluding so large a group of people from theoretical consideration, it is worth enquiring how well they would perform as leaders. This was precisely the focus of Kennedy's (1982) study, which involved the aggregation of several different samples for which LPC, situational control and performance data were available. Instead of the usual practice of considering just two groups, Kennedy trichotomized his sample so that 25 per cent (12.5 per cent either side of the sample mean) could be described as 'middle LPC' and the remainder as 'high' or 'low'. He then examined the performance of these three groups in the eight varieties of situational control. The results were both surprising and instructive. The 'high' and 'low' groups conformed more or less to the pattern predicted by the model – i.e. 'lows' performing better at either end of the continuum, 'highs' doing well in the intermediate octants. However, the 'middle' LPC group showed much less variability across situations and generally outperformed the other two groups regardless of situational favourability. This rather contradicts one of the central tenets of Fiedler's model since it suggests that the performance of leaders with no clear preferred style may be relatively *independent* of the situation, and not contingent upon it as the model implies. This conclusion is similar to that reached by the Ohio State and other studies considered earlier (Fleishman, 1973; Sorrentino and Field, 1986).

Although the most well known, Fiedler's model is by no means the only 'contingency' theory of leadership. Two other models that have also achieved some popularity are Hersey and Blanchard's (1993) Situational Leadership Theory (SLT) and Vroom and Yetton's (1973) model of optimal decision making (see also Vroom and Jago, 1988). Both of these share with Fiedler's theory the assumption that no one style of leadership will work for all situations, but differ greatly, both from Fiedler and from each other, in their analysis of the nature of this leader–situation interdependence.

SLT holds that leaders need to adapt their style to the 'readiness' of the group members to undertake the task at hand (Hersey and Blanchard, 1993). Readiness is conceived of as the combination of the group members' (or followers') ability, willingness and confidence to perform a given task. It is thought to be lowest where followers lack the appropriate skills, are unmotivated and, perhaps as a result, feel somewhat apprehensive about their ability to achieve anything. In such a situation the theory advocates a highly task-orientated approach by the leader, much as Fiedler's model does for the equivalent quadrant VIII in its situational taxonomy. At the other end of the spectrum – competent, committed and confident followers – a much less task-orientated style is thought to be appropriate since the leader can and should be able to delegate functions in such circumstances. But – and here the theory diverges from other models – such a decline in task-related activity by the leader in conditions of maximal follower 'readiness' need not be accompanied by any increase in socio-emotional orientation. In fact, the two leadership styles (task and socio-emotionally orientated) are thought to be independent of one another in this theory, rather than inversely related as they are in most other theories. It is at the intermediate levels of 'readiness' that a more relationship-orientated style is thought to come into its own, coupled with a modicum of task orientation. Thus, where the followers are able but unwilling or willing but unable, giving some attention to their socio-emotional needs (while remaining somewhat directive) is likely to pay the biggest dividends for the leader. Combining these elements produces a curvilinear relationship between follower readiness and leadership style (relationship- or task-orientated).

Some differences between SLT and Fiedler's theory should now be apparent. Although both emphasize that successful leadership is contingent on the match between the leader's style and the situation, in SLT it is assumed that leaders have the ability to adapt their behaviour to different contexts. Fiedler's account does not accord so much flexibility to leaders, assuming that their preferred style (as indicated by their LPC score) is relatively stable. In SLT there is much more emphasis on the followers and the leader–follower relationship. As we have seen, their ability and motivation to tackle the task are regarded as the principal antecedents of the leader's behaviour and should determine the nature of the leader–follower relationship. In Fiedler's theory, on the other hand, leader–member relations are just one element of the situation, which then help to identify which leadership style will be most effective.

What does the research evidence reveal about the validity of SLT? Although SLT is apparently widely used in commercial settings – Hersey and Blanchard (1993) claim that over a million leaders per year are exposed to training based on its principles – it has attracted relatively little attention from researchers, perhaps because of the complexity of the expected empirical relationships among the variables. (Essentially, a three-way interaction between follower readiness, socio-emotional orientation and task orientation is assumed to predict task performance.) One of the few systematic tests of SLT was conducted by Vecchio (1987) in a study of American high school teachers and their head teachers. Appropriate measures of teacher 'readiness' and performance were obtained from the heads, while the teachers themselves provided ratings of their heads' leadership style in terms of consideration and structure. The results were only weakly supportive of SLT. One set of analyses examining the precise three-way interaction specified by the theory found no statistical support at all; instead, one straightforward effect emerged of a very high correlation between teachers' 'readiness' and their performance, irrespective of their managers' style. An alternative analysis, which compared groups of teachers and heads who matched each other well (according to SLT) with those who did not, found some reliable differences in performance between the groups, particularly at low and moderate levels of teacher 'readiness'. For the high 'readiness' group, having the appropriate leader style was less important, however. A subsequent study by Blank et al. (1990) involving university hall of residence directors and subordinates also provided little support for SLT. The subordinates' performance was *not* found to depend on particular combinations of their 'readiness' and their director's style as the theory predicts. Only on job satisfaction was there some evidence of this interaction: low 'readiness' staff reported greater satisfaction with a highly task-orientated supervisor than with a less task-orientated one; high 'readiness' subordinates were largely unaffected by their director's behaviour. Thus, while seemingly successful in commercial terms, SLT remains unproven scientifically.

The leadership theories we have considered so far have been rather generic; they attempt to specify which leadership behaviour will be most effective across a wide range of task situations confronting a group. In contrast, Vroom and Yetton's (1973) theory confines itself to just one group activity, that of reaching a decision. It is concerned with trying to prescribe the optimal process to be adopted by the leader in various decision-making contexts. In particular, it seeks to define the amount of group consultation and participation the leader should encourage to produce the most effective decisions. An example will help to illustrate how the theory works.

Let us suppose you are chair of a trade union branch in a large factory. For some years you have led a committee composed of shop stewards from different sections of the factory, and you enjoy their respect and confidence. You have noticed that for some time membership and participation in the union have been falling, with negative consequences for your members' morale. You have to decide how to reverse this trend, a decision made the more urgent by a recent tougher style from management, a squeeze on wages in the factory and less favourable conditions of work. The question is: how should you as a leader proceed to make such a decision?

Vroom and Yetton (1973) identify five possible decision processes:

1   You could attempt to come up with a decision completely on your own without consulting anyone (A1).
2   Marginally less autocratically, you could obtain some ideas and information from your fellow committee members but still decide on a solution yourself (A11).
3   You could take the consultative process slightly further by sharing the problem with other shop stewards on a one-to-one basis, garnering suggestions from them but still ultimately making the decision yourself (C1).
4   You might decide there would be benefits in having some *collective* discussion of the problem, but you still retain the option of having the final say, being influenced (or not) by the rest of the group as you think fit (C11).
5   In a spirit of genuine group participation you could opt to try to resolve the whole problem in the group, hopefully arriving at a consensual collective decision (G11).

According to the Vroom–Yetton model, which process will work best (in terms of producing the most effective decision) depends on the nature of the decision task. Originally, they suggested that there were seven attributes (later modified to twelve – see below) that provided the necessary pointers as to which of those five processes the leader should or should not use. These pointers take the form of a series of nested conditional statements, which direct the leader towards an optimal decision-making style (or set of styles). The first and most fundamental attribute concerns the importance of the quality of the decision – does it matter that you get it right? Next, do you, as leader, have enough information and/or expertise to come up with a solution? Is the problem a well-structured one with recognizable steps to its solution? Having made a decision, is it important for its effective implementation that your group members accept it? Are they, in fact, likely to accept your decision? Do the group members share the wider goals of the group (in this case the trade union)? And, finally, is there likely to be some conflict among them over various options that might be considered?

Vroom and Yetton recommend that these questions be posed and answered sequentially in the form of a flow chart, as depicted in figure 3.4. You, as the would-be leader, work your way through the

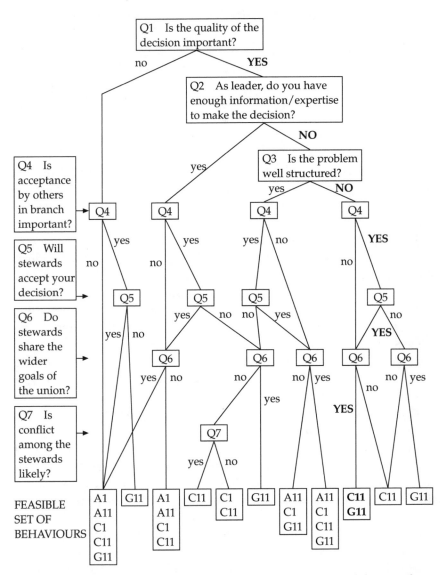

Figure 3.4 Application of the Vroom–Yetton model to a hypothetical decision about ways to increase trade union participation

questions, arriving at a prescribed decision process (or processes) at the bottom. This prescription is called the 'feasible set' of methods that the leader can adopt; those not so prescribed are presumed to fall outside the 'feasible set'. The options most likely to be taken at the various choice points in the diagram for this particular example are indicated in bold, which results in a feasible set of two decision processes, both of which call for participation by the other shop stewards in the decision (C11, G11). Although seemingly complex, the Vroom–Yetton model has a certain intuitive appeal, especially since it promises to provide a ready-made 'recipe' for a leader confronting any particular decision. It has also received some support from research. A typical method of testing the model has been to get leaders to identify various decisions they have had to make and then analyse these decisions in terms of the seven key attributes to allow the prescription of a feasible set of decision processes. This prescription is then compared to the *actual* process used to see whether the leader followed or departed from what was implied by the model (i.e. was the decision inside or outside the feasible set?). Finally, some judgement of decision effectiveness is obtained, often from the leaders themselves but ideally according to some independent criterion. Vroom and Jago (1988) located six studies that had tested the model in this way, involving a total of over 1500 decisions. Of those decisions that fell within their appropriate feasible set, over 60 per cent were successful; however, of those falling *outside* their feasible sets, over 60 per cent were *un*successful.

Although this seems like reasonable support for the theory, a closer look reveals some unexpected complexities. Vroom and Jago (1978), for instance, found that of self-reported (real) decisions made by managers that fell into feasible sets, over two-thirds were judged by the managers to have been successful. This success rate compared to one of only around 20 per cent for decisions deemed to have fallen outside feasible sets. However, it was also notable that participative decision processes themselves (especially C11) tended to be more successful, *whether or not they fell inside feasible sets*. This was particularly the case if 'success' was measured by degree of acceptance of the decision by subordinates, a point we will return to shortly. Field (1982) presented various hypothetical case studies to groups of business students, and instructed leaders to adopt one of the five decision processes on each (varying this systematically across cases). In this way he artificially (but randomly) contrived to have some decision processes within and some outside the feasible sets as specified by the Vroom–Yetton model. This had only a modest effect on decision effectiveness (as assessed by independent judges): of the feasible set decisions, 49 per cent were effective as compared to only 36 per cent of the decisions falling outside the feasible set, a statistically significant if small difference.

The Vroom–Yetton model seems moderately successful in prescribing some rough 'rules of thumb' for a would-be leader in trying to decide how far to involve group members in a decision. However, it is evident that these prescriptions are far from perfect: some successful decisions seem to be made despite their apparently flouting some of the criteria, and even following the prescriptions does not guarantee an effective or a socially acceptable decision. Part of the problem, as Vroom and Jago (1988) concede, is that particular branches of the decision tree do not lead to unique outcomes, leaving the leader still to decide between two or more courses of action (see figure 3.4). Such a decision may be determined by time pressure factors, the leader's past or future relationship with the group, or his or her personal beliefs. Inevitably, such imprecision takes its toll when the model is evaluated empirically. Furthermore, many of the choice points in the decision tree are posed in dichotomous terms when it would probably be more realistic to seek a graduated answer. For example, instead of 'Is acceptance of decision by subordinates important?' (Yes/No), ask 'How important is acceptance of decision by subordinates?' (not at all (1) to very (5)).

Such limitations of the original Vroom–Yetton (1973) model led Vroom and Jago (1988) to propose a revised version that incorporates more decision attributes (twelve instead of seven) and continuous instead of dichotomous decision tree responses. Although this greatly complicates the prescription process,[5] they claim that with the assistance of some relatively simple computer software, usable systems can be made available to leaders. The underlying logic of the new model is the same as in the original version: particular combinations of decision attributes prescribe one (or more) of five degrees of participation by group members. There has been little testing of the revised model but the initial indications suggest that it may be able to make more precise predictions than the original version (Field et al., 1990; Vroom and Jago, 1988).

Leadership as a process

In chapter 2 we saw the importance of norms in regulating behaviour in the group, and noted that everyone within the group was influenced by these norms with – in domains most central to the group – the leaders being more so than the followers. And yet, the whole discussion in the previous three sections has emphasized the leader as an agent of *change* in the group, a person who attempts to alter the prevailing norms and hence 'influence others more than he or she is influenced by them' (as we defined a leader earlier). This, then, raises a fundamental paradox: how can a leader be both a loyal group member (in adhering faithfully to the group's norms) *and* an effective and powerful deviate (in persuading the group to adopt new norms)?

The solution to this paradox was suggested by an early experiment by Merei (1949). This was carried out in a Hungarian nursery school, where Merei observed the behaviour of groups of young children when an older child was introduced to the group. This child was someone who had earlier shown characteristic leadership behaviours in the sense of having been an 'initiator' rather than a 'follower' in his or her own peer group. Naturally, Merei expected the newcomers to assume a dominant position in these new groups, if for no other reason than that children are very sensitive to age differences. However, what was of interest was the manner in which they achieved this leadership role. Would they assert their authority from the very beginning or would the process be more gradual? Merei concluded that those children who attempted the former strategy turned out to be unsuccessful leaders who were largely ignored by the other children. The successful leaders – as judged by how much they were eventually followed by the younger children – adopted a more cautious approach. To begin with they tended to follow the existing games and 'traditions' of the group, suggesting only minor variations. It was only after a few days of this accommodative behaviour that they began to suggest completely new activities or radical departures from the old routines.

This sequence of first conforming to the group norms and then introducing new ideas is central to Hollander's theory of leadership (Hollander, 1958; Hollander and Julian, 1970). Hollander suggests that what leaders must do in the early stages of their 'reign' is to build up 'credit' with the rest of the group. This 'credit' is what gives them the subsequent legitimacy to exert influence over those same group members and to deviate from existing norms. Hollander terms this 'idiosyncrasy credit' because it may eventually be expended in novel or innovative behaviour by the leader. Essentially, the more credit one builds up, the more idiosyncratic behaviour will be tolerated by the group. A direct test of Hollander's theory was provided by Estrada et al. (1995). They studied some student project groups longitudinally, obtaining both subjective measures of idiosyncrasy credit and leadership (as nominated by fellow group members) and objective measures of dominance and performance (as assessed by independent observers). As predicted, the idiosyncrasy credit accorded to each group member was reliably and positively correlated with the leadership indices (both subjective and objective) but *negatively* correlated with their attendance record (thus, supporting the notion of the leader as a 'good' group member). Interestingly, these relationships were stronger in high performing groups than in those that worked together less effectively. This suggests that the idiosyncrasy credit–leadership link is a hallmark of successfully led groups.

How does the leader establish a good credit rating with the group? One way, as Merei's (1949) findings suggest, is to adhere initially to the group norms. Hollander (1982) suggests at least three other sources of legitimacy for the leader. One stems from the methods by which the leaders achieve their position: were they elected by the group or simply appointed by an external authority? Hollander believes that the former method usually gives the leader greater legitimacy than the latter. The leader's competence to fulfil the group's objectives is also a critical factor. Someone seen to be exceptionally able in task-relevant behaviours will accrue more credits than the less able person. Finally, the leader's identification with the group may also be important. Those perceived to share the group's ideals and aspirations will have more legitimacy than those who are seen to identify more with some other grouping. Let us look at some of the research that has investigated these four factors.

Hollander (1960) examined the role of initial conformity in permitting the leader subsequently to influence the group. Experimental confederates were introduced into laboratory problem-solving groups. The groups had a series of problems to solve, and over the course of

113

these activities, false feedback from the experimenter established that the confederate was consistently suggesting correct solutions, thus giving him some initial legitimacy. Before each problem the group was required to discuss the best procedure for tackling the task. It was in this discussion phase that the critical variation in the confederate's behaviour was introduced. Every so often he would depart radically from the group consensus view as to the most appropriate procedure. Depending on experimental condition, this 'idiosyncratic' behaviour occurred *early* in the sequence of problems or *late*. The measure of his influence was the frequency with which the group followed his suggestions as to the correct solution to the problem. As predicted, when the idiosyncratic behaviour occurred early in the group's mini-history there was much less conformity to the confederate's suggestions than when it occurred later.

Hollander and Julian (1970) showed that the method by which the leaders achieved their position can also be important. In this experiment, leaders of groups who thought they had been elected to their position by their group were more likely to suggest solutions to the task problem which appeared to differ from the group's own solution than were leaders who thought they had been appointed by an outside expert. The 'elected' leaders believed they were more competent at the task and enjoyed more support from the group and thus, in Hollander's terms, had more credit to expend in suggesting controversial solutions.

The strength of the leader's identification with the group – the fourth of Hollander's proposed sources of legitimacy – has been little studied. One of the few attempts to investigate this was Kirkhart (1963), who examined choice of leader in predominantly black college fraternity houses. Those selected most frequently as leaders tended also to be those who identified most strongly with blacks as a social group. One of the interesting aspects of this result was that several of the hypothetical situations in which the students were asked to nominate leaders involved dealings with outside groups over issues concerning black–white relations. The fact that the social identification of the leaders was implicated in these kinds of *intergroup* contexts reminds us yet again of the close interdependence between intragroup and intergroup processes.

The obverse of a leader's identification with the group is the group's perception of the leader as representative or prototypical of it.

According to Hogg (1996), perceived leader prototypicality will have an important bearing on his or her acceptance by the rest of the group, particularly in intergroup contexts where it may be important to distinguish the ingroup from outgroups. This is facilitated by having a leader who somehow embodies the essential attributes of the ingroup, especially as these contrast with outgroup attributes. This was demonstrated by Hains et al. (1997), who simultaneously varied group salience, specific leader–group prototypicality (how closely the leader matched his or her particular group's characteristics) and generic leader–group stereotypicality (how closely the leader matched the general stereotype of a 'good leader'). In the high group salience conditions, which are of most interest here, it was clearly specific group prototypicality rather than general leader stereotypicality that had the most influence on the perceived effectiveness of the leader. Because prototypicality is not a fixed property – either of the leader or of the group – since it depends very much on the particular context confronting the group, it is possible that it underlies the attribute of 'charisma' discussed earlier. Perhaps a charismatic leader is someone whom the rest of the group regards as capturing the essence of that group, at least for certain tasks or social encounters.

A related source of leader legitimacy stems from the manner in which he or she exerts authority in the group. Tyler and Lind (1992) argue that leaders can concentrate on achieving good or equitable outcomes for group members (what they call distributive justice). But they can also emphasize the fairness of the procedures used to distribute those outcomes (called procedural justice). In several studies Tyler and Lind (1992) show how both are important for a leader to be perceived favourably by the group, but sometimes being seen to be fair can predominate. In other words, group members may forgive a leader for not giving them what they expect so long as he or she is perceived to have used an impartial procedure. It is important to note, however, that the effects of these perceptions of distributive or procedural justice are markedly affected by the context in which they are made. Platow et al. (1997) arranged for leaders to be seen to be acting fairly or unfairly in making an allocation *either* in an intragroup setting *or* in an equivalent intergroup situation. 'Fair' leaders were generally more strongly endorsed than 'unfair' leaders, as Tyler and Lind (1992) predict. However, the difference in endorsement between

115

fair and unfair leaders was smaller when they were making intergroup allocations. Indeed, in some intergroup contexts – particularly those involving an ingroup with whom people identify – the leader acting unfairly towards an outgroup was perceived as favourably, if not more so, than the 'fair' leader.

Overall, then, it can be seen that these approaches are all concerned with the changing relationship between leaders and their followers. In this, they contrast quite sharply with Fiedler's work. For Fiedler, the leader's style is seen as an enduring personality attribute, with his or her relationship with the group and position power as relatively static and independent components of particular situations. Hollander and others, on the other hand, view leadership as a much more dynamic process, in which the leader's power to influence the group changes over time *and* critically depends on the developing leader–member relations and the intergroup context. The significance of changing intergroup relations for the internal group hierarchy has already been noted more than once in this chapter: recall the Sherifs' summer camp experiments and their studies of adolescent gangs described above. What has been less often studied is the effect of a changing leadership position on the group's subsequent intergroup orientation.

This was the focus of Rabbie and Bekkers' (1978) experiment, which varied the stability of a leader's position and examined the effects of this on the leader's intergroup behaviour. They found that leaders who were rather uncertain of their position – they could be deposed easily by their group – were much more likely to choose a competitive bargaining strategy in a union–management simulation than those whose position was more secure. As Rabbie and Bekkers (1978) point out, their experimental findings have many parallels in international politics. Political leaders experiencing unpopularity on the home front will often need little excuse to engage in an aggressive foreign policy. Witness the British government's decision to send the Falklands invasion force in 1982, an event which coincided with the lowest poll rating for several months for the British prime minister, Mrs Thatcher. Similarly, in 1998, President Clinton, under threat from various legal investigations into his personal and financial relationships, adopted a bellicose attitude towards Iraq over its dispute with the United Nations weapons inspection team. Whatever the process at work here, it is becoming abundantly clear that our theories of leadership must recognize the important role that the intergroup situation plays in the internal workings of the group.

Communication Networks

Like many other large organizations, the university where I work has a very hierarchical and centralized decision-making structure. All major decisions about the university's present and future policy are taken by a small group consisting of the Vice-Chancellor and two or three of his colleagues, and these are disseminated downwards to heads of departments, thence to the staff belonging to these, and eventually to the students. In theory, decisions can also be made at these lower levels and communicated upwards through the hierarchy although, to those of us inhabiting these lowly quarters, this seems to be an ever more infrequent event. Furthermore, there are very few formal channels of communication that follow a *horizontal* course; they are nearly all up or down. Departmental heads report to Deans, Deans report to the Vice-Chancellor, and so on. What are the effects of organizing group communication networks in this way?

This was one of the questions that concerned Bavelas (1969). He suggested that a useful way of understanding the effects of different communication structures is to think of the group members as being related in terms of information 'linkages'. He pointed out that how these linkages are arranged topologically is much more important than knowing how close in units of physical distance various members of the organization or group may be. A direct telephone link between the White House and the Kremlin means that in communication terms the national leaders of the USA and Russia can be much closer to one another – if they choose to be – than they may be to most members of their own country, living many thousands of miles nearer. Borrowing from topological mathematics, Bavelas devised various quantitative indices by which it is possible to describe different kinds of networks. One of the most important of these is the notion of 'distance', which is simply the minimum number of communication links that must be crossed for one person in the group to communicate with another person. Thus, in figure 3.5d a person

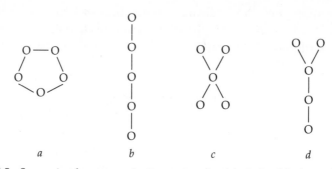

Figure 3.5 Some simple communication networks: (a) circle; (b) chain; (c) wheel; (d) Y-shaped

occupying the position at the join of the Y is linked to three of the other positions at a distance of 1, and to the person at the foot of the Y at a distance of 2. Using this system, one important measure for the system as a whole is the 'centrality index', which, in non-mathematical terms, is the extent to which the information flow in the group is centralized on one person or is dispersed more evenly among the members (Leavitt, 1951).

Armed with this analysis, Bavelas and his colleagues devised an experimental paradigm in which the effects of different communication networks could be studied. A typical experiment is that by Leavitt (1951). The members of a five-person group were seated around a table separated by wooden partitions. The partitions had slots in them so that written messages could be passed between the group members. The slots were also fitted with 'doors', which could be closed by the experimenter to constrain the communication in various ways. This allowed different networks to be created, and the four studied by Leavitt are shown in figure 3.5. In the 'wheel', for instance, the central group member could communicate to each of the others in the group directly but they could only communicate with each other through that central person. Each person was given a card with six symbols on it and the group's task was to discover which of these six was common to everyone's card, communicating only by written messages through the 'open' slots. The results were fairly clear. The groups arranged in a centralized fashion (networks b–d) made fewer errors on the task than the decentralized 'circle' arrangement. However, the morale and job satisfaction were higher in the latter, apparently because its members did not feel as 'left out' of things as did most of the members of the more centralized networks. Those in the central positions liked the task much more than the peripheral members and, interestingly, were almost invariably nominated as the group leader.

The conclusion that centralized groups performed more effectively was soon challenged, however. Shaw (1964), analysing 18 communication experiments, discovered that the nature of the task was a critical variable. In the early experiments the task was a very simple one involving a process of elimination and took just a few minutes to solve. In these kinds of tasks, as we have just seen, the centralized groups performed better. However, on more complex tasks the *decentralized* networks were clearly superior. Shaw showed that this was because the more difficult tasks required a much greater amount of information to be integrated for their successful solution. Since this integrative function typically fell on one person in a centralized network, this often resulted in 'cognitive overload' in that person and a consequent impairment of group performance. In the less centralized networks, on the other hand, although the group members needed to send more messages to one another, the load was shared more evenly among them, with a greater probability of a faster and better solution. Shaw also argued that centralized groups may result in lowered performance because of lowered morale and motivation among their members. Most people, he suggested, work better when they have some autonomy and this is denied to members of centralized networks since they are always dependent on someone else 'down the line' for information.

Of course, the networks used in these experiments are a far cry from the large and complex arrangements one finds in human organizations like the one I began this section by describing. Nevertheless, since the tasks faced by these real-life groups are many times more involved than even the most difficult of laboratory tasks, it seems safe to suggest that there are real dangers in centralizing the decision making of organizations to too great an extent. Most of these problems stem from the cognitive limitations of those placed in those key central positions. Without delegation of many of their functions, such leaders may simply be unable to assimilate and process the huge volume of information necessary for the group's effective performance. In addition, while coping with such problems may prove gratifying

119

to leaders' beliefs in their indispensability, the resulting lowered group member morale because of *their* sense of dispensability may be counterproductive. If we add to these difficulties other potential problems associated with collective decision making in the presence of powerful leaders – the so-called 'groupthink' phenomenon (Janis, 1972; see chapter 5) – we are forced to conclude that a highly centralized communication network is not the optimal arrangement for most human groups. Perhaps democracy has, after all, a pragmatic social psychological justification, quite apart from any political and ethical considerations.

Summary

1 Two fundamental aspects of group structure are role and status. Roles are behavioural regularities or expectations associated with particular group members. Two key roles in many groups are the task and socio-emotional specialists. Role differentiation can facilitate division of labour in the group as well as contribute to people's identities.
2 Group members enjoy different amounts of power and prestige, which gives rise to status hierarchies in groups. Such status differences can generate expectations for group members' behaviour that often turn out to be self-fulfilling.
3 Closely tied to status differentiation are social comparison processes, through which individuals can make appraisals of their abilities. Typically people choose similar others to compare themselves with, though there are self-esteem advantages in choosing someone slightly superior. Social comparisons may also affect task performance.
4 Those in high-status positions are often referred to as leaders, and it is often believed that certain individuals possess traits that equip them for this role. Most evidence suggests otherwise. Leaders are those who have attributes that can help the group to achieve particular task goals. Effective leadership involves both attention to the task and consideration for group members, though these may not coincide in the same person.

5 Good leaders are people whose personalities are well matched to particular situations. Where the match is poor the group is often less effective. Controversy exists over the extent to which leaders are able to change their behaviour to fit better with situations.

6 The process by which a leader acquires legitimacy in the eyes of the group is also important. Legitimacy can be acquired through task competence, initial conformity to group norms, identifying with the group, fitting well to the group prototype, and acting fairly in allocating rewards and sanctions to group members.

7 The network of communication in a group is another crucial aspect of group structure. It is helpful to view communication channels in topological terms – as linkages – rather than in units of physical distance. Networks that are highly centralized may be more efficient at solving simple problems, where the amount and complexity of information is not great. However, for more complex problems decentralized systems are superior.

Notes

1 Here we shall only be concerned with ability evaluation; validation of opinions is dealt with in chapter 4.

2 Although there are undoubtedly important developmental changes in social comparison activities over the first nine years of a child's life, we should be cautious in concluding that young children (i.e. less than five years) are not interested in or capable of social comparisons for self-evaluation purposes (Suls and Sanders, 1982). In fact, there is now ample evidence that children as young as three or four years are sensitive to relative performance information in both interpersonal and intergroup contexts (Chafel, 1986; France-Kaatrude and Smith, 1985; Yee and Brown, 1992).

3 I am grateful to Miles Hewstone for spotting this typically pithy Hansen character summation.

4 Note that Fiedler, like Bales, assumes the task and socio-emotional orientations to be bipolar opposites.

5 One estimate puts the number of possible decision scenarios in the new model at around 39 million (Field et al., 1990).

Further Reading

Cartwright, D. and Zander, A. (eds) (1969) *Group Dynamics: Research and Theory*, 3rd edn, chs 31, 35. New York: Harper & Row.

Fiedler, F.E. (1978) The contingency model and the dynamics of the leadership process, in Berkowitz, L. (ed.) *Advances in Experimental Social Psychology*, vol. 11. New York: Academic Press.

Hollander, E.P. (1978) *Leadership Dynamics: A Practical Guide to Effective Relationships*. New York: Free Press.

Shaw, M.E. (1964) Communication networks, in Berkowitz, L. (ed.) *Advances in Experimental Social Psychology*, vol. 1. New York: Academic Press.

Suls, J.M. and Wills, T.A. (eds) (1991) *Social Comparison: Contemporary Theory and Research*. New York: Hillsdale.

Vroom, V.H. and Jago, A.G. (1988) *The New Leadership: Managing Participation in Organizations*. Englewood Cliffs, NJ: Prentice Hall.

4

SOCIAL INFLUENCE
IN GROUPS

In chapter 2 we saw the crucial role that social norms play in group life both as cognitive 'signposts' for the individual and as social regulators for the group. An obvious indication that norms are at work is some uniformity of attitude or behaviour among the group members. Whether it be experimental participants observing a pin-prick of light in a darkened room, the behaviour of adolescent gangs in American cities or factory workers controlling the production rate in their 'shop', such uniformity is not difficult to observe. Once people get into collective settings they appear only too ready to conform to the majority in the group and to abandon their own personal beliefs and opinions. As we shall see in the first part of this chapter, this turns out to be a remarkably robust and culturally near-universal phenomenon.

One of the most persuasive attempts to explain this widespread prevalence of conformity is Festinger's social comparison theory, which we encountered in the previous chapter. In addition to making comparisons about abilities, argued Festinger, we also need to assess the correctness of our beliefs, and this too is accomplished primarily by reference to others. The information gleaned from these comparisons is particularly potent if it reveals the existence of a social consensus since that strongly implies a 'correct' way of looking at things. Accordingly, Festinger suggested that groups are motivated to establish and maintain uniformity in the group. From this he predicted a number of consequences for group cohesiveness and communication patterns in groups as the majority seeks to influence any dissenters to come around to its way of thinking.

So pervasive are conformity phenomena that for many years 'social influence in groups' was simply equated with 'conformity to the majority'. Little attention was given to the possibility that a dissenting minority might itself have some impact on the majority. However, the past thirty years have seen a number of empirical demonstrations of precisely that. Minorities, it turns out, are not completely passive recipients of influence from the majority but can elicit some change of opinion in that majority by behaving in a certain manner. One of the main architects of this growth of interest in minority influence has been Moscovici, and his work and that of his colleagues dominates the second part of the chapter. One of Moscovici's central arguments is that the processes of majority and minority influence are different in kind and effect. This claim will be examined and contrasted with another model of social influence which suggests that, on the contrary, majority and minority influence are essentially similar processes, and differ only in the strength of their social impact on group members. One other issue that recurs throughout the chapter is the importance of how the source of influence is categorized. Whether the source be a majority or a minority, if it is perceived to share category membership with the targets of its influence it is more likely to be persuasive than if it is seen to belong to some outgroup.

The Power of the Majority

A British television documentary examining the causes of civil aviation accidents ('The Wrong Stuff', BBC2, February 1986) attributed one of the major causes of such accidents to human error, particularly arising out of the group dynamics of the flight crew. In the programme, a serious airline accident was recreated using the actual sound recording of the final few minutes of interaction in the cockpit of the plane. The accident had been caused by the captain of the plane totally misjudging his landing approach. Only 8 miles from his destination he was approaching the airport 40 knots too fast and 200 feet lower than he should have been. Here is what took place between the captain (John), his co-pilot and the flight engineer as the co-pilot realized from his instruments that something was wrong and called the attention of the captain to the incorrect glide slope.

Co-PILOT (cautiously) Isn't this a little faster than you normally fly this, John?
CAPTAIN (confidently) Oh yeah, but it's nice and smooth. We're going to get in right on time. Maybe a little ahead of time. We've got it made.
Co-PILOT (uncertainly) I sure hope so.
ENGINEER You know, John, do you know the difference between a duck and a co-pilot?
CAPTAIN What's the difference?
ENGINEER Well, a duck can fly!
CAPTAIN Well said!
(Pause of several seconds)
Co-PILOT (anxiously) Seems like there's a bit of a tailwind up here, John.

CAPTAIN   Yeah, we're saving gas – helps us to get in a couple of minutes early too.
(Another pause)
CO-PILOT   John, you're just a little below the MDA here.
CAPTAIN   Yeah, well we'll take care of it here.

The captain then attempted to leapfrog the plane up over the glide slope to compensate for the incorrect altitude. This caused the plane to be too high for a safe landing and the accident was unavoidable.

The pervasiveness of conformity

If one had to choose a group that would be resistant to internal conformity pressures one might well have thought that a small group like this, consisting as it did of three highly skilled professionals, would be a safe bet. Each could clearly see the instruments revealing the danger signals and was well trained to respond to them. Yet only one of the three saw any cause for alarm and, significantly, the majority not only chose to ignore his increasingly anxious comments but actually ganged up together at one point to ridicule him. The dissenting voice, it seems, was as unwelcome here as it is in other groups the world over.

Real-life examples of conformity like this are inevitably complicated by such factors as the status relationships in the group and the personalities of those involved. Is it possible to demonstrate the existence of conformity to group pressure in conditions where such variables are either absent or experimentally controlled? This was the question posed, and answered, by Asch (1956) in some experiments that, like those of Sherif (1936) some years earlier, have rightly acquired classic status in the history of social psychology.

The basic procedure used in Asch's experiments is as follows: participants are recruited for what they are told will be an experiment in visual judgement. On arrival the participant is shown to a laboratory where a number of other participants are already seated. The experimenter explains that their task is to compare the lengths of some vertical lines. On each presentation there is a standard line and their task is to identify which of three comparison lines is the same length as the standard. They call out their answers in turn. This seems a simple enough task and, sure enough, in the first two trials everyone calls out the obviously correct answer. Then, on the third trial – and on eleven others occurring at intervals – the others in the room give what appears to be a completely wrong answer. What is more, they are unanimous in their error, giving their answers confidently and calmly. In fact, of course, those already in the room before the start of the experiment are confederates of the experimenter, who have been briefed to give incorrect answers on two-thirds of the trials. Asch's interest was in the behaviour of the one genuine participant: how would he or she react to the testimony from these apparently quite unexceptional people which contradicted so dramatically the evidence of his or her own eyes? Asch's findings were surprising: fully three-quarters of those 'naive' participants gave at least one incorrect response on the critical trials when the confederates went astray. Looking at the results another way, out of all the genuine participants' responses on the critical trials, over 36 per cent of these were either the same as or in the direction of the incorrect majority.

What gave these results such impact was the unambiguous nature of the task. There could be no doubt as to the correct answer since, in a control condition where people gave their answers alone, the number of errors was virtually zero. What Asch had demonstrated, therefore, was an apparent willingness on the part of people to deny this obvious veridical judgement in order to 'go along with' the majority. And that, according to Asch, was precisely the motivation behind most of the conforming responses. From detailed debriefings, Asch established that it was rare for the compliant participants actually to have 'seen' the lines as the same when they were different. Rather, they lacked confidence in their own judgement, assuming that the others in the experiment were privy to some additional information that was guiding their responses. Others, on the other hand, while not actually doubting what they saw, simply conformed so as not to be different. These reactions suggest that we should distinguish between conformity that involves a private perceptual or cognitive change – seeing the world differently – and conformity that is merely a behavioural or public compliance – 'going along with the others' (Festinger, 1953). The latter seems best to characterize the participants in Asch's experiments, while Sherif's (1936) experiments with the autokinetic effect seemed to elicit the former reaction (see chapter 2). It will be recalled that one of Sherif's interesting findings was that the group norm persisted even when the participants were subsequently tested on their own. Later in this chapter we shall encounter other examples of such internal changes.

In other experiments, Asch (1955) explored the effects of altering various aspects of his conformity-inducing situation. The most obvious factor to vary was the size of the confederate majority. Asch's results are shown in the solid curve of figure 4.1. From this, it seems that with just one confederate there is negligible conformity on the critical trials. However, with the addition of one or two further confederates the conformity level rises sharply, only to level off with the addition of further confederates. Indeed, Asch reported that fifteen confederates seemed to elicit slightly less conformity than four. This rapid increase in conformity with majorities of two to three has been confirmed in subsequent research, although the reduced conformity that Asch observed with large minorities has not generally been replicated. For example, Gerard et al. (1968), using a modification of Asch's paradigm but with a similar judgmental task, found an apparently linear effect of group size (dashed line in figure 4.1).[1] Milgram et al. (1969), in a naturalistic study of the influence on passers-by of differently sized crowds staring upwards apparently at nothing, found that the number of people who also looked up was linearly related to the size of the crowd, although there was a tendency for the relationship to flatten off with larger crowds (dotted line in figure 4.1).

A meta-analysis of over 100 experiments employing variants of Asch's paradigm confirms that, indeed, there is a linear relationship between conformity and the size of the majority, albeit not a very strong one (Bond and Smith, 1996). In general, then, larger majorities do elicit more conformity than small ones, although increasing group size beyond a certain point appears to have diminishing effects on the level of conformity.

Another variation that Asch (1955) introduced was to break up the consensus produced by the confederate majority, and this proved to be crucial. In one experiment, there were two naive participants facing the incorrect majority. Immediately, the level of conformity dropped to around 10 per cent. In another experiment, one of the confederates was instructed always to give the correct answer and this resulted in even less conformity, a negligible 5 per cent. However, it was clear

128

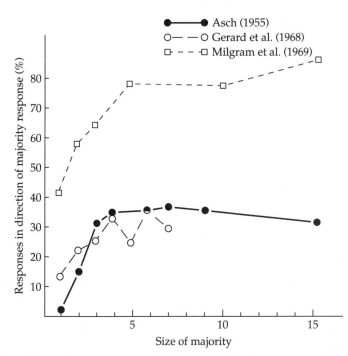

Figure 4.1 Group size and conformity (from Asch, 1955; Gerard et al., 1968; Milgram et al., 1969)

that it was the breaking of the unanimity that was the critical factor rather than simply the presence of an 'ally'. This was revealed in a third experiment in which one of the confederates was instructed to deviate from the majority but still give incorrect answers. Once again the level of conformity declined. Subsequent research has confirmed the importance of dissent for reducing conformity, although for some sorts of behaviours – particularly those involving subjective opinions rather than objective judgements – it is apparently necessary for that dissent also to support the participant's own position (Allen, 1965, 1975).

Exact replications and various modifications of Asch's experiments have been conducted in many different countries, and the basic conformity that he discovered seems to be remarkably prevalent. Although there are often substantial variations in the level of conformity observed, very few cross-cultural studies have failed to find any conformity at all (Mann, 1980; Smith and Bond, 1993). Perhaps more interesting than this near-universal occurrence of conformity are the reasons for the cultural differences in its manifestation. One intriguing theory has been advanced by Berry (1967), which relates the degree of conformity to the nature of the economy in different societies. Berry suggests that in societies whose economies require a high degree of interdependence – for example, high food accumulating cultures – there will typically be greater pressures to conformity (and socialization practices consistent with this) than in societies where food accumulation is less important and where people are more independent of one another. Adapting Asch's judgement task, Berry found evidence in support of this idea. The Temne of Sierra Leone, who depend on a single crop each year and are thus high food accumulators, showed substantially more conformity than groups of Eskimos, who rely on regular hunting and fishing trips for survival.

Berry's theory applies most readily to non-industrialized societies. Smith and Bond (1993) argue that such an analysis can be extended by considering the kinds of values that predominate in any given society. In individualistic cultures there is much emphasis on individual achievement, separation from and competition with fellow ingroup members, and a more general concern for self-determination and independence. Collectivist societies, on the other hand, tend to reward collective achievements, closeness to and cooperation with the ingroup, and a desire for consensuality (Triandis, 1989). As Hofstede (1980) and Schwartz (1994) demonstrated, it is possible to distinguish between cultures along this dimension and, it turns out, that dimension is also reliably correlated with the amount of conformity shown in the Asch paradigm (Bond and Smith, 1996). People in collectivist cultures (e.g. Brazil, Japan) tend to show higher compliance rates than those in more individualistic cultures (e.g. the UK, the USA).

Why do people conform?

Conformity is not restricted to the judgements of line lengths in experimentally contrived settings. A moment's reflection will confirm that we have a rather general propensity to change our attitudes and behaviour so as to bring them into line with others around us. This seems to be as true of the relatively minor issues of clothing fashion and musical taste as it is of more fundamental moral values and socio-political action. To underline this point let me consider briefly some research that has shown that people are prepared to administer what they believe is painful and potentially dangerous punishment to fellow research participants. Milgram (1963) devised a paradigm in which people taking the role of 'teacher' in a 'learning experiment' are requested to administer negative reinforcement (increasing voltage of seemingly real electric shocks) to the 'learner' (who is a confederate of the experimenter). Surprisingly large numbers of participants were prepared to obey the experimenter and go on to administer shocks of 400 volts or more (the obedience rates vary between 30 and 65 per cent). In two follow-up experiments Milgram showed the power of group influence on this antisocial behaviour (Milgram, 1964, 1965). In the first variant he had two further confederates assist the real participant in the learning experiment. These two stooges consistently suggested higher voltages and the experimenter announced that on any trial it was the lowest voltage mentioned by anyone that should be administered. It was thus open to the real participant always to propose a low voltage. In fact, though, just as Asch (1955) had found, the genuine participants consistently complied with the implicit pressure exerted by their two fellow 'teachers', over half of them administering 'shocks' of more than 210 volts; this compared to a paltry 2.5 per cent of a control group who participated in the experiment alone (Milgram, 1964). But group pressure can also be used to restrain antisocial behaviour, as Milgram (1965) subsequently showed. This time the unanimity of the two 'teacher' confederates was deliberately fractured by having one of them refuse to continue with the experiment once the shock level reached '150 volts', and the other withdraw at '210 volts'. The result of this 'group pressure to disobey' was that fewer of the real participants persisted in administering the 'very strong shocks' (see figure 4.2). It is tempting to dismiss Milgram's findings on grounds of the high degree of duplicity and artifice involved in his procedure and the difficult ethical issues that these raise. Nevertheless, the well-documented instances of group-instigated atrocities against civilians in Vietnam, former Yugoslavia and other war zones before and since suggest that social pressures to conform are both prevalent in their frequency and tragic in their consequences. The question is, then, what underlies this widespread tendency towards uniformity in groups?

131

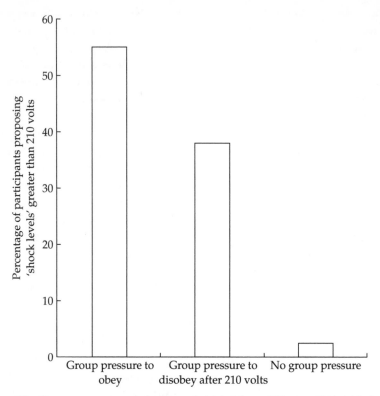

Figure 4.2 Group pressure and obedience (adapted from Milgram, 1964, table 3, and Milgram, 1965, table 1)

One of the most influential explanations of these conformity pressures has been put forward by Festinger (1950). He proposed that there are two powerful processes that result in individuals being influenced by the majority in the group. The first concerns the social construction of reality. Festinger started from an assumption that all of us hold a number of beliefs about the world. These act for us, he suggested, like mini-theories, guiding our actions and helping us to interpret social events. Because of this, it is important for us to have some way of verifying or testing our theories. But, unlike more formal scientific theories, we usually do not have any objective means or agreed procedures for doing so. Anticipating his later social comparison theory (Festinger, 1954; see chapter 3), Festinger hypothesized

132

that what we do instead is to turn to other people for information about the correctness (or otherwise) of our beliefs. Where everyone else appears to agree with us then that offers some reassurance that our beliefs are not completely at variance with reality. Festinger concluded that this validational function provided by social comparisons would mean that people will generally value uniformity in groups and will often behave so as to maintain it.

Pressures towards that uniformity are likely to increase in novel or ambiguous situations since there are fewer 'objective' cues to guide our judgements. Recall Sherif's (1936) autokinetic effect experiment. Here, it will be remembered, people in a completely dark room were asked to make a highly subjective judgement of how far a spot of light appeared to move. Faced with this uncertainty, their judgements quickly converged.

Social consensus becomes still more valuable when decisions also have important consequences. This point was neatly demonstrated by Baron et al. (1996). Using a clever adaptation of Asch's (1955) procedure, they modified the judgement task to resemble an identification parade: participants were shown a picture of a suspect and then asked in which of four other pictures the suspect appeared. The task was varied in difficulty by presenting the stimuli just once and briefly, or twice for a longer duration. The significance of the task was also manipulated by leading half of the participants to believe that they were participating in an important eye-witness testimony research project and that their data would contribute to new procedures used by the police and courts. Furthermore, they were offered the prospect of a substantial reward if they performed accurately. The remainder thought that they were taking part in a run-of-the-mill pilot experiment and were offered no rewards. As usual, two confederates of the experimenter gave consistently misleading answers on about half the trials. As expected, most conformity (about 51 per cent) was observed under conditions of high difficulty and high importance.

The second determinant of conformity identified by Festinger is the presence of some important group goal. When a group has a clearly defined objective this may, by itself, induce some uniformity of action among the group members, especially where achievement of the goal is dependent on the aggregation of their efforts. The effectiveness of a tug-of-war team, for example, critically depends on their success in maximizing and coordinating their pull on the rope. However, with more complex group tasks it is also vital that the group members can agree not just on the goal itself but on the means to the achievement of that goal. Without that uniformity of opinion the group members' efforts are likely to be fragmented and the attainment of the goal rendered less likely. This may be one reason why political parties devote so much time to appeals for unity in their ranks, particularly when confrontation with rivals is imminent at election time.

The power of a new goal to bring about attitude change in group members was convincingly demonstrated by Lewin (1965). As part of a health education programme after the war to persuade American families to eat more of various unfashionable, but nutritionally rich, cuts of meat (e.g. heart, kidney), Lewin compared the effectiveness of a lecture by a nutrition expert to a participative group discussion. In both cases the participants were housewives and the key measure was whether or not they would subsequently attempt a recipe at home with one of these novel ingredients. Nearly a third of those who had taken part in the group discussion were persuaded enough so to experiment, while a negligible 3 per cent of those who had only heard the lecture did so. One of the key differences between the two methods of persuasion was that in the discussion groups each session ended with the group deciding as a whole to give the new recipes a try; in the lecture, on the other hand, there was no such clearly defined group goal, merely an exhortation by the lecturer. Moreover, the active participation of the members of the discussion groups ensured that the group goal was internalized and not imposed from outside.

Both of these motives for conformity presuppose that the group has some initial attractiveness for its members. The other people in the group – and their opinions – matter to the person subjected to the influence. Presumably, the more they matter (i.e. the more cohesive a group is) the more conformity should occur. This seems to be the case. Festinger et al. (1950), investigating relationships in a student housing project, found a strong positive correlation between the degree of cohesiveness of student groups and how effectively group standards were maintained. This was confirmed by Lott and Lott (1961), who found a similar association between the cohesiveness of friendship cliques and the amount of conformity they showed in an experimental task. There was also a positive relationship between cohesiveness and the amount of communication in the group, suggesting how the conformity came about. Such pressures to uniformity can sometimes have unfortunate consequences. Crandall (1988) studied the incidence of eating disorders within friendship cliques in two American sororities. He noted how, over a period of six months or so, each woman's binge-eating level converged to that of her closest friends, suggesting that some form of social contagion through norm acquisition was responsible.

Important though these motives for conformity are, neither seems adequate to explain the compliance observed in Asch's experiments. In the first place, there was no ambiguity in the situation. People's opinions on the lengths of lines are easily and objectively verifiable; why then should the confederates' (incorrect) opinions have been so influential? Furthermore, there was no real or cohesive group. The participants were taking part in what they thought was an experiment in *individual* perception judgement; there were none of the usual criteria to mark a group's existence (interdependence, identification etc.; see chapter 1). Thus, pressures arising from attempts to achieve a group goal (the second of Festinger's proposed motives) should not have been present.

Noting these anomalies, Deutsch and Gerard (1955) suggested a third reason for conformity, which is really the obverse of the social reality function proposed by Festinger. People may have conformed, they suggested, not because they were relying on the confederates' judgements to define reality for them but rather to avoid the possibility of social ridicule, of being the 'odd one out'. There is a great deal of evidence that we are attracted to others with similar attitudes to us (Byrne, 1971) – or, perhaps more accurately, *repelled* by those with dissimilar attitudes (Rosenbaum, 1986) – presumably because of the social validation (or disconfirmation) such people provide. Thus, if we dislike others who disagree with us we may reasonably anticipate that others will dislike us if we express very different opinions from them. Assuming that most people prefer to be liked rather than disliked, then this might give them a motive to conform to the majority's opinion in Asch-type situations. Deutsch and Gerard (1955) labelled this form of conformity 'normative influence', to distinguish it from the 'informational influence' implied by Festinger's (1950) account. If such a motive is a reason for conformity then the amount of influence should be reduced if people make their responses privately.

Deutsch and Gerard (1955) designed an experiment that would simultaneously test this idea and the earlier hypotheses put forward by Festinger. The experiment involved several modifications to Asch's procedure. In one condition (the closest replication of Asch) participants gave their responses in a face-to-face situation where there was an incorrect majority of three. In half of the trials responses were made while stimuli were still visible; in the remainder the stimuli were removed before the judgements were made. This enhanced the ambiguity of the situation and hence should have increased the reliance on others for information. The next condition was identical to the first except that participants could not see each other and gave their responses anonymously. It was thought that this would reduce any conformity due to the need to be liked. In a third condition Deutsch and Gerard stepped up the conformity pressures by informing participants that they constituted one of twenty groups and that the five groups that made the fewest errors would receive an attractive prize. In this way a clear group goal was introduced, which was expected to increase cohesion and conformity. Finally, Deutsch and Gerard devised three conditions in which participants had to commit themselves by writing down their answers before hearing the responses of others and before giving their own responses. Some had to write their answers on paper which they subsequently threw away ('private commitment A'), some used a 'magic pad', which could erase their response on each trial ('private commitment B'), and some wrote their answers on notes which they signed and which they knew would subsequently be handed to the experimenter ('public commitment').

Deutsch and Gerard's results confirmed that all three motives were significant influences on conformity (see table 4.1). Notice, first of all, that as the group was made psychologically more significant by providing a collective goal, the number of errors (or level of conformity) increased. This was despite the fact that the group goal was to make the fewest errors. This supports Festinger's second hypothesis. It is also clear that Festinger's first hypothesis – the need for information in ambiguous situations – is supported by the greater conformity found in the more uncertain trials where stimuli were removed before responding. The need to be liked must also have been influential. With

Table 4.1 Mean number of socially influenced errors in Deutsch and Gerard's (1955) experiment (range 0–12)

Condition	Stimuli present	Stimuli absent
Group goal	5.7	6.9
Face to face	3.0	4.1
Anonymous	2.8	3.2
Private commitment A	0.6	0.7
Private commitment B	1.6	2.3
Public commitment	0.9	0.5

anonymous responding there was less conformity than in the face-to-face situation. This conformity dropped still further when participants first committed themselves by writing down their judgement. However, it is interesting that even in these prior commitment conditions conformity did not disappear completely, as it had in Asch's control conditions when no confederates were present. This strongly suggests that there was some residual influence due to the confederates, even though the stimulus situation was clear cut *and* the individuals could be assured of complete anonymity from their peers.

Such persistence of social influence when both 'informational' and 'normative' pressures for it are virtually absent poses something of a difficulty for the explanations for conformity we have considered so far. Turner (1987, 1991) has proposed a rather different explanation for conformity, which may help resolve this problem. Turner's starting point is to assume that a fundamental feature of group membership is that it provides people with a social identity – it helps them to define who they are. (This is already a familiar idea, which we discussed in chapter 2; it is one to which we will return in chapter 8.) When people identify with a group, argues Turner, they categorize themselves as members of it and, as a consequence, mentally associate themselves with the attributes and norms that they perceive as being part of that group. This process may be analogous to those actors who claim that their best performances occur when they quite literally become the person whose part they are playing. The outwardly visible aspect of the role – the spoken lines and costume – is reflected in an internal personality change as they attempt to assimilate the attributes of the character in the play. In Turner's theory, the script and the costume are the features of a social category, which become salient or 'visible' in certain situations. The corresponding internal change is the cognitive matching of oneself with the group's perceived characteristics, what Turner calls 'self-stereotyping'. It is this self-assignment of ingroup characteristics and behaviours that Turner believes is the key to understanding conformity. Thus, his explanation of the presence of conformity in Deutsch and Gerard's (1955) experiment is to assume that the participants believed that others in the experiment belonged to the same ingroup (they could reasonably infer that they were college students like themselves) and hence perceived their rather unusual actions as being normative for that group in that situation. Their self-categorization as 'college students' then led them to assimilate those same actions for themselves. Turner (1987) labels this form of influence 'referent informational influence' to distinguish it from the other types of influence we discussed earlier.

If this theory is correct then people should be much more affected by sources of influence that appear to come from their ingroup rather than from some outgroup. There is much evidence that this is the case. Abrams et al. (1990, experiment 2) used a modification of the Asch paradigm in which the confederates were perceived to be students studying the same degree (psychology) as the real participants *or* studying a different degree (ancient history). As a further independent variable, responses were given either privately or publicly. Overall, there was markedly more conformity to the confederates' responses in the ingroup condition (same degree subject) than in the outgroup condition (different degree), especially when participants were required to respond publicly and hence be more open to the scrutiny of others. Several other experiments have confirmed this greater influence exerted by ingroup sources (e.g. Van Knippenberg and Wilke, 1988; Wilder, 1990). There is more to conformity, it seems, than simply 'defining social reality'; it depends who is doing the defining.

At this point it may be instructive to consider conformity from a developmental perspective. Anyone who has enjoyed (or endured) the experience of bringing up children will readily affirm the importance of children's peer groups as a defining influence on their attitudes and behaviour. Adolescence can be a particularly testing time in this regard as the young person develops sometimes alarming new preferences in erotic behaviour, substance usage and musical styles – 'sex and drugs and rock 'n' roll', as it were. Such changes usually coincide with other new behaviours: endless telephone conversations with friends and much apparently aimless but seemingly deeply meaningful 'hanging out' on street corners and in pubs and clubs.

Psychological research has largely confirmed these parental observations. Costanzo and Shaw (1966) recruited young people between 7 and 21 years to participate in an Asch-type conformity experiment and found that, indeed, conformity to a group of confederate peers seemed to peak in early adolescence (11–13 years) and then decline. A similar inverted U-shape to the conformity–age relationship has been observed with more realistic social dilemmas (e.g. hypothetical scenarios involving the participant and two best friends who encourage him or her to undertake pro- or antisocial behaviour; Berndt, 1979; Brown et al., 1986). And studies of naturally occurring peer groups confirm their apparent ubiquity and psychological significance in the lives of adolescents (Kirchler et al., 1991; Sherif and Sherif, 1964).

However, peer group influence is by no means confined to adolescence and neither is it restricted solely to intragroup behaviours. One of the domains in which this is most obvious is gender. Gender segregation – a preference for own-gender playmates – occurs quite early in childhood, probably around three years of age (La Freniere et al., 1984; Maccoby and Jacklin, 1987). Maccoby and Jacklin (1987) argue that this behavioural segregation into groups of same-sex peers is crucial to the development of gender identity, helping to define who the child is and how he or she behaves towards members of the opposite sex category. And they are in no doubt that normative peer pressure plays a significant role in this. Here is one of their respondents, an 11-year-old girl, telling the interviewer what would happen if she played with the boys:

[they would] tease me. People would not be my friends. They would scorn me. *Nobody* who had any care of status would sit next to a boy if they could sit next to a girl. This teasing is worse because it lasts longer. It is sort of like being in a lower rank or peeing in your pants. You would be teased for *months* about this. (Maccoby and Jacklin, 1987, p. 245)

When we recall the various theories of social influence discussed in the previous section, perhaps it is not so surprising that conformity pressures should be felt particularly keenly in childhood and adolescence. After all, this is a period in people's lives when they are usually encountering many new social situations (e.g. different schools) when the need for information may be paramount. In several of these contexts there may be some emphasis on group tasks and activities with collective goals to attain. Emotionally, the need for affiliation is probably at its peak in these years, thus increasing the pressures of normative influence. And, given that several crucial identities are developed at this time (e.g. gender, ethnicity), the likelihood of referential influence is also likely to be high as children seek simultaneously to match themselves with those whom they see as prototypes of their category, and distance themselves from those who are not.

On being a deviate

The main result of conformity is, of course, greater uniformity among the group members.

How does this uniformity come about? In most experimental demonstrations we have discussed so far it seemed to happen as a result of individuals cognitively restructuring the situation, either to justify giving an 'incorrect' response or perhaps to reinterpret the meaning of the stimuli themselves (Allen and Wilder, 1980). But conformity is not always as private a phenomenon as this. Very often the majority will directly bring pressure on those with deviant opinions. This was another hypothesis to emerge from Festinger's (1950) theory. He argued that those in the majority would direct most of their communication towards those in the minority subgroup in an attempt to persuade them to change their position. The greater the discrepancy between minority and majority, the more communications one would expect. Since the object of these communications is to exert influence on the deviants, if these influence attempts are unsuccessful (that is, if the deviants maintain their non-conformist stand) Festinger believed that the other members of the group would come to dislike the deviants, even, in extreme cases, expelling them from the group altogether.

Schachter (1951) put these ideas to the test. He observed the behaviour of student discussion groups who had to solve a 'human relations' problem involving a delinquent boy and his family. Unknown to the half-dozen or so real participants in each group, Schachter introduced three experimental confederates. One was instructed to take up a deviate position in the group. Once the group's view began to crystallize, his job was to argue for a directly contrary point of view using some standard arguments. The second confederate was also to be a deviate initially but about a third of the way through the discussion he had gradually to change his position and come into line with the rest of the group. He was dubbed the 'slider'. The third confederate (the 'mode') had an easier role since he simply had to go along with the prevailing opinion in the group throughout. Schachter carefully monitored the number of remarks each person addressed to these three bogus group members, and the results are shown in figure 4.3.

As can be seen, most attention was paid to the 'deviate'. In the first ten minutes of the discussion each group member addressed about one communication on average to this confederate; by the end of the session the number of communications had risen to over twice that amount. In contrast, the 'slider', who initially received nearly as many communications as the 'deviate', was increasingly ignored, especially after he had apparently changed his mind. The 'mode' was virtually ignored throughout; since he already agreed with the group, there was no need for them to pay him any heed. These findings were neatly paralleled by some sociometric data that Schachter also collected. Everyone was asked to place their fellow discussants in rank order in terms of their desirability as group members. The mean ranks given to each confederate are shown at the bottom of figure 4.3 and it is clear that the deviate was given a consistently lower ranking than the other two, and well below the median rank of 5. Just as Festinger had predicted, the deviate who resisted the group's social pressure was not well regarded by his peers.

The discovery that deviates are not particularly liked has stood the test of time. Some years later, Schachter and seven colleagues conducted an enormous cross-cultural study that used a very similar procedure to the experiment just described, but which omitted the 'slider' and 'mode' roles (Schachter et al., 1954). Nearly 300 groups of schoolboys from seven European countries were observed discussing a project to build a model aeroplane. A number of prototypes were available. Most were highly attractive motor-driven models and were

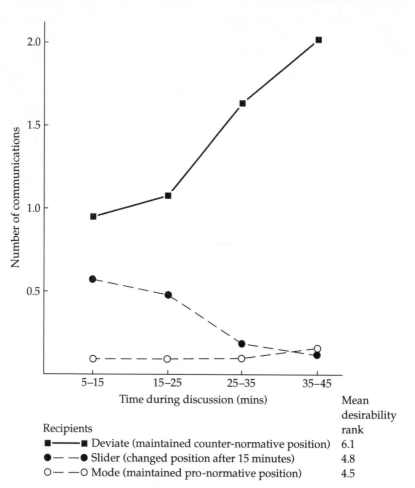

Figure 4.3 Number of communications (per person) addressed to 'deviate', 'slider' and 'mode' in Schachter's (1951) experiment

generally preferred by the boys. One of the models, however, was a glider and this was the model which the deviate always 'preferred' in the ensuing discussion to choose which model they would build. In the rank ordering measure at the end (this time to elect a group leader), although there were some slight national variations, the deviate's mean rank was below the median *in every country tested*, confirming once again that deviates are seldom very popular members of the group. Furthermore, as Mann (1980) has noted, there was a strong correlation between the tendency of groups to reach uniformity and rejection of the deviate.

There was one further intriguing result from the study of Schachter et al. (1954). In the first table of their paper the authors present the number sampled from the different countries. At the right hand margin of that table there is a column marked 'Additional groups', which, as the text beneath the table explains, shows the number of groups in each country in which the stooge was not a deviate. In such groups, 'either the subjects had not reached agreement among themselves or they were so enamoured of the glider that they eventually unanimously agreed with the stooge in his choice' (Schachter et al., 1954, p. 408). What is significant about this column is the number of groups it contains. There were in fact some 95 groups (or 32 per cent of the sample) which, in the researchers' view, could not be used because the deviate was not truly on his own against a consensual majority. Even more fascinating are some further findings presented a few pages later, which make it clear that of these 95 groups, fully 26 of them (or 9 per cent of the total) came around completely to the deviate's point of view and chose the glider, despite their initial preference for the motor-powered models. In other words, in a small but nevertheless not negligible proportion of the experimental groups it was a minority person who managed to persuade those in the majority to change their minds, and not the other way around. Quite how and when minorities are able to exert influence like this is the subject of the next section.

The Influence of the Minority

There is a particular irony that this little-known finding was reported in a paper that is so frequently cited as demonstrating the coercive power of the majority. Indeed, the study was specifically designed to test some hypotheses from Festinger's (1950) theory, which, as we have seen, stresses the dependence of the individual on the rest of the group. For Festinger, social influence is a unidirectional process: the deviant individuals are seen as the passive recipients of pressure from the rest of the group. But what those 26 influential deviates from Schachter et al.'s (1954) study show is that such a view of social influence may be neither accurate nor complete.

143

This, at least, is the contention of Moscovici (1976), who has inspired some radical changes in the way social influence should be understood. Moscovici begins by asking how change comes about in social systems. If groups are dedicated to achieving uniformity of opinion, as Festinger implies, how do their norms and values ever change? One immediate answer to this question is that groups change as a response to new *external* circumstances. If the situation confronting a group presents a new goal to achieve or task to perform (perhaps because of an altered intergroup relationship) then one would expect the group to adapt accordingly, which might result in changes within the group. Although these reasons for change are undoubtedly important, Moscovici points out that several historical examples of change cannot easily be explained by them. Take the change in popular and scientific thinking brought about by Darwin's (1859) theory of evolution, for instance. While his revolutionary ideas may not have been unrelated to social and economic changes occurring in nineteenth-century Britain, it is still the case that they were fiercely opposed by the majority view at the time, which was strongly dominated by traditional biblical views on the origins of humankind. Darwin himself was hardly a leading or powerful person in Victorian society and, as we know, his work was initially subjected to ridicule by the establishment (Desmond and Moore, 1991). According to Moscovici, the success of deviant viewpoints like the theory of natural selection in achieving acceptance owed much to the strategy adopted in their promotion. In particular, Moscovici believes that it was crucial that the minority proponents have typically been quite persistent in maintaining the validity of their theories, even in the face of the most virulent criticism from others. According to Moscovici, this consistency created conflicts with existing ideas, and it was from these conflicts that the changes sprang. Minority influence is possible, argues Moscovici, because no group is perfectly homogeneous; it always contains potential divisions. Deviants, if they act in a sufficiently consistent and convincing manner, make those divisions explicit and from the resulting conflict new norms may emerge.

In promoting these ideas Moscovici is a good advertisement for his own theory. For decades social psychologists had written about influence in groups as if it were synonymous with *majority* influence. It was against this dominant climate of opinion that Moscovici and a

144

few others started to publish their 'deviant' ideas, which they have continued to do in a consistent and persuasive fashion over the past thirty years.

An important initial task was to demonstrate that minority influence did indeed exist, and one of the first experiments to do this was by Moscovici et al. (1969). They used a similar procedure to that used by Asch. A group of participants was asked to make some perceptual judgements – this time about the colour of some bluish-tinted slides. However, Moscovici et al. turned Asch's set-up on its head by employing a *majority* of naive participants (four in all) and a *minority* of two confederates who had been instructed by the experimenter to call out the colour 'green' in response to the slides in a predetermined manner. In one condition, both confederates were consistent with one another, responding 'green' in every trial. In another condition, the confederates were not so consistent, sometimes calling out 'blue' along with the real participants. The primary measure of influence was how often the real participants responded 'green' also to the obviously blue slides. The results were clear. Around one-third of those in the first experimental condition made at least one 'green' response, and over 8 per cent of their responses overall were 'green'. This compares to the virtually zero 'green' response in the control condition (where there were no confederates), and a negligible 1 per cent of the other experimental condition, where the confederates behaved inconsistently. The figure of 8 per cent may not be very startling, especially when we compare it to the 36 per cent conformity rate reported by Asch (1956), but it must be remembered that this was achieved by a deviant minority against a majority twice its size. From this perspective, and in contrast to the dominant view that majorities are more powerful than minorities, that there was any influence at all is quite significant.

In an extension of this experiment, Moscovici et al. (1969) followed up their standard procedure with an individual assessment of the real subjects' colour thresholds. A second experimenter, supposedly conducting some independent research, entered the laboratory after the group perception task and administered a standardized test of colour discrimination. Each person was tested individually with no knowledge of other people's responses. The results showed that the experimental participants had a significantly lower threshold for the perception of green than the 'control' group: that is, blue–green slides were more likely to be seen by them as 'green'. These ancillary findings indicate that minority influence is effective not just in changing people's overt behaviour (their public responses in the first part of the experiment) but may have internalized cognitive consequences as well.

These findings were confirmed in a subsequent experiment, which compared directly the influence exerted by minorities and majorities. Using the same colour perception task, Moscovici and Lage (1976) employed three conditions of minority influence: one was identical to their earlier experiment (i.e. two confederates always calling out 'green'); one was a single confederate who was also consistent; in the third, two confederates were inconsistent with one another. There were also two conditions of majority influence, similar to those employed by Asch, i.e. a unanimous or a non-unanimous majority. Of the minority influence conditions only the consistent pair of deviates were able to exert any noticeable influence. Just over 10 per cent of the responses in this consistent minority condition showed evidence of conformity (versus 1 per cent in the 'control' group). While this was clearly less than the 40 per cent conformity rate in the unanimous majority condition, it was comparable to the 12 per cent found with the non-unanimous majority. However, in the subsequent colour discrimination test, those in the consistent minority condition were the *only* participants to change their blue–green thresholds significantly compared to the control baseline. So, despite the greater overt compliance found with majority influence, it was the *minority* that was apparently able to shift people's internal colour codes.

A recurring theme in minority influence research is that minorities seem to have their strongest effects *indirectly* – that is, after some delay, or on some dimension of attitude or behaviour that is related to but not necessarily identical to that exhibited by the influence source. As we shall see, the reason for this may be that minorities act as catalysts for change by provoking cognitive conflict in the majority. It may not be easy or possible to resolve these conflicts immediately or directly – for example, there may be normative pressures working against conceding ground to the minority too obviously, or the cognitive dissonance instigated by the dissent may take time to resolve – and so the change may only be latent or occur less overtly.

That minority influence may take some time to show its effects was observed by Perez et al. (1986). They presented their Spanish participants with arguments in favour of abortion, which was purported to be either a majority or a minority viewpoint. The participants' attitudes were then tested immediately, and again after a delay of three weeks, both on the focal issue of abortion and on a related matter, contraception. The majority had some influence in the initial post-test on both issues but this disappeared (and even appeared to 'boomerang' slightly) three weeks later; the 'minority message', on the other hand, while being relatively ineffectual immediately, showed clear effects after the temporal delay on both the abortion and contraception questions. This is strongly reminiscent of the 'sleeper effect', which has sometimes been observed in the literature on persuasion (Pratkanis et al., 1988).

In some ways, Perez et al.'s (1986) finding that a minority's arguments on one topic 'spill over' to affect people's opinions on another closely related topic is not surprising. After all, politically and psychologically there is usually considerable convergence of views on abortion and contraception. But what if the second topic is psychologically quite *un*related to the focal issue of the minority's message? For example, suppose one is exposed to a minority (or majority) arguing strenuously against allowing gay people to serve in the army. What effect might this have on one's attitudes to relaxing controls on the ownership of guns? This was the question posed by Alvaro and Crano (1997). Like Moscovici (1976), they assumed that minorities often have the power to stimulate thinking about the issue under discussion. Such cognitive work may involve the generation of counter-arguments to the minority's message but such counter-arguments are unlikely to be relevant to some unrelated topic and so they are 'vulnerable' to change on that, and not the focal, issue. This was, indeed, what happened. Alvaro and Crano first established that 'gays in the military' and 'gun control' attitudes were only weakly correlated. In the experiment proper, participants read a message, attributed to a minority or a majority, arguing strongly against allowing gay people to be soldiers. Subsequently their own attitudes were elicited on this and three other topics, including the question of increased gun controls. Little change was observed on the focal issue (gays in the military) but those exposed to the minority message did change their views significantly on the gun control topic. This suggests a rather intriguing persuasion strategy for would-be opinion-formers whose views are currently in the minority: first find a topic that is only loosely related to the issue you are really concerned with; concentrate your propaganda attempts on this topic; these will probably meet with considerable resistance from the majority but, surreptitiously, you may succeed in changing their minds on the matter you really care about.

There seems little doubt, then, that minority influence is a genuine phenomenon (Maass and Clark, 1984). Wood et al. (1994), in a meta-analysis of over 100 studies, confirmed this statistically, showing that, while generally less influential than majorities (except on indirect measures), minorities are nevertheless still persuasive when compared to 'control' conditions where no influence sources are present (again, especially on less direct indicators of attitude change). This forces us to accept Moscovici's contention that the traditional view of social influence as the exclusive preserve of the majority in the group is incomplete. Minorities, it seems, are not simply passive recipients of pressure from the group but may be active agents for change. This leads to a view of social influence as a bilateral process in which deviate individuals are both targets and sources of persuasion.

Although it is now indisputable that minorities can bring about change in the thoughts and actions of the majority, we need to remind ourselves that they do not always do so; there are limits to what they can achieve. History tends to concentrate on their success stories – for example, the Communist Party in Russia in the first two decades of the twentieth century or the pro-democracy movements in Eastern Europe in the past two decades – and often overlooks their failures – for instance, socialist political parties in the USA or the short-lived student revolt in China in the months following the Tiananmen Square massacre in 1989. Kelly (1990) recorded another such failure, albeit in a more parochial context. In 1988, Tony Benn, representing the minority left wing of the British Labour Party, challenged the then leader, Neil Kinnock, for the leadership of the Party. Kelly (1990) elicited views from ordinary party members on these two candidates and various policy issues that divided them over a three-month period in the run-up to the election (which Benn ultimately lost). Despite the fact that Benn and his supporters adopted 'classic' Moscovici influence strategies – presenting their ideas with admirable 'consistency' – Kelly's findings showed that they were remarkably ineffectual: on eight of the ten political issues she polled, the rank-and-file 'majority' members either showed no movement or actually moved to the right, and the two shifts to the left that might have been attributable to the Bennite campaigning were statistically unreliable. Still worse from the minority's perspective, the left-wing party members themselves moved to the right on *all* issues. In other words, the minority exerted very little influence and certainly much less than the majority, whose views ultimately prevailed.

There are several reasons why minorities like this may not succeed. One has to do with the amount of personal involvement the majority has in maintaining its view. In many experimental contexts where the judgement in question involves colours of slides or opinions on some question of only vague general interest, it may not 'cost' the majority so much to concede to the minority. On issues with more direct personal relevance (like one's political convictions) it may be quite another matter. Trost et al. (1992) certainly found this to be so in an experimental study where their student participants were presented with a persuasive message, purporting to be from a majority or a minority, arguing for the introduction of a compulsory new student exam. Half of the students were told that this new exam policy would not come into effect for several years and hence would be unlikely to affect them, while, for the remainder, it was perceived to be directly relevant since it would be introduced quite soon. When the latter message came from a minority it left the students quite unmoved – their attitudes to the exam did not differ from a 'control' (no message) condition. When it was less relevant their attitudes did change, and somewhat more so than those exposed to the same message apparently coming from a majority.

A second reason why some minorities may succeed and others not has to do with the prevailing climate of opinion in the group or culture concerned, the *Zeitgeist* or spirit of the times. Where there is already the beginnings of a groundswell of support for change in society at large, a minority endorsing that view against a local majority opposed to it may have more success than vice versa. Thus, the Labour Party in Britain during the 1980s was swinging to the right after a succession of electoral defeats at the hands of a very Conservative Thatcher-led government. Against such a climate of opinion the left-wing Benn challenge for the leadership was probably doomed to fail. Several experimental studies bear out this *Zeitgeist* effect. Maass et al. (1982), for example, found that groups of men exposed to a pair of deviates changed their views on one issue (abortion), for which there was some public support in the US at the time, but not on another issue (the death penalty), which was a more controversial matter. There was one other interesting variation in Maass et al.'s (1982) procedure, which paved the way for a new line of research. In some conditions the two confederates were male and hence could be seen as part of the ingroup of genuine participants. In others, however, they were female and hence constituted an outgroup. There were hints that the ingroup minority was more influential on the abortion issue than the outgroup although, in fact, the difference between male and female confederates was not reliable statistically.

Social categorization and minority influence

Nevertheless, as we know, those with minority views in society are not simply 'people who disagree' with us, they are often categorized as belonging to some outgroup as well. This was certainly true in the Labour Party during the 1980s, and is no less true in the more recent era of New Labour, where the left wing are routinely labelled as the 'loony left' or 'old Labour'. What effect does it have to categorize the source of minority influence as belonging to the outgroup in this way or alternatively as emanating from within the ingroup? Earlier in the chapter I discussed this issue in relation to majority influence and concluded that ingroup status conferred definite advantages for those seeking to influence others. A plausible explanation for this was provided by Self-Categorization Theory, which proposes that people generally gravitate *towards* those in their ingroup, especially prototypical ingroup members, but *away from* those in outgroups (Turner, 1991). The same reasoning should apply to minority influence: we should take much more seriously, pay more attention to and hence ultimately be influenced by minority persons with whom we believe we share category membership than by those we do not. David and Turner (1996) put this hypothesis to the test, combining the conventional minority versus majority influence source with their classification as ingroup or outgroup members. The study was set in the context of environmental debates in Australia over the wisdom of conserving (or harvesting for timber) rainforest areas. Participants, whose views on the conservation issue had been determined earlier, listened to a tape-recording which was said to be from a pro- (or anti-) conservationist pressure group, which was described as moderate (i.e. majority) or extremist (i.e. minority). Their own attitudes on the forest conservation issue were then elicited, both immediately and after a delay of 3–4 weeks. The purpose of this repeated attitude assessment was to test for the existence of any latent effects of influence, which have been attributed to minorities (Perez et al., 1986). As is apparent from figure 4.4, only the 'ingroup messages' had any positive effect on changing people's attitudes in their direction; all outgroup messages had a reverse or polarizing effect. The pattern of influence created by the ingroup messages is interesting: the immediate benefit is with the majority, while after a few weeks it is those who heard the minority message who show the greatest effects. Several other studies have confirmed this powerful effect of categorization on the magnitude and direction of social influence (Alvaro and Crano, 1997; Clark and Maass, 1988; Martin, 1988).

Nevertheless, there are some circumstances when it may be more efficacious to express a deviant point of view from outside the ingroup. One such circumstance is where that minority opinion is itself a deviant or unrepresentative position within the outgroup. For example, we may be sympathetic to a contrary argument that is expressed by one of our political opponents partly because it is an expression of dissidence in the 'other side', which may increase the unity of the ingroup; the same dissent from within the ingroup could have the opposite effect. Another reason why outgroup people can be influential is that they may become temporarily re-categorized as ingroup members, at least on the particular matter under debate. As Volpato et al. (1990, p. 129) observe, 'the enemy of my enemy is my friend'. Volpato et al. (1990) provided an experimental demonstration of this effect when they presented students from Milan with a message arguing for some innovations in the national school leaving examinations. For a third of the students this minority message was said to have emanated from a student committee in Milan (ingroup); another

151

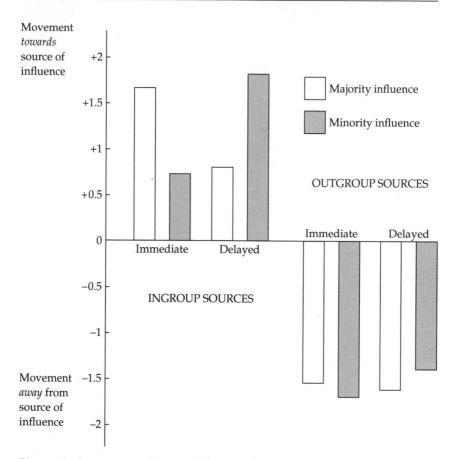

Figure 4.4 Immediate and latent influence of ingroup and outgroup majorities/ minorities (adapted from David and Turner, 1996, table 1)

third believed it came from a committee in Rome (outgroup); and the remaining (control) students received no minority influence at all. Of the three groups, those exposed to the outgroup minority showed the most influence. However, there were indications that the ingroup minority stimulated more creative thinking since participants in that condition generated more completely new proposals than in the other two. As we shall see in the next section, such innovatory effects of minorities are theoretically quite significant.

152

Two Influence Processes or One?

In the previous section I was concerned to demonstrate the existence of minority influence and examine the factors that seem to affect its strength and limit its sphere of application. A notable feature of several of the studies I discussed there was that the nature of this influence often seemed to differ from that exerted by majorities: it was delayed, or occurred more on related than on focal issues. This naturally raises the question as to whether the social psychological processes underlying majority and minority influence are the same or different. The answers to this question turn out to be quite complicated. On the one hand, Moscovici's (1976) original position and those of several of his associates (e.g. Mugny, 1982; Nemeth, 1986) are clear: there are qualitative differences between the two forms of influence, both in the factors that give rise to them and in the effects that they have. In recent years other 'dual process' theories of influence have been proposed, which although sharing nomenclature with the early models in fact make some diametrically opposed predictions (e.g. Bohner et al., 1995; de Vries et al., 1996). Then there are adherents of 'single process' models, who try to show that the differences between the two forms of influence are primarily differences of degree not of kind, and that the same fundamental processes are at work in both (Latané and Wolf, 1981; Tanford and Penrod, 1984). I want now to engage with this debate and examine the evidence that bears on it, beginning with the 'two processes' school of thought.

Moscovici, as already noted, believes that the means by which majorities and minorities come to have their effects are different. Following Festinger and others, he suggests that majorities primarily elicit *public* conformity from individual group members for reasons of social or informational dependence. By contrast, minorities, he believes, are successful mainly in bringing about *private* changes in opinion due to the cognitive conflicts and restructuring that their deviant ideas provoke.

Some of the earliest and clearest experiments documenting this distinction between influence in the public and private domains were performed by Maass and Clark (1983, 1986). In three experiments they examined people's attitude change (towards gay rights) after reading a summary of a group discussion in which a majority and a minority

153

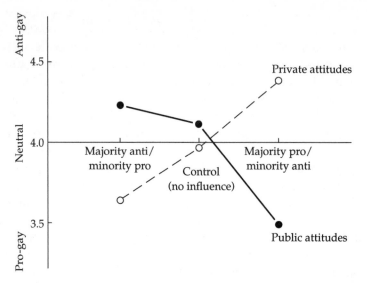

Figure 4.5 Public and private attitude change in response to majority and minority influence (from Maass and Clark, 1983, experiment 1)

viewpoint could be easily discerned. Whether these positions were for or against gay rights was systematically varied. The participants then had to indicate their own attitudes towards the issue. For half of them this was done anonymously and hence privately; the others believed that their responses would be seen by others taking part in the session with them. Attitudes in this public condition showed clear evidence of being influenced by the majority views they had read. When these were anti-gay their attitude hardened also; when the majority was pro-gay, so were they. However, those responding *privately* were influenced mainly by the minority view (see figure 4.5).

The distinction between the overt public compliance produced by majority influence and covert private conversion is central to the 'two processes' hypothesis. Remember that in the early demonstrations of minority influence by Moscovici et al. (1969) and Moscovici and Lage (1976), the effects of the deviant confederates were not restricted to the perception task, where responses were all made in public, but extended into the subsequent, and individually administered, colour discrimination test. An even more dramatic illustration that minority influence can bring about internal, and perhaps even unconscious,

154

changes which majority influence may be unable to do has been provided by a series of experiments by Moscovici and Personnaz (Moscovici and Personnaz, 1980, 1986; Personnaz, 1981). These experiments began with the blue–green colour task used in the earlier studies. As before, there was a confederate who always called out 'green' to the obviously blue slides. Participants were led to believe that this confederate was either representative of the general population (it was alleged that 82 per cent also tended to respond in the same way) or was unrepresentative (only 18 per cent responded in this way). In this manner the confederate seemed to be one of a majority or a minority. The ingenious twist that Moscovici and Personnaz now introduced into the procedure was to ask the participants, after each slide had been turned off, to report privately the colour of the after-image they saw on the blank screen. Now what most people do not know – and Moscovici and Personnaz stated that their participants did not know – is that the colour of an after-image is always complementary to the colour of the original stimulus. So, for blue slides an after-image should be yellow–orange; for green slides it would be red–purple. The results were truly remarkable. Those who had been exposed to a confederate thought to be from a majority showed little or no shift in their after-image colours, but those who believed that the confederate was a minority person reported after-image colours that were significantly further towards the *purple* end of the scale. Since this after-image colour is more complementary of green than blue, it suggests that they had undergone some internal shift in their perceptual system as a result of the minority influence. This shift persisted even when the confederate was absent. What gives these findings particular significance is that the after-image colours were different from the colours called out by the confederates and so there can be no question that the subjects simply 'copied' his or her response. Furthermore, Moscovici and Personnaz report that participants seemed quite unaware that any change had taken place. Indeed, very few of them ever responded 'green' themselves in their public responses.

Although Moscovici and Personnaz have now obtained similar results in four separate experiments, attempts to replicate these startling findings outside their laboratory have been less successful. In two close replications, Doms and van Avermaet (1980) observed a changed after-image colour after exposure to minority influence.

However, and problematically for the 'different processes' argument, they found equivalent changes in the majority influence condition also. Sorrentino et al. (1980) failed to find any reliable shift towards the red–purple after-image as a result of minority influence. However, an internal analysis of their data revealed that participants expressing more suspicion about the procedure showed the shift towards purple, while the less-suspicious participants did not. Finally, in the most sustained replication attempt to date, Martin (1998) reported five experiments that were exact or near replicas of the Moscovici and Personnaz (1980) procedure. In none of these was there any reliable difference between majority and minority influence conditions in the colour of after-image reported. However, confirming Sorrentino et al. (1980), a consistent finding in these experiments was that the more suspicious participants reported more purple-coloured after-images than less suspicious people. Sorrentino et al. (1980) suggest that suspiciousness tends to cause people to stare at the stimuli more intently and this more focused attention might generate a differently hued after-image.

Do these suspiciousness data offer us a way of making sense of all the conflicting findings? Could it be, perhaps, that there were subtle features of Moscovici and Personnaz's procedure that gave rise to greater suspicion in the 'minority' conditions? Unfortunately, such a neat resolution of the puzzle seems unlikely. For one thing, Martin (1998, experiment 5) reports that the bulk of the less-suspicious participants(over 90 per cent) actually came from the *minority influence* condition and all the more-suspicious participants came from the *majority influence* condition;[2] this is exactly the opposite pattern from what we speculated might have accounted for the original results. Moreover, Moscovici and Personnaz (1991) have devised a variation of their original after-image paradigm which, in my view, neatly side-steps this particular explanation. In these later two experiments an ambiguous line drawing of Lenin's face appears against a red background (in one experiment the picture of Lenin is gradually revealed; in the other it is always present). The confederate, who, as usual, is said to represent a majority or minority view, reports that she sees Lenin in the picture and the real participant has to give her response (in public). Then, in private, the participant has to report the colour of the background and, finally, the after-image created by this red hue.

156

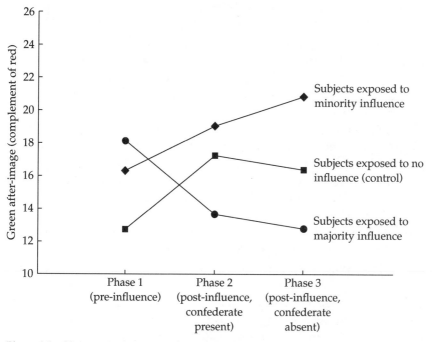

Figure 4.6 Changes in chromatic after-image created by colour associations of Lenin's portrait (from Moscovici and Personnaz, 1991, table 6, experiment 2)

Moscovici and Personnaz (1991) argued that Lenin is associated symbolically with the colour red and so any indirect effects of the confederate's influence should be indicated by a stronger perception of red as the background colour and a greener after-image (since green is the complement of red). According to their 'conversion theory', such changes should only occur among those exposed to minority influence. The results bore out their hypothesis. Both in their judgements of the background colour and their subsequent after-images, those in the 'minority' condition showed greater evidence of perceiving the Communist-associated colour of red than those in the 'majority' and 'control' conditions (see figure 4.6). Note that in these experiments there should be no question of any participant suspiciousness because the confederates are actually reporting a plausible – and correct – interpretation of the stimulus, unlike in the blue–green paradigm, where their responses are manifestly at variance with consensual reality.

Despite the unsatisfactory resolution of the conflicting findings from those after-image studies, there are other lines of evidence indicating that majority and minority influence instigate different socio-cognitive reactions in the minds of their recipients. Recall that Moscovici believes that minority influence can be a more potent agent of persuasion because, according to his model, the cognitive work it instigates results in internalized ('private') attitude change rather than superficial ('public') compliance. This is why his theory is often referred to as 'conversion theory' (Moscovici, 1980). He implies, therefore, that despite the fact that minorities may be disliked and initially disregarded, they are ultimately more thought-provoking than majorities. A few moments reflection might cause us to question this implication, however. Is it really plausible to suppose that participants in a typical social influence experiment, asked to name the colour of a slide, will think harder or more deeply when they hear that a small minority thinks that 'blue' is 'green' than if they learn that a vast majority do so? De Vries et al. (1996) argue that it is not. They analysed several experiments, predominantly concerned with attitude change, and concluded that, in fact, the opposite is more often true: people generally seem motivated to think more systematically about an issue when they believe that a substantial number of peers endorse a point of view at variance with their own than if only a handful of people hold that opinion. Mackie (1987) provided one of the clearest demonstrations of this. She asked participants to listen to a tape recording that contained two people offering an equal number of arguments for and against a topical issue. One of these disputants was alleged to represent a majority point of view; the other was said to be advocating only a minority opinion. The participants' own attitudes on this and a related issue were obtained both immediately after hearing the tape and a week later. The results were clear: the arguments supposedly put forward by the 'majority' resulted in much more evidence of attitude change, both immediately and after a delay, and on both the focal and related topics. In contrast, the 'minority' viewpoint caused very little change. Moreover, there was more recall of the 'majority' arguments and more evidence that they were elaborated in a favourable direction than was the case for the 'minority' arguments. Three other experiments provided broadly similar results, forcing Mackie (1987) to the conclusion that, contrary to Moscovici's hypothesis, it is the *majority* that tends to stimulate systematic processing in the minds of recipients, while minorities may evoke more superficial or 'heuristic' modes of thought (see Eagly and Chaiken, 1993).

If minorities do not necessarily provoke deeper or more careful cognitive consideration than majorities, it seems likely that they give rise to different *kinds* of thinking – the one more creative and divergent, the other more focused and convergent. Nemeth (1986) has suggested why this might be so. She points out that people's first reaction on hearing that a majority is adopting a view diametrically different from their own is to experience some anxiety. This follows directly from Festinger's (1954) original contention that people's default position is to accord some validity to consensual opinions and to feel uncomfortable in the presence of dissent. This heightened arousal, argues Nemeth, is likely to focus people's attention more closely on the truth or falsity of what the majority is expressing, to the exclusion of other possibly relevant issues. It has long been established that increased arousal has exactly such attention-narrowing effects on a range of tasks (Easterbrook, 1959; Zajonc, 1965). The result is a convergent mode of thinking, with much cognitive effort being expended on the majority's message and little on anything else. Exposure to a minority opinion is quite another matter. Here, we may feel quite relaxed since our initial comfortable position is that the minority is wrong and can be safely ignored. However, their persistent and confident espousal of such unpopular opinions, apparently to no personal benefit, at least causes us to think, if only of other possible alternative viewpoints to those the minority is adopting. Our more relaxed state of mind allows a more wide-ranging cognitive appraisal of the issues at hand, so that we may display more originality in any subsequent deliberations. Notice that Nemeth is not arguing that either form of influence necessarily has superior outcomes: in true 'horses for courses' fashion, in some tasks it is helpful to concentrate more closely on a small range of issues; in others a modicum of creativity can be beneficial.

Nemeth's ideas have stimulated much research, most of it broadly supportive of her hypothesis. One of the earliest experiments was by Nemeth and Wachtler (1983). They elaborated the usual Asch paradigm in which participants have to compare standard stimuli with others. In this experiment the stimuli were a series of embedded figures

Table 4.2 Conformity and originality as responses to majority and minority influence

	Majority influence[§]		Minority influence[§]		Control (no influence)
	Correct	*Incorrect*	*Correct*	*Incorrect*	
Conformity*	1.4$_a$	1.9$_a$	0.7$_b$	0.6$_b$	–
Originality[†]	1.7$_a$	3.8$_a$	5.1$_b$	4.8$_b$	2.8$_a$
Originality[‡] and correctness	2.5$_a$	5.6$_a$	9.3$_b$	7.0$_b$	3.9$_a$

* Number of figures chosen that were identical to those chosen by confederates.
† Percentage of novel responses, both correct and incorrect.
‡ Percentage of novel correct responses.
§ Means with different subscript are significantly different.
Source: Nemeth and Wachtler (1983), table 1

in which a standard pattern is hidden against a complex background, and the task was to identify which of six figures matches the standard (there might be more than one). One of the correct comparison figures was always easy to detect, two were much harder because they contained more distracting designs, and the other three were incorrect since they did not contain the standard pattern. As usual, there were confederates primed to give certain answers: *either* to respond correctly with both the easy and one of the difficult figures *or* to respond correctly with the easy figure but to make an incorrect choice from the difficult set. In half the groups there were two confederates and four naive participants (minority influence); in the remainder there were four confederates and two naive participants (majority influence). Those exposed to majority influence were more likely to copy the confederates' responses exactly, whether these were right or wrong. This is the usual conformity effect. However, when the participants' *novel* responses were examined, it was those in the minority influence condition who not only generated more new responses overall, but also produced a greater proportion of these which were actually correct, regardless of whether or not the confederates had given a correct answer too (see table 4.2). And, consistent with Nemeth's later (1986) theorizing on the role of arousal, those in the majority influence conditions reported feeling greater tension than those in the minority conditions.

Subsequent studies have confirmed this apparently stimulating effect of minorities on people's divergent thinking. Nemeth and Kwan (1985) found that those exposed to minority influence made more, and more original, colour associations than those exposed to majority influence.[3] De Dreu and De Vries (1993) found a similar result in the context of people's attitudes towards immigration: minority influence respondents generated more associations with the word 'foreigner' than those receiving a 'majority' message (see also Erb et al., 1998; Mucchi-Faina et al., 1991). Finally, Nemeth et al. (1990) observed that minority influence could improve recall in a verbal learning task. In the initial presentations of the material, participants discovered that one (or three) of their fellow participants had reported an unusual category as being the first thing they had noticed in the lists of words. This exposure to a minority (or a majority) adopting a surprising categorization affected their subsequent memory for the words: those in the 'minority' condition remembered more (over 60 per cent) than those in the 'majority' or 'control' conditions (around 55 per cent). The reason for this seemed to be that the exposure to the minority dissent caused more clustering of the recall responses than in the other conditions, and such categorical organization of material is usually helpful to memory.

All in all, then, there is considerable support for those who argue that minorities and majorities exert their influence in different ways and with different effects. What of the rival hypothesis that minority and majority influence are but two sides of the same coin, differing only in the strength of their effects? The clearest statement of this view has come from Latané and Wolf (1981). Drawing on Latané's (1981) social impact theory, they argue that the primary difference between majority and minority influence lies in the fact that in the former there are more sources of influence than in the latter. The importance of the number of sources stems from the basic proposition of social impact theory, which is that the impact of any social stimuli increases with their number, but in a negatively accelerating fashion. That is, the first stimulus has a large impact on a person; adding a second will increase the impact but by not quite as much as

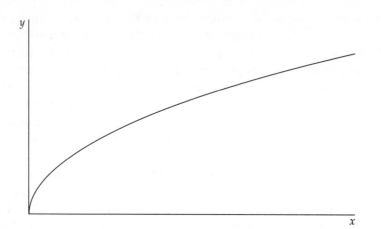

Figure 4.7 A typical negatively accelerating power function between two variables

the first; and subsequent stimuli will have only marginal additional effects.[4] In this formulation Latané draws a direct parallel with sensory experience data, where, since Stevens (1957), it has been reliably established that the subjective intensity of a sensation caused by a stimulus is a power function of the objective strength of the stimulus. If one plots the sensation against the magnitude or number of stimuli present then one typically gets a curve resembling that shown in figure 4.7. Thus, in a completely dark room the addition of one light source makes a large difference to the level of illumination. A second light increases the illumination still further, but the addition of nine more light bulbs does not make the room seem ten times brighter. By analogy, in Latané and Wolf's (1981) model of social influence, the 'light bulbs' are other people exerting influence on the experimental participant. The magnitude of their influence (or impact), as measured by the conformity shown, will thus depend on the number of them present. Because majorities contain more people than minorities, they should exert greater influence.

In support of their theory, Latané and Wolf (1981) have re-examined a number of studies that looked at the effects of varying the size of the majority on the level of conformity (see earlier). As predicted by their model, increasing the size of the majority does increase conformity but in a diminishing fashion. A comparison between figures 4.1 and 4.7 illustrates the resemblance between the observed relationships and the hypothetical one predicted by a mathematical power function. A meta-analysis has also been performed by Tanford and Penrod (1984). Although they used a different model to Latané and Wolf (1981), they came to essentially similar conclusions: increasing the number of source persons relative to recipients reliably increases the amount of influence exerted, though not in a linear fashion.

Crucial to Latané and Wolf's model is the idea that social influence – whether emanating from a minority or a majority – is a unitary process. Support for this was obtained by Wolf (1985) in an extension of her earlier study of minority influence in a simulated jury (Wolf, 1979). Using the same paradigm, she created mock juries in which participants thought they were either in a majority of three (against the deviate) or in a minority of one (against a majority of three). The participants' legal judgements were clearly affected in both conditions, but much more strongly in the latter. Since these judgements were always made in private – and hence should favour the operation of minority influence processes, according to Moscovici – Wolf argued that her findings supported the view that the two forms of influence differ in degree but not in kind (see also Clark and Maass, 1990, experiment 2).

If, as the single-process theorists believe, social influence is primarily controlled by the relative numbers of emitters and targets of influence, it should be possible to model its effects using computer simulations programmed with a few assumptions about the distribution of opinions in a population and how the holders of those opinions will affect each other (e.g. according to social impact theory). Nowak et al. (1990) did just this. They set up a hypothetical population of 1600 individuals in which the distribution of majority (70 per cent) and minority (30 per cent) opinions was randomized. Then, through successive iterations of the program according to certain rules – for example, the likelihood of any one individual unit changing 'opinion' depended on the numbers of people with different views in its vicinity – they showed that one quickly obtains stable configurations of opinion in the population that resemble a large consensual majority (usually around 90 per cent of the population) and a few discrete pockets (or 'groups') of minority opinion scattered about. Nowak et al. (1990) argued that such a process and outcome bears some resemblance to the emergence of minority groups in society. Since they achieved this with a single algorithm whose major parameters were the number of influence sources and their 'distances' from each other, they suggest that their unitary process model is at once a powerful and a parsimonious account of influence in the real world.

What can we say by way of a conclusion to this controversy? Supporters of the single-process hypothesis have amassed an impressive volume of evidence in support of their contention that the *quantitative size* of both minority and majority influence effects – particularly in the domain of overt public responses – *are* predictable from the same variable: namely, the number of those being influenced relative to the number doing the influencing. However, the single-process model is much less compelling when it comes to explaining the *qualitative nature* of majority and minority influence effects, particularly the difference between direct and indirect attitude change. It may be true, as Kruglanski and Mackie (1990) have argued, that these are not uniquely associated with one or the other form of influence, but still there is an accumulation of research suggesting that majorities are at their most influential in achieving immediate and overt change while minorities more usually bring about latent and less direct influence. Moreover, the idea that the primary causal factor at work is simply the size of the influence source is not compatible with the findings that changing the mode in which the influence is assessed (e.g. publicly or privately), or the direction in which it is exerted (e.g. with or against the *Zeitgeist*), or the category membership of the influence source (e.g. ingroup or outgroup) can all radically affect the magnitude of conformity, its direction and its cognitive effects. In these cases, the arithmetical ratios of influencers to influenced remain constant yet the outcomes are dramatically different. All this leads to the conclusion that while the numerical relationship between the minority and majority is clearly a significant feature of the group context which cannot be ignored, a proper understanding of when and how group members are able to influence each other will not be reached until we know a great deal more than we do about their various *social* relationships also.

Summary

1   The most easily observed kind of social influence is when individuals conform to the attitudes and behaviour of the majority. This can occur even to the extent that individuals are apparently willing to deny the evidence of their own senses in order to go along with the majority view. Such conformity is remarkably widespread and has been observed in many different countries.

2   The main explanations for this conformity to the majority (by Festinger and others) suggest that three main motivations are at work: the need to depend on others for information about the world and to test the validity of our own opinions, the achievement of group goals, which is facilitated by a uniformity of purpose, and the need for approval arising out of not wishing to seem different. These motives can be readily observed in peer groups during adolescence.

3   Pressures towards uniformity are most visible when reactions to deviates in the group are studied. Deviates attract the most attention from the majority as attempts are made to make them change their mind. They are also liked less than other members of the group.

4   However, deviates, especially when they are not completely isolated and when they act in a consistent fashion, can be shown to influence the majority. This is most evident on indirect or latent measures of influence. The categorization of the source of influence is also important: ingroup minorities typically bring about more change than outgroup minorities.

5   Controversy exists as to whether minority and majority influences are two separate processes with different effects or a single process with effects different only in magnitude. In support of the former view, different cognitive and attitudinal outcomes are usually obtained in the two domains. On the other hand, consistent effects of group size (of both majority and minority) on the magnitude of influence support a unitary process. While a rigid demarcation between the two modes of influence may not be tenable, there are sufficient qualitative differences in antecedents and outcomes to sustain a theoretical distinction between them.

Notes

1 Although, as Bond (1998) has pointed out, this experiment contained a confound between group size and gender: even-numbered majorities (e.g. 2, 4, 6 etc.) were always all male, odd-numbered majorities were always female. This may help to explain the rather jagged, if still statistically linear, shape of the size–conformity relationship observed.

2 Actually, it makes good sense that it was those of the 'majority' condition who were more suspicious. After all, they were confronted with an alleged majority (>80 per cent) who apparently saw a perfectly good blue slide as a shade of green. This would be more likely to raise doubts in their mind about the veracity of the information than the allegation that a minority (18 per cent) had such a perception. A small group like this could be more easily dismissed as having defective colour vision.

3 Intriguingly, the minority influence participants also excelled the control participants (exposed to no influence) in both quantity and originality. This result has important implications for theories of group productivity (see chapter 5).

4 Written mathematically, this relationship is a power function: $I = sN^t$, where I is impact, N the number of stimuli and t has a value <1; s is a constant which varies between situations and tasks..

Further Reading

Eagly, A. and Chaiken, S. (1993) *The Psychology of Attitudes*, ch. 13. New York: Harcourt Brace Jovanovich.

Kruglanski, A. and Mackie, D. (1990) Majority and minority influence: a judgmental process analysis, in Stroebe, W. and Hewstone, M. (eds) *European Review of Social Psychology*, vol. 1. Chichester: Wiley.

Moscovici, S. (1980) Toward a theory of conversion behavior, in Berkowitz, L. (ed.) *Advances in Experimental Social Psychology*, vol. 13. New York: Academic Press.

Nemeth, C. (1986) Differential contributions of majority and minority influence. *Psychological Review*, 93, 23–32.

Turner, J.C. (1991) *Social Influence*, chs 2, 4 and 6. Milton Keynes: Open University Press.

5

INDIVIDUALS VERSUS GROUPS

Are 'two heads better than one' or do 'too many cooks spoil the broth'? Do 'many hands make light work' or should you, in order to do something well, do it yourself? These various (and conflicting) adages reveal our society's long interest in the question of whether people work harder, think more clearly, learn more effectively and are more creative in the company of others or on their own. This interest is hardly surprising in view of the close interdependence between people that is one of the hallmarks of human existence; today, as they have for millennia, people work together, play together and make crucial life and death decisions together. It has thus been of no little practical importance to have known how best to organize ourselves to perform these tasks effectively. Reflecting these concerns, group psychologists have long argued about the respective merits of group and individual performance. Indeed, the earliest recorded social psychological experiments addressed just these issues. This chapter will examine some of these debates and review the enormous fund of empirical research that they have generated.

The first half of the chapter concerns some aspects of productivity. In other words, on tasks where there is some measurable index of performance, how do individuals and groups compare? As we shall see, there are a number of ways of answering this question and the outcome of the comparison very much depends on the method chosen. Nevertheless, across a range of tasks one finding seems to recur: groups often fail to operate as efficiently as one might have predicted from knowledge of the attributes of their individual members. Such findings have led some theorists to propose that groups are inherently unlikely to maximize their full potential, either because they fail to utilize and coordinate their resources in an optimal fashion or because factors within them lower people's motivation to perform well. As I hope to show, although much available data support these contentions, there are grounds for believing that they are unduly pessimistic about the capacity of groups to excel their potential productivity. Sometimes a group may, indeed, be more than the sum (or other combination) of its parts.

The second part considers the nature of group decisions and judgements on issues where there is no right or wrong answer, no larger or smaller outcome, but merely differences of opinion. What relationship does the group's collective voice have to its constituents' original views? Here the empirical conclusion is unequivocal: groups are typically more extreme in their views and behaviour than are their members considered individually. If the data are clear, the explanation for them remains controversial. As we shall see, a number of plausible theories have been proposed, and deciding between these viewpoints turns out to be a far from simple matter. Finally, the factors that affect the quality of collective decision making are discussed, and a theory suggesting that such decisions are prone to a detrimental set of symptoms known as 'groupthink' is examined.

Group Productivity

Does the presence of others help or hinder performance?

Whenever we undertake some group task one fact is inescapable: other people are present and may have the opportunity to observe and evaluate what we are doing. Thus, the most elementary question about group productivity is to ask whether the mere presence of others has any effect on performance. Indeed, it was exactly this question which was the focus of the first ever social psychology experiment (Triplett, 1898), and which seemed to preoccupy other social psychologists in the first three decades of the twentieth century (e.g. Allport, 1924; Dashiell, 1930; Moede, 1920–1). Triplett's study was inspired by his analysis of the record books of the League of American Wheelmen, the organization that apparently ran cycling competitions of various kinds in the United States at that time. Triplett noticed how time trials (in which cyclists raced alone against the clock) seemed invariably to yield slower performances than 'paced' events (in which the cyclist is accompanied by a series of pace-setters), which, in turn, were slightly slower than true competitions (cyclists racing against each other). Moved to explain these differences, Triplett devised a laboratory task (winding fishing reels) that could be undertaken alone or in competition with another. His results indicated that participants (mostly 9–12-year-old children) usually worked faster in competition than alone (Triplett, 1898; see also Moede, 1920–1).

That pioneering study was followed by many others, most notably by Allport (1924). Allport sought to remove the competitive element and asked people simply to carry out various cognitive tasks on their own or alongside (but not against) someone else also performing the task. The tasks ranged from relatively straightforward things like multiplication or vowel cancellation to more complex activities like thinking up counter-arguments to some philosophical position. Allport found that on simple tasks performance was facilitated by the presence of a co-actor, while on more difficult tasks it was impaired. In fact, this observation has stood the test of time, emerging clearly from the results of over 200 subsequent experiments examining the effects of social presence on various types of task performance (Bond and Titus, 1983).

For a long time, the fact that improvements in performance due to the presence of others – or, *social facilitation*, as it is known – were confined to tasks requiring simple repetitive or fast responses, and disappeared with activities that needed more careful or thoughtful action, remained a puzzle. Then Zajonc (1965, 1980) proposed an ingenious solution. He began by noting that the observed asymmetry between simple and complex tasks was by no means confined to humans. Bringing together data from a bewilderingly diverse range of species – including ants, chickens, cockroaches, fish, fruit flies, monkeys and, of course, humans – he argued that the simple versus complex task asymmetry had every appearance of being a universal law of social behaviour. To explain this consistency, Zajonc (1965) proposed that the presence of another member of the same species always had the effect of increasing an animal's arousal level (or drive), perhaps as an evolutionarily adapted response to prepare the organism for action (e.g. 'fight, flight, investigate'). According to classical learning theory (Spence, 1956), such increased drive should increase the likelihood of any well-learned or habitual response but *decrease* the probability of poorly learned or novel responses. Zajonc argued that the behaviour required for the successful completion of 'simple' tasks was of the former type since it usually involved some gross motor activity or very well-rehearsed mental processes. Hence, the drive induced by the presence of others should improve performance. On the other hand, 'complex' tasks, by definition, involve more complicated sequences of actions or less obvious cognitive strategies, none of which is likely to be well learned. In this case, then, the socially induced drive inhibits performance.

The scope and simplicity of Zajonc's (1965) theory proved an attractive combination and much of the next twenty years was devoted to testing, refining or reformulating it (e.g. Baron, 1986; Cottrell, 1972; Green and Gange, 1977; Guerin, 1986; Zajonc, 1980). Several difficulties soon emerged. First of all, the predicted effects of the mere presence of another were not always obtained. Other factors were often necessary to observe the classic social facilitation/inhibition effects (Guerin, 1986). This implied that the alleged drive-arousing properties of a conspecific might not be quite as universal as Zajonc had supposed. Second, even if arousal was involved in social facilitation, its origins seemed to be more complicated than Zajonc had assumed. Some argued that it was due to a concern with being evaluated by the other person (Cottrell, 1972), others suggested that it stemmed from the animal's difficulty in trying to monitor a potentially unpredictable conspecific (Guerin and Innes, 1982), while a third theory proposed that the increased drive was caused by the distraction inherent in attending both to the task and the 'other' (Baron, 1986). Third, the available physiological data were not very consistent with the drive explanation. The usual indicators of increased arousal (e.g. faster heartbeat, increased galvanic skin resistance) often did not respond predictably to the presence of another (Bond and Titus, 1983).

In addition to these problems, there was a growing sense that a 'drive' explanation was a rather impoverished account of social facilitation effects in humans because it tended to eschew cognitive–attentional factors and to overlook the social meaning implied by the presence of the other person (or persons). As a result, subsequent models of social facilitation/inhibition phenomena have moved away from a single biologically based explanation to more specific accounts based on higher-order psychological processes. Let us look at three of these more recent developments.

One idea, put forward by Monteil and Huguet (1999), rests on the hypothesis that, in so far as the presence of others is arousing, there should be a narrowing of the focus of attention (Easterbrook, 1959). Now, for very simple tasks such a narrowed focus might be beneficial since the relevant cues are few in number and easy to attend to. However, for more complex tasks, where several task features may require simultaneous attention, such 'tunnel vision' is likely to interfere with performance. To test this idea, Monteil and Huguet examined

171

the effect of the presence of someone else on performance in the Stroop (1935) task. This task involves the participant simply naming the colour of ink in which a word is written. As such, it clearly represents a 'simple' task within the conventional classification in the social facilitation literature. For some trials the word itself is either neutral or consistent with the ink colour (e.g. 'red' written in red ink). However, on key trials the meaning of the word is *in*consistent with the colour (e.g. 'green' written in red ink). Typically, response times are longer in these latter trials, presumably because of some semantic interference with the requested colour naming response. Monteil and Huguet (1999) found less interference when the Stroop task was performed in the presence of another person, particularly if that person was perceived to perform the same task slightly better. Apparently, the other person caused the participant to concentrate more closely on the required colour naming activity and somehow mentally to 'shut out' the potentially confusing effects of the word meanings. An intriguing aspect of these findings is that most analyses of the Stroop effect assume that attending to the word (rather than its colour) is the 'dominant' or habitual response. So Monteil and Huguet's finding that it is the non-dominant response (colour naming) that is socially facilitated is exactly contrary to the prediction from Zajonc's (1965) drive theory.

A second explanation for social facilitation phenomena suggests that people's performance in social tasks is determined by a combination of their own self-expectations and the potential for evaluation (through social comparison) implied by the presence of another person performing a similar task (Sanna, 1992; see chapter 3). Simple tasks should lead to high expectations, which are likely to be amplified by the evaluative presence of a social comparator; more difficult tasks may result in lowered expectations, which are then exaggerated further in co-action conditions. In two experiments, involving a vigilance task and a word association test, Sanna (1992) manipulated how well participants thought they had done in practice trials (poorly or well). Then, in the experiment proper, they undertook further trials alone or alongside someone else performing an identical task. As predicted, people's expectations as to how well they thought they would do (as generated by the practice feedback) strongly affected their actual performance. This was especially so for those in the co-action conditions,

172

who did particularly badly (or well) in the presence of another. For example, in the vigilance task, those in the 'low expectations' co-action condition made more than three times the number of errors than those in the 'high expectations' co-action condition. Interestingly, the same discrepancies in performance were not visible in other 'social performance' conditions where comparisons with the co-actor were impossible, thus preventing self-evaluations.

Are two heads better than one?

Towards the end of the nineteenth century, a French agricultural engineer called Max Ringelmann conducted a series of experiments designed to investigate the efficiency of various pulling techniques used in farming (Ringelmann, 1913; see Kravitz and Martin, 1986). In one of these experiments he asked agricultural students to pull horizontally on a rope that was connected to a dynamometer to record the force exerted. The students either pulled alone or in groups of various sizes. What Ringelmann discovered was that although, of course, the more people who pulled, the greater the force exerted, the force did not increase proportionately with the size of the group. Pulling on their own, the students managed to pull around 85 kg but when pulling in groups of seven they did not achieve anything like seven times that figure. In fact, they exerted a pull of around 450 kg, which is only about five times their average individual effort. Similarly, a 14-man group was able to achieve only just over 10 times the individual pull. Looked at another way, the groups appeared to be pulling at only 75 per cent of their full capacity. Somewhere along the line some of the individuals' combined strength seemed to have been dissipated.

This simple little experiment illustrates a number of the issues that crop up in research on group performance. How, for example, should one make the comparisons between individuals and groups? A straightforward comparison between the performance of individuals on their own and the combined product of a group of individuals will often yield the wholly unsurprising result that groups do better than individuals: Ringelmann's seven-man team pulled 450 kg; on average, an individual could manage less than 90 kg. Alternatively, one could hypothetically combine the performances of isolated individuals in some way (as if they were acting as a group), and compare that

173

Table 5.1 Problem solving by individuals and groups

	Problem 1	Problem 2	Problem 3
Individuals (*n* = 21)			
Proportion solving	0.14	0.00	0.095
Mean time taken (min)	4.50	9.90	15.50
Productivity (person-minutes)	4.50	9.90	15.50
Groups (*n* = 5 groups of 4)			
Proportion solving	0.60	0.60	0.40
Mean time taken (min)	6.50	16.90	18.30
Productivity (person-minutes)	26.00	67.60	73.20

Source: Shaw (1932)

pooled performance with the product of the real interacting group. This is what I did when I stated that Ringelmann's groups were only 75 per cent efficient: I computed what seven men *ought* to have been able to achieve (595 kg) and compared that to their *actual* performance (450 kg). This type of comparison between 'statisticized' and real groups is one of the most commonly used methods (Lorge et al., 1958; Hill, 1982). A third type of comparison is to take not the whole output from such statisticized groups, but merely the performance of their best members. For some kinds of tasks this test yields some interesting results, as we shall see. Finally, one may compute some measure of individual productivity: how much output per worker per unit time is being generated? In Ringelmann's experiment, as we saw, this appeared to decline as the size of the group increased.

Of all the kinds of tasks on which social psychologists have attempted to assess the relative performance of individuals and groups, those that involve some kind of logical problem solving have been the most popular. One of the earliest experiments was by Shaw (1932), who set her participants a number of reasoning problems to solve. Half worked on the problems individually, and half were allocated at random to four-person groups. Shaw observed whether or not the individuals and groups were able to solve the problems and how long they took. Her results from the first three problems are shown in table 5.1. Of the proportion of individuals and groups able to solve

174

the problems, the groups were superior (see the first row in each half of table 5.1). On two of the problems, three of the five groups were successful and on the third, two. This compares to three, zero and two individuals, respectively. However, the groups took a little longer on the task ('time taken' includes both successful and unsuccessful attempts). This difference, when translated into person-minutes, becomes quite substantial. In other words, if Shaw had been paying her participants by the minute to solve the problems, the group method of working would have proved much more expensive. But it is worth emphasizing again that, particularly on problem 2, at least for that extra money she would have obtained some correct solutions; none of the individuals working on that problem was able to come up with the answer.

Shaw (1932) did not compare her real groups with statisticized aggregates made up from combining individual performances. This was left to Marquart (1955), using very similar problems to those used by Shaw. As usual, half worked on the puzzles on their own, while the other half worked in groups. Just as Shaw had found, the groups were more likely to solve the problems although they took a little longer to do so. However, when Marquart randomly combined the individuals into hypothetical groups and examined how many of these statisticized groups would have solved the problems (i.e. how many contained a successful individual), she found no difference between their performance and that of the real interacting groups. The same technique was used in two experiments by Faust (1959), who set real and statisticized groups a series of seven problems to solve, four of which were spatial and the remainder verbal. On the spatial problems there was little difference between them, but on the verbal problems the real groups did better – significantly so in one experiment, marginally in the other.

Similar comparisons have been made in memory experiments. Perlmutter and de Montmollin (1952) asked their participants to learn some nonsense syllables and then tested their memory for these. Half of them did this task as individuals first and then in groups; for the other half, the sequence was reversed. The straightforward individual versus group comparison revealed that the groups recalled almost twice as much as the individuals although, at least on the early trials, they took a little longer about it. Such results do not seem to be

175

confined to the learning of nonsense syllables. Yuker (1955) tested people's memory for items in a short story and found that not only were groups superior to individuals on average, but also the group recall exceeded the initial recall of the 'best' individual in each group. Using the same short story, two studies by Stephenson and his colleagues confirmed these findings (Stephenson et al., 1986). They found that two- and four-person groups could remember more of the story than individuals. The groups were also more confident about the correctness of their answers, and this was true even when they got the answers wrong!

All the tasks considered so far have been of a convergent type where there has been an objectively right answer. How do groups fare on more open-ended activities, which call for creativity and imagination? One such task is 'brainstorming', an ideas-generating technique that is often used in business (Osborn, 1957). The essence of this technique is that people try to think up as many solutions as possible to the problem at hand. There should be no attempt at criticism or evaluation of the quality of these ideas; rather, participants are encouraged to free associate in response to previous suggestions. Intuitively, one might imagine that interacting groups ought to do very well at this kind of thing since they have a larger pool of original ideas to draw on, coupled with the mutual stimulation that group members should be able to generate. In fact, this turns out to be far from the case. Taylor et al. (1958) set individuals and groups (of four) to work on three brainstorming problems. While the interacting groups easily outshone the average individual in the number of ideas generated (by roughly 2:1), when those individuals were randomly formed into statisticized aggregates and the redundant ideas discarded, these statistical groups did far better than the real groups. On average, they produced around 68 novel ideas as compared to only 37 for the interacting groups. Furthermore, there was some evidence from a subsequent content analysis that this greater quantity was paralleled by superior quality also. These findings have been confirmed in other studies, which leads to the somewhat surprising conclusion that brainstorming is actually most beneficial when carried out initially in *private*, the interacting group then being used as a forum for combining and evaluating these individually produced ideas (Lamm and Trommsdorff, 1973; Mullen et al., 1991).

Potential and actual productivity: theories of group deficit

These findings on group performance present a rather confusing picture. Although groups seem to be generally superior in the simplest comparisons (i.e. groups versus average individual) when the performance of 'best' individuals or of statisticized groups is examined, the result often seems to go the other way, the extent of the deficit varying from task to task. One of the most influential attempts to bring some order to this complexity has been Steiner's (1972) theory of group productivity.

Steiner begins by proposing that a group's observed performance on a task will be determined by three factors: 'task demands', the 'resources' of the group and the 'process' by which the group interacts to accomplish the task. To understand what he means by these terms, it may be helpful to use and extend the culinary analogy, which he himself suggests. Imagine I am about to embark on the cooking of an elaborate dish. This is the *task* confronting me. Like as not, I will consult a recipe book, and there on the appropriate page I will find a description of the kind and quantity of ingredients needed, the various procedures required for their combination, and perhaps (if I am consulting a book guided by a particular culinary or nutritional philosophy) various rules to be followed in their preparation and cooking. All of these constitute the *task demands*.

Steiner suggests that the various kinds of tasks that groups have to undertake can be usefully classified according to a number of criteria. At the most basic level they may be *divisible* or *unitary*; that is, they can be divided into subtasks, each of which may be undertaken by a different person, or they are holistic tasks whose accomplishment is an 'all or none' affair. An example of a divisible task would be the manufacture of motor cars, where, since Henry Ford, the making of the finished vehicle is broken down into thousands of simple tasks performed on the assembly line. Another might be a collaborative learning exercise, where students are allocated to different tasks with a view to combining their efforts in some jointly produced project (see, for example, Aronson et al., 1978). Examples of unitary tasks would be Shaw's (1932) experiment, where the reasoning problems required some flash of insight for the answer and could not usefully be broken down into components. The second criterion for classifying

177

tasks is whether they are *maximizing* or *optimizing*. Does the task goal involve more quantity or speed (maximizing) or does it require the matching to some predetermined standard (optimizing)? Ringelmann's rope-pulling studies involved a maximizing task since the goal was to pull as hard as possible, whereas in Shaw's (1932) experiment the goal was to solve the problem (albeit as quickly as possible). Tasks may be *additive* (the contributions are simply added together as in brainstorming), *disjunctive* (where an either/or decision between different contributions is called for, e.g. reasoning problems), *conjunctive* (where everyone must complete the task, e.g. a group of mountaineers attempting a team conquest of a new peak) or *discretionary* (where groups can decide as they like how to accomplish the task).

If task demands constitute the recipe, then, to continue the analogy, *resources* are represented by the contents of my larder and my pretensions as a cook. As with task demands, resources will vary from task to task. In a tug-of-war presumably physical strength is at a premium, whereas in learning tasks people's short-term memory capacities are much more relevant. In a perfect world, the resources of the group would always be exactly matched to the task demands so that, in fact, the task can be successfully accomplished. Steiner proposes that this idealized scenario represents the maximum of *potential productivity* of the group. In our analogy it is, if you like, the glossy photograph in the recipe book, which shows me how the dish I am cooking should turn out.

The method of determining potential productivity depends on the nature of the task. Let us consider two simple cases, additive tasks and disjunctive tasks. With additive tasks, as we have seen, the group members' contributions are simply aggregated. Thus, the potential productivity of a group undertaking tasks like these is simply the sum of their maximum *individual* contributions. In the Ringelmann study the potential productivity of the seven-person team was around seven times the average individual person's pull capacity, i.e. 595 kg. Similarly, in Taylor et al.'s (1958) brainstorming study, since each individual could generate around twenty novel ideas a four-person group could theoretically produce eighty (assuming no redundancy between people).

For disjunctive tasks, the calculation of potential productivity is slightly more complex. Here, the solution is an all-or-none affair, and

Steiner suggests that it will be solved simply when one member of the group finds the answer. Hence, he proposes that the potential productivity for a disjunctive problem is equivalent to the probability of finding someone in the group who is able to solve it. To compute this one needs some idea of the prevalence of such people in the population from which your group is made up. Let us call that proportion P_i. From elementary probability theory it follows that the proportion of people in the population who *cannot* solve the problem is $1 - P_i$. Let us call that value Q. Knowing Q, as Lorge and Solomon (1955) pointed out, it is then possible to calculate the predicted probability that groups of any given size (n) will be able to solve the problem. Obviously, the larger the group, the more likely it is that it will contain someone who can solve the problem, and mathematically this can be expressed as $P_g = 1 - Q^n$. P_g is the expected proportion of groups able to solve the problem, and represents their potential productivity for that task. Let us quickly compute the potential productivity of Shaw's (1932) groups working on the first of her three problems. The proportion of individuals able to solve the problem was 0.14 (see table 5.1). Hence, Q, the proportion *unable* to solve the problem, is 0.86. It is then simple to work out that the potential productivity of her four-person groups is $1 - (0.86)^4 = 0.46$ (see Lorge and Solomon, 1955).[1] For the other tasks, the potential productivity figures are 0.0 and 0.33.

We now come to the crux of Steiner's theory. Just as the fruits of my labour in the kitchen almost always fail to match up to the picture in the recipe book, so Steiner proposes that a group's *actual productivity* (how it actually performs on the task) usually falls short of its potential productivity. This is, he says, because groups are seldom able to utilize their resources to the full; there are often losses due to processes within the group that impede the group's maximum attainment:

Actual Productivity = Potential Productivity minus losses due to faulty process. (Steiner, 1972, p. 9)

From this equation it is apparent that Steiner believes that, though groups can approach potential productivity in their performance, they can never actually exceed it.

179

What kinds of 'faulty process' are responsible for this failure of groups to achieve their potential? Some are straightforward to identify. In a tug-of-war, group members will find it difficult to synchronize their pulls perfectly and to pull along exactly the same line. Steiner calls this a problem of coordination and, as we saw from Ringelmann's results, such problems do appear to be real enough. It is likely that many of the drastic losses that occur in brainstorming groups can also be attributed to coordination problems, particularly those due to the difficulty of having to 'share the floor' with one's fellow group members. Since people cannot all speak at once – or, at least, not if their ideas are to be recorded – their production of ideas is somewhat 'blocked' by the other members of the group. No such blocking occurs for those generating their ideas on their own. Diehl and Stroebe (1987) showed that by systematically controlling the degree to which people could speak freely (e.g. in one condition participants were only allowed to speak when a light indicated that the floor was 'free') they could reliably alter the productivity of their brainstorming groups. Conditions in which there was 'blocking', whether naturally occurring or artificially introduced, yielded productivity figures of less than half of the 'unblocked' conditions.

Another source of faulty group process may be the social dynamics among the group members. Staying with the brainstorming example, it is likely that members of the real groups were affected by social comparison processes (see chapter 3) and monitored their output so as not to be too far out of line with the others (Paulus and Dzindolet, 1993). Indeed, giving people a higher comparison target to aim at, or even merely telling them that their scores will be compared against an (as yet undisclosed) standard, reliably improves their brainstorming performance (Paulus and Dzindolet, 1993; Szymanski and Harkins, 1987). It is also possible that participants in brainstorming groups feel inhibited from expressing some of their more bizarre or antisocial ideas out of embarrassment. Diehl and Stroebe (1987) found that having groups undertake the task apparently under the watchful eye of their peers or 'expert' judges produced markedly fewer ideas than those doing it alone.

So far, we have only considered examples of 'process loss', where the group has fallen well short of what it might have been expected to achieve. However, some of the studies considered earlier indicate that these losses can sometimes be minimal. In Marquart's (1955) and Faust's (1959) studies of problem solving, for example, there was little difference between real and statisticized groups, suggesting that once the correct answer became available in the group it was instantly recognized by the others. In Perlmutter and de Montmollin's (1952) memory experiment also, there were negligible process losses. Hoppe (1962) re-analysed their results by comparing their obtained group recall scores with those predicted by the Lorge–Solomon formula. He also ran a replication study of his own. In both sets of data the fit between the predicted and observed results was very close indeed, indicating that a group *is* sometimes able to utilize the pooled memories of its members efficiently.

Steiner's (1972) theory mainly emphasizes process losses due to problems that the group members may have in coordinating their activities or that arise from social influence processes within the group. There is another source of decrement which he identifies and that concerns motivation; perhaps people do not try as hard in a group as they do alone. Such a conclusion is suggested by some research by Ingham et al. (1974), which is one of only two published replications of Ringelmann's (1913) rope-pulling study. Having first replicated Ringelmann's results that groups do not pull as hard as the sum of their individual constituents, they modified the procedure slightly. Instead of using real groups to pull on the rope on each trial, they employed one naive participant and a number of confederates. Unknown to the real participant, who was always in the first position on the rope, the confederates had been instructed only to *pretend* to pull on the rope while making realistic grunts indicating physical exertion. In this way, Ingham et al. were able to construct 'pseudo-groups' of different sizes. Any decrement in pull from the real participant could only be attributable to motivation losses since no coordination losses could possibly exist. The results indicated that such a drop in motivation did indeed seem to occur (see figure 5.1).

A similar drop in effort on another kind of additive task was observed by Latané et al. (1979). They asked individuals and groups of different sizes to shout as loudly as they could and recorded the amount of noise produced. In line with Steiner's theory, they found that actual productivity did not match potential productivity. Groups of two performed at only 71 per cent of their individual capacity,

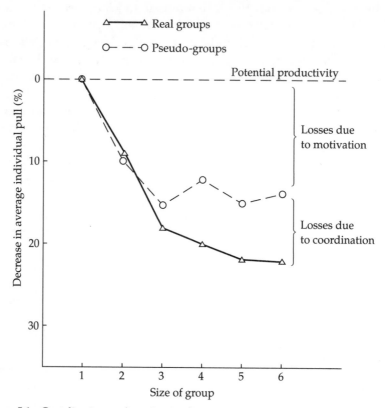

Figure 5.1 Coordination and motivation losses in group rope-pulling (from Ingham et al., 1974)

while a six-person group could only manage 40 per cent of their potential. Then, borrowing from Ingham et al. (1974), Latané et al. (1979) created 'pseudo-groups' to eliminate coordination losses. Participants were blindfolded and wore headphones playing constant 'white noise' so that they could neither see nor hear the others whom they were alleged to be shouting with. When told they were shouting with other people, their subjects still shouted less than when they believed they were on their own (at 82 per cent capacity for the 'groups' of two, 74 per cent for the 'groups' of six). These figures are an improvement on the real groups but still fall short of the potential productivity figure, indicating once again a lack of effort simply as a function of believing that one is doing a task with others. Similar results have been found with other tasks (e.g. Kerr and Bruun, 1981; Harkins and Petty, 1982; Harkins and Szymanski, 1989).

Latané et al. (1979) dubbed this slackening of effort in groups 'social loafing' and explained it in terms of Latané's (1981) social impact theory, described in chapter 4. They argue that the major source of influence in group performance experiments is the experimenter's instructions. When these are directed solely towards an individual then they will have maximum impact. With groups, on the other hand, the theory suggests that the impact of the instructions is 'divided' between the group members with corresponding reductions in output. According to the theory, as group size increases so impact *decreases*, corresponding to some power function (as discussed in chapter 4). Consistent with this account, most of the group size effects on productivity do seem to conform to the typical negatively accelerating power function curve (see Steiner, 1972; and figure 5.1, for example).[2] Thus, like Steiner's (1972) theory, social impact theory is essentially a theory of group *deficits* in performance. It presumes that, though steps can be taken to reduce social loafing (e.g. by making people's contributions to the group task more identifiable; see Williams et al., 1981), at the end of the day individual effort on collective tasks will never surpass solo efforts.

Social loafing certainly seems to be a pervasive phenomenon, at least on the mundane tasks and with the ad hoc groups that are commonly used in social psychologists' laboratories. Karau and Williams (1993) found 78 studies that had included comparisons of people working alone and collectively. Of these comparisons, nearly 80 per cent indicated the existence of some loafing, a highly significant overall effect. Nevertheless, in a careful analysis of the many factors that have been incorporated into such experiments, Karau and Williams (1993) identified several conditions in which social loafing is eliminated, and some, indeed, that provide hints that an inverse effect can be observed – what we might call *social labouring* (i.e. greater effort on group tasks). In Karau and Williams' (1993) meta-analysis the two key factors promoting social labouring were the importance of the task and the significance of the group to its members. When these were high, people seemed to work harder collectively than alone. Other variables that seemed to reduce loafing, if not actually to reverse it, were the opportunity for the group to be evaluated and the culture in which the study was carried out (there was generally less loafing in Eastern cultures). These qualifications to the general social loafing effect are important because they represent a direct challenge to the theories of group deficit that we have just considered. In effect, they suggest that process losses in groups may not be inevitable and that Steiner's (1972) equation linking actual and potential productivity should be amended to include 'process gains' (Hackman and Morris, 1975; Shaw, 1976). With such a formulation, if the gains outweighed the losses then the group could exceed its potential performance. In the next section, I want to consider the mounting evidence that now supports the validity of this idea.

Two heads really can be better than one: the benefits of working in groups

The two theoretical accounts of group productivity which we have considered so far – Steiner's (1972) and Latané's (1981) – both have a rather individualistic conception of human activity in group settings. For Steiner (1972), the performance of an isolated individual is always used as the 'benchmark' against which to measure behaviour in the group: although one can combine with one's fellow group members in various ways (according to the nature of the task), ultimately these co-workers are an impedance to the fulfilment of the group's true potential. Similarly, in Latané's (1981) view, the individual seems to be regarded as an 'effort economizer', looking to get away with the minimum exertion consistent with achieving some adequate level of group output. A similar emphasis is visible in those explanations that regard group productivity as a type of social dilemma in which individuals pursue their self-interests (of maximizing gains for minimum costs) in ways that are antithetical to the common good (Kerr, 1983; Shepperd, 1993). According to such perspectives, the solution to 'productivity loss' in groups lies in increasing the individual incentives for contributing while simultaneously decreasing the costs of doing so (Shepperd, 1993).

There is no doubt that for some kinds of group tasks such individualistic analyses are appropriate. It would be foolish to deny that personal motives and incentives play a part in determining how people will behave as group members. Nevertheless, such explanations over-look the possibility that people's motivation can be *socially* derived or that groups can provide 'added value' by combining individual con-tributions in ways that are not predictable from any prior assessment of them in a social vacuum. There are three lines of evidence leading in this direction: research that has examined different kinds of tasks than those typically used in group performance experiments; work that has studied the effects of working in groups that are psychologic-ally significant for their members; and investigations of the effect of different cultural values on individual and collective productivity.

First, we should note that the majority of research supporting the 'group deficit' point of view has employed rather trivial tasks, which are unlikely to have been very involving for the participants. Examples include clapping, shouting, brainstorming new uses for everyday objects, monitoring TV screens for the appearance of random visual signals, pumping air with a hand-held rubber bulb and rope pulling (Karau and Williams, 1993). Moreover, on few of these tasks was there any scope for correcting or complementing other people's con-tributions because the tasks were usually of an additive and maxim-izing nature, often requiring a very simple response. Faced with the prospect of undertaking such activities, perhaps it is not surprising that participants often did not feel greatly motivated to work any harder collectively than they did on their own. But what might hap-pen with more complex, and hence more involving, tasks, especially those that seem to call for some integration of the group members' contributions? The evidence from several different quarters all suggests that this has a facilitatory effect on group performance.

Let us begin with two studies we have already discussed: the experiments by Shaw (1932) and Faust (1959). In Shaw's experiment, the proportions of groups actually solving the three problems were 0.60, 0.60 and 0.40 (see table 5.1). As we then saw, the potential group productivity figures for these same three problems – based on the number of successful individuals – were 0.46, 0.0 and 0.33, respect-ively. In other words, on all three problems the *actual* proportions exceeded the theoretical maxima. Lorge and Solomon (1955) calcu-lated that the first and last differences were not significant but that the second *was*. Here, then, is one example of groups exceeding their potential productivity: on their own, no single individual could solve problem 2, yet three of the groups were successful. Similarly, Faust (1959) found that in one of his experiments his real groups outperformed his 'nominal' groups on a series of verbal problems. Shaw and Ashton (1976) found further evidence for what they called 'assembly bonus effects' using a crossword puzzle task. On simple puzzles, there was no difference between the observed and predicted performance, but with a more difficult puzzle the groups did significantly better than expected from the individual performance data. In all these experiments, there seems to have been some process in the group whereby group members have been able to facilitate each other's performance. Note that in all three of these experiments the group task was cognitively quite challenging and there was the possibility of amending or adding to the partial solutions afforded by others (see also Brickner et al., 1986; Harkins and Petty, 1982).

People can also be encouraged to surpass their individual efforts if they perceive that their co-worker in the joint task is, for some reason, less able than them to perform effectively. In such cases, people may feel they have to compensate for their collaborator in order for the group to do well. Once again, for such social compensation to occur it is important that the group members perceive the task to be sufficiently significant for them to care about the group outcome. Williams and Karau (1991) showed this with a brainstorming task which, for half the participants, was made out to be an important cognitive task related to intelligence; the remainder, on the other hand, were led to believe (somewhat more veridically) that it was a rather trivial task, and no mention was made of any association with intelligence. These different perceptions were bolstered by the verbal and non-verbal behaviour of the experimental assistants running the study. In addition, half the participants undertook the task with someone (actually a confederate of the experimenter) who professed to be 'not very good' or 'really good' at brainstorming tasks. In these ways, both task meaningfulness and partner ability were manipulated. Then, in the usual way, half of the participants performed the task under 'co-action' conditions, in which the ideas of each person generated were to be separately identifiable; the rest worked collectively, simply pooling their ideas. The results showed that for those in the non-meaningful task condition, social loafing was the order of the day, regardless of their partner's perceived ability. When the task was made to seem

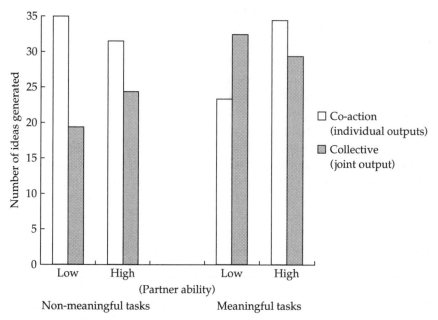

Figure 5.2 Social compensation on meaningful tasks when working with a 'low ability' partner (from Williams and Karau, 1991, table 3, experiment 3)

important, on the other hand, those who were teamed up with a 'low ability' person worked significantly harder in the collective task condition than in the mere co-action condition (see figure 5.2).

The compensation observed by Williams and Karau (1991) was by the 'superior' group member; he or she worked hard to 'make up for' the apparent deficiencies of the partner. However, it is also possible that for some kinds of tasks – particularly those involving physical persistence – the 'less able' co-workers may raise their output to the level of the highest performer, provided that that level is not too discrepant from their own. Underlying this upward movement of the lower performers could be a social comparison process (Stroebe et al., 1996). Recall from chapter 3 that Festinger (1954) speculated that there are pressures for uniformity in a group – in both opinion and ability – and that there is also a unidirectional drive upwards in most groups. Thus, lower-ability group members may be motivated to match the performance of their slightly superior peers, with a resultant increase in the overall group output. Where group members are too different

187

in ability, or too similar, this upward matching is less likely to occur. As noted in chapter 3, such a phenomenon was observed by Köhler (1926, 1927; see Witte, 1989; Stroebe et al., 1996). Köhler had members of a rowing club repeatedly lift heavy weights until they were exhausted. They did this alone, in pairs and in groups of three. The groups were arranged in such a way that they were composed of rowers of equal strength or of unequal strengths (in varying degrees). When the rowers' strengths were within 60–80 per cent of each other, the groups' output exceeded the sum of the individuals' outputs – a significant performance increment – but when their strengths were more disparate than this, or more equal, the groups tended to perform below potential, just as Ringelmann (1913) had observed a few years earlier. These results have been largely replicated by Stroebe et al. (1996), whose analyses make it clear that the increased group output was mainly due to the raised performance of the 'weaker' group member.

These different forms of social compensation may have important practical implications for education. They suggest that if learning tasks are organized into cooperative activities where several students are interdependent on one another for the achievement of a group goal, then a mix of abilities within that learning group may not be detrimental for effective performance. This might be particularly useful where students with learning disabilities are being integrated into mainstream schools, since it will allow them to participate more fully in the normal classroom activity instead of always being segregated into special classes. There is some evidence that such group learning techniques can benefit both mainstream children and those with disabilities. Armstrong et al. (1981) found that a four-week period of cooperative learning in an American elementary school benefited *both* groups of children: mainstream and learning-disabled students completed more assignments when organized into cooperative groups than when they learned on their own in the traditional way.

The second body of evidence that challenges the 'group deficit' perspective on group performance comes from research examining the effects of making the task group more salient for its members. Note that the bulk of studies that have found performance losses have employed groups that were purely ad hoc affairs. Typically, there is little or no interaction among the group members, there is no expectation of any future interaction as a group, and often there is no explicit group goal to try to attain. The absence of all these factors means that there is little possibility that the members of the groups will develop any identification with their group. In other words, psychologically speaking, most group performance studies have used physical aggregates rather than meaningful social groups. Why might this neglect be important? One answer comes from social identity theory (Tajfel and Turner, 1986; see chapter 8). Social identity theory assumes that a significant part of people's self-conceptions – their sense of who they are and what they are worth – derives from their group memberships. The theory goes on to assume that the social standing of these groups – how well they seem to be doing or how favourably they are viewed by others – is reflected in people's self-evaluations. Furthermore, since people are thought generally to prefer a positive rather than a negative view of themselves, this means that they will be motivated to find ways of enhancing their ingroup's status. Thus, in the context of the present discussion, it should mean that they will work harder on behalf of their ingroup if, by so doing, they can improve the position of that group relative to others.

The first intimation that this might be so came from an experiment by Harkins and Szymanski (1989). Using the by now familiar brainstorming task, they compared the performance of those who believed that their individual output would be monitored with those who thought that only the pooled group output was of interest. Crossed with this manipulation was the presence or absence of some comparison standard. Half of the participants were told that their performance would be compared against some criterion – either the average of 'other individuals' *or* the average of 'other groups' – while for the remainder no comparison was mentioned. The performance of the pooled group who believed they were to be compared with other groups was particularly interesting. According to social identity theory, such an explicit intergroup contrast should have heightened their (albeit mild) identification with their task group and motivated them to work harder for it. So it transpired: the output from these participants was the highest of all the conditions, even slightly (if not significantly) higher than the condition that social impact theory would have predicted would be most antithetical to social loafing (i.e. individual scores with an inter-individual comparison). Similar results were obtained by James and Greenberg (1989) using a real-life inter-group comparison between two universities.

Other findings underlining the importance of social identity for performance soon emerged. Perhaps the clearest came from an experiment by Worchel et al. (1998). In this study everyone first worked on an individual task (in this case, making paper chains), which provided a baseline against which to measure their performance on the same task when they worked as a group. Half the participants worked on their group task in the presence of another group, which, it was assumed, would heighten ingroup identification; the remainder worked only with their ingroup. In addition, for half the participants the salience of the group identity was heightened by giving the group(s) a name and having all the members of the ingroup wear the same coloured laboratory coat, which in the 'outgroup present' condition was a different colour from that worn by the outgroup. The remaining participants simply all wore different coloured coats. The results were clear cut: people worked consistently harder when there was an outgroup present, and they worked hardest of all when they were all wearing the same uniform but different from the outgroup (see figure 5.3). The pattern of results was particularly intriguing since there was clear evidence of social labouring (i.e. *increments* over the individual performance baseline) in a group task where no individual output was monitorable and where the group members were least identifiable (because they were all wearing the same coloured coats) (see also Karau and Hart, 1998). This is directly contrary to what social impact theory (and other individualistic accounts) would have predicted.

The third challenge to the assumption that group work inevitably involves some performance loss comes from cross-cultural psychology. As Smith and Bond (1993) warn, the fact that the vast majority of social psychological research findings emanate from Western industrialized cultures should lead us to be cautious about assuming that they are universally applicable. This warning is as apt for group performance research as it is for other fields; in Karau and Williams' (1993) comprehensive review, only 10 per cent of the data set involved non-Western participants. This cultural imbalance may be particularly important because it coincides with a difference in value systems,

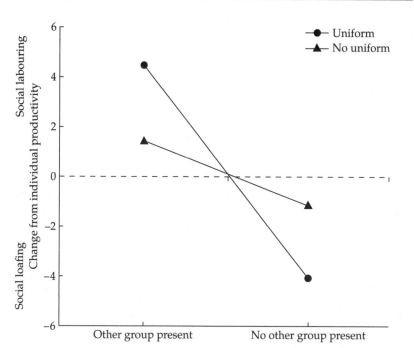

Figure 5.3 Mean difference in productivity change as a function of presence of an outgroup and wearing a group uniform (from Worchel et al., 1998, figure 3. Copyright © The British Psychological Society)

which has crucial implications for comparisons of individual and group productivity. It is well known that many Eastern cultures place considerable emphasis on collectivist values (Hofstede, 1980; Triandis, 1989). People in such collectivist cultures tend to feel very attached to their various ingroups (e.g. family, workgroup, village etc.), to define their aspirations and achievements in terms of these groups' outcomes, and hence to adopt a cooperative attitude to other ingroup members. In contrast, as we know, people in individualist cultures usually wish to preserve at least some independence from the group, and are inclined to pursue their own individual goals, often by competing with others. The implications of this collectivism–individualism distinction for working in group settings seem clear: in so far as the group has a well-defined task goal, this is more likely to be internalized and acted upon by collectivists than individualists, with the result that

191

performance decrements for the former (e.g. due to social loafing) should be the exception rather than the rule.

The evidence certainly seems to point that way. Matsui et al. (1987) asked individual and pairs of Japanese students to set themselves a performance goal for a simple number cancellation task. They then performed the task under conditions in which the best individuals (or pairs) would be rewarded. The pairs exceeded the goals they had set themselves (by about 6 per cent) while the individuals just failed to reach their targets (falling short by nearly 2 per cent). As a result, the output per person from the pairs was significantly higher than that of the individuals. Studies that have directly compared individual and group productivity across cultures have reinforced the role of collectivism–individualism in affecting group performance. In two studies, Earley (1989, 1993), using a more realistic office simulation task, found that managers and trainee managers in Israel and the People's Republic of China (two collectivist societies) worked harder in groups than they did alone; American managers, on the other hand, showed the usual social loafing effect. In the second of these studies, Earley (1993) included an additional group manipulation, whether the group with whom the participants believed they were working was from the same region as them and had many shared interests *or* was from a different region with whom they had little in common. This 'ingroup'–'outgroup' manipulation had a marked effect in the two collectivist samples (China and Israel), with people working reliably less hard in the 'outgroup' condition. In the more individual-ist American sample the same manipulation had no effect at all (see figure 5.4). Gabrenya et al. (1985) also found social labouring in Taiwanese children while American children on the same task ex-hibited social loafing (although cf. Gabrenya et al. (1983) for evidence of loafing in Taiwan).

In summary, then, as social psychologists have widened the scope of their investigations to include more complex tasks, or to involve groups with more significance for their members, especially in cul-tures with a strong collectivist orientation, it has become apparent that deficits in group performance and motivation are by no means inevitable. When what we are doing and who we are doing it with matter enough to us, we will work harder for our groups than we will ever do on our own.

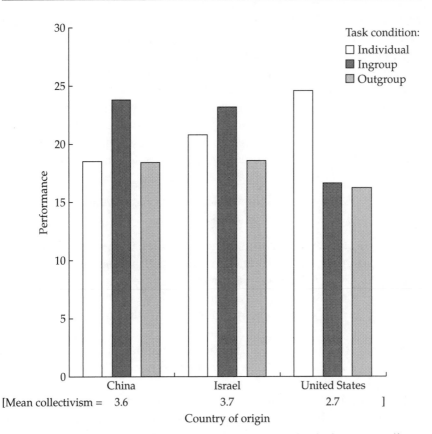

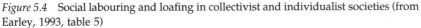

Figure 5.4   Social labouring and loafing in collectivist and individualist societies (from Earley, 1993, table 5)

Group Decision Making

Most of the tasks with which we have been concerned so far in this chapter have been ones for which there is some well-defined outcome: performance was measured as the ability to solve some logical puzzle, correctly recall some material or produce as large an output as possible. But many tasks that groups undertake in everyday life are not at all like this. Consider a family deciding where to go on holiday this year, a group of students trying to choose a topic for a cooperative learning project or a jury attempting to reach a verdict in a court case. In all of these (and countless other) examples of collective decision making there is no one objectively verifiable answer or unequivocal optimum performance. Rather, what the groups are faced with is making a choice among various options, each of which may have some subjectively perceived merit. Thus, in studying group judgements of this kind the question is not, as it was in the previous section, 'are individuals or groups superior?', but the more general problem, 'what is the relationship between individual opinions and the consensual view expressed by the group?'. Having once established that relationship, we can then investigate the social psychological processes that might underlie it.

Modelling group decisions: social decision schemes theory

In several of the comparisons between actual and potential productivity in the previous section we made use of a simple mathematical model to predict the potential productivity (e.g. assume the group can solve the problem if at least one member can; calculate the probability of finding such a person in the group). When actual productivity failed to match this, the presumption was that some factor had interfered with the operation of this 'ideal' model. Usually we are only able to guess what that factor might be and hence speculate about the actual process by which the group arrived at its answer. This imprecision, though undesirable, is understandable. Direct observation of groups at work can be difficult and, as seen in chapter 2, often produces quite complex data, which may be difficult to interpret. A way round this difficulty has been proposed by Davis and a number of others (Davis, 1973; Laughlin, 1980; Stasser et al., 1989a). Essentially, the method used by these theorists is to conduct a number of 'thought experiments' in which one imagines all the various ways groups might approach making a particular decision. These are formulated mathematically as different 'decision rule' models. One then feeds into these models some assumptions about the abilities or dispositions of people to make the decision. These may be hypothetical or they may be based on some previously collected data on the distribution of individual abilities or opinions. Through the application of some quite complex mathematical techniques, one then computes the probable outcomes from the different models. These hypothetical outcomes are compared to the actual results from some real sample groups. The

Table 5.2 Hypothetical possibilities of group solution under different decision rules

	Type of group composition										Theoretical probabilities of reaching
	Y_1	Y_1	Y_1	Y_1	Y_1	Y_1	Y_2	Y_2	Y_2	Y_3	
	Y_1	Y_1	Y_1	Y_2	Y_2	Y_3	Y_2	Y_2	Y_3	Y_3	
Type of decision rule	Y_1	Y_2	Y_3	Y_2	Y_3	Y_3	Y_2	Y_3	Y_3	Y_3	correct solution
Truth wins (TW)	+	+	+	+	+	+	–	–	–	–	0.6
Majority rule (M)	+	+	+	+	+	–	–	–	–	–	0.5
Unanimous verdict (UV)	+	+	–	+	–	–	–	–	–	–	0.3

+, Group solves problem.
–, Group fails to solve problem.

decision model which best 'fits' the observed pattern of data is then presumed to be the one that the groups used.

A very simple example will help to illustrate how this modelling paradigm works. The actual models and techniques used by social decision scheme theorists are actually far more complex than this, but the basic principles are not too dissimilar. Imagine a three-person group attempting to reach a decision on a problem with a right/wrong answer. Suppose, for the sake of argument, there are three types of person in the population: people who are able to solve the problem (Y_1), people who cannot solve it but who can recognize the correct solution when they see it (Y_2), and people who can neither solve it nor recognize the correct solution (Y_3). There are, of course, many other types of person imaginable. What are the various combinations of these three types of person that could occur in a three-person group? There are ten in all, as shown in the column headings to table 5.2. Now think of various ways that the group might come to a decision about the solution of the problem. Let us take three common rules that operate in groups (again, many others are possible): truth wins (TW) (i.e. a demonstrably correct solution will always prevail), majority rule (M) (i.e. a majority has to agree on the solution) and unanimous verdict (UV) (i.e. everyone must agree on the solution). Then determine whether each of the ten permutations of group members could or could not solve the problem under each of the three decision rules we have supposed might be operating. These are indicated by a plus or minus sign in table 5.2. We then have to make some assumptions about the distribution of our three types of people in the population, and also about the likely composition of our groups. To keep matters simple, I have assumed for this example that the three types are equally distributed throughout the population and also that the groups have been randomly formed. This implies that each of the ten group compositions will occur equally often. Again, we do not need to make such (probably rather unrealistic) assumptions, but other hypothetical distributions would complicate the example undesirably. It is now a simple matter to compute the theoretically predicted probabilities of reaching a solution under each of the decision rules. (For TW six out of the ten permutations solve the problem, so the probability is 0.6, and so on.) Notice that at this stage we have not actually observed a single live group in action. All the work has been done on paper or, rather, in a computer. It is only now that we go out and conduct the experiment with randomly formed groups of three persons. Suppose we employ 100 groups and observe that 59 of them are able to solve the problem. This gives us an 'observed' probability of solution of 0.59. The decision rule that produced the hypothetical probability closest to this figure was TW (= 0.6), and so we conclude that this is the group process that governs the solution to this particular problem.

One of the first attempts to use this modelling approach was by Davis and Restle (1963). They were interested to discover how groups went about solving logical problems that contained a number of steps. The two most likely models, they believed, were a *hierarchical* one, in which the most able members dominate the group and the less competent ones are excluded, and an *'equalitarian'* model, in which all members interact more or less equally, whether or not they are contributing effectively. The results strongly supported the second model: the observed data were very close to those predicted mathematically by the equalitarian process model, and the observational and sociometric data that were also collected seemed to support this too. What this experiment seemed to show, therefore, was that reason and logic do not always prevail in problem-solving groups.

This conclusion is reinforced by a series of modelling experiments by Laughlin and his associates (Laughlin, 1980). In these experiments,

196

usually six or more hypothetical decision schemes were tested against the results from actual problem-solving groups. For the kind of intellectual tasks we have been considering, one decision scheme consistently seemed to provide the closest fit with the observed data. That is what Laughlin calls the 'truth supported wins' model. In other words, the right answer will prevail in a group only if at least two members advocate it. In the three-person group of our very simple example in table 5.2, this also corresponds to the majority rule model. A single person suggesting the right answer (truth wins) is markedly less effective. The only exceptions to this conclusion seem to be for rather small groups (of two or three people) tackling difficult problems. Here, the TW model seems to apply rather better (Egerbladh, 1981).

However, once one moves away from decision-making tasks where there is a demonstrably correct answer then the decision rule that seems to prevail is some kind of majority verdict (Laughlin, 1996). For example, Davis et al. (1974) asked individuals and groups to rate the attractiveness of various monetary bets, in which the probability of winning was varied systematically. Although the groups were instructed to reach a unanimous decision (and many of the groups believed that this was what they had actually done), the hypothetical decision scheme that best fitted the actual data was a majority rule, i.e. the group went along with the bet advocated by most of the group. Majority decisions also seem to characterize other group judgements involving the expression of some collective attitude and decisions made by juries (e.g., Davis, 1992; Davis et al., 1975; Kerr et al., 1975).

How do individual and group decisions differ?

Until about 1960 the conventional wisdom was that a group opinion corresponded roughly to the average of the opinions of its constituent members. This common-sense view was undoubtedly influenced by the theory and research on conformity processes (in their heyday in the 1950s), which, as we saw in chapter 4, strongly suggested that group members are liable to converge on some agreed or normative position when asked to make a collective judgement. Thus, it was thought, a board of directors comprised of a number of people with varying views on the future direction of their company would compromise around the 'middle road'. Some even argued that such compromises usually resulted in rather cautious and unadventurous business decisions (Whyte, 1956).

Given this climate of opinion, perhaps it is not surprising that a series of experiments claiming that just the opposite was the case should have had such an impact on the field of group dynamics. The first of these – probably one of the most famous unpublished experiments in the history of social psychology – was by Stoner (1961), and, ironically enough, in view of Whyte's (1956) conclusions about the health of American corporations, it involved business students. Stoner asked his participants individually to make some judgements about some hypothetical social dilemmas. Each of these dilemmas involved someone having to make a choice between two courses of action, one of which (with the more desirable outcome) involved a higher degree of risk than the other. One of the dilemmas used was as follows: 'An electrical engineer may stick with his present job at a modest but adequate salary, or may take a new job offering considerably more money but no long-term security'. The participants were asked to judge the lowest acceptable level of risk for them to advise the main character in the scenario to give the riskier alternative a try. Participants were then randomly formed into groups and asked to reach a unanimous decision on each of the dilemmas they had considered individually. Stoner found to his surprise that these group decisions were nearly always riskier than the average of the individual group member pre-discussion decisions. These results were quickly replicated by Wallach et al. (1962), who also established that these shifts in group opinion became internalized because they reappeared when people were asked once more for their individual opinions *after* the group discussion. It was clear that these group decisions were *not* simply the average or compromise of the individual group members' initial positions; apparently, groups were willing to entertain greater risks collectively than they would as individuals.

In the several hundred studies that followed these two experiments, three other factors also became clear. The first was that the so-called 'shift to risk' that had been identified should more properly be called a 'shift to extremity'. Several experiments found that on some dilemmas groups regularly made more cautious or conservative choices than individuals (e.g. Stoner, 1968; Fraser et al., 1971). In other words, groups seem to shift away from the 'neutral' point of the scale towards the

198

pole initially favoured by the average of the individual choices. This polarization phenomenon (as it is now known) has proved to be remarkably general and robust, having been obtained in a wide variety of subject populations (Myers and Lamm, 1976). The second conclusion to emerge from the explosion of group decision-making research set off by Stoner was that the size of the group polarization shift was correlated with the average individual initial position on the scale (Teger and Pruitt, 1967). In other words, far from being constrained either statistically (by 'floor' or 'ceiling' effects) or psychologically (by wishing to appear moderate), the more extreme a group is to begin with, the more extreme it seems to become. The third important finding was that polarization effects are by no means limited to the choice dilemmas devised by Wallach et al. (1962). Moscovici and Zavalloni (1969) asked French school students to state individually their attitudes towards President de Gaulle and the United States. They were then formed into groups and the resulting consensually agreed attitudes showed evidence of polarization. Beforehand, their attitudes had been favourable towards de Gaulle and negative to the USA; in the groups they became even more pro-Gaullist and, somewhat less strongly, rather more anti-American. Similar attitude polarization effects were found by Doise (1969) and by Stephenson and Brotherton (1975). Polarization has also been observed in a variety of other domains including jury decision making, gambling decisions, estimates of auto-kinetic movements and judgements of physical attractiveness (Myers and Lamm, 1976; Isenberg, 1986). All in all, therefore, there are ample grounds for believing that polarization is a pervasive consequence of group interaction.

There is one cautionary qualification that needs to be added, however. This is that almost all the studies on which these conclusions are based were conducted in laboratory settings with ad hoc groups in which the decision-making task was a novel one and – even more importantly – in which the outcome was almost always hypothetical. The decisions seldom had any real consequences, either for those making them or for some other party. On those rare occasions when real decision-making groups have been studied, polarization has not always been much in evidence. Semin and Glendon (1973), for example, gained access to a job evaluation committee in a medium-sized business. The purpose of this committee was to decide on the grading of different jobs in the firm, which had direct implications for the status and pay of the incumbents of those jobs. Before the committee met, each member was required to allocate points to the jobs under consideration along a number of dimensions. During the committee deliberations, the individual ratings were made known to the other committee members and, after discussion, a committee recommendation was made on the point grading of each job. The procedure was thus almost an exact replica of the standard laboratory procedure. However, unlike groups in the laboratory, Semin and Glendon (1973) observed no polarization whatsoever in their decisions. After 28 decisions over a year, the average job evaluation made by the committee was virtually identical to the mean evaluations of the individual committee members.

On the other hand, Walker and Main (1973) analysed the judgements of American Federal judges, made alone or by a bench of three judges, and found that the collective and individual decisions differed markedly. Of the 400 or so cases tried by trios of judges, 65 per cent could be classified as libertarian, whereas only 30 per cent of the 1500 cases tried by single judges could be so classified. Clement and Sullivan (1970) also observed polarization among seminar groups of students trying to decide on what method of assessment should be used to evaluate their performance on a psychology course. Initially, they had a preference for a relatively conservative method, a tendency which became exaggerated after discussion with their fellow students.

An explanation for these discrepancies has been suggested by Semin and Glendon (1973). They point out that what distinguishes most real decision-making bodies from ad hoc laboratory groups is that the former are usually much more permanent affairs; they have a history and a future, while laboratory groups have only a transient existence. This means that they are much more likely to develop an internal structure (e.g. designated officers), adopt conventional procedures (e.g. written agendas) and establish norms about the decision issues, all of which might inhibit any 'natural' polarization from appearing. In this respect, the judges in Walker and Main's (1973) study, although they were certainly real-life groups, actually were rather more like laboratory groups in that they came together for only a single case and then disbanded. It may also be the case that polarization is more likely to occur in the early stages of a group's life or when it is confronted with a relatively novel or unusual situation. The groups in the studies that found no polarization had been extant for some time and also had considerable experience of the issues that they were deliberating. The same can hardly be said of a group of participants in a typical group decision-making experiment. Whatever the explanation for these anomalies between 'natural' and 'laboratory' groups, one thing is clear: group dynamics badly needs further research in which field and experimental methodologies are pursued in parallel.

Explanations of group polarization

Pushing the caveat about the possible unrepresentativeness of most group decision-making research to the back of our minds for the moment, how are polarization phenomena best explained? There are currently three main approaches to this question.

Polarization through comparison

One answer is provided by an extension of Festinger's (1954) social comparison theory (see chapters 3 and 4). Two prominent advocates of this approach have been Sanders and Baron (1977). According to them, polarization occurs in the following way: associated with any issue on which a group must reach a decision are likely to be a number of social values (e.g. caring for others, being adventurous, not taking risks with one's health, and so on). Taken together, these values will result in an initial social preference towards one decision outcome rather than another. Each individual, before the group discussion, will probably perceive him/herself as being somewhat further towards this socially desirable outcome than his/her peers (Codol, 1975). Once the group discussion gets under way – thereby heightening the salience of the relevant social values – some of these individuals discover that this was a misperception because there are others who endorse positions further towards the socially valued pole than them. The outcome of this social comparison is that they will then shift further in this direction in order to present themselves in a more favourable light. This is rather akin to the 'unidirectional drive upward' process, which Festinger suggested occurs in people's ability comparisons (see chapter 3). There will, of course, be some who find themselves already further towards the socially desirable extreme than most others in the group but, although conformity pressures may modify their opinion somewhat, they will have less reason to shift than their colleagues who are on the other ('wrong') side of the modal position. The net result is that the collective decision will be slightly more extreme than the average of individual positions and will come to represent more nearly the majority viewpoint in the group, as suggested by the social decision scheme analyses we discussed earlier.

The key factor in this social comparison explanation is people's knowledge of other group members' positions relative to the dominant social value(s) in question. It follows, then, that actually discussing the issues with those other group members may not be necessary to produce polarization, if one could provide the social comparison information in some other way. This is the rationale behind a number of experiments that have examined the effect of 'mere knowledge' on people's opinions. One of the first of these was by Teger and Pruitt (1967), who modified the usual paradigm to include a 'no discussion' condition, where group members were permitted only to hold up signs indicating their individual pre-discussion positions on each item. Sure enough, their subsequent decisions became more polarized after receiving this information, although not as strongly as those who had had the benefit of discussion as well. This polarizing effect of being exposed to other people's opinions was confirmed by Myers (1978). He found that simply presenting subjects with either the mean or the distribution of responses of apparently similar others was enough to shift their choices further in the initially preferred direction. Something similar has been observed in studies of gambling behaviour. Blascovich et al. (1973) found that people playing blackjack in groups made riskier bets than when playing as individuals, even when no discussion of bets was permitted. This was subsequently replicated even when participants used their own money to play with (Blascovich et al., 1975, 1976).

More direct evidence for the importance of social comparison processes has come from studies that have varied the salience of a social value directly. If it is, indeed, a movement towards a positively valued pole that underlies polarization then one should expect greater shifts as the value becomes more explicit. This is exactly what Baron and Roper (1976) found. Adapting Sherif's (1936) autokinetic effect paradigm, they suggested to participants that large estimates of movement of the light were indicative of superior intelligence. This, then, was the relevant social value. Upon hearing the responses of others in the 'public' trials of the experiment, people's estimates became significantly larger than those who always responded privately and were thus deprived of social comparison information.

Polarization through persuasion

The emphasis in the social comparison explanation is on the self-presentational or self-enhancement motives that are stimulated by comparisons with others. The focus is very much on relations among the group members; the actual *content* of the group discussion leading to the group decision is seen as irrelevant except as it affects these. In the second approach to be considered, this order of priorities is reversed. According to this view, the main causal factor – and in some strong versions of the theory, the *only* causal factor – underlying group polarization is the exchange of information and arguments that precede the collective decision. The champions of this 'persuasive arguments' theory (as it is known) have been Burnstein and Vinokur (1977), and they have accumulated an impressive array of evidence in its support. They begin by assuming, reasonably enough, that on any issue under deliberation it is unlikely that in the group there is a precisely equal balance of arguments and evidence for and against. Usually there will be a preponderance in one direction, presumably not unrelated to the dominant social values that are thought so critical for the social comparison explanation. Of course, each individual will not at first have access to all these arguments and nor will all the individuals in the group be aware of the same arguments. Once the discussion gets under way, all this different information comes out into the open; each person becomes acquainted with more of the arguments supporting the dominant view and perhaps one or two extra arguments against, although probably not as many. Burnstein and Vinokur (1977) suggest that the group members then act as rational 'information processors' and respond to the additional arguments and evidence supporting their initially preferred view by shifting their opinion further in that direction.

This idea that group decisions result from the pooling of individual contributions has received considerable support from studies that have either analysed or manipulated the argumentative content of group discussions. Vinokur and Burnstein (1974), for instance, counted up the number of pro-risk and pro-caution arguments that were generated over typically 'risky' or 'cautious' choice dilemma items. As they expected, the pro-risk arguments outweighed the pro-caution arguments on 'risky' items by about 6:4, and for 'cautious' items the ratio was reversed. When those arguments were subsequently rated for persuasiveness by independent judges, the arguments from the larger set on any item were also found to be more persuasive. Finally, Vinokur and Burnstein (1974) ran a small experiment in which participants were simply provided with prototypical arguments produced on different items, with no opportunity for discussion. The usual shifts occurred. These findings were confirmed by Ebbesen and Bowers (1974). Like Vinokur and Burnstein (1974), they found a correlation between the proportion of risky to cautious arguments produced and the average degree of polarization. They then went one step further and asked participants to listen to tape-recorded group discussions in which the proportion of risky to cautious arguments expressed was systematically varied. Irrespective of the particular items heard, changes in opinion were clearly related to the proportion of risky to cautious arguments in the discussion (see figure 5.5).

Not content with demonstrating the validity of their persuasive arguments theory, Burnstein and Vinokur (1973) have also attempted to show the *in*validity of the rival social comparison approach. They reasoned that if it is the persuasive content of arguments which causes polarization rather than comparisons between oneself and others, then it should be possible to produce shifts in opinion even when people are unable to infer the views of others, provided that the relevant arguments that emerge are sufficiently persuasive. On the other hand, even if people know where others stand on an issue, unless they are exposed to enough convincing arguments, they should not polarize. They then designed two ingenious experiments to put these hypotheses to the test. Both were based on the Wallach et al. (1962) procedure: participants initially answered choice dilemmas individually, discussed these same items in a group and then recorded their subsequent individual opinion. However, instead of the usual situation

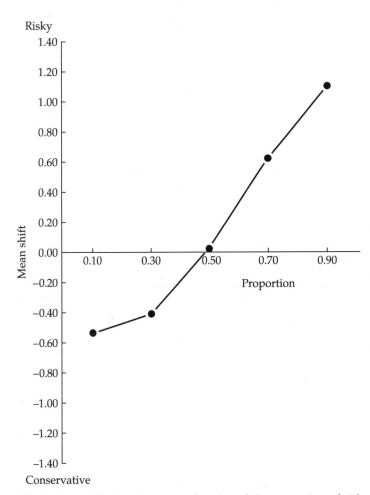

Figure 5.5 Average shift in opinion as a function of the proportion of risky arguments heard (from Ebbesen and Bowers, 1974. Copyright © 1974 by the American Psychological Association. Reprinted by permission of the author)

where everyone simply argued their own point of view, the experimenters announced that each person would be asked to argue a point of view provided by the experimenter. This might be the same as their own or it might differ and people would not know what others had been asked to do. In this way, social comparisons became impossible to make since other people's true opinions would be occluded.

205

Everyone was then given his instructions privately. In half the groups people were told to argue *for* their own point of view; the other half had to advocate a position directly contrary to what they really believed. The purpose of this manipulation was to vary the number and persuasiveness of the arguments generated. Burnstein and Vinokur (1973) assumed that people would have less to say and be less convincing when arguing for something they did not really believe in. In the second experiment, Burnstein and Vinokur informed the participants that everyone had actually been instructed to argue directly against their true views (and this was indeed what they were asked to do). Now social comparisons were possible again since people could infer each other's true positions simply by inverting whatever they said. However, the arguments generated here should not be plentiful or persuasive since, as in half the groups in the first experiment, people were being asked to play a devil's advocate role.

The main results from these two experiments provided a rather strong – not to say persuasive – argument for the validity of Burnstein and Vinokur's (1973) account. First of all, there was clear polarization in condition 1 of the first experiment where comparisons were impossible but where group members could be persuasive arguing for their own opinions. As usual, the polarization was negative on risky items and positive on cautious items. In condition 2, on the other hand, where people's arguments were presumably less persuasive, the polarization all but disappeared. The same was true for the risky items in the second experiment, where social comparisons were possible yet little polarization occurred. The only fly in Burnstein and Vinokur's ointment was the result from the cautious items in experiment 2. Unexpectedly, there was a significant shift in opinion here in the *risky* direction. Although this should not have occurred according to Burnstein and Vinokur's theory, it is equally inexplicable from the social comparison point of view since, if anything, the shift should have been in just the other direction.

Burnstein and Vinokur's (1973) competitive test of the social comparison and persuasive arguments explanations seemed conclusive. However, it is fair to say that other research that has compared the merits of the two approaches has been rather more equivocal. Zuber et al. (1992) found little support for the persuasive arguments theory. In their experiment, they asked participants to answer the

206

usual choice dilemma items twice individually *before* they entered the group discussion. In two of the conditions they were presented with a comprehensive list of the relevant arguments, relating to each item so that they were aware of them during one or both of these individual pre-tests. In the third (control) condition no arguments were presented prior to the group discussion. According to Burnstein and Vinokur, being made aware of the relevant arguments should cause a change in people's attitudes in itself, and little further polarization should happen in the group discussion phase. On the other hand, the social comparison view requires that they know something of their fellow participants' opinions, which, in this experiment, was only possible in the group discussion phase. The results supported the latter view. There was a significant shift going from individual pre-discussion to the group decisions, and this happened irrespective of experimental condition (i.e. it was as strong in conditions 1 and 2 as in the control condition). In other words, knowing where other people stood on the items seemed to be more important than knowing about the arguments.

A final difficulty for the persuasive arguments approach lies in its assumption that during the group discussion new information emerges to bring about the polarization. In fact, studies of how group members utilize both the shared and unshared information in the group suggest that this pooling of available arguments rarely happens. Imagine the following situation: four members of a personnel selection panel meet to discuss the relative merits of three candidates, A, B and C. On various objective criteria A is the stronger applicant, with (say) eight positive attributes, four neutral and four negative; B and C might have four positive, eight neutral and four negative characteristics. Now, if all members of the panel have access to all this information, there is little doubt that they should choose A for the job. But suppose not all the information about the candidates is shared, perhaps because the different panel members have been delegated different tasks during the selection process (e.g. one to review previous work experience, one to assess communication skills, one to evaluate team participation, and so on). Now, when they meet as a panel each person knows some positive and negative things about the candidates that may not be known by the others. If their discussion is optimal then all this unshared information will be revealed and candidate A will still be chosen. But groups do not often function in this optimal

Table 5.3 Effects of shared and unshared information on a group decision

	Condition	Candidate chosen (%)		
		A	B	C
Individual preferences (prior to group discussion)	Shared information	67	17	17
	Unshared information	25	61	14
Group preferences	Shared information	83	11	6
	Unshared information	24	71	5

Source: Stasser and Titus (1985), table 3

way. Instead, they tend to concentrate mainly on the information they have in common and overlook the 'hidden' non-shared information. The above example is taken from an experiment by Stasser and Titus (1985). In one condition, all information about these hypothetical candidates was shared. However, in a second condition, Stasser and Titus arranged for each member to have access to only two of candidate A's positive attributes, but all his neutral and negative attributes. However, the particular positive features known by each member were unique to that person (i.e. unshared). In a parallel way, *all* of candidate B's positive attributes were shared, but his neutral and negative features were spread around the four panellists. For candidate C, both the positive and negative attributes were unshared while his neutral aspects were held in common. Note, that the total amount of information (positive, neutral and negative) about the candidates was identical in the 'shared' and 'unshared' conditions; only its distribution among the panel members differed. The effects of this one difference were dramatic, as can be seen in table 5.3. Prior to the group discussion there was a strong preference for candidate A in the 'shared' condition, a preference which was magnified in the final group decision. This outcome accurately reflected the objective merits of the candidates. However, note what happened in the 'unshared' condition. Initially, candidate B was preferred, a consequence of the biased information each panel member had at his or her disposal. But the group discussion, far from correcting this misleading impression by revealing all candidate A's 'hidden' talents, actually resulted in an even stronger preference for the less well qualified candidate B. Subsequent experiments confirmed that, indeed, much more of the group's time is typically spent discussing (and reiterating) the information they all already possessed than in discovering any new information (Stasser et al., 1989b; Stasser and Stewart, 1992).

There are important theoretical and practical implications of this observation that group members may not spontaneously exchange all the knowledge they possess. It casts some doubt on Burnstein and Vinokur's (1973) hypothesis that group polarization can be entirely explained as the outcome of acquiring and processing new information during collective deliberations. It also provides a clue as to how groups like selection panels and other committees can act so as to improve their decision making. We will discuss this in more detail in the next section but, for the moment, we can simply note that they may be well advised to implement procedures that work against too early an achievement of consensus. For, as Stasser and his colleagues have shown, such consensus is occasionally attained at the expense of objectivity.

Polarization as intergroup differentiation

For the persuasive arguments explanation, the actual discussion in the group is more important than the person who puts forward the argument; the information content – and hence persuasiveness – of the arguments expressed is presumed to be a property of the arguments themselves and is independent of their source. But are we really as receptive to arguments from people we see as our opponents as we are to those from our friends? This brings us to the third of our explanations of group polarization, an explanation which invokes social identification with the group as the key process (Wetherell, 1987). Drawing on Turner's (1987) self-categorization theory, outlined in the previous chapter, Wetherell argues that what is happening when a group polarizes is that the group members are attempting to conform more closely to the normative position that they see as prototypical for their ingroup. When the situation makes their ingroup

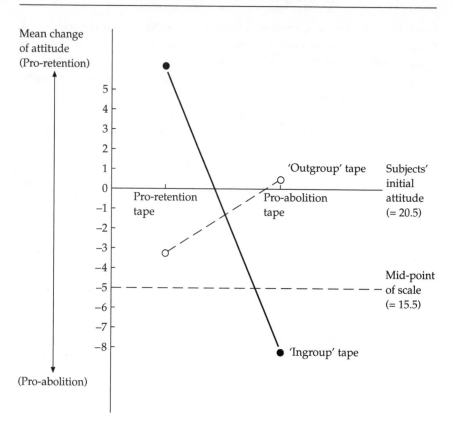

Figure 5.6 Intergroup effects on attitude polarization (from Mackie and Cooper, 1984)

identity more important – say, for example, when an intergroup relationship comes particularly to the fore – then the relevant ingroup
norms are likely to become more extreme so as to be more clearly
differentiated from outgroup norms, and the within-group polarization will be enhanced.

This was the idea tested by Mackie and Cooper (1984). They found
that students' attitudes towards the use of standardized tests for
university entry could be dramatically altered after hearing a taped
'ingroup' arguing for the retention (or abolition) of these tests, but
were much less affected when the tape was alleged to be of an outgroup (see figure 5.6). Notice that initially the students were mildly in
favour of retaining the entrance tests, a tendency that was exaggerated after hearing the pro-retention 'ingroup' tape. But on hearing the

pro-*abolition'* 'ingroup' tape their attitudes switched completely and actually fell below the mid-point of the 31-point scale. The changes after hearing the same arguments attributed to an 'outgroup' were much smaller and were generally in the reverse direction. In subsequent experiments, Mackie (1986) found that the same effects could be obtained even without the element of intergroup competition; it was sufficient to maintain that one of the tapes was from a collection of individuals (and not an outgroup) to eliminate the polarization. In line with Turner's (1987) theory, Mackie also found that people's estimates of what the taped group's normative position was were more extreme when they believed they would be joining it – and hence might have identified with it – than when they believed it was irrelevant to them.

Several other studies have confirmed that the psychological presence of a category in a group discussion – learning that some discussants share an ingroup membership while others belong to an outgroup – nearly always generates polarization (Abrams et al., 1990; Turner et al., 1989; van Knippenberg and Wilke, 1988; but cf. Reid and Sumiga (1984) for a contrasting result).

Concluding remarks on group polarization

Let me now summarize these three approaches and assess their competing merits. The social comparison explanation is at its strongest in explaining polarization in domains where there is little opportunity to exchange arguments but where, nevertheless, there is some information available as to the socially preferred way of behaving and as to how others actually are behaving. Decisions in blackjack gambling or estimates of autokinetic movement do not seem readily amenable to the very cognitive information processing approach advocated by the persuasive arguments theorists and yet, as we have seen, polarization can be observed as clearly here as with more verbal discussion tasks. On the other hand, in the latter situations, the persuasive arguments approach convincingly shows that it is the content of the messages exchanged during the group discussion that determines the extent of polarization (and *not* the positions taken up by the message senders). Both the social comparison and persuasive argument approaches seem most applicable when one initially knows little about one's fellow group members, or where the decision taken is a novel one. After all, if one knows everybody's views about an issue and one is well acquainted with all the relevant arguments it is hard to see why either process should come into play. Perhaps that is why polarization has not been so easy to observe in real-life groups that have been in existence for some time. The essence of the third approach is that group members have some knowledge of their group's main attributes and characteristic normative attitudes, and then shift towards these as their group membership becomes salient or threatened in some way. It seems difficult to explain the differential polarization caused by exposure to 'ingroup' or 'outgroup' arguments in any better way than by such a social identity perspective. Certainly, such findings are especially difficult to reconcile with the persuasive argument approach since the actual information content of the messages is always held constant. However, powerful though these intergroup effects are, it is less easy to imagine how they would come into play in (say) a jury, where there is not an obvious outgroup against which to define the prototypical ingroup norm.

We are left, then, with the theoretically inelegant but nevertheless probably correct conclusion that all three types of process are present to some degree in most decision-making situations in the real world. Their relative weights may vary from situation to situation but it seems unlikely that any one operates to the complete exclusion of the others.

The quality of the decision-making process

So far, I have said little about the *quality* of group decisions. This is because if we think simply in terms of outcomes we usually do not have any straightforward criteria against which to measure quality. Who knows whether an appointment committee offered the job to the best candidate or whether the jury returned the 'true' verdict? However, if outcomes are difficult to assess, perhaps it is possible to evaluate the decision-making process that led to those outcomes. According to one influential theorist, it is possible (Janis, 1982). Janis analysed a number of American foreign policy decisions made between 1940 and 1980 and came to the conclusion that where these turned out 'badly' for the decision makers (i.e. where American interests were damaged), the decision process was marked by five features. First, the group making the decision was very cohesive. Second, it was also typically insulated from information outside the group. Third, the decision makers rarely searched systematically through alternative policy options to appraise their relative merits. Fourth, the group was often under some stress caused by the need to reach a decision urgently. And last, but by no means least, the group was nearly always dominated by a very directive leader. These five conditions, Janis believed, generate strong conformity pressures in a group and it is these 'concurrence seeking tendencies' that lead to defective decision making, or what Janis called 'groupthink'.

What are the symptoms of 'groupthink'? Janis lists several, some of which will be familiar from our earlier discussions of social influence (chapter 4) and group performance (this chapter). First, a very cohesive group is likely to exert pressures on dissenters to conform to the consensus view. Some of this pressure may be implicit, but often the leader or other members of the group will take it upon themselves to bring the deviates into line and reject them if they do not do so. Arising out of this pressure towards uniformity is the second 'groupthink' symptom: an illusion of unanimity and correctness. As seen in chapter 4, other people often provide very powerful sources of reality construction. If they all give the appearance of total agreement on some issue, then we may be led to the conclusion that this view is the only valid one. Such a state of mind is likely to inhibit any creative search for other opinions, and even to lead to a positive rejection of those opinions and a ridiculing of their sources. Since some of these may emanate from outside the group, a third symptom of groupthink is a negative stereotyping of outgroups. This is particularly likely to occur in political decision making, which is nearly always conducted in a conflictual intergroup context. As we shall see in chapter 6, a common consequence of intergroup conflict is derogation of the outgroup and glorification of the ingroup.

The picture that Janis (1982) painted, therefore, is of a tightly knit group, isolated from outside influences, converging rapidly onto a normatively 'correct' point of view and thereafter being convinced both of its own rectitude and of the inferiority of all other competing opinions (or groups). He argued that such a set of symptoms is almost exactly the opposite of what should characterize good decision-making process (namely, the rational weighing of possible options in the light of all the available evidence), and hence where they occur one should expect the outcomes to be less than ideal.

Janis believed that the link between process and outcome may not be a perfect one since other factors may intervene to rescue a 'faulty' decision or abort a 'good' one. Nevertheless, other things being equal, poor decisions are likely to lead to poor results, and he presented evidence from such American misadventures as the attempted invasion of Cuba at the Bay of Pigs in 1961, the bombing of North Vietnam in 1965 and the Watergate scandal in 1973, which indicates that in each of these events groupthink may have occurred among key decision makers. Nor is it just American governments who seem to be liable to groupthink. Consider the following description of decision making in the British Cabinet during Mrs Thatcher's period as Prime Minister:

It is January 1984. The place is No. 10. The forum is the Cabinet's Overseas and Defence Committee. The subject is the possibility of an attempt to normalize relations with Argentina . . . Sir Geoffrey Howe is four minutes into the Foreign Office paper on the need to open exploratory talks with the Alfonsin Government. Mrs Thatcher cuts in, 'Geoffrey, I know what you're going to recommend. And the answer is 'No!'.

End of item: nobody argues with the boss. (Anonymous source quoted in Hennessy, 1986, p. 99)

If true, this account bears more than a passing correspondence to Janis's description of 'groupthink'.

Janis (1982) contrasted various fiascos, which he believed were preceded by groupthink, with other events in which he believed the groups engaged in vigilant decision making. In these instances, apparently, the leader adopted a more neutral role, encouraged the expression of minority viewpoints, and even appointed independent experts or *devil's advocates*, whose job was to provide a critical appraisal of the group's currently preferred decision. One of the best examples of this, in Janis' view, was the Cuban missile crisis of 1962 where President Kennedy and his advisors engaged in some brinkmanship diplomacy with the Soviet Union over the siting of missiles in Cuba. This was a particularly interesting case since it involved the same group of officials who had perpetrated the Bay of Pigs fiasco a year

214

earlier. But from published accounts of the second crisis it seems that Kennedy took active steps to avoid the blinkered vision that had led to the earlier disaster. He encouraged his Executive Committee to debate policy options freely, even absenting himself from some meetings to encourage greater dissent. His brother Robert Kennedy, the Attorney General at the time, was unofficially assigned the devil's advocate role and apparently spent most of his time ruthlessly criticizing other people's ideas. Although decisions taken during the thirteen-day crisis came perilously close to initiating a major military conflict between the USA and the USSR (hardly a 'successful outcome'), the *way* the decisions were reached was markedly superior to the other incidents documented by Janis.

For his evidence, Janis relied almost exclusively on historical material, usually eyewitness accounts by participants. Although such case studies often make plausible reading, as objective evidence they inevitably have their limitations. Participants in events can only ever give partial – and sometimes deliberately censored – descriptions of them, and the over-reliance on such archival evidence may, in any case, lead to a kind of 'hindsight wisdom', as Fischhoff and Beyth-Marom (1976) have noted. Other analysts, coming from a different perspective, may reach rather different conclusions. Kramer (1998), for example, has re-analysed two of the events presented by Janis (1982) as prime examples of groupthink leading to fiascos, the Bay of Pigs mission instigated by Kennedy and the escalation of the Vietnam War ordered by Johnson. In the light of subsequent records of these presidential decisions, Kramer argues that they were driven as much by political considerations as any faulty group dynamics in the Kennedy and Johnson cabinets. Hart (1990) is similarly sceptical about the utility of Janis' model to account for the Dutch government's lack of preparedness for the German invasion of the Netherlands in 1940. In these and other instances, Janis may have exaggerated the importance of social psychological processes at the expense of wider socio-political factors.

This is not to argue for the complete abandonment of archival sources in social psychological research, however. It is possible to use them to explore theoretically interesting questions, especially if they are analysed systematically with quantitative content-analytic techniques. A good example of how this can be done has been provided by Tetlock et al. (1992). They took published accounts of eight of

215

Janis' (1982) cases (six thought to display groupthink, two which he believed showed 'vigilant' decision making) and asked independent judges to rate[3] these on a large number of attributes, many of which were relevant to the groupthink model (e.g. group cohesion, strength of leader, conformity, etc.). When they compared 'groupthink' events with the 'vigilant' events the results broadly supported Janis' model, with one glaring exception. Thus, the groups involved in the groupthink instances tended to have a stronger leader, and to show greater conformity and more rigidity than those showing 'vigilance'. However, they were actually rated as *less* cohesive and not more, as Janis would have predicted. Furthermore, when these various indicators of decision-making process were correlated with one another (controlling for the effects of other variables), only those relating to procedural or structural defects of the group (e.g. leadership style) were strongly associated with symptoms of defective decision making; cohesiveness and exposure to threatening circumstances were not (Tetlock et al., 1992). Using the same technique, Peterson et al. (1998) compared the modus operandi of the management teams of seven prominent companies during 'successful' and 'unsuccessful' periods of trading. Problematically for Janis' theory, successful economic performance tended to be associated with a more cohesive management team (and not less) and with a strong (rather than a weak) chief executive (although this second result may be more consistent with the groupthink model than it first appears, as we shall see). In summary, then, careful analysis of historically documented examples of political and commercial groups provides some support for Janis' intuitions about factors associated with faulty decision making but reveals that a high level of cohesiveness is not one of them.

The same picture emerges from experimental and field studies of decision-making groups. Flowers (1977) created groups of high and low cohesiveness with leaders who had been trained to use either a non-directive participative style or a directive and task-orientated approach. The groups were asked to role play a committee of school administrators facing a delicate but urgent personnel problem. An analysis of committee deliberations showed that, contrary to Janis' hypothesis, the level of cohesiveness had no effect on either the number of different solutions proposed or the number of facts considered in reaching a decision. The leadership style, on the other hand, *was* influential. More solutions were produced and more information was considered with the open, non-directive leaders than with the more directive kind. Very similar results were obtained by Fodor and Smith (1982) when they compared leaders previously classified as high or low in 'need for power', again in cohesive and less cohesive groups. The less power-hungry leaders elicited more relevant information and a greater number of alternative proposals during the group discussion than did those scoring high in need for power. But the cohesion of the groups made no difference. In fact, experiments showing deleterious effects for group cohesion on decision-making quality are extremely rare, and even then additional factors – for example, some threat to the group's identity – may need to be present (Turner et al., 1992).

The importance of the leader and the relative *un*importance of cohesiveness have been confirmed in field studies of naturally functioning groups. Vinokur et al. (1985) studied the process and outcome of National Institutes of Health conferences in which a panel of experts and consumers meet to evaluate new medical technologies. From the participants of six such conferences, Vinokur et al. (1985) obtained various measures on the decision-making process, ratings of the chairperson, assessments of the amount and quality of information exchanged and, lastly, the outcome measure: an evaluation of the quality of the final policy statements. Consistent with Janis' theory, Vinokur et al. found that one of the variables most highly correlated with the quality of outcome was that dealing with the facilitative role played by the chairperson in encouraging full participation among the experts. However, contrary to Janis' theory, cohesiveness was a much less predictive variable and, if anything, was also *positively* correlated with the quality of decision (where Janis predicts the reverse). Moorehead and Montanari (1986) similarly found that the cohesiveness of student project groups was unrelated to their performance.

I have dwelt at some length on the potential hazards of collective decision making. How can these be avoided? Clearly, the answer is *not* simply to leave all important decisions to a single individual. Leaving aside the ethical and political difficulties in delegating such powers to one person, there are several practical disadvantages to such a solution. First, as we saw in chapter 3, any problem of even moderate complexity is likely to prove more than can be handled by one person's cognitive capacity; some division of labour is essential in most important decisions. Allied to this are the benefits that accrue from the pooling of ideas, information and experience, which, as we saw earlier in the chapter, can lend groups an advantage even if they do not always fully exploit it. The combining of individual ideas may also lead to a cancelling out of idiosyncratic biases and prejudices which, if left unchecked in any individual decision maker, must surely be detrimental. Finally, as I showed earlier, there are potential motivational gains from the cohesion and identification provided by a group that are not available to a lone individual. The question is not, therefore, how we can dispense with group decision making, but how we can capitalize on its advantages while circumventing its defects.

The key to answering this question lies in devices and procedures that maximize the effective participation of all group members to ensure greatest exposure of relevant ideas and information. Three factors seem to be particularly important. The first, as correctly noted by Janis (1982), concerns the style adopted by the leader. As we have just noted, there is ample evidence that a leader who is too directive, who promotes his or her own point of view too forcefully and who discourages the expression of alternative opinion and criticism is liable to be detrimental to effective decision making. By implication, therefore, leaders should adopt an approach that is the opposite of this, and this meshes well with some of the conclusions that emerged from our discussion of leadership in chapter 3. However, two qualifications should be added. One is that, as we saw in chapter 3, the most appropriate leadership style may depend somewhat on the situation confronting the group. So, while there may be some generic advantages associated with a more participative style of leadership, there can be circumstances when a more directive approach is called for. Second, it is important to distinguish between directiveness that is associated with outcomes (i.e. the leader attempting to achieve his or her particular goal), and that associated with the group process (i.e. ensuring that everyone in the group is able to have their say). Peterson (1997) showed that these two kinds of directiveness have very different consequences for the quality of the subsequent group decision. After many years of chairing trade union meetings and university committees, I cannot but agree. All too often, a firm hand is needed to deal with one's more unruly colleagues to ensure that they do not drown out the contributions of the shyer members of the group.

A second factor relevant to effective group decision making is the cohesiveness of the group. It clearly is not the case, as Janis (1982) had surmised, that cohesion leads to poor decision making. Indeed, all the evidence suggests that it is either unrelated to decision quality or may even be associated with *better* decision process (Courtright, 1978; Moorhead and Montanari, 1986). And surely this makes sense: are not group members more likely to feel comfortable about expressing their views if the group is cohesive than if it is loose-knit and fragmented? If cohesiveness plays any role, perhaps it is, as Steiner (1982) suggested, more in the *desire* for it than its actual presence. Maybe it is only when groups are desperately seeking to manufacture unity that they become prey to the concurrence seeking defects that Janis identified; having once achieved it, the pressure for unanimity will be more than outweighed by the security it provides to allow criticism and dissent.

Third, and probably most importantly, groups need to find ways to reduce the tendency for non-shared information to remain hidden. Research following Stasser and Titus' (1985) discovery of this pluralistic ignorance phenomenon has provided some helpful pointers. One useful technique is explicitly to assign different roles to the various members of the decision-making group *and* to ensure that everyone is aware of this division of labour and expertise. In the hypothetical example of a personnel selection panel that I gave earlier, if one person is charged with the task of researching candidates' prior experience, another with evaluating their current job skills, and so on, then each panel member should feel a greater responsibility for ensuring that all the information they possess is made known to the rest of the panel. Experimental research bears this out. For example, Stasser et al. (1995), using a mock homicide investigation in which several critical clues were distributed among the members of the 'investigation team', found that when the group members had been informed of the fact that each of them possessed unique information they were much more likely to discover the culprit than when they were not so reminded. In fact, such 'role assigned' groups did almost as well as control groups in which members shared all the information.

There is also evidence that groups can be trained in better decision making (Larson et al., 1994). Using a similar paradigm to that developed by Stasser and Titus (1985), Larson and his colleagues

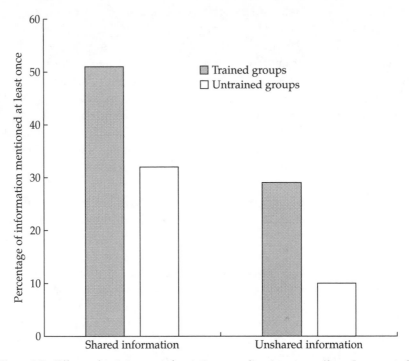

Figure 5.7   Effects of training on information sampling in groups (from Larson et al., 1994, table 1)

exposed half the groups in their experiment to a short training regime, which required that they took a few minutes at the start of their discussion to plan how they would make their decision and which also reminded them of some of the common pitfalls of collective decision making (e.g. inadequate information search, too strong an adherence to the first solution thought of, etc.). The remainder received no such instruction. The effects of this brief training were to increase the overall amount of information mentioned quite considerably (from 28 per cent to 40 per cent), and this benefit was as true for the redundant shared information as it was for the unshared information (see figure 5.7). It seems that decision-making committees, particularly those meeting for the first time or which may be otherwise inexperienced in decision making, would do well to invest a small amount of time at the beginning of their deliberations to reflect on how they will proceed, and be self-conscious about the dangers they should be on the lookout for as they do.

Summary

1 In studying group performance the most basic issue concerns whether the mere presence of another person helps or hinders task performance. The evidence suggests that there is mild facilitation of performance for simple tasks but inhibition for more complex tasks. Zajonc's influential explanation for this phenomenon in terms of physiological arousal is now less well favoured than accounts that emphasize cognitive and attentional capacity.

2 The question of the relative superiority of individual or group performance depends entirely on the mode of comparison. In the simplest contrast – between groups and the average individual – groups invariably outperform individuals. However, if the comparison is made with statisticized groups – formed by pooling individuals' performances statistically – then real interacting groups usually, but not invariably, perform less well on a range of tasks.

3 Two influential theories that have tried to explain this apparent deficit are Steiner's theory of group productivity and Latané's social impact theory. In Steiner's theory, actual productivity is thought never to exceed potential productivity because groups usually fail to utilize their resources in the optimum way for a given task. In Latané's theory, the deficits are attributed to a lack of motivation, which is thought to occur in groups. This happens, it is supposed, because the impact of the experimental instructions is 'diluted' among the group members.

4 Although much of the group performance literature supports the group deficit theories, there is no doubt that group interaction can also lead to process *gains*. This seems to occur for complex or highly involving tasks, or when the group is psychologically important for its members, or if the prevailing values favour collectivism rather than individualism.

5 Group decision making is a special form of group performance. A useful method for studying group decision making is social

decision schemes theory. This is a mathematical modelling approach which attempts to simulate various possible methods of combining individual contributions to the group decision. The hypothetical combination rule that generates predictions closest to observed group decisions is assumed to be the one that is operative. For a number of intellectual tasks it appears that a 'truth supported wins' model is the best 'fit' with the data. For tasks where there is no demonstrably correct decision some form of majority decision rule is more likely.

6   When groups make decisions on such judgmental tasks they nearly always exhibit polarization: the collective view is more extreme than the average of individual opinions in the same direction. This has been found in many laboratory experiments although less consistently in naturalistic studies.

7   There are three main current explanations of this group polarization phenomenon: social comparison theory, persuasive arguments theory and social identity theory. Social comparison theory proposes that polarization is caused by group members competing with one another to endorse the socially most desirable viewpoints. Persuasive arguments theory emphasizes the role of information exchange. Polarization occurs, according to this view, because new arguments and evidence come to light during the discussion. The social identity approach proposes that polarization is due to group members' conforming to ingroup norms in contrast to outgroup norms. Each perspective finds much supportive evidence and it is probable that more than one of the processes underlies polarization.

8   Groups can sometimes make bad decisions by not considering all the relevant information and not appraising the full range of options available. Janis called this 'groupthink' and believed that it is caused by a cohesive group being led by an over-directive leader. Several historical examples seem to support his analysis, although more controlled research suggests that only the leadership factor is crucial. Techniques are available that can aid decision making by increasing the amount of unshared information made available to the group.

Notes

1   Actually, Steiner (1972, p. 20) erroneously computes this figure to be 0·596, and does not mention the values for the other two tasks. As we shall see, this mistake and omission have important implications for his theory of process loss.
2   Of course, figure 5.1 appears to be the exact inverse of the hypothetical curve shown in figure 4.7. This is because it plots average output per person along the ordinate instead of total group output. It is easy to verify, however, that re-plotting the graph for total output against size would show the typical negatively accelerating shape.
3   Actually the procedure used was more complicated than this. It involved the judges sorting the attributes – there were a hundred of them – into something resembling a normal distribution for each case study to indicate how characteristic each one was in the case study they had read. From these Q-sorts (as they are called) it is possible to derive composite scores for each event, comparable to an overall rating judgement (see Tetlock et al. (1992) for details of the technique).

Further Reading

Group productivity

Steiner, I.D. (1972) *Group Process and Productivity*, chs 1–3. New York: Academic Press.

Stroebe, W. and Diehl, M. (1994) Why groups are less effective than their members: on productivity loss in idea-generating groups, in Stroebe, W. and Hewstone, M. (eds) *European Review of Social Psychology*, vol. 5, pp. 271–303.

Williams, K., Karau, S. and Bourgeois, M. (1993) Working on collective tasks: social loafing and social compensation, in Hogg, M.A. and Abrams, D. (eds) *Group Motivation*, pp. 130–48. Hemel Hempstead: Harvester Wheatsheaf.

Group decision-making

Baron, R.S., Kerr, N.L. and Miller, N. (1992) *Group Process, Group Decision, Group Action*, ch. 6. Milton Keynes: Open University Press.

Brown, Roger (1986) *Social Psychology*, 2nd edn, chs 6, 8. New York: Free Press.

Organizational Behaviour and Human Decision Processes (1998) 73(2–3) (special issue on groupthink).

Stasser, G. (1992) Pooling of unshared information during group discussions, in Worchel, S., Wood, W. and Simpson, J.A. (eds) *Group Process and Productivity*, pp. 48–67. London: Sage.

Turner, J.C. (1991) *Social Influence*, ch. 3. Milton Keynes: Open University Press.

6

INTERGROUP CONFLICT
AND COOPERATION

So far, I have been mainly concerned with processes *within* the group: the ways people behave towards and influence other members of the ingroup. In this and the next two chapters, the focus shifts to the *intergroup* domain: to the factors governing people's behaviour and attitudes towards members of outgroups. However, this change of emphasis is not complete. Just as we have seen that in various aspects of intragroup dynamics intergroup relations cannot be ignored, so too we will discover that intergroup phenomena are not easily separable from what goes on inside the group.

This chapter is about conflict and cooperation between groups. It will cover a wide range of issues, starting with the origins of social discontent and collective protest. For a long time it was believed that such unrest was caused by frustrating events, either in people's past or as currently experienced. Such frustration, it was thought, led inexorably to various forms of aggression directed either towards the source of the frustration or, more commonly, onto some scapegoat target such as a minority group. However, empirical and theoretical difficulties led this frustration–aggression hypothesis to be largely abandoned. Instead of viewing frustration as an *absolute* deprivation of basic needs, an alternative theory conceived of it as a state of *relative* deprivation. In other words, people are discontented not necessarily because they are hungry or poor, but because they are hung*rier* or poo*rer* than they believe they should be. This relative deprivation theory has proved to be a powerful explanation for the incidence of many forms of intergroup violence and collective protest.

The discussion then broadens out to consider other kinds of intergroup relationship, both conflictual and harmonious. It is possible to analyse these various forms of intergroup behaviour – whether competitive or cooperative – as the response of people to their real or imagined ingroup interests. Where these are incompatible with another group, so that what the outgroup seeks is at the expense of the ingroup, then the outcome is likely to be mutual antagonism and discrimination. On the other hand, where the interests are concordant – both groups working towards a common objective – then a more amicable relationship is more probable. This idea that goal relationships can be important determinants of intergroup behaviour crops up frequently in the social sciences and led Campbell (1965) to dub it the realistic group conflict theory. Within social psychology the best-known proponent

226

of this approach is Muzafer Sherif, whose work we have already encountered more than once in this book. It is Sherif's work, therefore, that serves as the point of departure for the second half of the chapter.

Deprivation and Discontent

The study of intergroup prejudice has a long history in social psychology, dating back sixty years or more. Although prejudice has been variously defined over that time, for my current purposes I will regard it as the holding or display of derogatory attitudes, negative affect or discriminatory behaviour towards members of an outgroup because of their membership of that outgroup (Brown, 1995). Here are some examples of prejudice recorded in Margate, a seaside resort not far from where I live. Margate is a socially and economically depressed town with high levels of unemployment and above average scores on various ill health and deprivation indicators. It has also been the temporary home in recent years of a number of asylum seekers from such places as Afghanistan, Czechoslovakia and Kosovo. Unfortunately, I am ashamed to say, these refugees are often made less than welcome by the citizens of Margate, as these comments reveal:

I tell you exactly what I think. They should fucking send them back where they come from. Put them in a big boat and push it out to sea.

They're hassling the young girls and molesting the children.

Don't get me wrong, I'm not racist. We need the Pakis to run the corner shops and the Chinese to do the take-aways. But this riff-raff – who needs them? (remarks reported in the *Observer*, 4 October 1998)

Frustration, prejudice and intergroup aggression

How can we explain these naked expressions of intergroup hostility? According to one of the earliest theories of prejudice, it is all due to frustration (Dollard et al., 1939). In this frustration–aggression theory, Dollard and his colleagues attempted to provide a single explanation for aggression between individuals, and aggression between groups in the wider society. Their hypothesis was that 'the occurrence of aggressive behaviour always presupposes the existence of frustration and, contrariwise . . . the existence of frustration always leads to some form of aggression' (Dollard et al., 1939, p. 1). By frustration they meant any interference with the satisfaction of some basic need (e.g. hunger, thirst), and they believed that this caused a build-up of some arousal – an instigation to aggress. This aggressive 'energy' had to be expended to remove the source of the interference. If not, it did not simply dissipate but remained within the person, ready to burst out at the first opportunity.

Often the aggression may not be directed at the real source of the frustration but may be 'displaced' onto some alternative target. When my children were young, on those occasions when I remonstrated with them over some misdemeanour, they usually did not express their annoyance at me directly but would kick a football violently into a neighbour's garden. Dollard et al. argues that such displaced aggression occurs either because the frustrated person may have learned some inhibitions against attacking a more powerful target (at that time I was bigger and stronger than my children, after all[1]), or because the true source of the frustration is not immediately obvious. To the poor or dispossessed, the real perpetrators of their condition may not always be visible or accessible. Whatever the reason for its diversion, the aggression must still find an outlet and so it is displaced onto substitute targets, usually those for whom there are fewer associated inhibitions because they are seen as weaker or less able to retaliate – for example, members of minority groups.

Thus, to return to those bigots of Margate, frustration–aggression theory would attribute their xenophobia to the economic and social privations of living in a rundown area. Such hardship would probably generate considerable frustration, which, in turn, gives rise to feelings of aggression. These are then vented on a conveniently visible group of newcomers to their town, the refugees.[2] Dollard et al. (1939) applied this kind of analysis to explain the growth of anti-Semitism in Germany between the two world wars. That Hitler was able to find such a receptive audience for his racist ideology was due, they argued, to the previous decade of frustration caused by the collapse of the German economy in the 1920s. One study that supported this hypothesis was by Hovland and Sears (1940). Concentrating on the southern states of the USA between 1882 and 1930, they correlated an economic index (the price of cotton) with an index of racial aggression (the number of lynchings of black people). As expected, the two indices were negatively related: as the economy declined and times got hard, so the number of lynchings increased[3] (see also Hepworth and West, 1988).

Other attempts to verify this so-called 'scapegoat' theory of prejudice have met with mixed success. Miller and Bugelski (1948) conducted an experiment with a group of young men at a summer camp. On the evening when the men were eagerly anticipating a night out on the town, the camp authorities suddenly announced that they would be required to stay on at the camp to take some uninteresting and difficult tests. This constituted the frustrating experience. Before and after this frustration they were also asked for their attitudes towards two minority groups. Analysis of these intergroup attitudes revealed that after the frustration their stereotypes of the outgroups became less favourable; a control group experiencing no frustration showed little such change. This seemed like a classic demonstration of displacement. Although, understandably, the men were angry at the real agents of their frustration (the camp authorities), this anger also appeared to have 'spilled over' onto the minority groups, who could have no conceivable responsibility for the men's plight. However, Stagner and Congdon (1955) found no evidence for increases in prejudice in students following the frustration of failing in some academic tests. On the other hand, Cowen et al. (1958), using a similar methodology, *did* find some increase in anti-black feeling after failing some puzzles, although on a more general measure of ethnocentrism against all minorities there was little change. Finally, just to add to the complexity, Burnstein and McRae (1962) found that doing badly in an experimental task had just the opposite effects on the evaluation of a black team member. Far from displacing their anger at performing poorly onto him, the white subjects actually saw the black confederate *more* favourably, and this was especially evident in highly prejudiced subjects who should have been the most eager to derogate him.

One of the problems with the displacement explanation is that it is difficult to predict with any certainly which target will be chosen as the scapegoat. Miller (1948), one of the authors of the original theory, suggested that targets that are neither too similar nor too dissimilar to the real source of frustration would be selected. He derived this hypothesis from considering how the contradictory processes of 'generalization' (the association of a learned response to a new stimulus similar to the original conditioned stimulus) and 'inhibition' (the suppression of a response to a stimulus due to its association with punishment) would combine. Because the processes operate in opposite directions – one tending to elicit aggression with increasing similarity, the other tending to prevent it, also as a function of similarity – the situation producing the highest likelihood of aggression is when outgroups are of intermediate similarity (Brewer and Campbell, 1976; Brown, 1984b). However, this analysis often proves rather difficult to apply outside the laboratory. For instance, Horowitz (1973) has identified a number of examples of civil unrest where the violence has been directed not against the original cause of the strife, but against some third party. One of these took place in Burma in 1938, a country which was at that time under British colonial rule. After the break-up of a demonstration by British police, there was extensive rioting. This uprising, however, was not directed against their colonial oppressors but against Muslim Indians; Hindu Indians were much less affected. Although this looks like a prime example of displaced aggression, as Horowitz (1973) points out, simply from the point of view of 'stimulus similarity', the Hindus should have been as good a displacement target as the Muslims. And yet, in the event, they escaped quite lightly. In discussing several other historical examples, Horowitz points out that, although *after the event* it is usually possible to suggest that the conflicts were a result of displaced aggression, the specific choice of outgroup in each case is as well explained by historical and cultural factors as by any single psychological motivation like frustration.

In addition to these difficulties, frustration–aggression theory ran into other obstacles. Perhaps the most fundamental of these was the discovery that frustration was neither necessary nor sufficient to cause aggression; several studies reported that aggression had occurred with no prior frustration or, alternatively, that frustration had been experienced and no overt aggression had resulted (Berkowitz, 1962; Bandura, 1973). These findings led Berkowitz (1962) to propose a major reformulation of the theory. The first change he suggested was to stress the importance of situational cues to release the aggression that had been engendered by frustration. These cues were stimuli in the social environment that had been associated with aggression in the past. Applying this idea to the scapegoat theory of prejudice, Berkowitz reasoned that the likely choice for a scapegoat is an outgroup with prior associations of conflict with or dislike for the ingroup. The second modification Berkowitz made was to redefine the concept of frustration. Dollard et al. (1939) tried to define frustration in objectively observable terms, 'an interference with a goal response'. But it soon became apparent that this was inadequate. The same frustration event can lead to aggression or not, depending on how it is interpreted (Pastore, 1952). Accordingly, Berkowitz widened the meaning of frustration to include a cognitive element: frustration, he believed, is not just some state of objective deprivation, it is also the thwarting of people's expectations – whether they *think* they are deprived. But this was not all. Berkowitz had also found that a whole range of other things seemed to give rise to aggression – for example, pain, extreme heat or cold, and other noxious stimuli – even though, strictly speaking, they were not interferences with goal responses. This led him to propose that the general cause of aggression was not frustration itself, but 'aversive events'. For Berkowitz, frustration was just one of a number of unpleasant experiences likely to give rise to anger and aggression (Berkowitz, 1989).

This revamped frustration–aggression theory proved to be almost as influential as its predecessor. Scores of experiments successfully demonstrated the importance of environmental cues and cognitive mediators in controlling the amount or direction of aggression (Berkowitz, 1974). The theory was given additional support by studies that linked collective violence to adverse meteorological conditions. Baron and Ransberger (1978), followed by Carlsmith and Anderson (1979), showed that riots in American cities were much more likely to occur in very hot weather (i.e. more than 29°C) than when the temperatures were more moderate (i.e. less than 20°C). In Berkowitz's terms, the extreme heat (probably coupled with high humidity) was an aversive stimulus which increased city dwellers' arousal levels, and hence their propensity to violence.

But whether this arousal factor is the only or even the major cause of prejudice and other forms of intergroup aggression is another matter (Billig, 1976). First, there is the problem of translating the separate individual states of frustration into collective acts of aggression. Frustration–aggression theory assumes that whenever there is an outbreak of prejudice or discontent then several hundred (or thousand) people are simultaneously in roughly the same emotional state of anger arousal and coincidentally select the same targets for the discharge of that anger. Elsewhere, I have used an analogy to show the implausibility of this assumption (Brown and Turner, 1981). Imagine a student cafeteria at 1 p.m. during term-time. It is probably crowded with a hundred or more customers. Are they all there at the same time and in the same place because, and only because, they are all hungry, as a simple arousal explanation would have us believe? Of course, people do eat because they are hungry, but the simultaneous choice of time and location must also surely have at least something to do with such social factors as patterns of mutual influence ('Are you coming for lunch, then?'), the availability of other places to eat and the scheduling of classes in the institution concerned. So it is with aggression. The patterning and selectivity of intergroup antagonism suggest that over and above the mere anger of the individuals concerned, factors like social norms and collective goals must also be involved. (This point is explored more fully later in the chapter.)

A second problem with the idea that prejudice is simply the aggregation of individual emotional states is that it implies that conflict between groups is seldom guided by any deliberate strategy on the part of the group members involved, but is rather an irrational affair. Again, such a conclusion seems unwarranted. Fogelson (1970), in his analysis of the American race riots of the 1960s, observed that one noteworthy feature of these riots was that the violence, though widespread, was not completely arbitrary or directionless. Particular stores and houses were selected for looting and arson; others were left virtually untouched. The rioting was also confined to particular geographical areas – usually the home territory of the rioters. All this led Fogelson to suggest that the rioting, though it gave some appearance of irrationality, was actually consciously directed towards particular ends – namely, the publicizing of the rioters' state of deprivation and the defence of their neighbourhood. As we saw in chapter 1, exactly the same conclusion was reached by Reicher (1984a) in his study of a minor disturbance in Britain in 1980. Such observations suggest a degree of cognitive control by the participants which is inconsistent with the idea in frustration–aggression theory that such events are caused simply by the welling up of anger in individuals. If this is true for the extreme behavioural manifestations of discontent that occurred in these riots, then it is plausible to suppose that milder forms of prejudice might also contain similar 'rational' elements such as the perception of some intergroup competition over jobs or housing, or the attempted preservation of deeply held cultural values and practices.

A final difficulty with the frustration–aggression hypothesis is its inability to explain or predict positive instances of intergroup behaviour – friendliness and cooperation. To be sure, an absence of frustration should mean an absence of aggression, but is that the same thing as making positive overtures towards outgroups? More likely it would imply a neutral or indifferent attitude, which is a different matter altogether. And yet, as we shall see, groups do sometimes enjoy mutually favourable relations when they see it in their interests to do so.

Relative deprivation and social unrest

Talking once with a miner I asked him when the housing shortage first became acute in his district; he answered, 'When we were told about it', meaning that 'till recently people's standards were so low that they took almost any degree of overcrowding for granted. (Orwell, 1962, p. 57)

This excerpt from Orwell's brilliant essay on the condition of the British working class in the 1930s, *The Road to Wigan Pier*, makes an important point about the origins of discontent. Deprivation, he implies, is not an absolute condition but is always relative to some norm of what is considered acceptable. This is the idea that lies at the heart of several explanations of social unrest, known collectively as relative deprivation theory.

The central proposition in relative deprivation theory is that people become discontented and rebellious when they perceive a discrepancy between the standard of living they are currently enjoying and the standard they believe they *should* be enjoying. For Gurr (1970), who has done much to formalize the theory, it is precisely this gap between attainments and expectations, or 'relative deprivation', that is the motor force for collective violence. The bigger the gap the greater the likelihood of unrest.

233

Gurr's version of relative deprivation theory, as he acknowledges, is a direct descendant of the frustration–aggression theory discussed in the previous section. Probably because of this, Gurr placed much emphasis on the individual's direct experience of relative deprivation: what person X is experiencing relative to what person X expects. However, others have pointed out that there is another kind of deprivation, a deprivation derived from people's perception of the fortunes of their group. The most prominent of these is Runciman (1966), who suggested that in collective movements the most important factor is a sense that the ingroup is deprived, relative to some desired standard. Runciman labelled this 'fraternalistic (or collective) deprivation' to distinguish it from the other form, 'egoistic deprivation'. Of the many lines of evidence which Runciman draws on to support this distinction, perhaps the most telling is his observation that participants in uprisings are seldom the most deprived *individuals*. Caplan (1970), for instance, noted how supporters of Black Power during the American race riots of the 1960s were drawn mainly from middle- and upper-income blacks and rather less from the poorest (and most egoistically deprived) blacks. Slightly privileged though they may have been relative to others in their (black) ingroup, as members of that disadvantaged *group* they experienced relative deprivation just as keenly as the most destitute of their fellows.

What gives rise to a perception of relative deprivation? At the most general level, as noted above, relative deprivation is caused simply by a gap between expectations and achievements. Cantril (1965) conducted a large cross-national survey in which, among other things, he asked respondents to indicate how they valued their past, present and future life as compared to their 'ideal' good life. The difference between each respondent's actual rating and their ideal aspiration represents a direct measure of relative deprivation. Gurr (1970) correlated the mean relative deprivation scores from each of the thirteen nations in Cantril's study with indices of 'turmoil' derived from archival records of incidents of civil unrest in these same countries. Just as the theory predicted, the correlation between relative deprivation and internal turmoil was strongly positive. Crawford and Naditch (1970) used exactly the same measure of relative deprivation in a survey of black residents in Detroit shortly after a large-scale riot in the city. The respondents' attitudes towards the rioting, Black Power

Table 6.1   Black militancy and relative deprivation

Attitude item		Relative deprivation* %	
		Low	High
Do you think that riots help or hurt the Negro cause?	Help	28	54
	Hurt	60	38
Do you approve or disapprove of Black Power?	Approve	38	64
	Disapprove	36	22
Will force or persuasion be necessary to change white attitudes?	Force	40	51
	Persuasion	52	35

* Perceived discrepancy between 'actual' and 'ideal' life.
Source: Crawford and Naditch (1970), table 1 ('don't knows' omitted)

and militant political action generally were strongly influenced by their level of relative deprivation, as can be seen in table 6.1. Those indicating a large discrepancy between their present and ideal lives were much more likely to endorse support for violent protest.

So, people's expectations are clearly implicated in their support for social change. The next obvious question is: what governs people's expectations? One possibility is past experience. Davies (1969) has suggested that people tend to extrapolate from their own recent experiences of affluence or poverty and expect the future to be similar. If, for example, their standard of living has risen steadily over previous years this will generate an expectation of future gains. Starting from this assumption, Davies (1969) proposed his famous J-curve hypothesis. This states that rebellions are most likely to occur not after a period of prolonged deprivation, but after a period in which the general standard of living has risen for a number of years and then takes a sudden downturn. This sharp decline after a period of relative prosperity produces the requisite gap between actual and deserved living standards for the arousal of relative deprivation.

In support of his theory, Davies (1969) cites mainly historical evidence. Pointing to major upheavals such as the French and Russian revolutions, the American civil war, the rise of Nazism in Germany in the 1930s and the growth of Black Power in the 1960s, he argues that before each of these events there had been a period of 20–30 years of gradually increasing prosperity followed by a steep economic recession. The evidence for Davies' hypothesis is rather mixed. Hepworth and West (1988) re-analysed the same data set used by Hovland and Sears (1940), which linked lynchings of black people to economic indicators (see above). While confirming Hovland and Sears' correlation, albeit at a lower level, Hepworth and West also found an association between one year's lynchings and the *decline* in prosperity from the previous year. On the other hand, Miller et al. (1977) disputed Davies' (1969) analysis of black urban rioting in the USA in the 1960s, claiming that the drop in black prosperity occurred too early (in the late 1950s) to have generated the subsequent black dissatisfaction (cf. Crosby, 1979; Davies, 1978, 1979; Miller and Bolce, 1979).

If comparisons with the past do not always generate thwarted expectations, comparisons with other groups can be a much more potent source of relative deprivation. A classic demonstration of this was provided by Runciman's (1966) survey of English class attitudes. He found that a sizeable number of better-off white-collar workers felt aggrieved at the relative prosperity of those working in blue-collar occupations. Despite their objectively superior position, these white-collar respondents clearly felt that they were not getting as much as they deserved. Such intergroup comparisons were also much in evidence in Vanneman and Pettigrew's (1972) study of prejudice in the US. They surveyed over 1000 white voters and elicited their perceptions as to whether they felt they were doing better or worse economically than other whites like themselves (egoistic deprivation) and blacks (collective deprivation). On the basis of these two questions Vanneman and Pettigrew divided their sample into four groups according to whether they were 'gratified' (doing better than others) or 'deprived' (doing worse), either egoistically or collectively (see table 6.2). Those who were collectively or doubly deprived showed the most prejudice. Those who experienced only egoistic deprivation showed little or no prejudice; their discontent with their personal lot, since it was not combined with a group-based dissatisfaction, did not translate into intergroup prejudice. Notice that in both these studies it is members of 'superior' groups (on various objective economic indicators) who are experiencing relative deprivation.

Table 6.2 Collective and egoistic deprivation and prejudice

Type of deprivation	Prejudice score*
Doubly gratified	−20.9
(doing well personally *and* as a group)	
Egoistically deprived	−13.9
(doing poorly personally but well as a group)	
Collectively deprived	+14.3
(doing well personally but poorly as a group)	
Doubly deprived	+29.1
(doing poorly personally *and* as a group)	

* Typical items included: 'would object if a family member wanted to bring a
Negro friend home for dinner'; 'would mind if a Negro family with about the same
income and education moved next door'; 'thinks white and black students should
go to separate schools'. High score indicates agreement with items.
Source: Vanneman and Pettigrew (1972), table 9

More typically, of course, it is members of subordinate groups who
feel the most deprived. Abeles (1976) found that American blacks'
support for black militancy was correlated with collective deprivation. In India, Muslims, who are a socially disadvantaged minority
group there, have been found to show much more biased attitudes
towards Hindus to the extent that they are collectively deprived
(Tripathi and Srivastava, 1981). Likewise, in South Africa the relative
deprivation experienced by black and Indian people may be related
to their negative attitudes towards other ethnic groups (Appelgryn
and Niemwoudt, 1988; de La Rey and Raju, 1996; but cf. Appelgryn
and Bornmann (1996) for a contrary finding).

In Vanneman and Pettigrew's (1972) study, as we saw, there was
an important distinction between collective and individual deprivation. This is a recurring theme throughout much of the subsequent
research. Guimond and Dubé-Simard (1983) observed that among
French Canadians in Quebec, only measures of collective deprivation
were consistently correlated with support for Quebec nationalism;
measures of egoistic deprivation, on the other hand, showed rather
weak associations. Likewise, Walker and Mann's (1987) study of unemployed workers in Australia found that it was principally those

who felt a strong sense of collective deprivation who were prepared to contemplate militant protest activities, such as participating in demonstrations, breaking the law and destroying public and private property. Those who felt egoistically deprived, in contrast, tended to report more symptoms of individual stress such as headaches, indigestion and sleeplessness (see also Koomen and Fränkel, 1992).

If there is one group that has good cause to feel relatively deprived it is women. Despite decades of equal pay legislation in many countries, women continue to earn less on average than men and are concentrated in lower status occupations (Grubb and Wilson, 1992). For example, according to recent government figures, average salary levels for women in the UK are only around 70 per cent of the levels for men (New Earnings Survey, 1998). This inequality persists into the domestic domain, where women typically undertake the majority of household chores even when both partners are working (Biernat and Wortman, 1991). It is thus rather surprising that several studies have reported that women do not always report much dissatisfaction with this sorry state of affairs (Biernat and Wortman, 1991; Crosby, 1982; Major, 1994). For example, Crosby (1982), in a survey of working women, found that, despite the fact that they were aware of the general disparity between men's and women's pay, her women respondents did not feel that it applied to them personally and hence expressed relatively low levels of discontent. I shall consider possible explanations for this apparent paradox shortly.

Even if women's *general* level of relative deprivation is not as high as one might expect, for those women who do feel the injustice of their position keenly there is evidence that this translates into a desire to try to rectify things. Tougas and Veilleux (1988), in a survey of Canadian women, found a clear link between their feelings of collective deprivation and their support for affirmative action policies aimed at redressing gender inequalities. In an interesting comparison with Crosby's (1982) findings, in a later study Tougas et al. (1991) found that the sense of collective deprivation was driven, at least in part, by women's personal frustration that employment equity programmes had been of little benefit to them. As we saw in Vanneman and Pettigrew's (1972) study, such 'double deprivation' (egoistic and collective combined) seems to be a particularly potent stimulus for protest. Foster and Matheson (1995) found that women students who

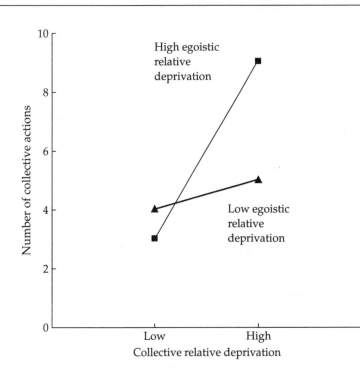

Figure 6.1 Double deprivation and collective action (from Foster and Matheson, 1995, figure 1. Reprinted by permission of Sage Publications)

felt both personally aggrieved that men were paid more than them *and* aggrieved on behalf of women in general were the most likely to have participated in various feminist protest activities in the previous six months (see figure 6.1).

Of course, in Foster and Matheson's (1995) study we cannot be sure of the causal direction: did the deprivation give rise to the protest activity (as relative deprivation theory assumes), or did some accidental involvement in collective action cause a change in their attitudes? That it was the former rather than the latter is suggested by the findings of a rare prospective study, in which respondents' views on their job situation (including both personal and gender-based dissatisfaction) were collected one month *before* a behavioural questionnaire was administered in which their involvement in various personal career development and collective protest activities was investigated (Hafer and Olson, 1993). Feelings of *personal* discontent were only associated with

239

more attempts to change jobs or obtain further qualifications and training and not at all with any collective action. On the other hand, *collective* discontent was strongly linked to involvement in affirmative action programmes and strikes, and only weakly to career improvement (see also Olson et al., 1995). Finally, Kelly and Breinlinger (1996), in another longitudinal study of women activists, found that relative deprivation was only reliably associated with participation in women's group activities for those who showed a strong sense of identification with women as a group. As we shall see, group identification probably plays an important role in translating relative deprivation into collective action.

In all these studies, the link between relative deprivation and collective discontent has been correlational, with all the usual difficulties of causal interpretation that implies. However, experimental evidence also exists which points directly to deprivation being a determinant of derogatory intergroup attitudes and behaviour. A colleague and I asked groups of women students to work on a task in which they had to generate ideas for increasing female participation in senior university jobs (Grant and Brown, 1995). For this they each expected to receive around $10, although they were warned that this payment would depend on the evaluation of their performance by another group. That evaluation formed our experimental manipulation of deprivation: half the groups learned that they had been given a poor evaluation and would receive only $4; the remainder were evaluated positively and would receive their expected $10. The participants reacted strongly to this manipulation. Compared to those who received what they expected, the deprived groups showed markedly higher levels of ingroup bias against the other group, expressed more dislike for them and, from careful observation of their videotaped interactions, made more derogatory comments about them and were readier to engage in collective protest against what they saw as an unfair judgement.

Relative deprivation theory, then, has been quite successful in helping us to understand when and where social discontent will arise. However, in the thirty years since its appearance there have been some qualifications to it, which have improved its explanatory power still further. Four issues in particular are worthy of note.

The first concerns the role of group identification. The importance of social identity processes to intergroup relations will be discussed in chapter 8, but here it is worth recording that people's identification with their ingroup seems to be a crucial precursor to developing a strong sense of collective deprivation to motivate group action. We saw this in Kelly and Breinlinger's (1996) study. Further evidence of this link was provided by Gurin and Townsend (1986), who found that women's gender identity – particularly a sense of sharing a common fate with other women – was strongly related to both collective discontent and the endorsement of collective efforts by women to achieve social change. Likewise, Abrams (1990) found that Scottish teenagers' support for the Scottish Nationalist Party (which has long campaigned for political independence from the rest of the United Kingdom) was correlated with their sense of deprivation in relation to the English (particularly regarding pay differentials), and that this deprivation was connected to the strength of their Scottish identity. Finally, in an experimental study, Smith et al. (1994) found that psychology students' sense of grievance at being arbitrarily deprived of their experimental payment was magnified if they had first spent a few minutes describing psychologists as a group, thereby priming their professional identity.

A second factor that seems to be important in transforming people's responses to inequality into collective protest is the belief that such action will bring about some social change (Klandermans, 1997). However angry disadvantaged groups may feel, if they do not see some practical means of redress they may not be willing to do much about their plight. This was well illustrated in an experiment by Martin et al. (1984), which had women workers taking the part of a female sales manager in a company. This manager was depicted as being slightly to greatly underpaid relative to comparable male managers, thus creating different levels of relative deprivation. The organization was also described as one in which the female managers had (or had not) regular contact with each other, had vital skills that could not easily be replaced, and had organized themselves into a formal group with the aim of rectifying gender inequalities. In this way the experimenters hoped to create the impression that the disadvantaged group of women managers were (or were not) able to mobilize resources to change their situation. Asked to image that they were such a manager, the participants responded to the different levels of male–female pay inequality in an entirely predictable fashion: the larger it was, the more discontented they felt. On the other hand, this had little effect on what kinds of protest they might engage in. This was determined much more by whether or not they believed that the collective efforts of women managers could be effectively marshalled. In a real-world parallel of this, Klandermans (1997) investigated the reasons why Dutch trade union members elected not to participate in a strike. Despite the fact that they believed that an all-out strike would result in clear benefits to union members, nearly half of these non-participants felt that it would not make much difference whether or not they joined in and, even more significantly, over 80 per cent believed that the general support for the strike would be poor and hence, by implication, the strike would be a failure (Klandermans, 1997, p. 77). In short, some sense of perceived efficacy may be as important – if not more so – as a perception of being relatively deprived (Bernstein and Crosby, 1980).

A third issue concerns the nature of the perceived injustice that underlies relative deprivation. As traditionally conceived, and as all the examples I have considered above indicate, a sense of relative deprivation is engendered when people experience some discrepancy between the outcomes they are receiving and those to which they feel entitled. In other words, they perceive some injustice in the distribution of material goods. Tyler and Smith (1998) have argued that, important though such *distributive* justice concerns are, they can sometimes take second place to a sense of *procedural* injustice – a feeling that the methods for deciding about and allocating material goods are unfair (independently of the ingroup's actual outcomes). According to this point of view, what you get may not be as important as the way that you get it. An example of this tension between procedural and distributive justice is provided by Lind et al.'s (1993) analysis of litigants' acceptance (or not) of arbitration decisions handed down by some American courts adjudicating in civil law suits. After the court's initial decision (which was not binding unless both parties accepted it), those involved were asked for their evaluations of the fairness of the court procedure and the favourability of the outcome to themselves. Lind et al.'s findings suggested that the principal determinant of whether the parties accepted the arbitration decision was their positive assessment of the fairness of the court's proceedings. Their subjective view of the outcome was generally unrelated to their acceptance of the arbitration, although the objective outcome (awarded by the court) did have an influence. Although these results provide a reassuringly benign view of dispute resolution ('it matters not who wins or loses, but how the game is played'), I suspect that they may be restricted to the legal context in which they were obtained. In other less-regulated intergroup contexts it may be much more difficult to separate procedural and distributive concerns. After all, why do subordinate group members feel relatively deprived (i.e. perceive unfairness in group outcomes such as inequalities in earnings)? Is it not usually because they see that the *methods* of allocating those outcomes have been illegitimate (i.e. procedural irregularities such as employment discrimination)? Indeed, there is considerable evidence from interpersonal contexts that distributive and procedural injustice may interact in exactly this way (Brockner and Wiesenfeld, 1996). It seems to me likely that a similar relationship will hold in intergroup settings also.

The final matter concerns the thorny question of who is chosen as comparator. Social comparisons, as we have seen, are an important source of relative deprivation since they often provide the means by which people assess their group's standing and progress in society. But whether those comparisons lead to feelings of deprivation – or its converse, gratification – obviously depends entirely on the group we choose to compare with. I have in front of me this year's pay claim for my trade union. In it our case for a large salary increase is presented in various ways, one of the most persuasive of which (at least to me) is a figure portraying the change in average earnings of various occupational groups over the past ten years. The graph for university lecturers' pay is an approximately horizontal line, showing no increase in real terms over the decade. However, the graphs for hospital doctors, civil servants and MPs all reveal steady increases of varying magnitude over the same period (especially MPs: a growth of 30 per cent). So, of course, as a university academic, I feel seriously deprived and more than a little aggrieved. However, noticeably missing from that same pay claim are the salary levels of nurses or school cleaners, in comparison to whom university salaries look positively exorbitant. So, what governs people's choice of comparison group?

Early relative deprivation theorists suggested that we tend to use 'similar others' for comparison purposes, an idea familiar to us from Festinger's (1954) theory (Gurr, 1970; Runciman, 1966). Major (1994) argues that this provides part of the solution to the 'paradox of the contented female worker' noted by Crosby (1982). Major suggests that the reason that women seem surprisingly unperturbed by glaring gender pay inequalities is that they typically compare themselves to *other women* rather than to men. In other words, they make intragroup comparisons among similar category members rather than intergroup comparisons with a different outgroup. Major argues that this is for a variety of structural, social and ideological reasons. For example, many occupations are still markedly skewed in gender composition, which makes other women the most available comparison target for the majority of female workers. Added to this is the fact that many women have long-term personal relationships with men, which may somewhat inhibit too frequent a comparison with them at an intergroup level. Finally, there is a pervasive belief in Western societies that people generally get what they deserve (Lerner, 1980) so that, in Major's words, 'what "is" has a marked tendency to become what "ought" to be' (Major, 1994, p. 294). Such an ideology is hardly likely to promote a questioning appraisal of the many differences in economic status between men and women.

Nevertheless, groups do not always restrict themselves to within-group comparisons and nor do they necessarily focus only on outgroups that are similar to them. If this were the case, there would never have been the revolution wrought in South Africa by Nelson Mandela and his comrades in the African National Congress. The whole basis of their successful struggle against apartheid was the iniquity of the huge disparities between the dominant white minority and the underprivileged black majority, two very *different* groups. In this instance, the strong consciousness among black South Africans of themselves as a group, the near universal condemnation of apartheid as an illegitimate political system, and the increasing instability of the South African economy were all factors that precipitated comparisons between such manifestly dissimilar groups. I will consider these factors again in more detail in chapter 8 when I discuss the consequences for social identity of belonging to groups of superior or inferior status.

Intergroup Behaviour and Real Group Interests

The very first Israelis I ever saw were soldiers. They came to my village and entered the school. I think there is nothing good to be said about them. When I see any soldiers, I think that those soldiers will be killed some day . . . There will be no peace. Some day there will be another war, and the Arabs will be successful. We will take back all of Palestine. (Najeh Hassan, 20-year-old Palestinian)

You have to understand the Jewish people. We are a small people; our identity in the past was a persecuted people, a hated people. Young Israelis like me feel that it is about time Israel is not oppressed but a nation that is independent and controls its own destiny . . . [A Palestinian] is someone who is poor, weak physically and mentally. I don't mean stupid, but I wouldn't say brilliant either. A simple worker whose mentality is directed towards how to make a profit. (Yaacov Leviatan, 20-year-old Jew)

According to the newspaper report from which these comments were taken (the *Observer*, 31 May 1987), Najeh Hassan and Yaacov Leviatan were born within days of each other and not many miles apart in June 1967. In the same week, the Israeli government launched a major military offensive against its Arab neighbours, which resulted in the Israeli occupation of East Jerusalem, the West Bank and the Golan Heights. Why should these two young men living in the same country have such hostile attitudes, if not actually towards each other, then certainly towards the group to which the other belongs? One answer is to be found later in the same newspaper article in a remark by Yaacov's father, Shlomo Leviatan: 'There is a basic conflict of interest between the Palestinians and us: what is good for us is bad for them, and what is good for them is bad for us'. This, in a sentence, is Sherif's (1966) theory of intergroup conflict, a theory that has had seminal influence on the whole field of intergroup relations since the War.

Conflicting goals and intergroup competition

At the heart of Sherif's theory is the proposition that group members' intergroup attitudes and behaviour will tend to reflect the objective interests of their group *vis-à-vis* other groups. Where these interests conflict, then their group's cause is more likely to be furthered by a

245

competitive orientation towards the rival group, which is often easily extended to include prejudiced attitudes and even overtly hostile behaviour. In the Israeli–Palestinian example above the conflict of interest is plain. The groups are disputing over an area of land, for which each claims sole historical, political and religious ownership and rights. At the same time, the ingroup's success in achieving the goal is likely to be furthered by very positive attitudes towards other ingroup members, thereby engendering high morale and cohesion. Where, on the other hand, the groups' interests coincide, then it is more functional for the group members to adopt a cooperative and friendly attitude towards the outgroup. If this is reciprocated then a positive joint outcome is more probable.

To demonstrate the validity of this perspective Sherif and his colleagues conducted three famous field experiments, which have come to be known as the 'summer camp' studies (Sherif and Sherif, 1953; Sherif et al., 1955, 1961). Although these experiments differed slightly from one another, they are similar enough in conception and outcome for us to be able to consider them together. They were longitudinal (lasting some three weeks) and were designed to show systematic changes in behaviour as a result of changing intergroup relations. The full design included three stages: group formation, intergroup conflict and conflict reduction.[4] To effect this design, Sherif and his colleagues arranged for the experiments to be conducted in the context of a boys' summer camp. In fact, as far as those participating in the experiments were concerned, that is exactly what it was since all the activities were exactly the kinds of things that went on in American summer camps in the 1950s (and probably still do!). The difference was, of course, that, unknown to the boys, the adults running the camp were all trained researchers making careful observations of all that went on. The boys themselves – all white, middle class and aged around twelve years – had been carefully screened before being invited to the camp, and only those who seemed to be psychologically well adjusted and from stable homes were accepted. In addition, none of the boys knew each other before coming to the camp. Although this was a highly select and unrepresentative sample, it did ensure that any behaviour they subsequently exhibited could not be attributed to a prior history of social or psychological deprivation, or to pre-existing personal relationships between the boys.

In the first stage of the experiments the large group of 22–24 children was split up into the two experimental groups of the study. Care was taken to match these two groups as carefully as possible. In the first two experiments, in addition to matching on various physical and psychological characteristics, it was also arranged to have the majority of each boy's best friends in the *out*group.[5] In the third experiment the boys never actually met each other before the groups were formed and initially were camped some distance from each other, unaware of the other group's presence. For some days, the children engaged in various activities in these groups without, however, having much to do with the other group. Very quickly, the groups developed an internal structure and evolved mini-cultures of their own with their own group symbols and names, and norms of appropriate behaviour. Although the other group did not figure much in their thinking, it is interesting to note that in the first two experiments the observers did record some instances of comparisons between the groups and in these comparisons 'the edge was given to one's own group' (Sherif, 1966, p. 80). Furthermore, in the third study, where the groups did not know of each other's existence at this stage, on being informed of the presence of the other group several boys spontaneously suggested to the camp authorities that the other group be challenged to some sporting contest. As we shall see, it is significant that these expressions of ingroup favouritism occurred *before* the intergroup conflict phase of the experiment had actually been introduced.

The second stage then began. It was announced to the boys that a series of intergroup contests would take place, e.g. softball, tug-of-war etc.). The overall winner of these contests would receive a cup and each member of this successful group would be given a gleaming new penknife – just the kind of prize every 12-year-old boy covets. The losers would receive nothing. In this way, an objective conflict of interest was introduced between the groups. In technical terms, they had moved from being independent of one another to being negatively *interdependent* – what one group gained the other lost. With the advent of this conflict stage the boys' behaviour changed dramatically. Whereas in the first stage the two groups had coexisted more or less peaceably, they were now transformed into two hostile factions, never losing an opportunity to deride the outgroup and, in some instances, physically attack it.

247

In a variety of micro-experiments, disguised as games, Sherif and his associates were able to document systematic and consistent ingroup favouritism in judgements, attitudes and sociometric preferences. One of these experiments was designed as a bean-toss game in which a large number of beans were scattered over the grass. Each team member had a set time to pick up as many beans as possible. Each boy's pickings were then displayed on a screen by means of a projector (or so it seemed to the children), and everyone estimated how many each had collected. In fact, through some sleight of hand, the experimenter contrived always to project the same number of beans onto the screen. Despite this constant 'stimulus', the boys' judgements showed consistent bias in favour of their own group. These biases are shown in figure 6.2, where it can be seen that both groups overestimated the performances of their own members as compared to those in the outgroup. Notice also that the winning group showed even more bias than the losing group.

Changes took place *within* the groups too. They invariably became more cohesive and the leadership structure sometimes changed, with a more aggressive boy assuming dominance. When asked to nominate their best friends, over 90 per cent of the children in both groups chose people in their own group. This was all the more remarkable when it is remembered that, in the first two studies at least, every boy's best friends had been placed in the *other* group. How fragile those initial interpersonal relationships proved to be in the face of the changing intergroup relationship!

On the face of it, these experiments seemed to provide strong support for Sherif's theory. The behaviour of these ordinary well-adjusted children was shown to vary systematically with the nature of the intergroup relation. These changes in the boys' behaviour were too widespread and too rapid to be attributable to any enduring personality disposition. Moreover, members of the winning group, who were presumably less frustrated than the losers, actually seemed to show *more* evidence of outgroup derogation than those who really had been frustrated by being denied the prizes. Such a finding is rather problematic for the frustration–aggression theory that we considered earlier.

Subsequent research largely confirmed Sherif's findings. In a series of experiments by Blake and Mouton (1962) it was found that groups

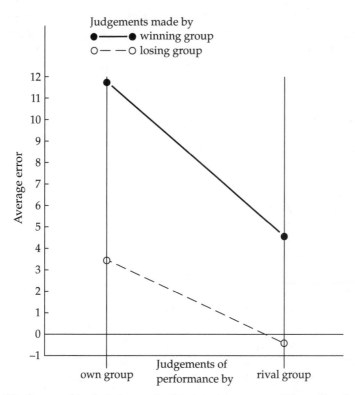

Figure 6.2 Ingroup bias in judgements after intergroup competition: errors in estimating a performance by victors and losers (from Sherif, 1966, p. 84, figure 5.2. Copyright © 1966 by Houghton Mifflin Company, Boston. Used by permission)

in competition with one another consistently over-evaluated their own group's product in comparison with that of the outgroup. In one of these experiments, 48 groups (mainly of managerial staff) were asked to solve an organizational problem. The groups were arranged in competitive pairs. Afterwards, each group evaluated both its own solution and that of its rival. Of the 48 possible group judgements, 46 favoured the ingroup solution, two reckoned the solutions to be equal, and not one of them conceded any superiority to the outgroup! (Blake and Mouton, 1962). Similar results were obtained by Kahn and Ryen (1972) when they asked groups to engage in a simulated 'football' game in the laboratory. Despite the fact that members of their own team were unknown to them and could not even be seen throughout the session, they were rated more favourably than members of the opposing team. Also, just as Sherif had found, winning teams showed much more evidence of this ingroup bias than losing teams. In a subsequent experiment, Kahn and Ryen also found bias favouring the ingroup even when they asked members merely to *anticipate* taking part in such an intergroup encounter. The bias in this experiment was strongest when anticipating competition but, somewhat surprisingly, it was still visible when the groups were asked to imagine *cooperating* with another group.

The readiness for people to show partiality for their own group (and its products) over outgroups (and theirs) is not confined to artificially created groups in experiments, however. Prevailing national stereotypes often undergo sharp changes for better or worse according to developments in international relations as new alliances are forged or wars declared. For example, Seago (1947) found that American stereotypes of Japanese people became very much less favourable after the Japanese attack on Pearl Harbor in 1941. During the Gulf War of 1990–1 Haslam et al. (1992) recorded Australian students' perceptions of the United States, a rather negative outgroup for Australian students. Between September 1990, just after Iraq invaded Kuwait, and February 1991, when they finally withdrew, the stereotypes of Americans became significantly less positive, particularly on such traits as 'arrogant' and 'scientifically minded'.

Studies of ethnic, occupational and religious groups have also confirmed the link between ethnocentric attitudes and functional relations between groups. Brewer and Campbell (1976) conducted an ethnographic survey of thirty tribal groups in East Africa. Respondents from these different groups rated their own and other groups on a number of indices. Of these groups, 27 gave higher ratings to themselves than to any other group. The degree of this ingroup bias in relation to particular outgroups was weakly related to their proximity: nearby outgroups seemed to be derogated somewhat more than further distant groups. This correlation is consistent with Sherif's realistic conflict approach since it would be expected that neighbouring groups would be more likely to become involved in disputes over grazing land, access to water and other scarce resources. Brown et al. (1986) studied workgroup relations in a large factory. As is often the case, when we asked workers to judge their own and other groups' contributions to the running of the organization, they almost invariably favoured the ingroup. In addition to eliciting people's attitudes, we also asked them to characterize each intergroup relationship on a harmony–conflict dimension ('two teams pulling together' versus 'two groups on opposite sides working against each other'). This index of conflict was strongly correlated with the amount of bias shown against each outgroup: those outgroups with whom a conflictual relationship was perceived were thought to contribute less to the organization than those who were seen to be working *with* the ingroup. As a final illustration of the importance of conflicting group interests, consider the relationship between Orthodox and Reform Jews in Israel, a relationship which is at best tense and which has, on occasion, degenerated into outright hostility (see, for example, the *Independent*, 13 September, 1997). This intergroup situation was the focus of a study by Struch and Schwartz (1989). They examined the aggressive intentions of secular Israelis towards ultra orthodox Jews. These were measured by various items, including, at the mildest pole, some social distance measures (e.g. willingness to have as neighbours), some items concerned with electoral opposition to projects of special interest to such religious groups and, strongest of all, the endorsement of certain actions aimed directly as penalizing the sect (e.g. boycotting their stores). The best single predictor of this aggression was the respondents' answers to two questions concerning conflicts of interests between the groups: the more conflict they perceived, the more aggression they expressed. Interestingly, this correlation was strongest among those respondents who themselves identified strongly with some religious (but not ultra orthodox) group. In other words, the social identity of the group members had an effect on how much psychological impact the conflict of interests between the groups had, a result which recalls similar findings from some studies of relative deprivation discussed earlier.

I began this section with one real-world intergroup conflict; let me finish with another. In 1984, British coal miners went on strike over the threatened closure of a number of mines. The strike lasted for twelve months, during which time there were several violent confrontations between striking miners picketing pits and power stations and the police attempting to prevent them. Viewed in Sherif's terms we could describe this as a classic example of a 'realistic conflict'. In

251

any specific incident we could regard the miners and the police as disputing the territory outside the pit gates but, more generally, we might say that they were engaged in a political 'win–lose' struggle over the conduct of industrial disputes. The dramatic effect that this conflict had on miners' attitudes towards the police is graphically described in this bitter comment from a South Wales miner during the strike: 'We've always been brought up to respect policemen but I've got no respect for any of them now. There was a time when if I saw a policeman have a hammering I'd go and help him. I'd walk past and spit in his eye now' (quoted in *Striking Back* by the Welsh Campaign for Civil Liberties, 1984, p. 182).

Superordinate goals and intergroup cooperation

Conflicting goals, as we have seen, lead quickly to the development of hostilities between groups, the arousal of competitive ingroup-favouring biases and internal group cohesion. What about the other side of the coin? How may cooperation and friendliness between groups be induced? According to the realistic group conflict approach outlined at the start of this chapter, the solution is clear. A way must be found to replace the objectively conflictual relationship between the warring groups with one in which they are *positively* inter-dependent, each needing the other for the attainment of some desired objectives.

This, at least, was the strategy adopted by Sherif and his colleagues in the summer camp studies. Having so easily generated such fierce competition between the boys, the researchers attempted to reduce the conflict by introducing a series of *superordinate goals* for the groups – that is, goals that both groups desired but which were unattainable by one group by its own efforts alone (Sherif, 1966). One such superordinate goal was engineered by arranging for the camp truck to break down some miles from camp. Since it was nearly lunchtime, the children had a clear common interest in getting the truck started to return them to camp. However, the truck was too heavy to be push-started by one group on its own. Only by both groups pulling on the tug-of-war rope attached to the front bumper (the same rope they had used in *contest* just days earlier!) could the truck be moved. After a number of scenarios like this, a marked change was observed in the boys' behaviour. They became much less aggressive towards members of the other group and on a number of quantitative indices showed a clear reduction in the amount of ingroup favouritism.

Several subsequent experiments have confirmed these effects of introducing superordinate goals (Turner, 1981). To give just two examples, Ryen and Kahn (1975) found that bias in people's intergroup evaluations was reduced (though not eliminated) after a cooperative intergroup task as compared to a competitive task. They also observed that members of the two groups sat closer to one another after the cooperative encounter than after competition. In an experiment I conducted with a colleague, we found similar effects for cooperative goals, independently of any interaction between the groups (Brown and Abrams, 1986). In this study the groups (of schoolchildren) taking part never actually met but believed that they were linked cooperatively (or competitively) with another school. Making the intergroup goal relationship a cooperative one in this way led them to believe that they would like members of the other school more, work together with them better and feel more cooperative towards them.

So far, the implementation of superordinate goals looks to be a powerful recipe for the reduction of intergroup antagonism; working together for such jointly valued objectives seems invariably to promote harmony and to reduce discrimination. But before leaping to that conclusion, we must look at some other research, which has identified some important limitations of the superordinate goals strategy. The first of these studies concerns the *outcome* of the cooperative endeavours and has been investigated extensively by Worchel and his colleagues. Noting that in the summer camp studies the cooperative episodes between the groups were always successful, Worchel et al. (1977) reasoned that it may have been this successful outcome rather than the cooperation itself that led to the reduced hostilities. Accordingly, they designed an experiment in which they arranged for two groups working together on two tasks either to succeed or to fail. This cooperative encounter was preceded by a period of interaction in which the groups had variously been competing, cooperating or working independently on two other tasks, the outcome of which was never made clear to them. Worchel et al. suggested that this prior 'history' of intergroup relations might have an important impact on the groups' subsequent reaction to failure in the later cooperative task. So it turned out. After the first phase of interaction, attitudes were predictably affected by the nature of the intergroup goals: those cooperating showed the most favourable attitudes towards the outgroup, the competitive groups the least, and the independent groups falling in between. Attitudes towards the ingroup showed exactly the opposite pattern. As usual, competition elicited greatest ingroup attraction (or cohesion), with slightly less in the other two conditions. However, after the second phase – where, remember, all groups had been cooperating – there were some rather different reactions. Attitudes towards the ingroup hardly changed at all, but in all the experimental conditions except one the groups showed increased attraction towards the *outgroup*. Irrespective of whether they succeeded or failed, those who had previously been cooperating or working independently became friendlier towards those in the other group. The exception occurred among those groups who had previously been competing with one another. If the cooperation in phase 2 was 'successful' then, like the other groups, they too were more favourably disposed towards the outgroup. But those who 'failed' in the cooperative tasks showed a sharp decrease in their outgroup attraction ratings (see figure 6.3). It was as if they wished to blame the outgroup for their joint failure to achieve the superordinate goal (see also, Worchel and Norvell, 1980).

It is not just the outcome of the cooperation over superordinate goals that affects intergroup attitudes. Sometimes people seem to react adversely to the convergence or blurring of boundaries implied by that cooperation. Blake et al. (1964) report how in a chemical plant attempts to reduce interdepartmental rivalry by imposing company-side superordinate goals were not always successful in eliminating friction. I made a similar observation in the course of a case study of an aircraft engineering factory (Brown, 1978). I asked the respondents (shop stewards working in the factory) to imagine a situation in which the management announced a 10 per cent redundancy programme across the whole factory. For active trade unionists, as these men were, such a situation represents a clear and common threat to all groups of workers in the factory, one which they could most effectively deal with by a concerted and joint programme of inter-union action. To my surprise, however, only one-fifth of my respondents reacted to this hypothetical situation by talking of developing a joint strategy and cooperative links between the different sections of the

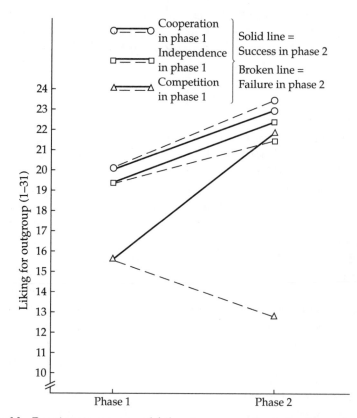

Figure 6.3 Reactions to success and failure in a cooperative task with a prior history of cooperation, competition or independence (from Worchel et al., 1977)

workforce.[6] Most seemed to see the threat as one that would have to be dealt with by defending their own area in isolation. The atmosphere of intense rivalry between some of the departments rendered the possibility of collaborative action difficult. Here is how one of the respondents summed up these difficulties:

I should think that would be about one of the only things that maybe could pull the two main factions together that you've got here – you've got Production and Development ... if they knew that they were all in the same boat and that they were all going to suffer. Because at the moment, I've got to admit, it's 'us' and 'them'. They sort of [two-fingered gesture made by S] at us and we do the same thing ... It's bad, it really is bad ... I never realized it was that bad until I actually became a steward . . . I should think that would be their only answer. If they tried – I say 'they' – if *we* then tried to do it in our separate areas; Christ! We'd be lost wouldn't we? You'd have not only men fighting the firm for a job, you'd have men fighting men for a job, which is not on is it? Not to my way of thinking anyway. (Brown, 1978, p. 425)

I found evidence of similar reactions to a superordinate goal in two laboratory experiments (Deschamps and Brown, 1983; Brown and Wade, 1987). In both we created a cooperative situation in which two groups had to work together for a considerable financial reward. The task was to rework some factual material into a lively and interesting article suitable for a popular magazine. Their joint success at this would be judged by an expert journalist. However, we varied the manner in which the two groups worked together. In some conditions, the two groups were given very *distinctive* roles to play: one had to concentrate on the text, the other on the figures, pictures and headlines. In other conditions they were given very *similar* roles: each was given roughly half the materials to work with. Finally, in the Brown and Wade (1987) study, we made the groups' roles still more similar or ambiguous in a third condition by not allocating any sub-tasks whatsoever. In both experiments, we found that varying the distinctiveness of the groups' roles in this way had reliable effects on their friendliness towards the other group. Despite the fact that they were all cooperating towards the same superordinate goal, those with distinctive roles showed greater friendliness towards the outgroup than those whose group contributions were not so easily distinguishable. However, subsequent research has indicated that the positive effects of distinguishing task roles clearly may be confined to cooperative encounters that are strictly at an intergroup level. Marcus-Newhall et al. (1993) introduced some modifications to the paradigm we had developed to allow a more personalized interaction. In these circumstances, allocating particular activities to each group produced slightly more bias than an arrangement where the tasks were distributed across the two groups (see Brewer (1999) for further analysis of the effectiveness of superordinate goals in promoting cooperation).

These findings suggest that groups which have a common interest in uniting or even just working together more closely may be well advised to think carefully about how to allow each group to retain something of its identity in the joint operation. A good example of how this can be achieved is provided by Hartley et al. (1983) in their study of the 1980 national steel strike in Britain. In the steel industry there are at least six different trade unions representing various occupational groups. When the strike began, a joint trade union strike committee was set up in each area to coordinate the activities of the strikers. Hartley et al. (1983) report how the advent of the strike brought about close inter-union cooperation as they attempted to attain their superordinate goal of a better pay award from their employers. One of the ways in which this cooperation was achieved is interesting and confirms the experimental findings I have just presented. As Hartley et al. describe it:

Inter-union cooperation was also the product of an emergent division of labour, especially on the Rotherham Strike Committee. URTU (the road haulage union) representatives were extremely knowledgeable about the local haulage industry (by contrast with ISTC – the main steel workers union) and their contributions concerning it were highly valued. By confining their contributions to this, and rarely participating in the major tactical debates, the URTU members adopted a specialist role on the Rotherham Strike Committee which was conducive to cooperation. (Hartley et al., 1983, pp. 130–1)

Realistic group conflict theory: an evaluation

Realistic group conflict theory, as we have seen, offers a powerful explanation for both the positive and the negative sides of intergroup behaviour. Its principal strength is that it can account for the ebb and flow of prejudice over time and across different social contexts since it shows how these can often be attributed to changing economic and political relations between the groups concerned. Moreover, as we shall see in chapter 8, it provides the main plank for successful interventions aimed at improving intergroup attitudes, particularly those based on the contact hypothesis. Nevertheless, despite its undoubted merits there are, as Turner (1981) has noted, a number of empirical and theoretical difficulties with the perspective which mean that it is unlikely by itself to provide a complete account of all aspects of intergroup relations.

One problem is that while it is clear that intergroup competition leads to more negative and biased attitudes than cooperation, such biases do not disappear altogether in the latter type of situation. One only has to think of the tensions that persist in coalitions of political parties or in corporate or institutional mergers to be reminded of this. Indeed, a number of experiments have shown that ingroup favouritism is remarkably hard to eradicate even when groups have a material interest in its elimination (Brown, 1984a; Ryen and Kahn, 1975).

A second difficulty is that an explicit conflict of interest may not be necessary for the arousal of ingroup bias and intergroup discrimination. Ironically enough, one of the first hints of this came from the 'summer camp' studies that Sherif and his colleagues conducted. Recall Sherif's (1966) observation that, even before the competition phase had been introduced, the boys had shown an interest in trying to 'best' the other group in various activities. As we shall see in the next chapter, such apparently gratuitous intergroup rivalry now has considerable experimental documentation.

A final ambiguity is whether the negative interdependence that the theory assumes to underlie intergroup hostility need always be based on real conflicts over such concrete issues as land, money or political power. Perhaps, instead, it could derive from *perceived* conflicts of interests or even from competition over such intangible assets as social status. Sherif himself was vague on this point, defining group interests as:

a real or *imagined* threat to the safety of the group, an economic interest, a political advantage, a military consideration, prestige, or a number of others. (Sherif, 1966, p. 15)

Allowing perceived conflicts to have similar causal status to actual conflicts helps us to understand why some manifestations of racism (for example) take the form of, 'they (immigrants) are taking all our jobs/houses etc.' even though unemployment and homelessness among immigrant groups are usually higher than those of the host community. What people believe may be more important than the demographic facts.

However, if perceptions of conflicting goals can underlie intergroup prejudice, and if those perceptions do not always veridically reflect the groups' actual relations, where do they come from? One hypothesis is that such beliefs derive from ideological attempts by dominant groups to manufacture social divisions (and obfuscate others) as part of some long-term 'divide and rule' political strategy (Billig, 1976; Reicher, 1986). Such an argument has a ring of plausibility, particularly in relation to those real-world intergroup tensions that are not obviously founded in objective conflicts or, in the opposite case, where there is little discord *despite* the presence of an objective subjugation. However, it is not one for which it is easy to find conclusive empirical support. Moreover, the occurrence of such 'non-realistic' perceived conflicts, even in the ideologically aseptic environment of the social psychologist's laboratory, suggests that there may be other processes underlying such subjective orientations. These are discussed in the following two chapters.

Summary

1 One theory links intergroup prejudice and social discontent together by considering them both to be a product of frustration. According to this frustration–aggression theory, both kinds of phenomena are examples of displaced aggression caused by the frustrations endemic to social life. In times of economic depression, these frustrations are intensified still further and the resulting aggression (or prejudice) is more violent and more widespread. This theory was subsequently modified by Berkowitz to incorporate cognitive factors and to attempt to predict which 'scapegoat' would be chosen as the target of prejudice. However, even in its revised form, frustration–aggression theory still posits individual anger arousal as the main cause of collective discontent. Such a view may be difficult to reconcile with the seemingly uniform and goal-directed nature of much intergroup aggression.
2 A direct descendant of frustration–aggression theory is relative deprivation theory. The core idea of this theory is that people become discontented when they perceive a negative discrepancy between their current standard of living and the standard of living they believe they deserve. Relative deprivation is this

gap between attainments and expectations, and has been found to correlate with various societal indices of disorder. One of the most important causes of relative deprivation is a negative comparison between the ingroup and other groups. In various contexts these have been found to be associated with dissatisfaction in both high- and low-status groups. Recent developments in relative deprivation theory have concerned the role of group identification, the perceived feasibility of achieving any change through protest, the fairness of procedures used to allocate group outcomes (as well as the fairness of the outcomes themselves) and, most important of all, how to predict the choice of comparison groups. Often this is determined by similarity but occasionally very dissimilar groups engage in mutual comparisons.

3   A major determinant of intergroup behaviour is the nature of the goal relationships existing between groups. Where these are conflictual – what one group gains another loses – intergroup competition and antagonism are likely to result. Alongside these negative orientations run biases and misperceptions favouring the ingroup. Such discriminatory or biased intergroup attitudes may be functional in assisting the group to achieve its objectives.

4   If conflictual goal relationships generate hostility and competition, then common or superordinate goals should lead to friendliness and cooperation. Much evidence supports this. However, it is important that the outcome of the cooperative endeavours is successful. If the superordinate goal is not achieved, then there is a danger that the failure may be blamed on the outgroup, with negative effects on attraction to that outgroup. Furthermore, it is often helpful if groups can make distinctive contributions to joint ventures so that their identities are not threatened by the blurring of group boundaries which may occur with superordinate goals.

Notes

1   But, alas, no longer! And, as our roles have become less unequal, both my attempts at remonstration and their assaults on neighbouring greenhouses have become much less frequent.

2 Ironically, of course, the refugees themselves are likely to be much more frustrated than those who disparage them. Most of them are fleeing from situations of extreme poverty or persecution far worse than the good people of Margate could ever imagine.

3 As with any correlational analysis, causality is difficult to establish here.

4 This last stage was not included in the two earlier experiments and is discussed in the following section. There were also some differences in the group formation phase, which will be noted presently.

5 These friendships had formed in the first few days of the camp.

6 In the event, the situation proved to be more real than hypothetical. In the years following the study, the company in question implemented several job-cutting programmes on a much wider scale than I had outlined in my 'imaginary situation'.

Further Reading

Berkowitz, L. (1989) Frustration–aggression hypothesis: examination and reformulation. *Psychological Bulletin*, **106**, 59–73.

Billig, M.G. (1976) *Social Psychology and Intergroup Relations*, chs 4–5. London: Academic Press.

Major, B. (1994) From social inequality to personal entitlement: the role of social comparisons, legitimacy appraisals, and group membership, in Zanna, M.P. (ed.) *Advances in Experimental Social Psychology*, vol. 26, pp. 243–8. San Diego, CA: Academic Press.

Olson, J.M., Herman, C.P. and Zanna, M.P. (1986) *Relative Deprivation and Social Comparison*. Hillsdale, NJ: Lawrence Erlbaum.

Sherif, M. (1966) *Group Conflict and Cooperation*. London: Routledge and Kegan Paul.

Turner, J.C. (1981) The experimental social psychology of intergroup behaviour, in Turner, J.C. and Giles, H. (eds) *Intergroup Behaviour*, pp. 66–101. Oxford: Blackwell.

Worchel, S. and Austin, W. (eds) (1986) *The Social Psychology of Intergroup Relations*, 2nd edn, chs 5, 16. Chicago: Nelson Hall.

7

THINKING ABOUT GROUPS

Throughout this book, and especially in the previous chapter, we have considered many different examples of intergroup situations. These have involved ethnic groups, trade unions, sports teams, laboratory groups and others besides. Some of these relationships have been conflictual, imbued with hostility and distrust, others were more cooperative and harmonious. Cutting across this tremendous diversity, though, was one common feature: the participants were viewing each other in categorical terms, as members of two or more groups. Indeed, as I explained in chapter 1, this is one of the defining characteristics of intergroup behaviour. Given that the process of categorization is always invoked in intergroup encounters, it is reasonable to ask what determines its likelihood of use and what are its cognitive and behavioural consequences. In short, what leads us to think about people as group members, and what happens when we do? These are the questions that will concern me in this chapter.

The first half of the chapter is devoted to an analysis of social categorization, what I call the foundation stone of all intergroup behaviour. Psychologists, whatever their specialism, all agree that human thought and perception would not be possible without the ability to simplify and systematize the world into categories. The process of categorization gives rise to two inevitable consequences: a sharpening of the perceived differences *between* categories and a levelling of the distinctions *within* categories. These twin processes of accentuation and assimilation serve to make categories more functional for their owner by helping to discriminate better between members who belong to one rather than another.

A first important question is to understand the factors determining which of several potentially available categories will actually be used in any situation. As we shall see, these include people's habitual dispositions, their particular goals at that moment, and also the composition of the people to be categorized. In general, we can say that categories will be chosen which make the most sense of the situation that confronts us. Such 'sense making' may go on deliberately and consciously but may also occur automatically, outside of our awareness. But whether under our control or not, there is no doubt that social categorization is a generic process, observable in adults, young children and infants alike.

I next consider two of the more important *social* consequences of categorization. One is that it gives rise to behavioural discrimination in which members of our own category are typically treated more favourably than members of an outgroup. This happens even when the basis of the categorization is so trivial as to be virtually meaningless. A second is that it gives rise to perceptions of homogeneity within groups that are seldom symmetrical. An analysis of the circumstances in which the ingroup is seen as more (or less) variable than the outgroup concludes the first half of the chapter.

In the second half, I turn my attention to group stereotyping, the attribution of a set of characteristics to all or most of the members of a category. Stereotypes are seen as necessary concomitants to the process of categorization. They provide the expectancies that guide our judgements of and behaviour towards other people. One important way they do this, particularly in intergroup contexts involving groups of different status, is to provide ideological justification for maintaining current inequalities. Often they achieve this by being biased in favour of confirmatory evidence: information that is consistent with stereotypes is generally perceived and recalled more readily than that which disconfirms them. Since stereotypes often reflect existing intergroup relationships, this means that they will generally function so as to reinforce rather than undermine those relations. Finally, I consider how stereotypes have a self-fulfilling quality, often creating the very 'reality' that they purport merely to represent.

Social Categorization: The Foundation Stone of Intergroup Behaviour

It is probably no exaggeration to say that categorization is one of the most fundamental processes studied by psychologists. Open a textbook in any field, be it in perception, cognition or social interaction, and you will soon encounter it as a key explanatory mechanism. It is, as Bruner (1957) suggested some years ago, an inescapable feature of human existence. Why is this? It is so because the world is simply too complex a place for us to survive without some means of simplifying and ordering it first. Just as scientists use classification systems to reduce nature's complexity to a more manageable number of categories, so too do we rely on categories in our everyday lives. We simply do not have the cognitive capacity to respond uniquely to every single person or event that we encounter. Moreover, even if we had such an unimaginable limitless capacity, it would be highly dysfunctional to perceive, store or respond to each 'stimulus' separately because stimuli – be these physical objects or people – possess many characteristics in common with each other, as well as attributes that distinguish them from other stimuli. By assigning them to categories based on these similarities and differences, we can deal with them much more efficiently. Furthermore, without categories we would be unable to communicate with each other through language because, above all, linguistic systems permit the ready reference to whole classes of people and objects without the constant need for particularistic description.

To give a simple example, suppose I visit some foreign city. If (as frequently seems to happen to me on such occasions) I lose my way, it is very useful to me to be able to recognize particular categories of people (e.g. police, taxi drivers, local residents) to ask for directions. I will find my way to Notre Dame or Piazza San Marco much more quickly by using social categories like these than by simply asking the first person I meet (usually an equally lost fellow tourist). What is a matter of mere convenience in this mundane example can literally become a question of life or death in more threatening environments. To be able to recognize and behave appropriately towards members of 'our' and 'their' sides in Kosovo or Rwanda can make the need for fast and accurate categorical judgements more than a little important for one's personal survival.

If social categories are to be useful simplifying and ordering devices then it is important that they help us discriminate clearly between those who belong and those who do not. One of the first people to recognize this important point was Campbell (1956), who demonstrated that enhancement of contrast was a rather basic consequence of categorization by eliciting it in a simple physical judgement task. He asked his participants to learn the physical location of some nonsense syllables. (On every trial a given syllable was always presented in the same position along a horizontal line.) Within the stimuli there were two implicit categories of nonsense syllable, one in which the central letter was always 'E' and another that always ended in 'X'.

The 'E' group was always presented towards the left, the 'X' group to the right, although they overlapped in the middle. Campbell found that perceivers made consistent errors in estimating the position of these overlapping syllables – the 'E' stimuli being moved to the left, the 'X' stimuli to the right – so that the physical locations of the two categories of stimuli were more clearly separated.

This principle was later formalized by Tajfel (1959) into two hypotheses. The first of these was that if a category is imposed on a set of stimuli – whether these be physical objects, sensory events or people – such that some of the stimuli fall into class A and the remainder into class B, then this will have the effect of enhancing any pre-existing differences between the two categories. The second hypothesis, really a corollary of the first, was that differences *within* the categories will be attenuated. Or, put less formally, members of different groups will be seen as more different from each other than they really are while members of the same group will be seen as more similar.

In a test of these hypotheses, Tajfel and Wilkes (1963) found that people's estimates of lengths of lines were influenced by labelling half of them (the shorter lines) as 'A' and the remainder as 'B'. The effect of this simple categorization was to cause an accentuation of the perceived differences between the longer and shorter lines. There was less evidence of the expected within-category assimilation in this experiment, although, as we shall see shortly, this effect has been observed by others. A similar phenomenon has been observed in a variety of other tasks, including judgements of sound patterns in speech phoneme categories, recollection of monthly variations in temperature, impressions of faces and the evaluation of attitude statements (see Doise, 1976; Eiser, 1971; Krueger and Clement, 1994). Moreover, at least two experiments have confirmed the existence of the intracategory assimilation effect. McGarty and Penny (1988) found that political statements purporting to come from the same authors were judged to be more similar to one another than when those same statements were evaluated in the abstract (i.e. with no author attribution). And Doise et al. (1978), using a more realistic task of asking children to form personality impressions from photographs, found both category differentiation *and* assimilation. Half the children knew in advance that they would be judging both boys and girls and hence the category was salient for them; the remainder were unaware while rating the first three photographs that three others of the opposite sex would follow. When the gender category was salient more *different* traits were used to describe the male and female photographs, and more *identical* traits were used to describe the photographs of the same gender.

In summary, one of the important functions of the categorization process is to sharpen the distinctions between different groups and to blur the difference within them so that the recognition of and response to members *and* non-members of those categories is facilitated. In this way both our mental and social worlds can be better organized and comprehended.

Factors affecting category use

Picture the following scene. You enter a cafeteria of a student union. It is quite full, this being lunchtime in the middle of term. At first glance, there appear to be roughly equal numbers of both sexes, mostly aged between 18 and 25 but with a sprinkling of older people and one or two children running around as well. A number of different ethnic groups also seem to be represented, since several languages, accents, skin colours and dress styles are immediately audible or visible. At one table, you notice a group of sportsmen who seem to be celebrating something, at least to judge from the increasingly raucous songs they insist on subjecting their neighbours to. In this everyday situation there are obviously several categorical dimensions that you, the observer, might use – for example, gender, age, ethnicity and so on. Which of these will you be most likely to use, and what factors govern that choice?

To answer this question we need to know more about you (what are your habitual ways of perceiving social situations? What are your needs and goals?), and more about the situation you are confronted with (what are the actual similarities and differences among the people in it?). These insights were provided by Bruner (1957), who suggested that the categories most likely to be used are those that are most 'accessible' to a person – this is shorthand for the first set of questions – and those that best 'fit' the situation he or she is faced with – the second kind of questions (see also Higgins, 1989; Oakes et al., 1994). To illustrate these concepts of 'accessibility' and 'fit', let us re-examine our opening scenario. We can imagine a number of reasons for you being there or characteristics that you possess which will influence your behaviour. For instance, perhaps you are there to meet a friend who has just picked up their child from the nursery. In that case, a rapid scanning of the room by age may be the most efficient way to locate any young children and their parents. Alternatively, you may be there on a romantic mission, hoping to meet the partner of your dreams. For such purposes, gender would be a more functional category. Or then again, possibly you have just come from a demonstration against racism, which might sensitize you to the variety of ethnicities which seems to be present.

But whatever categories you bring with you because of some personal predisposition or temporary task goal, they will only be useful to you if they roughly correspond to the actual people in that cafeteria. Thus, the categories of stockbroker or bus-driver are unlikely to be used, simply because most student cafeterias are peopled with so few members of those categories for it ever to make sense to do so. On the other hand, categorization by gender or nationality does correspond to some real differences among the participants. Some of these differences are more clear cut than others, and many social stimuli form only very fuzzily defined groupings. Campbell (1958) analysed the factors that lead discrete entities (that is, individual people) to be seen as groups. These are common fate, similarity and proximity. People who do things together or to whom similar things happen (common fate) are more likely to be perceived as a group. Likewise, people who share common characteristics (similarity) like a language or dress style will probably be classified together. And those who are physically near one another (proximity) may also be regarded as a group.

On all three counts the group of sportsmen in the cafeteria might well be categorized together. In short, there are real physical, psychological and cultural differences between people to which categories must correspond if they are to be functional to us.

The most complete analysis of category accessibility and fit is provided by self-categorization theory (Oakes et al., 1994; Turner et al., 1987). In this theory it is noted, first of all, that the two concepts are neither fixed nor independent of one another. Which categories are most accessible to the observer can change from situation to situation (according to varying temporary goals), and this naturally has implications for their fit with real differences among those being perceived. Second, not all categories are psychologically equivalent: we belong to some and not to others. According to self-categorization theory, the categorical dimension most likely to be adopted in any particular instance is that which simultaneously *minimizes* the difference between self and the most prototypical member of the ingroup category and *maximizes* the difference between that prototypical ingrouper and the prototypical outgroup member. This is an expression in social psychological terms of the processes of category accentuation and assimilation that Tajfel (1959) had earlier formulated at a more abstract or purely cognitive level. Self-categorization theory has formalized this principle into what is termed the optimal 'meta contrast ratio', a symbolic computation in which the average intercategory difference forms the numerator and the average self – 'ingroup other' difference constitutes the denominator. This is not a fixed formula for every situation. If, for some reason, a different ingroup identity becomes salient for the perceiver, a different meta contrast ratio comes into play. As we saw in the example earlier, depending on whether our observer's identity as a (would be) lover or anti-racist protester was uppermost, very different categories would be likely to be activated.

Let me now move from these hypothetical cases to some of the empirical research that has investigated this question of the choice of categorization. First, I deal with some features of the immediate situation that seem to affect the 'fitness' of some categories rather than others. Then I turn to the 'accessibility' issue by examining those aspects of the perceiver that have been found to influence category usage.

Category fit

As we have seen, Campbell (1958) suggested that the way people (as stimuli) actually stand in relation to one another influences whether they are seen as members of the same group. He called this perceived entitativity. One of the clearest demonstrations of this was provided by Gaertner et al. (1989) in a study investigating how ingroup bias can be reduced. Gaertner et al. reasoned that if members of two categories could be perceived as belonging to a single superordinate group

Table 7.1 Situational effects on perceived entitativity (percentage of subjects in each condition choosing each cognitive representation of the situation)

	Experimental condition		
Cognitive representation	*Two-group*	*One-group*	*Separate individuals*
Two groups	80.0	21.7	16.7
One group	18.9	71.7	15.8
Separate individuals	1.7	6.7	67.5

Source: Gaertner et al. (1989), table 1. Copyright © 1989 by the American Psychological Association

or, alternatively, simply as separate individuals then any ingroup bias associated with these categories would be reduced. Accordingly, in three different experimental conditions they sought either to maintain a group division, to subsume it in a larger category or to eliminate group cues altogether. Using artificial group labels (different colour tags), six participants were initially assigned to one of two groups and had to work in those groups. The two groups were then brought together to work in a further task, and the nature of this encounter was systematically varied. In the 'two-group' condition the members of the group sat opposite each other at a table, keeping their original group labels, and interacted mainly among each other with a view to winning a prize for the best solution to the task. In contrast, in the 'one-group' condition the members of the two groups sat in alternate places around the table, devised a new group label for the larger entity formed by the joining of the groups, and worked with each other to win a prize for the best *joint* group solution to the task. In the 'individual' condition each person sat at a separate table, was asked to think up an idiosyncratic name, and worked towards the best individual solution. Notice how this experimental manipulation incorporated all three of Campbell's (1958) criteria for entitativity: physical proximity (where they sat), similarity (the labels) and interdependence of fate (the reward outcomes). Table 7.1 shows how the manipulation affected participants' perception of the situation. It is clear (from the percentages along the upper left to the lower right diagonal) that it had a marked effect on the way they categorized each other. (I shall return to this experiment in chapter 8, when I discuss methods of reducing intergroup prejudice.)

Another situational factor that may affect which categories get used is the perceptual distinctiveness of certain people. Kanter (1977), for instance, has suggested that people who constitute a numerical minority in an organization (for example, women in a male-dominated profession) can become the focus of attention from the majority. Kanter's ideas were followed up by some experimental studies by Taylor and her colleagues (Taylor, 1981; Taylor et al., 1978). In these experiments participants listened to a tape-recorded discussion of six people whose pictures were shown during the recording to coincide with their oral contributions. The composition of the group was systematically varied. In one experiment it consisted of one black and five whites, five blacks and one white, or three of each (Taylor, 1981). In another, gender was the categorization variable and the group consisted of single-sex participants and all other possible sex ratios (Taylor et al., 1978). Both studies provided some, but not unequivocal, evidence of the cognitive drawing power of numerical distinctiveness. A further investigation of the alleged distinctiveness of 'solos' was by Biernat and Vescio (1993). In two studies using the same paradigm as Taylor et al. (1978), with black and white participants, they found only ambiguous results for the hypothesized category distinctiveness of the 'solo' person. The pattern of memory errors seemed to indicate that the black–white category was actually more likely to be evoked in the 'balanced' conditions since the difference between 'within-race' and 'between-race' errors – a key indicator of category usage – appeared to be greater there than in the 'solo' conditions (Oakes, 1994; Biernat and Vescio, 1994).

Thus, it seems that simply being in a minority is not a very reliable source of distinctiveness. There are other sources, however. People with a physical disability or some visible stigmata often complain about how frequently they are stared at. One reason for this may be that for most people the sight of a disabled person may be a fairly novel event and this novelty may itself catch people's attention. This was the thinking of Langer et al. (1976) when they displayed various photographs of disabled and non-disabled people in a public foyer. They unobtrusively measured how long passers-by stopped and looked at the pictures, and found that those of people with a physical disability (a woman in a leg brace or a hunch-backed man) were consistently looked at longer than those of non-disabled people.

Category accessibility

It is not just the stimulus properties of the situation that can activate one category rather than another, however. What the person brings to the situation also contributes to the ease or difficulty with which categories are accessed. Three factors in particular have been found to be important: the nature of the immediately preceding events, the personal disposition of the perceiver, especially as this affects their tendency to use some categories habitually, and the current task or goal of the person doing the categorizing.

If something has occurred very recently that is evocative of a particular categorization then it is likely that subsequent events will also be interpreted in terms of that same category system. On the day I am writing this, findings of a public inquiry into the police investigation of a brutal murder of a black teenager, Stephen Lawrence, have just been published (Macpherson, 1999). The inquiry report was unequivocal that both the murder itself and subsequent police behaviour were racially motivated. This inquiry, just like the abortive murder trial that preceded it, has received enormous media coverage. My guess is that this will heighten everyone's sensitivity to ethnic issues in subsequent reports of police malpractice. We will be more ready to look for evidence of racial discrimination than had there not been this publicity.

In technical terms, this is known as 'priming', and the effects of priming on category activation have been extensively studied by social psychologists. For example, Skowronski et al. (1993) studied the effect of presenting various adjectives or labels evocative of the category 'mentally handicapped' on people's recall and impressions of a person described in a short vignette. These words were embedded among a large number of neutral words that participants were exposed to before they read the vignette. Participants exposed to such primes recalled more stereotypical attributes about the character in the vignette and generally evaluated him more negatively. There is even evidence that the activation of a category by a prime can occur unconsciously. Devine (1989) presented participants subliminally with various words that are stereotypically associated with the category 'Blacks' (e.g. 'niggers', 'lazy', 'athletic'). The exposure time was only 80 ms and each word was immediately 'masked' by a string of meaningless letters. Under such conditions it is virtually impossible to detect the words. Half of the participants were presented with a high proportion (80 per cent) of ethnically associated words, the rest a much lower proportion (20 per cent). In a subsequent impression-formation task in which they were asked to make some judgements about an ambiguously described person, the former group rated this target person significantly more negatively than the latter. Devine concluded that in the more concentrated priming conditions the category 'Blacks' had been subconsciously activated and that this category was then used to judge the target in a manner consistent with the black stereotype (e.g. 'aggressive').

Devine (1989) had also pre-tested her participants for their levels of prejudice but found that this made little difference to their susceptibility to the priming stimuli. However, there are now grounds for doubting this last finding, as we have recently discovered (Lepore and Brown, 1997). When we inspected Devine's priming procedure carefully, we noted that it contained not just category labels (e.g. 'Blacks') but also much obviously stereotypic material (e.g. 'lazy'). We believed that it may have been the latter that generated the subsequent derogatory impression for the 'high prime' participants, irrespective of their prejudice level. What would happen, we wondered, if only categorical material was used as primes with no accompanying negative attributes? When we conducted this experiment using a similar procedure to Devine (1989), we found that, in fact, high- and low-prejudiced participants formed very different impressions of the target person. The high-prejudiced people reacted to the primes by judging him more negatively but the low-prejudiced people's judgements became more positive (see figure 7.1). Our explanation of this divergent effect of category activation for people differing in prejudice is that the mental picture evoked by the category 'Blacks' in high- and low-prejudiced people is quite different. For prejudiced people who, we may surmise, habitually make negative judgements every time they are confronted with a black person, there are stronger cognitive connections between the category 'Black' and negative characteristics. For less-prejudiced people, on the other hand, the habitual

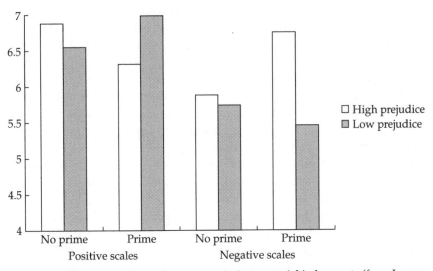

Figure 7.1 Effects of subliminal category priming on social judgements (from Lepore and Brown, 1997, figure 1)

judgements are more favourable, resulting in stronger links to positive attributes (see also Locke et al., 1994; Wittenbrink et al., 1997).

The fact that high- and low-prejudice people respond differently to ethnic primes at an unconscious level suggests that there may be some people for whom a given categorization is perpetually or 'chronically' accessible. This is particularly likely to be the case for the more prejudiced, for whom any situation will be interpreted via their favoured categories. Early evidence was provided by Allport and Kramer (1946). They presented equal numbers of photographs of Jewish and non-Jewish people to participants who had earlier been tested for their level of anti-Semitism. The more anti-Semitic participants identified a greater number of photographs as Jewish than the less-prejudiced participants, and were also more accurate. In our terms, ethnicity was a chronically accessible categorization for the prejudiced people and, as a consequence, they applied it more readily – and, it seems, more precisely – than the less-prejudiced participants (Tajfel, 1969).

People's susceptibility to apply one set of categories rather than another does not have to be a stable disposition as indicated by their measured level of prejudice; it can also vary as a function of immediate task demands. This was demonstrated by Oakes and Turner (1986).

Using the same name-matching paradigm as Taylor et al. (1978), they showed how giving participants certain instructions can override any distinctiveness properties associated with 'solo' stimuli. Like Taylor et al., Oakes and Turner varied the sex composition of a tape-recorded discussion group. Half the listeners were warned, as in Taylor et al.'s experiment, that they would be asked to describe just a single person; the remainder were told to concentrate on the group as a whole. In the latter conditions, reasoned Oakes and Turner, the sex category would be most likely to be used not in the 'solo' case, but in the 'balanced' (three male versus three female) groups, where it would be a better fit for the task at hand. This, indeed, seemed to be the case. The evaluation of the same male target was more stereotyped in the 'balanced' than in the 'solo' conditions, implying that the sex category had been more readily accessed there (see also Biernat and Vescio, 1993).

It is important to realize that the perceiver's goals can be changed quite subtly, with equally subtle effects of which they may be unaware. Pendry and Macrae (1996) showed this by asking participants to watch a short video clip under three different instructions. Some were to form an impression of the person in the video and were informed that they would subsequently have to explain how they had reached that judgement to another member of the psychology department. The implication was that they should pay careful attention to the target person since they would be accountable for their judgement. In a second condition, participants were asked to estimate the target person's height, a simple physical characteristic strongly correlated with gender. In a third condition, they were asked merely to report on the picture quality of the video, with no reference to the target person. Finally, there were some (control) participants who did not watch the video at all. The video itself portrayed a professional woman apparently hard at work in an office. Pendry and Macrae were interested to discover whether the specific category of 'businesswoman' was activated by watching the video or, instead, merely the more generic category of 'woman'. They predicted that the first set of instructions would induce a more attentive frame of mind, which would lead to the use of the more informative 'businesswoman' subcategory; the other participants, in contrast, would probably only activate the broad gender category because they were attending to other features of the situation. To measure category activation Pendry

Table 7.2   Category activation influenced by different processing goals

| Trait word type | Lexical decision times (ms) for processing goal | | | |
	Accountable	Height	Picture quality	Control
'Woman'	571	549	556	613
'Businesswoman'	537	598	589	599
	*	*	*	n.s

* indicates significant difference.
Source: Pendry and Macrae (1996), table 2. Reprinted by permission of Sage Publications.

and Macrae used a lexical decision task in which participants simply had to report (as quickly as possible) whether or not a word appearing on a computer screen was a real word. Some of these words were stereotypic of businesswomen (e.g. 'confident', 'ambitious', 'assertive') but not of women; others were stereotypic of women but not really of businesswomen (e.g. 'caring', 'emotional', 'warm'). They reasoned that if the 'businesswoman' category had been activated while watching the video, participants should respond faster to the former set of words than to the latter. Activation of the 'woman' category would be indicated by exactly the opposite pattern. Participants' decision times (measured in milliseconds) showed clearly that the different processing goals provided by the experimental instructions had had an effect (see table 7.2). Note that in the first condition ('accountable') they responded faster to the 'businesswoman' traits than to the 'woman' traits; in the other two video conditions they were faster responding to the 'woman' traits. It is particularly noteworthy, I think, that these temporal differences (of 30–50 ms) are much too small to suppose that the participants could have exerted any conscious control in bringing them about. Apparently, the category activation and subsequent stereotypic associations had occurred automatically.

Social categorization in children

Thus far, all the examples and research evidence documenting the ubiquity and importance of categorization in social perception have involved adults. Yet, if categorization is really indispensable to social life we should expect to see it in operation in young children. Presumably their need to simplify and understand their environment is no less than that of their parents, caretakers and teachers. This point was brought home to me many years ago when one of my children went into hospital for an operation at the age of four. Lying in the hospital bed, he began to make sense of this novel and somewhat threatening situation. At one point he observed a man in a white coat entering the ward and asked if this was one of the doctors coming to see him. His chosen and highly functional method of simplifying the hospital context was to assign all men to the category 'doctors' and all women to the category 'nurses'. As elsewhere, in this hospital the correlation between gender and occupation was extremely high and hence gender acted as a convenient and highly economical category for subsuming all the different varieties of doctors and nurses he had encountered hitherto.[1]

There is, in fact, considerable evidence that children from a very early age indeed are remarkably sensitive to the major social divisions in their world and, moreover, that their awareness and use of different categories is affected by the particular context in which they find themselves rather than being a fixed propensity to classify in a certain way. An early study by Horowitz and Horowitz (1938) presented white American children with several series of five pictures, of which three were similar on two criteria and the remaining two differed on one criterion. For example, there might have been three white males, one black male, and one white female. Which is the odd one out? By combining ethnicity, sex, age and socio-economic status in different ways, Horowitz and Horowitz were able to discover which category was most salient for the children. Ethnicity seemed to predominate, followed by sex, with economic status being the least important. Other studies in the US have confirmed the presence of ethnic awareness in children as young as four years (Williams and Moreland, 1976). Gender is also an early and well-used category. Thompson (1975) found that over 75 per cent of two-year-olds whom he studied could correctly classify photographs by male and female, a figure rising to 90 per cent a year later. Other research confirms this (Duveen and Lloyd, 1986; Slaby and Frey, 1975; Yee and Brown, 1994).

Outside the United States, ethnicity and gender also tend to be the most widely used categories, but not invariably so. Davey (1983) asked 7–10-year-old British children to sort a series of photographs into groups that 'belong together' or 'look alike'. Within these, there were pictures of different sex, age, ethnicity and style of dress (to convey socio-economic status). The most frequent sorting criterion by far was ethnicity, used first by nearly half the children. Sex was the next most popular, and age and dress style much less so. However, changing the nature of the task had a strong effect on the children's categorization strategies. In a subsequent test, Davey (1983) asked the children to sort the photographs according to who would play together. In this task, gender emerged as much more important than ethnicity. In the terms we used earlier, for play behaviour gender is more 'accessible' than 'ethnicity' (see also Verkuyten et al., 1995). However, Bennett et al. (1991) found little evidence of sorting by ethnicity in a study carried out with 8–11-year-olds in an area of Britain with a low proportion of non-white residents. Instead, the children seemed to focus on more incidental features, such as facial expression or how the person was seated. When they repeated the study in an area of North London where significant numbers of ethnic minorities live, they found greater use of ethnicity, at least among their younger (8-year-old) participants. Presumably, in this ethnically more diverse environment an ethnic categorical structure provided a better 'fit' to the people whom the children encountered in their daily lives.

The context specificity of preferred categorizations was also revealed in a study we carried out in a primary school which had strong links with a special school for children with profound physical and learning disabilities (Maras and Brown, 1996). We asked the mainstream children to sort a number of photographs portraying boys and girls with and without disabilities (e.g. some children were shown wearing hearing aids or sitting in a wheelchair). Early in the study all the children tested tended to classify by gender (boys versus girls) and disability (non-disabled versus disabled). Three months later these same categories were used but, at least for a group of children who had had regular contact with the special school, in a more refined way. These children, probably because of their greater exposure to different kinds of disability, now looked to subdivide the 'disability' category instead of seeing it as a homogeneous entity. At the same time their attitudes towards the disabled children also changed.

There is also evidence that even infants of a few months old are capable of making categorical distinctions. For example, it is generally well recognized that by six months they can discriminate between categories of phonetic, colour and shape stimuli (Durkin, 1995). The same may also be true for social categories. Fagan and Singer (1979) employed a technique known as a habituation paradigm with babies of 5–6 months. In a habituation paradigm one stimulus is shown repeatedly to the infant to get him or her used (or habituated) to it. Then the same stimulus and a 'test' stimulus are presented simultaneously and the time the baby stares at each is measured. If the test stimulus is looked at longer then it is assumed that they have seen something novel or different about it and hence have made a discrimination. Fagan and Singer matched photographs of a man or a woman, or an adult and a baby so that they were as similar as possible on various facial features. They also matched *same* sex or age photographs so that they were less similar to one another than the male–female or adult–baby combinations. The infants spent longer looking at the test stimulus when it was of a different category (despite being objectively more similar) than when it was of the same sex or age (see also Langlois et al., 1987, 1991). That such young children have the ability to make such classifications makes sense once we reflect on the nature of their social world. At that phase of human development, age and sex categories probably provide very functional means for sorting out where different forms of nurturance and stimulation are likely to come from.

Some consequences of social categorization

In my analysis of realistic group conflict theory in chapter 6, I noted that one of its difficulties is that conflictual goals seem not to be necessary to elicit ingroup bias in people's judgements. Sherif himself had observed occasional instances of spontaneous intergroup rivalry even before the competition phase of the experiment had been initiated. The ease with which ingroup-favouring judgements can be elicited is by now a well-documented phenomenon. In a meta-analysis of three decades' worth of intergroup relations research, we found that across all of the studies where an ingroup evaluation had been compared to an outgroup evaluation, 75 per cent of them revealed a bias in favour of the ingroup (Mullen et al., 1992). This accumulation of evidence has led researchers to ask whether the mere fact of being categorized as belonging to a group is sufficient to trigger intergroup discrimination.

Mere group membership and intergroup discrimination

Rabbie and Horowitz (1969) were the first to investigate this question. As we saw in chapter 2, they found that dividing schoolchildren into two arbitrary groups produced only very slight ingroup-favouring biases in their intergroup ratings (Horowitz and Rabbie, 1982). When that group division was accompanied by some interdependence of fate, then those biases became much more evident. However, Tajfel et al. (1971) took this paradigm one stage further and showed conclusively that mere categorization *was* sufficient to elicit intergroup favouritism. Moreover, this favouritism took the form not of mere bias in pencil and paper judgements but of clear-cut behavioural discrimination in the allocation of rewards. Like Rabbie and Horowitz, they assigned schoolboys to one of two groups on a very arbitrary basis: their alleged preference of one of two abstract artists, Paul Klee and Vassilij Kandinsky. However, in this experiment the children knew only which group they themselves had been assigned to, the identity of their fellow ingroup and outgroup members being kept hidden by the use of code numbers. Then, under the general pretext of the experiment ('a study of decision making'), the children were asked to allocate money to various recipients using specially prepared booklets of decision matrices (see table 7.3 for examples). The identity of the recipients on each page was unknown but their group affiliation was revealed. To eliminate self-interest as a possible motive in the allocations, the children were never able to award money to themselves directly.

The results were clear. Although they made some effort to be fair in their allocations, the children showed a persistent tendency to award more money to ingroup recipients than to those they believed belonged to the other group. Thus, in matrix 1 in table 7.3, over 70 per

Table 7.3 Two sample matrices from minimal group experiment

	Reward numbers													
Matrix 1														
Member 72 of Klee group	18	17	16	15	14	13	12	11	10	9	8	7	6	5
Member 47 of Kandinsky group	5	6	7	8	9	10	11	12	13	14	15	16	17	18
Matrix 2														
Member 74 of Klee group	25	23	21	19	17	15	13	11	9	7	5	3	1	
Member 44 of Kandinsky group	19	18	17	16	15	14	13	12	11	10	9	8	7	

On each page subjects must choose one pair of numbers.

These are two of several different types of matrix used. Matrix 1 was designed to measure general ingroup favouritism, while matrix 2 was designed to measure the tendency to maximize the difference between ingroup and outgroup recipients. In the experiment, these matrices would be presented to each subject at least twice: once as above, and once with the group affiliations of the two recipients reversed.

In the original experiments 1 point = 1/10p. Given that each booklet contained some sixteen pages (each with point values ranging from 1 to 29) the total amount of money which each boy thought he was dispensing was not inconsiderable. In 1970 this probably amounted to about £0.50 which, at today's prices, is probably equivalent to around £3.00.

Source: Tajfel et al. (1971)

cent of the participants made choices favouring their own group, with a mean response from people in the Klee group (say) of between the 14/9 and 13/10 boxes. This was true even when, in absolute terms, the ingrouper might be worse off. For example, in matrix 2 in table 7.3 the mean response from people in the Kandinsky group was somewhere between the 13/13 and 11/12 options. Notice that this choice results in the Kandinsky recipient actually receiving 6 or 7 points *less* than he might otherwise have done but, crucially, he thereby receives more than the Klee recipient. The results are rather surprising when one considers how sparse this social setting was. The children were allocated to two meaningless groups on a flimsy criterion. They did not interact with members of their own or the other group. The two groups had no current or past relationship with each other. And yet, when asked to allocate sums of money to anonymous others, the children consistently favoured ingroup members over outgroupers. Simply being assigned to a group does, after all, seem to have predictable effects on intergroup behaviour.

Intergroup discrimination in this minimal group situation has proved to be a remarkably robust phenomenon. In more than two dozen independent studies in several different countries using a wide range of experimental participants of both sexes (from young children to adults), essentially the same results have been found: the mere act of allocating people to arbitrary social categories is sufficient to elicit biased judgements and discriminatory behaviour (see Brewer, 1979; Diehl, 1992; Tajfel, 1982b).

Despite this empirical consensus, the minimal group paradigm has attracted controversy. This has focused on the interpretation of the observed data as revealing discrimination or fairness (Branthwaite et al., 1979; Turner, 1980, 1983a; Bornstein et al., 1983a), possible demand characteristics associated with the paradigm (Gerard and Hoyt, 1974; Tajfel, 1978), statistical treatment of the data (Aschenbrenner and Schaefer, 1980; Brown et al., 1980), rival ways of measuring intergroup orientation (Bornstein et al., 1983a,b; Turner, 1983a,b), doubts about the paradigm's external validity associated with its obvious high degree of artificiality (Aschenbrenner and Schaefer, 1980; Brown et al., 1980), and the extent to which economic self-interest can explain the typically observed discrimination (Rabbie et al., 1989; Turner and Bourhis, 1996).

Space does not permit me to discuss all of these issues here. However, it is worth making the following observations on two or more important issues in question. The first concerns whether or not participants in these experiments are really showing ingroup favouritism or, alternatively, are displaying behaviour better described as some form of 'fairness'. My view is that while it seems clear that people do show a clear propensity towards equalizing ingroup and outgroup outcomes in these situations, it is nevertheless true that they are nearly always more 'fair' to ingroupers than to outgroupers. In other words, although people's choices cluster around the centre or 'fair' point (e.g. 13/13 in matrix 2), when an ingroup member is the recipient on the top line the responses tend to be on the *left* of centre; when an outgrouper is the beneficiary on the same line the responses move to the right of centre. Furthermore, the evidence for this persistent bias is derived not just from particular reward allocation matrices but from a variety of other dependent measures, which have also shown that ingroup members or products receive more favourable ratings than equivalent outgroup stimuli (Brewer, 1979; Brown et al., 1980). Again, this is seldom very extreme in its extent, but it is both reliable and pervasive.

An interesting exception to this pervasive minimal group discrimination is when the decisions involve the distribution of penalties or aversive stimuli. Hewstone et al. (1981) modified the normal paradigm by asking participants to withdraw money from ingroup and outgroup members (who had earlier been given an initial sum). The subsequent levels of bias, though visible, were lower than usually found. Then Mummendey and her colleagues, in a series of experiments which involved the distribution of negative outcomes (e.g. short duration of an unpleasant noise; working on a boring task), found that intergroup discrimination *completely* disappeared and that strategies of equalizing the outcomes or minimizing the total amount of aversive stimulation were more prevalent (Mummendey et al., 1992; Otten et al., 1996). Intergroup discrimination re-emerged only in certain circumstances – for example, when the participants were in a subordinate or minority-status group. In chapter 8 we will consider some possible explanations for this asymmetry between discrimination with positive and negative outcomes.

The second issue concerns whether the manifestation of intergroup discrimination in the minimal group paradigm can be explained via the operation of self-interest motives (Rabbie et al., 1989). At first glance, this seems paradoxical since the paradigm was devised to eliminate self-interest by preventing participants from giving any money to themselves. However, Rabbie et al. (1989) argue that, while such direct self-interest may be excluded, participants may still believe that members of each group will tend to favour each other. In other words, there may be some perceived interdependence and so people will respond to this by maximizing the benefits to fellow ingroup members and hence, by reciprocity, to themselves. To test this idea, Rabbie et al. (1989) added two variations to the standard minimal group paradigm. In one they specified that participants would only receive what other ingroup members gave them; in the other, they could only get what outgroup members allocated. This had a predictable effect on participants' reward distributions: those dependent solely on the ingroup increased their ingroup favouritism somewhat compared to the normal condition, while those wholly dependent on the outgroup decreased it and mainly showed outgroup favouritism. Others, too, have found that linking people's fortunes directly to others substantially reduces, though does not always eliminate, ingroup favouritism (Diehl, 1989; Sachdev and Bourhis, 1985).

These experiments show that people respond to self-interest considerations when these are made explicit. However, they are hardly conclusive in demonstrating that self-interest accounts for the discrimination typically observed in the conventional minimal group paradigm, as Turner and Bourhis (1996) have forcefully argued. For one thing, it remains to be explained why being categorized as a member of a group should in itself generate particular expectations of others' behaviour. Second, Diehl (1989) showed that the link between reciprocity expectations and actual behaviour is not a simple one. In this experiment participants were given false feedback about outgroup members' intended (and not actual) allocation strategies. They were then asked of their own intentions as well as actually to distribute the rewards. There was some correlation between participants' own intentions and their assumptions about what outgroup members would do. But when it came to their actual behaviour there was no reliable difference between those who expected the outgroup to be fair and those who anticipated it being discriminatory. Finally, there is evidence that when the economic interests of minimal group members are fully satisfied (by telling them that they will receive full payment for participation irrespective of anyone else's allocations), they still show intergroup discrimination (Gagnon and Bourhis, 1996). Thus, while perceptions of interdependence and mutual reciprocity can play a role in guiding group members' behaviour in certain circumstances, they do not provide a complete explanation for the minimal intergroup discrimination. In chapter 8 I will consider other, more promising, accounts.

Perceived intragroup homogeneity

As we saw earlier, two consequences of categorization are the exaggeration of intergroup differences and the enhancement of intragroup similarities. In this section I want to focus on the second of these, and, in particular, on what seems to be a consistent asymmetry in judgements made in intergroup settings: the ingroup and outgroup are seldom perceived to be equally homogeneous.

Common-sense wisdom has it that people generally see members of an outgroup as more similar to one another than members of the ingroup: *'they* are all alike, but *we* are all different'. John Motson, a well-known (white) football commentator, caused some mild controversy recently when he admitted that he sometimes found it difficult to distinguish black players:

There are some teams where you have got players who from a distance, look almost identical. And, of course, with more black players coming into the game, they would not mind me saying that that can be very confusing. (The *Independent*, 5 January 1998)

Although he was roundly criticized for these remarks, Mr Motson was doing no more than articulating what some social psychologists believe to be a general principle of group perception (e.g. Ostrom and Sedikides, 1992; Quattrone, 1986). However, although I have no reason to believe that Mr Motson was anything but sincere (if somewhat tactless) in his confusion, it turns out that the outgroup homogeneity effect (as it is known) is far from being the universal characteristic of intergroup variability judgements that it is sometimes claimed to be.

One of the first attempts to study this phenomenon systematically was by Jones et al. (1981), who asked members of university clubs to rate members of their own club as to how similar they were on a number of trait dimensions. The exercise was repeated for the members of other clubs. Jones et al. found a consistent tendency for members of outgroups to be seen as more similar to one another than members of the ingroup. Similar results have been obtained in several other studies (Linville et al., 1989; Quattrone, 1986).

What is the explanation for this outgroup homogeneity effect? One view is that it stems from the different amount of information we have about ingroup and outgroup members (Linville et al., 1989). We usually know more individuals in our own group, we may interact with them more often and, as a result, be more aware of the differences among them. Members of the outgroup, on the other hand, because they are less well known, are likely to be seen in a more global and undifferentiated fashion. This model, then, stresses the importance of differential familiarity with members of ingroup and outgroups. A second model takes a different view, suggesting that it is not information about a number of specific exemplars which is important, but the nature of the category as a whole (Park et al., 1991). According to this perspective, people hold in their heads not a tally of specific ingroup and outgroup people known, but more abstract conceptions of the categories as a whole, modelled on the prototypical member of each and some estimate of the variability around this typical person. The reason that the ingroup may be seen as more variable is that the conception of that category is both more important (because it contains the self), more concrete (again because we have at least one case very well known to us) and more provisional (because of a presumed greater motivation to form an accurate impression about those close to us psychologically).

Although intuitively plausible, the first view – call it the familiarity hypothesis – does not have much empirical support. Linville et al. (1989) did find that over the period of a semester members of a university course rated their classmates as increasingly more variable, and then demonstrated in a computer simulation that greater perceived variability can be associated with changes in familiarity. However, these findings stand against a number of other studies which have either found no effects for familiarity or even an inverse correlation (e.g. Brown and Smith, 1989; Jones et al., 1981; Simon et al., 1991). Another problem for the familiarity hypothesis is that the outgroup homogeneity effect can still be observed in minimal group situations where there is equal and near zero information about both ingroup and outgroup because the groups concerned are anonymous (Wilder, 1984a).

Even more problematic is evidence from several studies that have examined variability judgements during the process of group formation. For example, Brown and Wootton-Millward (1993) studied groups of student nurses over a year of their training. These groups were small (typically less than 20 in each) and their members had extensive daily face-to-face contact with one another. If Linville et al. are right, the greater mutual acquaintanceship afforded by this experience should have led to enhanced perceived variability within the ingroup over time, and thus a more pronounced outgroup homogeneity effect. In fact, there was *no* consistent tendency towards greater perceived ingroup variability over time, and – still worse for the familiarity hypothesis – on at least two judgmental dimensions it was the ingroup, and not the outgroup, which was seen as more homogeneous. A similar increase in ingroup homogeneity with greater familiarity was observed by Oakes et al. (1995) when they elicited group similarity judgements from members of small Outward Bound training groups. Ryan and Bogart (1997) also observed relative ingroup homogeneity (i.e. the ingroup seen as more similar than the outgroup) in a longitudinal study conducted among new recruits to four university sororities. This ingroup homogeneity declined somewhat over a period of six months but, interestingly, this was due to the outgroup being seen as more homogeneous rather than to any increase in the perceived heterogeneity of the ingroup. In fact, the perceived homogeneity of the ingroup hardly changed at all over this time, despite the fact that they reported significantly greater familiarity with their fellow sorority members.

In fact, these findings are just some from a whole series of studies that have shown that the outgroup homogeneity effect is by no means the rule in intergroup perception (Devos et al., 1996; Simon, 1992). One important factor in determining whether it is the ingroup or the outgroup which is seen as more homogeneous is the relative size of the groups concerned. This was shown by Simon and Brown (1987). Reasoning that where an ingroup is in the minority it may feel its identity under threat from the larger minority group, we believed that such threat might lead to a greater need to protect the integrity of the ingroup by seeing it in more homogeneous terms – a kind of psychological closing of ranks. Using a minimal group paradigm, we independently varied the size of both the ingroup and outgroup and found, as we expected, that those who found themselves in a relatively smaller group showed clear ingroup homogeneity; those in the non-minority groups showed the usual outgroup homogeneity effect (see figure 7.2). Two further details from the experiment confirmed our suspicion that people's identities might be involved in this reversal. One was the data from the control conditions, in which exactly the same judgements were made but with one crucial difference – the participants were not themselves allocated to a group and hence were acting as neutral 'observers'. These participants showed no tendency to see smaller groups as more homogeneous, thus ruling out the possibility that our results could be explained as simply an effect of group size (Bartsch and Judd, 1993). A second and clinching point was the

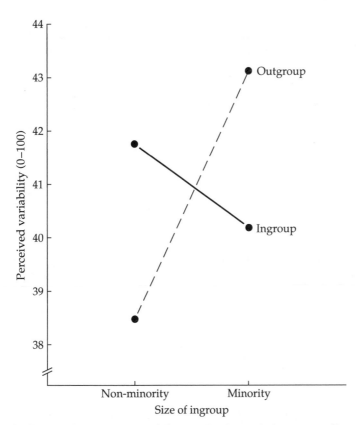

Figure 7.2 Perceived intragroup variability in minority–majority contexts (from Simon and Brown, 1987, derived from table 1)

finding that those in the minority groups identified more strongly with their ingroup than members of larger groups (see also Brown and Smith, 1989; Simon et al., 1991 for real-world replications of these minority–majority effects).

We have seen, then, that people's personal knowledge of ingroup and outgroup members cannot satisfactorily explain the asymmetry in perceptions of intragroup homogeneity. Moreover, the existence of *ingroup* homogeneity in certain intergroup contexts also raises problems for the second explanation, which posits more abstract conceptions of ingroup and outgroup (Park et al., 1991). Another explanation is suggested by the supplementary findings from some of these studies, which revealed that identity was more important for minority than for majority group members (Simon and Brown, 1987; Simon and Pettigrew, 1990). As I noted earlier, Turner et al. (1987) have suggested that the process of identifying with a group involves the simultaneous operation of two processes: the matching of oneself to what are seen as the key defining, or 'criterial', attributes of the ingroup prototype, and the maximizing of the distance between this and the outgroup prototype. To the extent that people strive to make themselves more similar to some idealized conception of what a 'good ingroup member' should be, this will tend to induce an enhanced perception of ingroup similarity – at least along certain dimensions (Haslam et al., 1996).

The dimensional specificity of homogeneity perceptions is now well established. Kelly (1989), in a study of British political parties, found that party members saw their own party as more homogeneous on those issues central to their party's ideology, but as less homogeneous on more generalized criteria. Similarly, in our study of student nurses, we found ingroup homogeneity on nurse-relevant dimensions ('care and understanding', 'communication') but the opposite on criteria more relevant to the doctor outgroup (e.g. 'professional independence') (Brown and Wootton-Millward, 1993). Both of these studies replicate the same basic pattern found in more controlled laboratory conditions. All in all, therefore, it seems reasonable to suppose that an important factor contributing to asymmetries in group homogeneity perceptions are processes stemming from people's identities as members of certain groups and not others (see chapter 8).

Stereotypes: The 'Pictures in our Heads'

In the previous section, I noted that an inevitable consequence of categorical thinking is that perceived differences among members of the same group become blurred. This, of course, is exactly what happens in the process of group stereotyping. When we stereotype people we attribute to them certain characteristics that are seen to be shared by all or most of their fellow group members. Stereotypes, then, are the inferences that we make, the images that spring to mind once a particular category is evoked. They are, if you like, the 'contents' of the categorical boxes to which we assign people when we seek to make sense of any given social situation. The term 'stereotype' was introduced to the social scientific community by Lippmann (1922), a political journalist. Appropriating the word from its origins in the printing industry, he described stereotypes as the cognitive moulds that reproduce mental images of people – what he called 'pictures in our heads' (Lippmann, 1922, p. 4).

A year or two ago I came across an article in a newspaper which will serve nicely as a point of departure for our discussion of inter-group stereotypes. Under the headline 'RAF finds few women make good pilots', the article reported how senior (male) officers running the Aircrew Aptitude Testing Centre for the Royal Air Force believed that women lacked the natural ability to become good pilots. According to one such officer:

There is no polite way of saying it, but females wanting to become pilots show emotions not seen in men and, because of this, quickly lose their concentration. We do have a few who are first class but they will remain a minority. (*Daily Telegraph*, 24 November 1997)

The traditional gender stereotypes (women as emotional and unable to concentrate, and men, by implication, the opposite) are obvious here and presumably have corresponding implications for the career chances of male and female RAF personnel. Indeed, the same article reports that only 10 per cent of the women applicants passed the pilot aptitude test compared to 40 per cent of the men.

How can we understand such stereotypical thinking from a social psychological point of view? The analysis of the origins, functioning and consequences of stereotypes has become a central preoccupation of social psychologists over the past twenty years, so much so that it is impossible to do justice here to all the complex issues involved. In any case, comprehensive treatments of the topic are readily available elsewhere (Fiske, 1998; Macrae et al., 1996). Instead, I want to focus on what I think are three particularly important features of stereotypes from the point of view of intergroup relations: legitimating beliefs, expectancies and self-fulfilling prophecies. I have concentrated on these because they relate most closely to the *social* aspects of stereotypes – that is, how they derive from and help to perpetuate the very intergroup relationships in which they manifest themselves. This means I will be rather cursory in my discussion of the more individual functions of stereotyping and the cognitive processes underlying it (again, see the sources cited above for more detail on these aspects; see also Brown, 1995).

Stereotypes as legitimating beliefs

Stereotypes, just like the categories they are associated with, are mental representations that provide meaning and order to our world as individual perceivers. So, to those RAF officers earlier, a simple (not to say simplistic) rule of thumb for pilot suitability might be 'men good, women poor'. Such a simple mantra would obviously result in great economies of cognitive effort for them, as well as providing an efficient model of personnel selection. However, over and above such psychological functions, a belief in the inherent inferiority of women pilots also serves the *social* function of perpetuating the occupational status quo in which flying is a predominantly male affair. In other words, whatever else it does and whether or not it is based in any objective reality (a point to which I will return shortly), such a stereotype helps to justify keeping women on the ground, literally and metaphorically below their male counterparts. That stereotypes can serve this function of ideological justification has long been recognized by social psychologists (Allport, 1954; Jost and Banaji, 1994; Tajfel, 1981). Let me now consider some of the research supporting such a claim.

To begin with, we should note that most meaningful group stereotypes are held more or less consensually by members of a society or a subgroup within society. I am sure that that RAF officer is not alone in thinking that 'women are emotional'; in fact, research on gender stereotypes reveals that this is quite a widespread belief (Williams and Best, 1982). And, of course, many national and ethnic stereotypes also seem to be endorsed by substantial majorities, even if social norms may occasionally inhibit their public expression (Dovidio and Fazio, 1992; Karlins et al., 1969; Katz and Braly, 1933). The significance of these findings is that it suggests that stereotypes serve more than purely individual psychological functions for those who hold them; it implies that some social factor is also at work. Otherwise, one would expect that each person would process a more or less unique constellation of stereotypes presumably derived from their own personal experiences with the outgroups concerned. A second piece of evidence supporting the argument that stereotypes are often used to justify the ingroup's behaviour towards the outgroup is that they can be observed to change quite rapidly with changes in the intergroup relationship. As I noted in chapter 6, when two countries become embroiled in war, the stereotypes of the 'enemy' typically become very negative, and usually begin to reflect themes of 'cruelty', 'aggression' and 'deceit' (e.g. Seago, 1947). It is not difficult to see how perceptions of the outgroup in such terms would legitimate a bellicose attitude by the ingroup in retaliation.

The fact that the content of outgroup stereotypes is sensitive to variations in the nature of intergroup relationships also suggests that stereotypes can derive, however tenuously, from aspects of social reality. This does not mean, let me hasten to add, that any particular stereotype is objectively 'true' in the sense of accurately describing that group's actual characteristics. Rather, the suggestion is that a group's culturally distinctive behaviour patterns or the particular socioeconomic circumstance in which it finds itself could provide the basis for the development of stereotypic perceptions. For example, suppose a given group in a society has a poor standard of living, high rates of unemployment and low levels of educational achievement. It is easy to see how these visible indicators of the group's social status might get translated into perceptions of it as 'poor', 'lazy' and 'stupid'. Moreover, since 'what is' has the disconcerting habit of coming to be regarded as 'what should be', as Major (1994) has observed, such stereotypic perceptions may be used by more privileged groups to justify to themselves the perpetuation of the inequalities that gave rise to the stereotypes in the first place. Some evidence for this socioeconomic basis of stereotypes was obtained by Brewer and Campbell (1976) in a study of 30 ethnic groups in East Africa. One of the more economically developed of these groups, the Kikuya tribe in Kenya, was consistently described by the other groups in the area as 'intelligent' and 'progressive' or, less flatteringly, as 'pushy' and 'proud'.

A similar kind of explanation sees the origins of stereotypes in the over-representation of various groups in certain socially prescribed roles. Eagly and Steffen (1984) have shown that the gender stereotypes of women as 'kind', 'warm' and 'understanding' may derive more from the fact that statistically they are more likely to fulfil the traditional roles of 'homemaker' and 'caregiver' than from any inherent attributes possessed by women themselves. In a social judgement study, they found that such stereotypically feminine characteristics disappeared if the woman concerned was also described as being an employed person. Similarly, men were described as being just as 'sensitive' as women if they were also labelled as 'homemakers'.

Hoffman and Hurst (1990) extended the logic of this argument by presenting participants with a hypothetical society, supposedly on a distant planet, peopled by 'Orinthians' and 'Ackmians'. The participants read short descriptions of 15 members of each of these groups, which contained information about each person's occupation ('city worker' or 'child raiser') and different personality characteristics that they possessed ('active', 'logical', 'sensitive', 'warm' etc.). Across the 30 target people there was no correlation at all between the possession of particular characteristics and either group membership or occupation. Orinthians and Ackmians were described on average by the same kind of attributes as were 'city workers' and 'child raisers'. The only difference in these descriptions was that a majority (80 per cent) of one group was described as 'city workers' and a majority of the other as 'child raisers'. Having read these descriptions, the participants were asked to rate on a number of personality traits (half of which had not appeared in the target description) 'Orinthians in general' and 'Ackmians in general'. Half the participants were also invited to explain why Orinthians and Ackmians might tend to occupy the particular social roles they did; the remainder did not have to provide any such account. The participants' ratings of Orinthians and Ackmians showed how easily they leapt to (erroneous) stereotypical conclusions based on the prevalent occupation in each group. Despite the fact that the individual targets had been described in exactly equivalent terms, the group with a majority of city workers was seen as decidedly more 'agentic' (e.g. 'assertive', 'forceful', 'logical', 'self-reliant') than the group containing a majority of child raisers, which was perceived as more 'communal' (e.g. 'considerate', 'kind', 'warm', 'patient'). Moreover, the participants who had been asked to explain the group–occupation link provided even more stereotypic group judgements than those who had not been asked for such an explanation

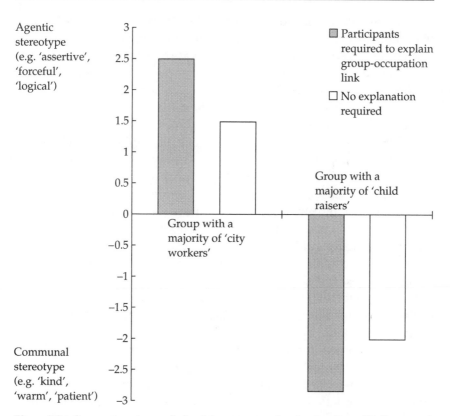

Figure 7.3 Group stereotypes derived from occupational roles (from Hoffman and Hurst, 1990, adapted from table 1)

(see figure 7.3). The process of having to account for an occupational imbalance, even in a purely fictitious society like this, seemed to be associated with the generation of more clear-cut group stereotypes. Once again, we see the link between stereotyping and the legitimation of the status quo.

Stereotypes as expectancies

We have seen, then, that stereotypes can serve not only to reflect social reality, but also to *refract* it in a way that is likely to lead to a perpetuation of the existing status relations between groups. In order for this to happen, stereotypes should presumably influence the judgements of individual actors – for example, a personnel officer making a hiring or promotion decision when faced with applicants from different social categories, or an estate agent choosing (or not) to let a property to clients from one ethnic group rather then another.

There are many ways that stereotypes can affect social judgements like these but a recurring theme is that they act to bias what the perceiver *expects* of the group (or group member) in question. Thus, that RAF officer whom we saw earlier articulating his belief about the aeronautical ineptitude of women will doubtless anticipate that, in the next batch of women applicants for pilot training, a majority will again fail to make the grade. Can we be sure that he will be completely neutral and unbiased in that future judgement, uninfluenced by his current expectancies? Probably not, if the research on stereotype usage is any guide.

Let me begin with a very simple example, the association between a person's sex and their height. There is a widely held stereotypic belief that men will be taller than women. Such an expectancy, though, can lead us to make mistakes in particular instances, as Nelson et al. (1990) discovered. They have found that people's estimates of the heights of women and men portrayed in photographs were reliably influenced by the sex of the person depicted, even when there was no actual sex difference in the stimulus photographs themselves. Indeed, so powerful was this particular – and in other contexts, usually rather accurate – stereotype that it persisted even when the researcher pointed out the absence of an overall sex difference in the stimuli and even when participants were offered a substantial cash prize to be accurate.

Of course, in many real-life situations a person's category membership is not the only information available to us when making judgements. We may know about their educational qualifications, prior experience and various personal attributes they possess. Such individuating information has to be integrated with the categorical knowledge associated with the person's group membership, and occasionally it will prove as powerful, if not more so, than the stereotypic expectancies in guiding our judgement (Locksley et al., 1982). Nevertheless, there is little room for complacency here. Glick et al. (1988) presented business managers with realistic appearing curricula vitae (CVs) of potential applicants for different kinds of jobs. The CVs implied a predilection for traditionally masculine, feminine or neutral activities and also, of course, indicated the applicant's sex. As expected, the individual characteristics of the applicants influenced the managers' views on the suitability of each person for different jobs, but so too did their sex: male applicants were more likely to be short-listed for a sales manager job and females for a dental receptionist post.

Likewise, Darley and Gross (1983) found that social class stereotypes can influence judgements of academic performance. In their experiment, participants were first shown a videotape of a girl. This depicted her as either coming from a deprived working-class background or as enjoying a more privileged middle-class environment. This was designed to generate negative and positive expectancies with respect to her academic performance because of the well-known correlation between class and educational achievement. The impact of these stereotypical expectancies was assessed in two separate conditions: one in which no further information was available, the other in which a second tape was shown in which the girl undertook some tests but which presented a rather ambiguous and inconsistent picture of her abilities. In all cases, participants were asked to predict her likely future performance in different academic domains. In the second condition, participants had some further and potentially individuating information, and so we might expect to find less impact of the social class stereotype among them. In fact, exactly the opposite happened. Those who had access to the additional information contained in the second tape projected their class stereotypes on to the girl's future performance more strongly than those who only ever saw the first tape. For the former group, the 'middle-class' girl was estimated to achieve a whole grade point higher then her 'working-class' counterpart. Darley and Gross (1983) concluded from their experiment that we do not use stereotypes in an undiscriminating or unthinking way; rather, stereotypes serve as tentative hypotheses for which we then seek out further information. Without that further information, as in the 'no information' conditions of that experiment, we hesitate to apply them too firmly (see also Leyens et al., 1994).

Unfortunately, people are usually rather selective about the information that they will look for: typically they are biased in favour of things that confirm their expectancies and will all too readily overlook information that is inconsistent with them (Stangor and Ford, 1992). A vivid demonstration of this phenomenon was provided by

Snyder and Swann (1978). They led interviewers to believe that the person they were about to interview was an extravert or an introvert. Then, during the interview itself, the interviewers could select from a range of questions in order to discover whether the target person really did fit the designated personality type. Those holding the 'extravert' hypothesis systematically chose more questions likely to reveal extravert tendencies (for example, 'what would you do it you wanted to liven things up at a party?'); those holding the alternative hypothesis chose more questions indicative of introversion (for example, 'what factors make it hard for you to really open up to people?'). Such confirmation-seeking tendencies persisted even when, in another experiment, participants were offered a substantial reward for the most accurate diagnosis. And, perhaps most disturbing of all, in a further study the interviewees themselves started to display the very behaviours the interviewers had been primed to expect, even though, of course, everyone (both interviewers and interviewees) had been randomly assigned to the different expectancy conditions.

Stereotypes influence not only our experiences for the future but they can also bias our recall of the past. This was shown by Hamilton and Rose (1980), who presented participants with a series of slides depicting some occupational groups (for example, stewardess, salesman) associated with some traits (for example, 'attractive', 'talkative'). In the slides, each trait appeared with each occupation exactly the same number of times. However, when asked to recall what they had seen, people erroneously remembered more stereotypical associations (for example 'attractive stewardess') than non-stereotypical pairings (for example 'attractive salesman'). Information consistent with their occupational stereotypes was more readily remembered – even over-remembered – than inconsistent information. Notice that in table 7.4, the frequency estimates along the falling diagonal (where the traits are stereotypic of the occupation) are all well above the true value of 2.0.

The selective effects of group stereotypes on memory occur even in the most primitive conditions. Howard and Rothbart (1980) asked participants to recall various statements about behaviours that had previously been associated with members of two experimentally created groups. The participants themselves had been assigned to one of these two groups also. The behaviours to be recalled were both favourable and unfavourable, and, of course both types were exactly

Table 7.4 Stereotypes as illusory correlations: mean frequency estimates of stereotypic and neutral traits associated with different occupational groups in a recall task

| Occupational category | Traits stereotypic of | | | |
	Accountant/ librarian (e.g. perfectionist/ serious)	Doctor/ stewardess (e.g. wealthy/ attractive)	Salesman/ waitress (e.g. talkative/ busy)	Neutral traits
Accountant/librarian	2.7*	2.0	2.2	2.3
Doctor/stewardess	2.2	2.7*	2.4	2.1
Salesman/waitress	1.9	2.1	2.9*	2.3

* Indicates match between stereotypic traits and occupational categories. The true value in all cells should have been 2.0.
Source: Hamilton and Rose (1980), table 1. Copyright (1980) by the American Psychological Association. Reprinted by permission of the author

balanced between the two groups. However, the participants' memories were not so well balanced. While they were equally good at recalling the group origin of the favourable behaviours, when it came to the unfavourable behaviours they were much better at recalling those associated with the outgroup than the ingroup (see figure 7.4).

Stereotypes, as we have seen, are the association of specific attributes with a social category. This experiment of Howard and Rothbart (1980) reminds us that, very often, these expectancies we hold of different groups are evaluatively loaded as well: generally, more positive traits and fewer negative traits are associated with the ingroup, while the reverse may hold for the outgroup, although less strongly (Brewer, 1979). There is now mounting evidence that these stereotypic biases can be automatic in their operation; quite literally, we may not even need time to think to display some of these group-based expectancies. The first hint that this might be so came from Gaertner and McLaughlin (1983), who measured how long (white) participants took to decide whether two strings of letters presented on a screen were real words. Some of them were actually nonsense syllables (e.g. ZUMAP), but others were real words, including BLACK, WHITE,

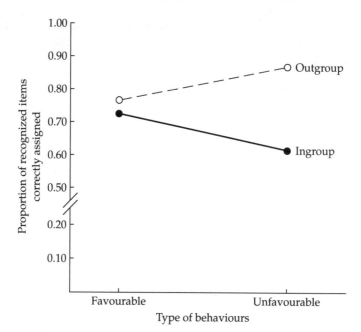

Figure 7.4 Selective recall for ingroup and outgroup information (from Howard and Rothbart, 1980, figure 1). Copyright © 1980 by the American Psychological Association.

three positive adjectives (e.g. CLEAN) and three negative adjectives (e.g. STUPID). The key question was how long participants would take to acknowledge the pairing of BLACK and WHITE with these negative and positive words. In the event there was no difference in reaction time to the negative pairings with the ethnic labels, but real *positive* words associated with WHITE were responded to consistently faster than when they were associated with BLACK. Notice that the task was very easy: the participants were not required to say that they endorsed any of the word pairings, only to identify them as real words or not. And this was easier when there was the familiar and psychologically comfortable expectancy involving the ingroup and things positive (see also Dovidio et al., 1986).

More compelling still are some experiments by Perdue and his colleagues, which suggest that the presence of differentially valenced expectancies associated with the ingroup and outgroup is both a generic cognitive tendency and one that may occur subconsciously. In one study they presented participants, who were all relatively young students, with the category label 'young' or 'old' (Perdue and Gurtman, 1990). But the exposure time for this was so brief (55 ms) and immediately overwritten on the screen by another word that it was almost impossible to detect what had been presented. The participants' task was simply to indicate as quickly as they could whether that second word was a positive or a negative trait label. Their response times indicated that that decision was reliably affected by the first subliminally presented category label: negative words were responded to more quickly when preceded by 'old' than 'young'; for positive words exactly the reverse occurred. In subsequent experiments, similar effects have been found by replacing the age category labels with the more generic ingroup and outgroup pronouns 'we' and 'they' (Perdue et al., 1990) or with faces of black and white people (Dovidio et al., 1997).

That stereotypic expectancies can sometimes operate automatically, outside our conscious control, should not mislead us into thinking that they always do so. A recurring theme of both this and the previous section is the idea that stereotypes are essentially guides to social action: they lead us to expect some things of groups and not others, and they help to justify some kinds of behaviours towards those groups and to exclude others. As a final illustration of this, let me turn to the eminent American lawyer Patricia Williams, who recently gave the BBC Reith lectures (Williams, 1997). She relates how she once tried to obtain a mortgage to buy a house. All the initial negotiations for the loan were completed over the telephone and, because she appeared to be an ideal 'low-risk' applicant as far as the bank was concerned (impeccable middle-class credentials, at least to judge from her job – Columbia Law Professor – and her accent, educated 'northeastern'), the loan was approved without further ado. Only a few written formalities remained, including the completion of an 'ethnic monitoring' form required by law and intended to discourage racial discrimination in housing. To her surprise, the last form had already been partially completed by some bank official, the box marked 'white' having been ticked. The coincidence of her high-status occupation and 'educated' accent has led to the obvious inference that she must be Caucasian. The slight snag, of course, is that Professor Williams is actually an African American. So she corrected this ethnic misclassification and returned the forms to the bank. Suddenly the previously agreed loan ran into difficulties. The bank wanted a bigger deposit, proposed a higher rate of interest and generally changed its whole demeanour from obligation to obstruction – and all because the lady was black.

Stereotypes as self-fulfilling prophecies

So far I have concentrated on stereotypes from the point of view of those who hold them – how they influence judgements of others and justify actions towards them. However, stereotyping is not just a one-way process; those who are stereotyped are prone to react to their treatment by others and in doing so they may ironically reinforce the very stereotype that provoked their reaction in the first place. In other words, stereotypes can turn out to be self-fulfilling prophecies (Darley and Fazio, 1980; Snyder, 1981). Before I review the research that has documented this, let me return one last time to that RAF pilot selection centre with which we began. Remember that the officer in charge of the centre believes that women are 'too emotional' to make good pilots. We have no record of women RAF personnel's reaction to this judgement of their capabilities, but it is not too fanciful to suppose that their response might be something other than a calm acceptance. Indeed, one can easily imagine a 'full and frank exchange of views' were they to meet the man in question. And, of course, such a heated reaction on their part would probably confirm his original stereotype that women are, indeed, 'too emotional'. And so it goes.

An early demonstration of this dynamic quality of stereotyping was provided by Word et al. (1974). Here, white participants had to role-play the position of a job interviewer. Half of the interviewees were white and half black, but in either case they were confederates of the experimenters, who had carefully trained them to react in a standardized way. Careful observation of the interviewers' behaviour revealed that they acted in a subtly different way with the black as compared to the white interviewee: they sat further from them and tended to lean further back in their seats; the interviews were also fully 25 per cent (or three minutes) shorter and contained more speech disfluencies (for example, stuttering, hesitations). One can easily imagine what effect these differences in non-verbal behaviour might have on a real job interviewee but Word et al. did not leave this to our imagination. In a second experiment, they reversed the roles.

302

This time the *interviewers* (always white confederates) were trained to act in one of two ways: *either* to sit closer to the interviewee, make fewer speech errors and make the interview last longer *or* to do the opposite. These were, of course, the very differences in behaviour elicited by the black and white confederates in the first experiment. This time it was the behaviour of the interviewees, again all white, which was carefully monitored by independent judges. The striking finding was that their behaviour seemed to reciprocate that of the interviewers: when the interviewer sat closer and talked more fluently, they responded in the same way, and noticeably differently from the other experimental condition. As a result, they were judged to be reliably calmer and also to be more suitable for the 'job' for which they were being interviewed. A similar self-perpetuating effect was observed by Snyder et al. (1977). They led male participants to believe that the person they were speaking to on the telephone was either an attractive or an unattractive woman. The men's image of their partner seemed to elicit different behaviours from her: her interaction style was subsequently judged by independent observers to be more friendly, likeable and sociable in the 'attractive' than the 'unattractive' condition (Snyder, 1981).

There is evidence that these self-fulfilling effects can occur without the perceiver being aware that the stereotype has been activated. Chen and Bargh (1997) presented white participants with subliminal images for white or black faces during a dot estimation computer task. The faces were on the screen for just 13 ms, too short a time to detect their presence. Shortly afterwards these 'primed' participants had to play a session of 'Catch Phrase' with another white participant, who had also completed the dot estimation task but without the subliminal images. The conversation of these two people, as they tried to guess words from the clues provided by their partner, was tape-recorded and then played back to independent judges, who had to rate the hostility displayed by each person. Incredibly enough, both the participant who had been surreptitiously primed with the black faces and his or her partner (who had not) were more hostile towards each other than people (and their partners) who had been primed with white faces (see figure 7.5). Chen and Bargh (1997) argued that those in the 'black prime' condition had had the stereotype of African Americans automatically activated. Part of this stereotype is hostility,

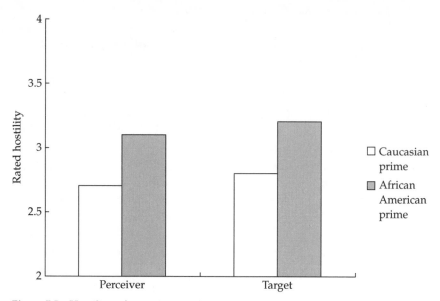

Figure 7.5 Hostility of perceiver and target after subliminal priming of perceiver with African American and Caucasian faces (from Chen and Bargh, 1997, figure 1)

which emerged in their interaction with their partner, who, in turn, behaved aggressively back.

The self-fulfilling nature of stereotypic expectancies has been observed in naturalistic contexts also, most notably in schools. In a famous experiment, Rosenthal and Jacobson (1968) led teachers to believe (falsely) that some of their students showed exceptional promise. In a follow-up test a year later, these students scored significantly higher than those who had not been so labelled. These increases could only be attributable to the teachers' expectations because only they knew the identities of the allegedly 'bright' children. Crano and Mellon (1978) found a similar effect of teacher expectancies in a large longitudinal study conducted in British primary schools. The teachers' expectations of their pupils' abilities at the start of the study turned out to be predictive of the pupils' subsequent performance a year later, and this held true even when the pupils' initial academic achievement level was statistically controlled for (Jussim, 1989).

Institutional practices within schools may compound expectancy effects and may even create some of their own. For instance, in many schools there is streaming by ability. In such situations students from socio-economically disadvantaged backgrounds, which will often include disproportionate numbers of ethnic minorities, are usually over-represented in the lower ability groups. There is thus some correspondence between the academic categorization ('slow' band) and other category labels (for example 'working class', 'black'), thus helping to preserve the negative stereotypes of intellectual inferiority associated with the latter. This problem is well illustrated by the evidence from Epstein's (1985) study of a large number of American schools, which found that teachers with more negative ethnic attitudes were also more likely to use some kind of 'tracking' system in their classrooms. Such practices would inevitably place more blacks (and other minority groups) in the 'slower' tracks, thus conveniently bolstering the teachers' prejudiced stereotypes.

In all of these examples the presumed instigator of the self-fulfilling prophecy has been the person holding the stereotype: some action by him or her is thought to provoke the confirmatory behaviour in the target person. However, evidence is beginning to emerge that the target person's own awareness of a prevailing stereotype about their group can contribute to them behaving in a manner consistent with that stereotype – a self self-fulfilling prophecy, as it were. Steele and Aronson (1995) have brought this to our attention in an ingenious series of experiments involving the performance on standard educational tests by black and white students. Steele and Aronson hypothesized that when black students become self-conscious about their academic achievement as *black students*, this reminds them of the cultural expectation (at least in the United States) that in general black people perform worse than whites. This awareness – what Steele and Aronson call 'stereotype threat' – then interferes with their academic test performance, perhaps because they perceive standardized tests to be biased against them, or because of heightened arousal (see chapter 5), or by diverting cognitive resources onto task-irrelevant matters or even, conceivably, because they may internalize the cultural stereotype into their own conception of themselves. To demonstrate this process, Steele and Aronson (1995) asked black and white participants to take a test comprising items taken from a widely used examination used for entry to graduate school. Half of the students were told that the test was, indeed, highly diagnostic of academic success; the remainder were told instead that it was merely part of a research programme into problem solving. The researchers predicted that, in the first condition, the black students would be more apprehensive about their performance because of their knowledge of the cultural assumption about underachievement of black students, and would actually perform worse as a result. So it proved. The scores of the black students in the first, stereotype threat, condition were markedly lower than those of their white counterparts – on average 5 items were correct versus 11 – while in the other condition there was no difference (both scored around 9). A subsequent experiment revealed that taking a test under such implicitly threatening conditions also heightened black students' awareness of their ethnicity, increased their self-doubts, and also led them to provide more self-handicapping explanations for their likely performance (e.g. they typically reported having had 2 hours less sleep the night before than participants, black or white, in the other condition).

Summary

1   A key feature of human cognition is people's need and ability to categorize the world. This arises because of the amount and complexity of information they must deal with. An inevitable consequence of categorization is a cognitive accentuation of the differences between categories and an assimilation of the differences within categories.

2   The use of one categorization rather than another in a given situation depends upon the degree of its fit with the actual similarities and differences among the people in the situation, and upon the ease of its cognitive accessibility to the person concerned. Factors affecting fit and accessibility include features of the stimuli such as proximity, interdependence and novelty, and the person's needs, goals and habitual dispositions.

3   Two important intergroup consequences of categorization are, first, that it can lead to behavioural discrimination in the treatment of ingroup and outgroup members. Simply being classified as a category member, on however trivial a basis, can generate

biased reward allocations which favour the ingroup. A second consequence is that the ingroup and outgroup are rarely seen as equally internally homogeneous. From the perspective of a majority group, usually the outgroup is seen as more homogeneous than the ingroup, especially on judgmental dimensions peripheral to its identity. But minority groups, or groups at early stages of their formation, will typically see themselves as more homogeneous than outgroups, particularly on identity-relevant criteria.

4   Stereotyping is the attribution of common characteristics to members of a group. It arises directly from the categorization process, particularly the assimilation of within-group differences, and serves to guide and justify people's behaviour in intergroup settings.

5   Three important aspects of stereotypes are their role in legitimating existing intergroup inequalities, their nature as expectancies that bias judgements and recall in favour of confirmatory information, and their self-fulfilling quality in the way they can instigate in the group being stereotyped the very behaviour that constitutes the stereotype in the first place.

Note

1   The fact that on this occasion the person happened to be a male nurse understandably caused him some consternation.

Further Reading

Devos, T., Comby, L. and Deshamps, J.-C. (1996) Asymmetries in judgements of ingroup and outgroup variability, in Stroebe, W. and Hewstone, M. (eds) *European Review of Social Psychology*, vol. 7, pp. 95–144. Chichester: Wiley.

Diehl, M. (1990) The minimal group paradigm: theoretical explanations and empirical findings, in Stroebe, W. and Hewstone, M. (eds) *European Review of Social Psychology*, vol. 1, pp. 263–392. Chichester: Wiley.

Macrae, N., Stangor, C. and Hewstone, M. (1996) (eds) *Stereotypes and Stereotyping*, especially chs 1, 5, 8 and 9. London: Guildford Press.

Oakes, P.J., Haslam, S.A. and Turner, J.C. (1994) *Stereotyping and Social Reality*, especially chs 5–8. Oxford: Blackwell.

Operario, D. and Fiske, S.T. (in press) Stereotypes: processes, structure, content and context, in Brown, R. and Gaertner, S. (eds) *Blackwell Handbook of Social Psychology*, vol. 4. Oxford: Blackwell.

Tajfel, H. (1981) *Human Groups and Social Categories*, chs 4–6. Cambridge: Cambridge University Press.

8

SOCIAL IDENTITY AND INTERGROUP RELATIONS

A recurring theme throughout this book has been the psychological importance that people attach to their membership of various groups. In chapter 4 we saw how people were decidedly more influenced by those who belonged to their ingroup rather than an outgroup. In chapter 5 we discussed how a strong attachment to a group can have powerful motivating properties, overcoming the otherwise common tendency to slacken one's efforts when undertaking collective activities. Then, in the previous two chapters, we explored some of the implications of group membership for our behaviour and attitudes towards other groups, whether as a response to disparities and conflicts in the intergroup situation or as a consequence of various socio-cognitive processes. As we saw, group members seem to show a remarkably consistent tendency to favour their own group in their perceptions, judgements and behaviours. Often those ingroup biases are traceable to objective factors – for example, competing with an outgroup for some scarce resource – but not always; mere categorization seems to trigger ingroup-favouring responses by itself. As I tried to show in the previous chapter, the ubiquity of this intergroup differentiation can be understood once we appreciate how fundamental categorization and its by-products are for human social existence. Nevertheless, despite the undoubted importance of these cognitive processes, they cannot by themselves explain the pervasive asymmetry in people's intergroup attitudes – that it is generally the ingroup (and not the outgroup) which comes off best. Theoretical models based solely on cognitive processes can explain why groups are perceived as more different from each other than they really are, and why they may be seen in crude and over-simplified terms. But they cannot so easily account for the consistently positive light in which the ingroup is viewed and the negative or, at least, less positive flavour so often attached to the outgroup. To understand this we need a further concept, that of social identity.

Social identity processes, then, are the focus of this chapter. I begin with a brief exposition of an important theory – social identity theory, as it is known – which has done much to elucidate the nature of these processes and to spell out their implications for intergroup behaviour. As I will show, the theory is helpful in explaining a wide range of intergroup phenomena, from discrimination in minimal group settings to the subtleties of language use by different ethnic groups. In all these contexts, a common theme is the tendency of groups to seek out and maintain some positive distinctiveness from each other. Social identity theory presumes that this search for group distinctiveness is functional for individuals because, in this way, they can achieve some positivity for themselves via their association with a favourably regarded ingroup. This has its most obvious consequences in the fostering of conflictual intergroup relations. However, as will become apparent in the second half of the chapter, a better understanding of social identity processes also has important applications in the promotion of tolerance and harmony between groups.

Social Identity and Intergroup Conflict

In chapter 7 I argued that dividing the social world into a manageable number of categories is indispensable for us to be able to simplify and make sense of it. But, of course, it is not just others who are so classified; we also locate ourselves in some groups and not in others. It is this act of self-categorization that forms the basis for all of our many social identities. As one of the architects of social identity theory defined it:

[social identity is] that part of an individual's self concept which derives from his knowledge of his membership of a social group (or groups) together with the value and emotional significance attached to that membership. (Tajfel, 1978, p. 63)

In other words, we invoke a part of our social identity whenever we think of ourselves as belonging to one gender/ethnicity/social class rather than another.

Social identity theory

This idea that social identity derives from group membership has a long history (e.g. Mead, 1934), but it was not until the 1970s that it was realized that social identity processes might have implications for intergroup behaviour (Tajfel, 1978; Tajfel and Turner, 1986). This can happen if we assume, with Tajfel and Turner (1986), that by and

311

large people prefer to have a positive self-concept rather than a negative one. Since part of our self-concept (or identity) is defined in terms of group affiliations, it follows that there will also be a preference to view those ingroups positively rather than negatively. But how do we arrive at such an evaluation? Tajfel and Turner (1986) extend Festinger's (1954) social comparison theory (discussed in chapters 3 and 4) and suggest that our *group* evaluations are also essentially relative in nature; we assess our own group's worth by comparing it to other groups. The outcome of these intergroup comparisons is critical for us because indirectly it contributes to our own self-esteem. If our own group can be perceived as clearly superior on some dimension of value (like skill or sociability) then we, too, can bask in that reflected glory. Cialdini et al. (1976) found evidence of exactly this phenomenon among college football supporters. On the days following a victory by their side, college scarves and other insignia – all indicating heightened pride in college membership – were much more in evidence than on days following a defeat (see also Snyder et al., 1986). Because of our presumed need for a positive self-concept, it follows that there will be a bias in these comparisons to look for ways in which the ingroup can, indeed, be distinguished favourably from outgroups. Tajfel calls this 'the establishment of positive distinctiveness' (Tajfel, 1978, p. 83). Note that here again is a further parallel with Festinger's (1954) theory, for Festinger suggested that ability comparisons within the group would be subject to a 'unidirectional drive upwards' (Festinger, 1954, p. 124). However, Festinger believed that the kind of comparisons we are discussing here are rarely made (Festinger, 1954, p. 136). As we shall see shortly, and as I already noted in chapter 3, there is no lack of research demonstrating people's readiness to engage in intergroup comparisons and, more often than not, these comparisons result in the ingroup being viewed more favourably than the outgroup (Mullen et al., 1992).

How can social identity theory help to explain the persistent tendency for people to display intergroup discrimination, even in as barren a context as the minimal group paradigm? Consider again the situation: participants have been allocated to one of two equally meaningless groups. Indeed, so meaningless are they that there is literally nothing to differentiate them except the group labels and the fact that they themselves are in one group and not the other. They are referred to by code numbers, thus leading to feelings of anonymity. Given this anonymity the only possible source of identity, primitive though it may be, is their ingroup. However, that group is initially indistinguishable from the other group and hence, according to the theory, contributes little positive to its members' self-esteem. Accordingly, pressures for distinctiveness come into play and members of both groups seek to differentiate their own group positively from the other by the only means possible: by allocating more money or points – it does not matter which (Turner, 1978) – to fellow ingroupers than to outgroupers. Recall, also, that they will often do this even at the cost of some absolute gain to the ingroup (the maximizing difference strategy).

The presumed link between intergroup discrimination and self-esteem was demonstrated by Oakes and Turner (1980). They found that participants in a minimal group experiment who were not given the usual opportunity to make intergroup reward allocations showed lower self-esteem than those who were. In a follow-up experiment, Lemyre and Smith (1985) confirmed this result and established that it was indeed the opportunity to display *intergroup* discrimination that elevated self-esteem. Control participants who, although having been categorized, could only distribute rewards between two ingroupers or two outgroupers, or who could not distribute rewards at all, showed lower self-esteem than those able to make *inter*group decisions. I shall return to this link between self-esteem and discrimination later because it turns out that it is not as straightforward as social identity theory and these initial studies imply.

But how can social identity theory account for the *absence* of discrimination in the minimal group paradigm when negative outcomes are at stake (see chapter 7)? At first glance, such a finding would appear to contradict the search for positive distinctiveness that the theory presumes to exist in intergroup situations. If group members can feel better about their ingroup by rewarding it more, why should they not feel the same about punishing it less? The precise reasons for the observed asymmetry between discrimination with positive and negative outcomes are not yet fully understood. Mummendey and Otten (1998) have advanced three varieties of explanation for this asymmetry, the most promising of which actually relies on social identification as its primary motive. The argument goes like this: when participants find themselves in a minimal group situation and are asked to do something quite unusual (e.g. inflict mild punishment on others), they will probably regard this as a rather inappropriate form of behaviour (Blanz et al., 1997). Thus, the experimenter's request that they do so may generate a 'common fate' experience which leads them to redefine the situation as one in which the artificial categories (e.g. Klee and Kandinsky) are subsumed within a new superordinate category ('we the experimental participants' versus 'The Experimenter', who is asking us to do these unpleasant things). Such a recategorization would be expected to lead to lessened ingroup bias because former outgroup members become reclassified as fellow members of a new superordinate category (Turner, 1981).

We put this explanation to the test (Gardham and Brown, in press). In our experiment we created minimal groups in the usual way and then, depending on experimental condition, participants were asked to allocate or to remove either rewards (small sums of money) or punishments (short bursts of unpleasant 'white noise'). In this way, we could directly compare two kinds of socially inappropriate behaviour (allocating punishment or removing rewards) with two less inappropriate activities (allocating rewards or removing punishments). We guessed that the former two cases would create the recategorization that Mummendey and Otten (1998) had hypothesized would occur, and hence we would observe little ingroup favouritism. In contrast, the other two conditions might be regarded as less socially undesirable and so the 'usual' ingroup favouritism would be shown. To check on the participants' identity processes we included a measure of superordinate group identification (the school they belonged to) and subgroup identification (the minimal group they had been assigned to in the experiment). The results bore out Mummendey and Otten's (1998) prediction (see table 8.1). As can be seen, the levels of ingroup bias were lowest (in fact, they were statistically not different from zero) in the socially 'inappropriate' conditions (upper right and lower left cells of table 8.1). Furthermore, it was precisely in those conditions where superordinate group identification was highest relative to subgroup identification. In the other two conditions (upper left and lower right cells), the bias was much more in evidence and the superordinate identification relatively weaker.

Social identity theory, then, seems to provide a plausible account of people's readiness to favour these most minimal of ingroups. But its

Table 8.1 Explaining positive–negative asymmetry in intergroup discrimination by means of social identification

		Rewards	*Punishments*
Allocate	Ingroup bias*	2.1	0.6
	Comparative identification[†]	0.2	2.3
Remove	Ingroup bias*	−0.8	1.1
	Comparative identification[†]	2.5	0.4

* Measured on an index of maximum difference between ingroup and outgroup.
[†] Superordinate group identification *minus* subgroup identification.
Source: Gardham and Brown (in press), tables 1 and 5

applicability is not limited to these rather contrived experimental situations; part of its attraction has been its ability to make sense of a wide range of intergroup phenomena in natural contexts, particularly where the ingroup favouritism observed appears to have no obvious rational or material basis. I shall focus on examples from just three domains: the world of work, the use of language in intergroup relations, and gender segregation in young children. For others, see Abrams and Hogg (1990), Capozza and Brown (1999) and Tajfel (1978, 1982).

The search for group distinctiveness

Occupational groups have proved a fertile source of data for researchers interested in the links between social identity processes and ingroup favouritism. One example is provided by the well-known tendency for groups of workers to be concerned about the size of wage relativities *vis-à-vis* other groups of workers. This was particularly prevalent in the British engineering industry in the 1970s but, historically, examples of disputes centring on differentials go back at least as far as the early nineteenth century. What is interesting about these industrial conflicts is that they may have little 'realistic' basis in the sense that there is rarely an explicit conflict of interest between the groups concerned. Often, indeed, the workers may have different employers and may work in a completely different industry. The

Table 8.2 Matrix used to measure intergroup differentiation in wage comparisons

	Wages				
Toolroom group	£69.30	£68.80	£68.30	£67.80	£67.30
Production and Development groups	£70.30	£69.30	£68.30	£67.30	£66.30

Source: Brown (1978)

other important aspect of differentials disputes is – as the words imply – that they are about the *difference* between groups rather than about their levels of wages in absolute terms. These two points were borne out very clearly in a study of an aircraft engineering factory which I conducted some years ago (Brown, 1978).

In this factory, there were three main groups of workers: Production, Development and the Toolroom. For many years these three groups – who, incidentally, belonged to the same trade unions – cooperated well together, presenting a united and often highly militant front in their negotiations with management. However, a few years before the study this unity had largely disappeared, resulting, as I was to discover, in a fairly tense network of intergroup relations. I interviewed a number of shop stewards from each of these departments, quizzing them about their intergroup attitudes. One of my questions asked them to suggest new wage levels for the groups. I found that although the existing wage structure was generally maintained, each group sought to modify it so that its own position relative to the other groups was improved. The Toolroom respondents were particularly notable in desiring a differential over the nearest group which was over three times larger than the existing gap. And it was clear that it was the difference that mattered as much as the absolute wage level. I was able to establish this using some matrices adapted from the minimal group experiments. An example is shown in table 8.2. Respondents had to choose one of the five pairs of options. When presented with this array of wage relativities, members of the Toolroom were virtually unanimous in choosing the extreme right-hand pair. Notice that this meant a sacrifice of as much as £2 per

Table 8.3 Ingroup bias in intergroup perceptions of Dutch nurses

Respondents	Theoretical insight		Interpersonal relations	
	BN	SPN	BN	SPN
Baccalaureate nurses (BN)	+0.9	−0.6	−0.2	+0.5
Social psychiatric nurses (SPN)	+0.1	−0.6	−0.8	+0.4

The higher the score, the higher the evaluation.
Source: van Knippenberg and van Oers (1984), table 2

week in absolute terms in order to establish a £1 differential over the other groups. That this intergroup differentiation cut across the groups' 'real' interests was realized by one of the stewards:

Your sectarian point of view is going to cost *you* money and *save* the company money. (Brown, 1978, p. 423)

But, as one of his colleagues commented:

The purchasing power of the money, you see, very often doesn't come into it. It's a question of status – I suppose we're all snobs at heart, or whatever – but honour and status does seem to come into it. (Brown, 1978, p. 419)

Observations such as these seem much more explicable by social identity theory than the realistic group conflict theory discussed in chapter 6.

For a further example, consider another occupational group, nurses, people who are more usually associated with caring and self-sacrifice than with group favouritism and animosity. And yet there is evidence that nurses too are quite ready to display ingroup bias, particularly in relation to their nursing colleagues. For example, van Knippenberg and van Oers (1984) in their study of academic and psychiatric nurses in the Netherlands found clear evidence of ingroup bias on attributes specific to each group, e.g. theoretical insight versus interpersonal relations (see table 8.3). As can be seen, there was some agreement between the groups as to their respective merits and these attributes: the Baccalaureate nurses (BN) are generally regarded as having superior theoretical insight, while the social psychiatric nurses (SPN) are seen as having better interpersonal skills. However, the ratings also showed that the concession that an outgroup might be superior on one set of dimensions was considerably outweighed by the claim to *ingroup* superiority on the other set. The degree of ingroup bias on the latter was generally twice as high as the amount of outgroup bias on the other attributes. Moreover, van Knippenberg and van Oers (1984) also found that the dimension on which each group showed the most ingroup bias (i.e. theoretical insight for the BN group and interpersonal relations for the SPN group) was also the aspect of nursing that each group regarded as most important. This selectivity in making positive intergroup comparisons has been found in other studies also (e.g. Mummendey and Schreiber, 1984; Stewart et al., 1990), and reminds us that the pursuit of positive distinctiveness is not an unthinking or generalized group response but is always relative to the particular intergroup context in which people find themselves.

As a second illustration of social identity processes at work in the real world, we can turn to language usage in intergroup settings. Note, first of all, the attempts by various national and ethnic groups to maintain the integrity of their language (Giles, 1977). Examples abound. In Europe, one thinks immediately of the Flemings and the Walloons in Belgium, the Catalans in Spain, the Bretons in France, and the Welsh in Britain. Elsewhere in the world, examples are scarcely less numerous – for instance, the importance of French in the political movement for an independent Québec in Canada, or the role of Hebrew in the establishment of the state of Israel. In all these cases, we see attempts by groups to make themselves distinct from other groups in one of the most fundamental ways of all – language. It is fundamental in two ways: first, because our membership of ethnic/national groups is intimately connected with the use of language or dialect. It is part of our cultural heritage and, indeed, may even be a defining attribute for group membership. In other words, our social identities may be directly expressed through language. But language is important to intergroup relations in another way: it is also the prime means of communication with outgroups. Depending on the language, dialect or accent we choose to use, we can communicate more or less effectively with members of the outgroup: attempt to integrate or cut ourselves off. These considerations have led Giles and his colleagues to explain the behaviour of ethnolinguistic groups in terms of social identity processes (Giles and Johnson, 1981). Where identity is threatened, efforts to establish distinctiveness may take the form of linguistic divergence, and two experimental studies have found exactly that (Bourhis and Giles, 1977; Bourhis et al., 1978). Both were set in the context of a language laboratory, and in both the language students were confronted with an outgroup speaker who threatened their linguistic identities. Evidence of language divergence by the students was found, either by broadening their accent or by them switching languages altogether. In fact, in one of the studies covert recordings of their reactions captured muttered insults and obscenities directed towards the outgroup person, *but in the ingroup language*. This differentiation is particularly significant since, as some earlier work of Giles had established, in most inter*personal* contexts people tend to converge in their language use (Giles and Powesland, 1975). That in intergroup contexts the opposite can happen is indicative that different (identity) processes may be at work (see chapter 1).

Biases can creep into intergroup language in subtle ways too; the very form in which we explain other people's behaviour can differ according to whether it is an outgroup or an ingroup person we are describing. The credit for this discovery should go to Maass and her colleagues, who, in a series of ingenious studies, have identified what they describe as a linguistic intergroup bias which seems to be rather prevalent in intergroup communications (Maass, 1999). To document this bias, Maass et al. (1989) asked members of rival quarters (*contrade*) of an Italian city to describe what was happening in some cartoons depicting members of their own and the other *contrada*. The studies were conducted in the weeks prior to an annual horse race involving intense competition between the *contrade*. When the descriptions were analysed linguistically it became apparent that positive ingroup behaviours – for example, an ingroup member shown comforting someone in distress – were described using words more indicative of enduring dispositional states (e.g. 'he is compassionate') than were the same behaviours by outgroup members. The latter tended to be depicted in more concrete and situationally specific terms (e.g. 'he is hugging her'). For negative behaviours exactly the opposite occurred. A similar

319

phenomenon was observed in newspaper reports of an anti-Semitic demonstration at a basketball match involving an Italian and an Israeli team (Maass et al., 1994). Jewish newspaper accounts of the demonstrators were more likely than non-Jewish reports to use more abstract descriptions, implying some deeper-rooted and less transitory explanation for the event.

One explanation for linguistic intergroup bias is in terms of social identity processes. By seeing negative ingroup behaviours concretely and positive ingroup behaviours more abstractly, a favourable image of the ingroup can be maintained, especially relative to a more dispositionally negative and only temporarily positive conception of the outgroup. Such an explanation received support from a subsequent study by Maass et al. (1996) involving groups of wild game hunters and environmentalists. Prior to being presented with the cartoons, members of these two groups received a message, apparently from the other group, which was either identity threatening or conciliatory in tone. Sure enough, those who had read the threatening communication showed much more marked linguistic bias than those in the other condition. Moreover, this bias was correlated with their level of collective self-esteem, an association consistent with social identity theory's hypothesis of a link between ingroup bias and a positive self concept. Nevertheless, it is unlikely that identity protection mechanisms are the only processes underlying linguistic intergroup bias. In another study, Maass et al. (1995) showed that, in less conflictual intergroup contexts (e.g. northern versus southern Italy), what may drive the bias are differential *expectancies* about ingroup and outgroup behaviours, rather than an inevitable value-laden preference for ingroup-positive and dissociation from ingroup-negative. They showed this by including in the stimulus cartoons activities that were both typical and *un*typical of northern and southern Italians. These activities were also balanced for desirability (i.e. equal numbers of positive and negative behaviours were included). If identity motives cause the bias, they should have found the usual effect for this latter factor (e.g. ingroup-positive and outgroup-negative acts being described more abstractly). In fact, no such bias was visible; the principal finding was that typical behaviours, whether from ingroup or outgroup and whether positive or negative, were described more abstractly than untypical behaviours.

320

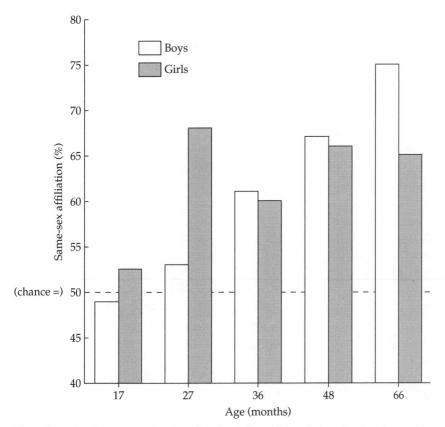

Figure 8.1 Gender segregation in children at play (adapted from La Freniere et al., 1984, figure 1)

A third example of intergroup differentiation that seems to have its origins in social identity processes comes from the children's playground. As anyone who has had anything to do with children will tell you, young children are remarkably choosy about their playmates. From the age of three years – and even younger in girls – they show a marked preference for their own gender. One of the clearest documentations of this gender segregation was obtained in a Canadian day-care centre, which took children from 18 months to over 5 years (La Freniere et al., 1984). The researchers observed these children over several months and noticed a sharp gender cleavage in their affiliative behaviour (see figure 8.1). From as early as three years, or

321

2¼ in girls, they directed many more affiliative acts towards members of their own sex than they did towards children of the opposite sex. Such own-gender bias is a remarkably prevalent phenomenon, having been found in many different contexts with a variety of research methodologies (e.g. Harkness and Super, 1985; Maccoby and Jacklin, 1987; Yee and Brown, 1994).

In seeking the explanation for this early form of gender discrimination, Maccoby and Jacklin (1987) examined and rejected a number of plausible hypotheses. For instance, it seems unlikely that it can be traced to any direct socialization pressures from adult caretakers. Gender segregation in play persists even if adults are not present and, if anything, may be less evident, not more, when they are. Moreover, there appeared to be little relationship between how sex-typed parents are and the degree of own-gender preference displayed by the child. Maccoby and Jacklin (1987) speculate that gender segregation may have its origins in the pervasive and highly functional categorization by sex, a classification that includes both self and others (see chapter 7). From an early age, children acquire a primitive gender identity based on this self-categorization (Duveen and Lloyd, 1986; Slaby and Frey, 1975; Thompson, 1975). One way this identity can be made more distinctive, argue Maccoby and Jacklin (1987), is by developing attitudes and behaviours that emphasize the differences between the sexes. An effective way of achieving this intergroup differentiation could be by favouring single-sex play groups, each with its distinctive styles of social interaction (see Durkin, 1995, ch. 5). The fact that girls seem to show gender segregation earlier than boys might be attributable to a 'defensive' reaction by them against the typically more boisterous rough-and-tumble play of their male peers (Di Pietro, 1981).

Responses to status inequality

The real-world examples I chose to illustrate social identity processes all had one other feature in common: they all involved groups of unequal status. The groups of engineering workers and the different categories of nurse enjoyed different amounts of prestige and possessed much less power and status than their employers. Minority group languages or dialects are nearly always devalued by the dominant linguistic group (Giles and Powesland, 1975). And, of course, it is well known that men and women can expect very different career opportunities in later life, even if in the nursery and school playground it is to be hoped that the status difference between the sexes has not yet developed into its full-blown adult form. Let us then consider what happens when people belong to a group of dominant or subordinate status.

Let us consider the case of the high-status group first. Obvious examples of such privileged groups would be those in managerial positions in business, those working in professions (e.g. medicine, law), white ethnic groups in many Western societies, and people who work (as opposed to those who are unemployed). On a whole host of comparative criteria such groups emerge as superior to other groups in society. Thus, following the logic of social identity theory, members of such groups should have few identity problems. They can satisfactorily view their ingroups as enjoying the desired state of positive distinctiveness in relation to other groups, a perception that has comfortable ramifications for their own view of themselves.

At first glance, then, one might expect members of dominant groups not to manifest much evidence of intergroup differentiation. However, while this does follow strictly from the social identity hypothesis, there are other reasons why we should not expect this outcome. How are intergroup attitudes usually elicited? Group members are typically asked to evaluate their own and other group(s) on a number of valued dimensions (for example, 'how intelligent/industrious/friendly are the groups?'). To such questions, which implicitly or explicitly refer to the comparative worth of the groups, members of high-status groups are likely to give answers which reflect their (to them) self-evident superiority. In other words, they are likely to show clear signs of positive ingroup bias. In fact, research on intergroup attitudes in hierarchical situations confirms that this generally happens. High-status groups do tend to show more ingroup bias than low-status groups (Mullen et al., 1992). This effect was more pronounced in laboratory experiments where, usually, status differences can be more unambiguously determined. Also, in more naturalistic settings other important variables may be at work which, as we shall see, can radically interact with the effects of status itself.

To illustrate this general trend a study by Sachdev and Bourhis (1987) will serve well. They modified the minimal-group paradigm so that the groups were of equal or unequal ability on a creativity measure. The subjects then had to evaluate the creativity of the groups on another task. As can be seen from figure 8.2, both the high- and equal-status groups showed very clear ingroup bias in their evaluations, while the lower-status groups tended to favour the outgroup. Notice, too, that the members' satisfaction with their ingroup (roughly equivalent to their strength of identification) was also correlated with status (lower part of figure 8.2).

The fact that the equal-status groups in this study showed almost as much bias as the high-status groups suggests that the intergroup differentiation (or bias) revealed by these two groups may be serving rather different functions. For the high-status groups it may be merely to maintain their already secure dominance; for equal-status groups, on the other hand, it may be to *achieve* some distinctiveness, as I suggested earlier in putting forward the social identity explanation of discrimination in the minimal group situation. Indeed, it could be argued that it is precisely in circumstances of status equality that one might expect the greatest intergroup rivalry (and hence discrimination) since it is there that groups have the least positive distinctiveness (Brown, 1984b). A 'needle match' between two sports teams adjacent in a league is likely to elicit much more competitiveness than a game between two teams at opposite ends of the table.

It was this idea that formed the basis of a series of experiments I conducted on the effects of intergroup similarity (Brown, 1984a; Brown and Abrams, 1986). In these experiments schoolchildren believed that they were undertaking a task in conjunction with members of another school. That school was described as being variously rather similar to them in status (they were alleged to be about as good as them at various academic disciplines) or better or worse than them. In addition, the prevailing attitudes towards those school disciplines at the other school were depicted as either similar or different. We found three main results. The first was that when the children believed that the other school held similar attitudes to them they thought they would like them better than when the outgroup attitudes were different (Brown, 1984a; Brown and Abrams, 1986). This parallels similar findings obtained at the interpersonal level and is predictable from

324

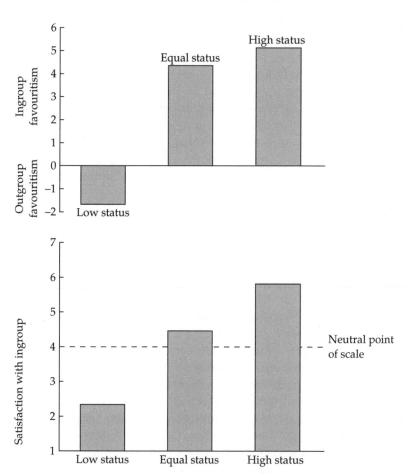

Figure 8.2 The effects of a group's status position on ingroup bias and satisfaction with the ingroup (from Sachdev and Bourhis, 1987, ingroup favouritism derived from three measures of bias in table 1; 'satisfaction' from first three rows of table 2)

Festinger's (1954) social comparison theory (Byrne, 1971; see chapter 4). It was also rather against the social identity hypothesis that similarity might provoke a search for distinctiveness, which might then lead to a greater distance between groups.

A second finding was that when the children believed that they were about to engage in a cooperative task with the other school their levels of ingroup bias in performance evaluations were *moderated* when they believed that the outgroup was of equivalent status to their school

325

(Brown, 1984a). Again, this was rather against the social identity prediction. However, a third result was somewhat more in line with the idea of the pursuit of distinctiveness. This was obtained in the Brown and Abrams (1986) experiment, where we found that when the outgroup became very similar to the ingroup (similar attitudes *and* similar in status), then the amount of ingroup bias *increased*. It was as if a certain threshold of similarity had been crossed beyond which the ingroup felt threatened by the psychological proximity of the outgroup (see also Diehl, 1988; Rocca and Schwartz, 1993).

Now let us turn our attention to the groups at the other end of the spectrum. What are the consequences of belonging to a group of subordinate status? At first glance these seem negative. Members of such groups will frequently discover that they have lower wages (if they have a job at all), poorer housing, fewer educational qualifications and are consensually regarded as being inferior on a number of criteria. Thus, not only are the worse off in a direct material sense, but psychologically too they may well be disadvantaged. If identity is indeed maintained through intergroup comparisons, as social identity theory suggests, then the outcome of the available comparisons is unremittingly negative for their self-esteem.

Tajfel and Turner (1986) suggest that one response to this situation is for members of such groups to abandon their current social identity. Thus, in a spirit of 'if you can't beat 'em, join 'em', they may seek to leave their ingroup and join another apparently more prestigious group. Recall how the lower-status group members in Sachdev and Bourhis's (1987) experiment expressed markedly lower levels of satisfaction with their ingroup. Examples of members of 'inferior' groups distancing themselves physically or psychologically from their group are not hard to find. In their classic studies of ethnic identification, Clark and Clark (1947) found that black children in the USA showed identification with the preference for the dominant white group, a finding replicated with minority groups in other countries (e.g. Vaughan, 1964; Morland, 1969; Milner, 1975).[1] Interestingly enough, the tendency of children to 'disaffiliate' from socially disadvantaged groups may undergo a curious curvilinear change between 3 and 9 years. In chapter 2 I described a study of ours in which we experimentally created high- and low-status teams of young children (Yee and Brown, 1992). Generally, the children preferred to be in the higher status group and those that were in it showed more ingroup bias than those who were in the low-status team. However, in the 5-year-old age group there was much less evidence of this abandonment of the 'sinking ship'. Unlike their younger and older peers, they continued to wish to remain in the low-status group and to evaluate it more favourably than the other, consensually more prestigious, team (see also Aboud, 1988, for other evidence of this socially 'critical period' between 5 and 7 years).

Disidentification with the ingroup is by no means a phenomenon restricted to children, as Lewin (1948) noted of American Jews who attempt to 'pass' into Gentile society. Nevertheless, members of subordinate groups may not always be so willing (or able) to reject their identity. For instance, if the boundaries between the categories are fixed and impermeable, as is the case with many ascribed group memberships like gender and ethnicity, then the option to leave the subordinate group may not be open. Ellemers and her colleagues have shown that the mere knowledge that passage from one group to another is possible has the effect of lowering subordinate group members' level of identification with their group (Ellemers et al., 1988). But even in cases where movement out of the group is an option, if group members have a sufficiently strong identification with or attachment to the ingroup they may not abandon it even if it is not doing well. Although the size of following of football clubs is undoubtedly correlated with their success, most loyal fans do not cease supporting their club just because it fails to win the league or, still worse, avoid relegation. Ellemers et al. (1997) experimentally misled participants into thinking they were either weakly or strongly identified with an artificial group, which then appeared to perform badly in a task. Those who believed that they were highly involved with their group (strong identity condition) showed less inclination to leave it than those in the weak identity condition. In a real-world analogue of this situation, Abrams et al. (1998) found that employees' stated intentions to leave their workplace (companies in Japan and Britain; higher education institutions in Britain) were strongly and *negatively* correlated with their strength of identification with the organization in question; the more they identified the less they wanted to leave.

In cases where mobility is psychologically difficult or practically impossible, Tajfel and Turner (1986) suggest that other tactics may be adopted. One is to restrict the comparisons to other similar subordinate-status groups so that the outcome of those comparisons is more favourable to the ingroup. Rosenberg and Simmons (1972), for example, found that self-esteem among blacks who made comparisons with other blacks was higher than in those who compared themselves with whites. On the other side of that ethnic divide, it is often reported that white respondents from poorer socio-economic backgrounds show more overt prejudice than more middle-class samples (Brown, 1965; Vollebergh, 1991). Such 'poor white racism', as it is sometimes called, may also be motivated in part by the desire to avoid identity-damaging comparisons with wealthier social classes and to seek positive distinctiveness in relation to a similarly deprived group.

Another strategy is to side-step those dimensions of comparison on which the subordinate group is regarded as inferior and to find new dimensions, or new values of the old dimensions, so that the group can achieve some prestige. Lemaine (1966), in a study conducted – like Sherif's – in a children's camp, found that the potential losers in a hut-building contest discovered additional attributes to emphasize (for example, the hut's surrounding garden). I observed something rather similar in the aircraft factory study I briefly described earlier (Brown, 1978). One member of the lower-status Production group, conceding that the Development workers might have a higher level of skill, introduced a new argument in Production's favour: the extra responsibility of producing airworthy engines:

because it was Development, you could leave several bolts out here and there, you know, it was a gash set up. That is why *we* claim as Production workers that *we* build an engine that goes upstairs in the plane. When *they* build one it goes over the test bed, and all that can do is ruin the test bed. If it goes up there – well that's the end of it if it falls out of the sky. Concorde? You can forget it if *it* falls out the sky; that's the end of it. The Yanks would love that! . . . That adds strength to the fact that the Production side are as good as Development. (Brown, 1978, p. 416)

The lifestyles of subcultural groups like the 'punks' of the 1980s or the 'hippies' of the 1970s, which were characterized by a complete negation of the dominant society's values in fashion, music and morality, may be other examples of the same phenomenon. Experimental evidence supports this creative search for alternative modes of intergroup comparisons by low-status groups. Jackson et al. (1996) led members of artificial (over/underestimators) and real (smokers) groups to believe that not only was their group socially devalued but that it would be very unlikely (*or* distinctly possible) that they could leave it if they wished. The participants then evaluated the ingroup on various dimensions, some directly relevant to the defining criteria for their group and some unrelated to it. Jackson et al. (1996) observed a more positive evaluation of the ingroup on some of the unrelated dimensions, especially when exit from the group was seen as improbable (see also Ellemers et al., 1997; Mummendey and Schreiber, 1984).

None of these responses, with the possible exception of this latter one, is completely satisfactory for members of a lower-status group because they leave the unequal relationship between themselves and the dominant group essentially unchanged. Hence, the possibility of unfavourable comparisons with that group remains, with all the likely consequences for social identity that they entail. Why, then, do they not confront directly the dominant group's superiority by agitating for social and economic change and by refusing to accede to the consensually accepted definitions of their respective groups' worth? Such a competitive intergroup orientation would be the most obviously predictable reaction from the premise of social identity theory that people generally strive for a positive identity and avoid a negative one. It turns out that subordinate groups *do* sometimes opt for this strategy – for instance, the various movements for civil rights in the 1960s instigated by black people in the USA, followed by Maoris in New Zealand and aboriginal people in Australia and Canada, and, most dramatically of all, the abolition of apartheid in South Africa brought about by the African National Congress in the 1990s. However, for this to happen it may be necessary that members of those lower-status groups can conceive of some alternatives to the current state of affairs (Tajfel and Turner, 1986). Until they can imagine that the old order is neither fair nor inevitable, they may be unlikely to engage in psychologically risky comparisons with the 'superior' group. What are the circumstances that encourage the generation of these 'cognitive alternatives'? There are probably several but, to date, the three most powerful factors have been found to be, first, that the boundaries between the groups be relatively impermeable; second, that the status differences between them be somewhat unstable; and, third, that those differences be perceived as illegitimate, founded on unfair and arbitrary principles (Tajfel and Turner, 1986).

An experiment by Ellemers et al. (1993) provides a nice demonstration of the importance of all three variables. The experiment used a management–worker simulation. After being divided into two groups and taking a test of organizational problem solving, the participants were led to believe that one group had been allocated the higher-status management role, the other the worker role. (In fact, by some experimenter sleight of hand, everyone was assigned to the latter lower-status group.) However, the basis for this allocation varied. Some groups were told that the assignment had been done fairly on the basis of their test performance, and were also led to believe that their fellow group members accepted this as reasonable. Other groups were told that the allocation had been made solely on the basis of the *number* of test items completed rather than their correctness and, moreover, it was indicated that their fellow group members thought this was a pretty unfair way to do things. In this way a legitimate or illegitimate status relationship between the groups was created.[2] Further information was then forthcoming. Half the groups were told that the status positions of the two groups could change later in the experiment ('unstable' condition); the remainder were told that they would not ('stable' condition). Finally, some believed that if they performed exceptionally well individually they would have the opportunity to join the management group ('permeable' group boundaries); others believed that the group compositions would not alter ('impermeable' condition).

The effects of these different manipulations were remarkably consistent. Not surprisingly, those in the illegitimate conditions felt angrier than those in the legitimate conditions. Moreover, it was the latter participants who showed the most interest in finding some alternative criteria than the one used for evaluating the groups. This corresponds to the second of the identity-maintaining strategies that I noted earlier: the seeking out of new comparative dimensions when the current one is unfavourable to the ingroup. The group members' identification with their ingroup was affected by all three variables (see figure 8.3). Those in groups with impermeable boundaries showed higher identification than those who thought they could change groups. Those in

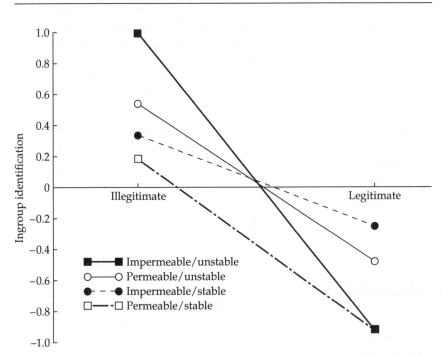

Figure 8.3 A subordinate group's reaction to status illegitimacy, instability and permeability of group boundaries (from Ellemers et al., 1993, adapted from figure 1, illegitimate and legitimate conditions only. Copyright © 1993 by the American Psychological Association)[3]

'illegitimately' inferior groups showed higher identification than those whose position was 'legitimate'. And stability, too, had an effect, albeit in conjunction with the other two variables. Highest identification was shown by those in the illegitimate, impermeable and unstable condition, lowest by those in the legitimate, permeable and stable condition. Faced with the identity-threatening prospect of having been assigned, apparently justifiably, to a subordinate group with little prospect of changing its position, group members who see the possibility of leaving it for another seem psychologically disposed to do so. At the other extreme, where the basis for their inferiority is obviously unfair, there is a real chance of the groups' positions reversing in the near future but no chance of escaping from their group (even if they wanted to), their identity needs are best met by sticking with their group and taking on the outgroup on its own terms.

Ellemers et al. (1993) were concerned mainly with the *intra*group reactions of subordinate group members to different socio-structural conditions. Their *inter*group measures showed generally rather weaker effects. However, other experiments, also concerned with the effects of illegitimate and unstable status relations, have consistently found that such changes elicit strong intergroup responses too, mainly in the form of greatly increased levels of ingroup favouritism but sometimes by engaging in collective protest against their treatment (Brown and Ross, 1982; Ng and Cram, 1988; Turner and Brown 1978; Wright et al., 1990). One other noteworthy feature of several of these studies is that these effects are often observed as strongly in the 'superior' group as in the 'inferior' group, suggesting that destabilizing and delegitimating status relations present a threat to the higher-status group's identity and they react with enhanced attempts to defend their now fragile superiority. These findings from the laboratory have been largely confirmed in field studies. Simon et al. (1998) were interested in people's readiness to participate in social protest aimed at redressing current discrimination and grievance. The particular social movements they studied were the Grey Panthers – an organization campaigning for elderly people – and the Gay Rights movement. Having first established that participants perceived their current intergroup standing as unjust and potentially open to change – two of social identity theory's preconditions for motivating people toward social change – they examined various likely correlates of their willingness to get involved in collective action for their group (e.g. campaigning for better facilities for elderly people, taking part in gay rights civil disobedience activities). In both studies a reliable predictor of collective action was people's level of identification with the organization in question, and this was true even after other relevant variables, like endorsement of the political goals of the movement (also a strong predictor) and personal rewards and costs, had been controlled for. Kelly and Breinlinger (1996) found similar effects of group identification on participation in trade union activity or the women's movement.

The reunification of East and West Germany in 1989 has also provided a fascinating context for studying the consequences of membership in a low-status group. Although formally the two regions belong to the same nation state, socio-economically East Germans are still second-class citizens. Their social psychological response to this

332

situation has been studied by Mummendey and her colleagues (Blanz et al., 1998; Mummendey et al., 1999). Blanz et al. (1998) surveyed East Germans as to their attitudes towards current developments in Germany and their endorsement of different social and psychological strategies. Consistent with social identity theory, these attitude responses fell into distinct and recognizable clusters. For example, individual mobility was one (e.g. 'in future I would like to regard myself as a West German'); preference for alternative comparison dimensions (e.g. 'social relationships') or different comparison groups (e.g. 'a country belonging to the former Eastern community') was another; direct competition with West Germany was also an option (e.g. 'we will make it clear to the West Germans that we are the more efficient Germans'). In addition, other tactics could be seen, including making comparisons with the past or evaluating one's group with reference to absolute standards (see also Brown and Haeger, 1999). Mummendey et al. (1999) then tried to predict which of these strategies would be endorsed most from measuring participants' levels of identification (with East Germany), their perceptions of legitimacy, stability and permeability of the East–West relationship, and various measures of relative deprivation. Several of the associations they observed were consistent with social identity theory. For instance, permeability of the East–West boundary was negatively correlated with identification (Ellemers et al., 1988); perceived illegitimacy was negatively associated with attempts at individual mobility (Ellemers et al., 1993); and relative deprivation was directly linked with a competitive orientation towards the 'superior' outgroup (Grant and Brown, 1995). However, other correlations were more surprising, either in their direction or by their absence. For example, perceived stability and permeability were both *negatively* correlated with individual mobility, when one might have expected the reverse, and creative strategies like changing the nature of the group comparisons were not related systematically to any identity or deprivation variable.

The nature and consequences of social identification: some further issues

Earlier in this chapter I noted that Tajfel and Turner (1986) defined social identity as deriving from people's group memberships, and

333

proposed that a central motive underlying intergroup discrimination and ingroup bias was presumed to be a need for a positive social identity. From these simple ideas it proved possible to make sense of a wide variety of intergroup phenomena, as we have just seen. Nevertheless, despite social identity theory's undoubted success as an explanatory and generative model, the research it has inspired has thrown up some additional complexities (Brown and Capozza, 1999). Three issues, in particular, are worth discussing here: the relationship between self-esteem and intergroup discrimination; the hypothesized link between strength of group identification and ingroup bias; and the homogenous concept of the 'group' employed by social identity theory.

Self-esteem and intergroup discrimination

A key idea of social identity theory is that biased intergroup comparisons or allocations are motivated by a desire to be able to view one's ingroup, and hence oneself, positively. In other words, there is presumed to be a causal connection between intergroup discrimination and self-esteem. As Abrams and Hogg (1988) have pointed out, this link could take two forms. It could be that people show discrimination in order to raise their self-esteem because a positive self concept is generally preferred to a neutral or negative one. Alternatively, it could be that prior low self-esteem, perhaps stemming from belonging to a low-status or stigmatized group, causes intergroup discrimination in order to raise it to 'normal' levels. The evidence for both of these processes is equivocal, although, on balance, the first hypothesis has received rather more support than the second (Rubin and Hewstone, 1998). Thus, as discussed in a previous section, in minimal group settings participants who discriminated showed higher self-esteem than those who were denied the opportunity to do so (Lemyre and Smith, 1985; Oakes and Turner, 1980). In fact, of 12 attempts to test the first hypothesis, 9 yielded supportive evidence (Rubin and Hewstone, 1998). On the other hand, studies investigating the opposite direction of causality have generally produced a less positive outcome, with most (16/19) failing to support the supposed link (Rubin and Hewstone, 1998). For example, it is usually groups with *enhanced* social status – and hence presumably higher self-esteem – who show greater ingroup favouritism (Mullen et al., 1992; Sachdev and Bourhis, 1985). Moreover, and contrary to both possible causal links, correlations between the amount of ingroup bias and levels of self-esteem are sometimes close to zero (Hogg and Sunderland, 1991; Hogg and Turner, 1987).

What are we to make of this confusing picture? At least some of the difficulty can be attributed to the plethora of instruments that have been used to measure self-esteem in these experiments (Rubin and Hewstone, 1998). Sometimes people use scales that tap *personal* feelings of self-worth which may not relate simply to positive feelings based on one's *group* membership; the scales may assess generic feelings of positivity instead of situational specific self-evaluations, or, even if they are addressing collective sources of self-esteem, the measures may refer to all groups and not some particular group. As Long et al. (1994) found, these different kinds of self-esteem have quite different correlations with ingroup bias and may interact with each other in quite complex ways.

A second reason for the mixed pattern of findings could be that the measures of self-esteem and ingroup bias may be strongly influenced by social desirability factors (Farnham et al., 1999). After all, it is hardly the done thing to say one is feeling too negative (or too positive) about oneself, nor, in the polite society of the laboratory, should one brag too much about one's own group at the expense of another. Such constraints are likely to depress any real correlation that might exist between self-esteem and ingroup favouritism. In an attempt to circumvent these self-presentational concerns, Farnham et al. (1999) advocate the use of more subtle measures where it is not obvious what is being investigated. One such technique is the Implicit Attitudes Test (Greenwald et al., 1998). In this test participants are asked simply to categorize as quickly as possible a word that appears in the centre of a computer screen. In the first set of trials the stimulus words are all obviously positive or negative (e.g. 'joy', 'vomit') and the task is simply to assign them to an 'unpleasant' or 'pleasant' category. In the next set of trials the words are all pronouns (e.g. 'me', 'they') and participants have to classify them as self-relevant ('me') or irrelevant ('not me'). Then, in the next two steps, these classifications are combined so that stimulus words must be categorized as 'unpleasant *or* not me' versus 'pleasant *or* me' (phase 3), and 'unpleasant

335

or me' versus 'pleasant *or* not me' (phase 4). The average response time per word is computed for each step and a typical finding is that, where the two dimensions of classification are psychologically consistent (phase 3), the reaction times are typically a few hundred milliseconds quicker than when they are *in*consistent (phase 4).[4] Greenwald et al. (1998) argue that this bias results from automatic mental association between certain stimuli (e.g. 'myself', 'ingroup') and positive attributes. Such cognitive links mean that we find it much easier to make a conjunctive classification when the two coincide than when they do not. Farnham et al. (1999) found that such implicit measures of self-esteem, ingroup bias and group identification were correlated with each other.

Aside from these methodological concerns, a more fundamental reason for the absence of a consistent self-esteem–bias relationship could be that other motives, apart from a positive self-evaluation, come into play when people identify with a group. Hogg and Abrams (1990) suggest that being categorized as a member of a group in a minimal group experiment invokes a 'search for meaning' as the participants attempt to reduce the uncertainty created by the rather unusual experimental procedures. The discrimination that the participants typically manifest can then be viewed as their attempt to clarify what is otherwise an ambiguous situation rather than, necessarily, an attempt to feel good about themselves. The fact that self-esteem may sometimes increase following such discrimination (Lemyre and Smith, 1985) may thus be attributable to this greater self-certainty rather than to a more positive ingroup evaluation. In support of this idea, Hogg and Mullin (1999) found that giving participants some prior exposure to the minimal group procedures consistently reduced the levels of intergroup discrimination they showed. However, the corresponding changes in self-esteem were somewhat less reliable.

Group identification and ingroup bias

A second issue is related. If biased intergroup evaluations and decisions are motivated by social identity concerns, then presumably one should expect to find a positive correlation between the strength of people's group identification and their levels of ingroup bias. However, this correlation has proved to be rather unstable (Hinkle and

Brown, 1990). In fact, of the 14 separate studies which we were then able to locate, only 9 revealed a positive median correlation between identification and bias, and many of these were quite weak (typically less than 0.3). Furthermore, some of these medians disguised a considerable variation in the direction and magnitude of the consistent correlations. What might account for this variability? Two possibilities have been mooted. The first is methodological, and concerns the ways in which group identification has typically been measured. The second explanation is more radical and suggests that the psychological processes proposed by social identity theory may not be equally operative in all groups. Let me consider each in turn.

Recall, first of all, Tajfel's (1978) definition of social identity with which I began this chapter. It has three components: a *cognitive* aspect (awareness of group membership or self-categorization), an *evaluative* aspect (how good or bad the group is considered to be), and an *emotional* aspect (feelings of attachment to the group). Most measures of group identification combine two or more of these separate components into a single score measuring overall strength of identification (e.g. Brown et al., 1986). Now, according to Ellemers et al. (1999), such a conflation may be a mistake because the three aspects of identity may function relatively independently of one another and hence have different consequences for the amount of ingroup favouritism displayed. For example, a person might be highly aware of belonging to a group and yet not be very committed to it. In such a case, one would not expect much of a relationship between overall identification and any bias towards an outgroup. In fact, Ellemers et al. (1999) speculate that it is especially the more affectively toned group commitment component that is most likely to be correlated with positive intergroup differentiation. In an experiment involving artificial groups of supposedly different problem solving styles they found that, indeed, the group commitment measure correlated significantly with ingroup favouritism while the cognitive and evaluative measures of identity did not.

An alternative explanation for the inconsistent relationship between identification and bias is that the proposed link between identity maintenance and intergroup comparisons may not hold equally well in all group contexts or apply as strongly to all group members (Hinkle and Brown, 1990). We have suggested that the prevailing levels of

337

individualism or collectivism in a group (or its members) and their inclination (or not) to engage in intergroup comparisons will be important factors in determining whether group identification will be associated with ingroup bias. Our hypothesis is that one would only expect a strong link between identification and bias in groups that can be simultaneously characterized as 'collectivist' – that is, where there is an emphasis on intragroup cooperation and group achievements – and 'relational' – that is, where there is a concern for one's group's standing or performance relative to other groups. On the other hand, for more individualistically orientated groups (or people) in contexts which favour an asocial method of evaluation – for example, in comparison to some abstract standard or to a level in the group's past – the correlation between identification and bias is likely to be much lower, if it exists at all. In such groups, we speculate, identity is sustained in ways *other than* making intergroup comparisons. In three studies we classified group members as individualists or collectivists and as preferring a relational method of group evaluation or an autonomous one. We then correlated the levels of group identification and bias in each of these four categories and found strong support for our hypothesis (Brown et al., 1992; see figure 8.4). Notice that the correlation is highest in the upper right cell of the diagram, lowest in the bottom left, and intermediate in the remaining two. Although subsequent studies have not always found this same pattern (e.g. Brown et al., 1996), there is now accumulating evidence that the hypothesized link between social identity and biased intergroup comparisons proposed by Tajfel and Turner (1986), while undoubtedly a potent motivator of intergroup behaviour in some contexts, may not be quite as generic as they had originally assumed.

Recognizing group diversity

The finding that group identification is not always strongly related to ingroup favouritism raises a third interesting issue for social identity theory, which is whether all groups are equivalent, psychologically speaking, in the manner in which they provide their members with a social identity. In other words, when I identify with my family, my profession or my football team, are the processes by which I sustain that identity the same? In social identity theory no differentiation is

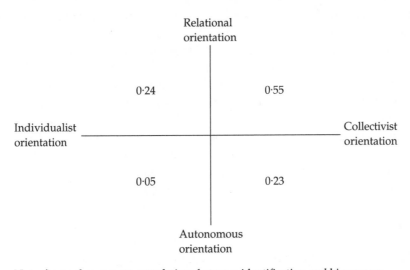

Note: figure shows mean correlations between identification and bias across three independent studies.

Figure 8.4 The association between group identification and ingroup bias, as moderated by different social orientations (from Brown et al., 1992, tables 2, 3 and 5)

made between different kinds of group. To be sure, it is recognized that each group has its own prototypical attributes and that its status position in society has repercussions for the identity strategies likely to be adopted by its members, but ultimately it is assumed that 'a group is a group is a group' as far as the basic social psychological mechanisms are concerned.

There are grounds for doubting this assumption, however. In the study by Brown et al. (1992) I have just described, we allocated individuals to different categories based on their scores on particular measuring instruments. However, it is also possible to locate discrete groups that differ markedly in their levels of collectivism, as we showed in a subsequent study (Brown and Torres, 1996). For example, when people identify with a religious group they regard it in a more collectivist manner than when they identify with their subject of study. As expected, the correlation between religious identification and bias against other sects was reasonably strong and significant, while the same association for the academic group tended to be weaker. Importantly, though, people's strength of identification with these different groups was equally strong; it was the manner in which the identity was expressed which differed.

This idea that identity processes may vary across types of group is supported by some research by Deaux and her colleagues (Deaux et al., 1995, in press). In one study (Deaux et al., 1995), they asked participants to sort a large number of different social categories into clusters on the basis of perceived similarity. These categories ranged from personal or family relationships (e.g. brother, friend, lover) through various occupations (e.g. secretary, teacher, gardener) and religious or ethnic groups (e.g. unemployed, person with AIDS). These same categories were rated by a second group of judges for the extent to which they could be described by various social and psychological characteristics (e.g. desirable–undesirable, achieved–ascribed, individualist–collectivist). Deaux et al. (1995) found that their motley collection of categories could be reduced to five basic types of groups: relationships, occupations, political organizations, stigmatized groups and religion/ethnicity. Moreover, these different kinds of groups were clearly perceived differently by the second set of judges, with each cluster receiving rather disparate ratings on various dimensions. For example, some were perceived to be more concerned with socio-emotional processes, others to be more task-orientated; some more collectivist, others more individualist. In a subsequent study, Deaux et al. (in press) asked members of some of these types of groups to report on the important aspects of that group membership using a standardized questionnaire. They found these different aspects – or identity functions, as Deaux et al. (in press) call them – could be grouped into seven broad factors: providing self-insight, facilitating intergroup comparisons, ingroup cohesion, a source of collective self-esteem, permitting downward interpersonal comparisons, opportunities for social interaction, and for romantic involvement. Notice that some of these are completely consistent with social identity theory's conception of identity (e.g. the second and fourth), but others seem to be serving quite different psychological needs. Deaux et al. (in press) also observed that groups scored very differently on these seven identity functions. For example, members of a sports team tended, not surprisingly, to emphasize intergroup comparison, collective self-esteem and social interaction. On the other hand, a religious group placed more stress on self-insight, ingroup cohesion and collective self-esteem. Similar differences in

340

identity functions have also been found among trade unionists, foot-ball supporters and students (Aharpour and Brown, 1997).

It seems clear, then, that there is more to social identification than meets the eye. People identify with groups for a variety of reasons and, as a result, they maintain that identity in more ways than by making biased intergroup comparisons, common though these un-doubtedly are. What now needs to be done is to understand better how these different identity functions affect other forms of intergroup behaviour, including those less likely to lead to tension and conflict between groups. Although we are not yet in a position to provide that kind of fine-grained analysis, it is nonetheless true that consider-able attention has been paid in recent years to how social identity processes more generally are implicated in harmonious and cooperat-ive intergroup relationships. It is to that topic that we now turn.

Social Identity and Intergroup Harmony

From a casual reading of the last two and a half chapters, it would be easy to reach the conclusion that social psychologists have been pre-occupied with studying the darker side of intergroup relationships – conflict, prejudice and biases – to the exclusion of more positive aspects such as cooperation and mutual tolerance. I want now to redress that imbalance somewhat by considering in this, the final section of the book, some of the factors that are likely to promote intergroup harmony rather than conflict. I begin with a brief dis-cussion of the contact hypothesis, an idea that forms the basis for all serious attempts to improve fraught intergroup relations. I then dis-cuss several developments that grew out of that work, all of which involve the manipulation or reconfiguration of social identities. I con-clude with a consideration of some practical implications for today's multi-ethnic society.

Reducing prejudice through intergroup contact

In 1954, in the case of *Brown v. Board of Education, Topeka*, the United States Supreme Court ruled that school systems which segregated black and white students violated important articles of the American constitution. That decision proved to be a historic one since it paved the way for the comprehensive desegregation of the American education system over the next three decades. An important ingredient of that legal judgment was the belief that the continued separation of white children from black (or Hispanic or Chicano) children was detrimental to the life chances of those minority groups and instrumental in perpetuating ethnic prejudice and intolerance. The corollary of this belief was that the increased contact between such groups brought about by school desegregation would reverse these harmful effects (Cook, 1979).

In the same year, there was another significant landmark in American race relations. This was the publication of a book entitled *The Nature of Prejudice* by Gordon Allport (1954). In that book Allport provided not only a seminal analysis of the origins of intergroup prejudice but also a series of influential policy recommendations for its elimination. Taken together, these recommendations have come to be known as the contact hypothesis, since underlying all of them is the idea that bringing members of different groups into contact with one another in various ways is the best way of reducing any tension or hostility that might exist between them. In Allport's view, however, it was not enough just for groups to see more of each other; contact alone would not guarantee intergroup harmony. He provided a list of conditions that he believed needed to be satisfied before one could expect it to have its desired effects. Of these, the most important are as follows: first, the contact between the groups should be prolonged and involve some cooperative activity rather than be casual and accidental. Without the incentive provided by the presence of a common objective, the interaction is unlikely to generate very much change in attitude (see chapter 6; Cook, 1978). Second, there should be a framework of official and institutional support for the new policy of integration. The establishment of Equal Opportunities Commissions or Race Relations Tribunals may not in itself be effective in outlawing discrimination but such bodies do help to create the kind of social climate in which more tolerant norms can emerge. Thus, the significance of that *Brown v. Board of Education* decision may have derived less from its immediate effect on other state education systems (many of which resisted any change for several years) but more from the impact that it had on social attitudes, an effect which came to full fruition in the civil rights movement of the 1960s. Third, the contact should ideally involve people of equal social status. It is little good, Allport contended, having extensive contact between members of two groups if those groups are fundamentally unequal in status and power. Such encounters are only likely to reinforce prejudiced and derogatory attitudes in the dominant group. The relationship between slaves and their owners, often one involving a high degree of contact, is the obvious example here. On the other hand, if contact takes place between equal-status groups, then improved intergroup attitudes can result (Clore et al., 1978; Blanchard et al., 1975). With these (and some other) qualifications, Allport argued that such policy interventions as the establishment of integrated housing schemes, the abolition of discriminatory and separatist employment practices, and the introduction of properly desegregated education and leisure facilities could all contribute effectively to the reduction of prejudice and the improvement of intergroup relations.

The forty years since the publication of Allport's theory have seen much research aimed at testing and verifying its main tenets, most of which has had at least some measure of success. Provided that the contact takes place under the favourable circumstances he specified, hostile intergroup attitudes and behaviour do seem to diminish (Amir, 1976; Hewstone and Brown, 1986; Pettigrew, 1998). Nevertheless, despite its empirical support, the theory still continues to attract interest as attempts are made to understand the processes by which contact has its positive effects, and the scope and limits of these effects (see, for example, Miller and Brewer, 1984; Gaertner et al., 1993; Hewstone and Brown, 1986). In a moment I shall be examining the key issues that are currently under debate but, before doing so, I want to reconsider an old question: the role of intergroup contact in dispelling ignorance about the outgroup. Stephan and Stephan (1984), for instance, argue that ignorance is an important element in prejudice and that programmes for improving intergroup relations should focus on providing information about the outgroup that highlights similarities between ingroup and outgroup. The rationale behind this is the belief that the discovery of such group similarities will lead to attraction between the respective group members, much as attitudinal agreement between individuals leads to interpersonal liking (Byrne, 1971).

This idea has long formed part of the contact theory (Pettigrew, 1971). Now, although Stephan and Stephan (1984) present some evidence supportive of a relationship – albeit a weak one – between knowledge of an outgroup and positive attitudes towards that group, there are grounds for doubting whether that relationship is central to the successful implementation of contact policies. To begin with, it is surely misguided to teach people that others are similar in all respects and to ignore obvious differences. This will only create more difficulties when these differences become apparent as, for example, when Muslim schoolgirls in Britain appear for physical education lessons wearing long trousers, while others are wearing shorts.

Furthermore, one of the presumed consequences of contact – i.e. the discovery of similarities between groups – may sometimes be rather unlikely to occur, for the groups concerned may often, in reality, turn out to have rather *dissimilar* values and attitudes. For instance, many ethnic groups differ fairly fundamentally in their cultural beliefs and practices. Contact in cases such as these is likely to reveal these differences and hence, according to the causal process alleged to underlie the contact hypothesis (i.e. similarity-attraction), should result in *less* intergroup liking, not more.

Finally, there is now ample evidence to show that intergroup discrimination and hostility are caused by factors *other* than a mere lack of knowledge or inaccurate perceptions. Thus, as we saw in chapter 6, objective conflicts of interests are a potent source of mutual derogation. Alternatively, the mere fact of categorization or factors that affect the identity of group members can be sufficient to trigger discrimination (chapter 7). All of these factors, rooted as several of them are in objective features of the environment, are unlikely to be affected by any new knowledge resulting from contact between groups, even under the ideal conditions specified by Allport (1954).

Cross-cutting group memberships

When groups come into contact with one another – for example, in a desegregated school or in a multi-national company following the merger of two or more smaller organizations – one thing is very likely to happen: the pre-existing groups of, say, ethnicity or nationality are likely to be overlaid by other dimensions of categorization

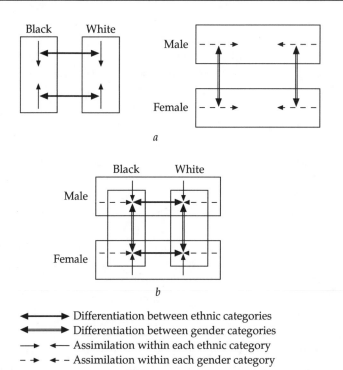

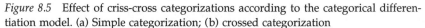

Figure 8.5 Effect of criss-cross categorizations according to the categorical differentiation model. (a) Simple categorization; (b) crossed categorization

– for example, gender or workgroup. That is, two people who are in different groups in one respect (e.g. black and white) may be in the same group from another perspective (e.g. both women). Doise (1976) has argued that in cases like this where two categories cut across each other, any discrimination in terms of the original categories will be reduced because of the simultaneous operation of between- and within-category effects on both dimensions. As figure 8.5 illustrates, the differentiation and assimilation processes involved in categorization (see chapter 7) should cancel each other out and the end result should be lessened bias in terms of gender or race.

There is a good deal of evidence supporting this hypothesis. Social anthropologists, for example, have often noted how societies that have cross-cutting kinship and tribal systems seem to be less prone to internal feuding than those with a more pyramidal structure (Gluckman,

1956). In experimental settings, when people are classified on more than one dimension one typically observes less bias against those with whom at least one identity is shared (Deschamps and Doise, 1978; Vanbeselaere, 1991). Note, however, that if the two crossing categories result in a double ingroup identity being opposed to a double outgroup, then the outcome will be *enhanced* rather than reduced differentiation (Brown and Turner, 1979; Urban and Miller, 1998). These findings are interesting because of their potential significance for policies aimed at reducing prejudice. They suggest that if we can arrange social situations so that at least two (and perhaps even more) categorical dimensions cut across one another then, in principle, the likelihood of persistent prejudice between groups along any one of those dimensions should be reduced. Unfortunately, in the world outside the laboratory, where group memberships are likely to be much more meaningful and where they may differ in status and size, such superimposition of categories can have more complex effects. For instance, because of contextual factors one category dimension will often dominate over others, thus weakening any effects associated with their criss-crossing. This was shown clearly in a study conducted in Bangladesh where the relevant dimensions were religion (Muslim and Hindu), nationality (Bangladesh and Indian) and language (Bengali and Hindi) (Hewstone et al., 1993). Consistent with an earlier study conducted in India (Hagendoorn and Henke, 1991), Hewstone et al. (1993) found that respondents' intergroup evaluations were strongly determined by religion, rather less so by nationality and almost not at all by whether a group spoke the same language or not. The net result of this was that people of a different religion *and* nationality were strongly derogated by respondents, especially in comparison to compatriots of the same religion. Thus, while the crossed categorization strategy clearly has some possibilities for conflict reduction, it cannot be relied on to eliminate all manifestations of ingroup favouritism.

Changing the salience of group identities

Earlier, I noted how promoting intergroup contact under the right conditions can be a powerful weapon in the fight against bigotry and intolerance. There is no doubt that most effective policies for desegregating schools and integrating housing and employment owed their success to the implementation of some or all of Allport's (1954) contact criteria (Pettigrew, 1998). Nevertheless, one problem has recurred time and again in research on and application of the contact hypothesis, and that is the problem of generalization. Many studies reported that it was not too difficult to change people's attitudes towards the particular outgroup members that they had actually encountered; much harder was to effect a shift in their attitudes and stereotypes towards the outgroup as a whole, especially those many hundreds (thousands?) of outgroup strangers that they run across in their daily lives or hear about on their televisions or in their newspapers (Cook, 1978).

In the past twenty years there have been three new developments of the contact hypothesis, all of which attempt to tackle this issue of generalization (Brewer and Miller, 1984; Gaertner et al., 1993; Hewstone and Brown, 1986). Each of these three approaches has its origins in social identity theory since they all recognize that group memberships get incorporated into people's self-concepts and that these social identifications have important consequences for behaviour. Moreover, they all propose that to optimize the effects of contact and to promote generalization one must try to change the salience of existing group identities. However, despite this common theoretical base, the three models offer rather contrasting prescriptions for arranging intergroup contact.

Brewer and Miller (1984) take as their starting point the phenomena of enhanced intergroup discrimination and stereotyping that are frequently attendant on social categories becoming psychologically salient (see chapter 7). It follows from this, they argue, that during the contact the boundaries between the groups should be made less rigid, ultimately to be dissolved altogether. In this way the situation should become 'decategorized' and all interactions should take place on an interpersonal level. In this 'personalized' form of contact the participants should be more likely to attend to idiosyncratic information about each individual and be correspondingly less attentive to group-based – that is, stereotypical – information. Repeated interpersonal contact of this kind is thought to result in the disconfirmation of pre-existing (negative) stereotypes of the outgroup, which ultimately is:

more likely to generalize to new situations because extended and frequent utilization of alternative informational features in interactions undermines the availability and usefulness of category identity as a basis for future interactions with the same or different individuals. (Brewer and Miller, 1984, pp. 288–9)

Perhaps President Clinton had this idea in mind when he developed his 'Coming Together Fellowship' scheme for improving American race relations. In this policy black and white individuals who belong to existing clubs and groups are set the challenge of getting to know each other better, 'the principle being that relations will improve only when contacts are people to people, not "race to race"' (the *Independent*, 3 December 1997). In support of this model, Brewer and Miller have carried out a number of studies using a similar paradigm (Bettencourt et al., 1992; Miller et al., 1985). Typically, two artificial categories are created (for example, 'overestimators' and 'underestimators'). Then members of these two categories are brought together into cooperative work groups so that both overestimators and underestimators are represented in each group. The subjects are given different instructional sets for the group tasks: some are encouraged to focus on each other to find out what the 'fellow team members must really be like' (Bettencourt et al., 1992, pp. 305–6); others are told to concentrate particularly on the task at hand. In this way it is hoped to 'personalize' or 'depersonalize' the contact situation, respectively. After the task the subjects allocate rewards to the members of their team and also to members of another team unknown to them, portrayed on a short video clip. The key dependent measure in these experiments is the degree of bias in these allocations between over- and underestimators, both for the known team members and the 'strangers' shown on video. A consistent finding has been that those undertaking the task with the 'personalization' instructions show less bias than those who are concentrating much more on the task, although a recent study suggests that the beneficial effects of 'personalized' contact may be restricted to majority groups; minorities in this experiment showed more bias under 'personalized' conditions than with those receiving the 'task' focus instructions (Bettencourt et al., 1997).

An interesting variant on the 'personalized' contact idea has been proposed by Wright et al. (1997). Noting that trying to stimulate cross-group friendships on a large scale may not be very practicable, Wright et al. (1997) suggest that an alternative may be to try to provide publicly visible ingroup role models who have a close relationship with a member of the outgroup. The knowledge that ingroup members can apparently be friends with an outgroup member is thought to provide important new information about the nature of the intergroup relationship and it may stimulate the generation of a more tolerant normative climate, particularly if the role models concerned are perceived as reasonably typical of their groups (a point I will return to shortly). Wright et al. (1997) offered both laboratory and field evidence in support of this process, what they call the 'extended contact effect': those knowing of or observing ingroup–outgroup friendships showed less prejudice or ingroup bias than those who did not. That this idea might have some practical application is indicated by Liebkind and McAlister's (1999) evaluation of an educational intervention in Finland. Several schools participated in a programme in which student role models led class discussions based on 'real-life' stories of friendships between young Finnish people and foreigners. The school students exposed to this programme showed significantly less xenophobia than those in 'control' schools who had not.

Starting from the same premises as Brewer and Miller (1984), Gaertner et al. (1993) reach a different conclusion. They too are mindful of the biases that seem to be so readily generated by the presence of category divisions. But their solution to this problem is not to try to eliminate the categories; instead, they suggest that cognitively or physically redrawing the category boundaries will be a more productive strategy. The aim of this is to subsume the previous ingroup and outgroup into a new superordinate category so that the former outgroupers can be perceived as fellow ingroupers. Thus, rather than attempting to eschew group references altogether, Gaertner et al. hope to harness the power of a common ingroup identity to reduce pre-existing intergroup differentiation. Where Brewer and Miller propose *decategorization*, they advocate *recategorization*. I found a telling example of this recategorization idea in the press coverage following the referendum in Northern Ireland, which endorsed the Good Friday agreement of 1998. A primary school headteacher commented on the result:

The referendum will not change anything overnight. A lot of people say peace will never come to the North. We hope for a united Ireland, *but we are all Europeans now*, as well as Irish. (The *Observer*, 24 May 1998, my emphasis)

Notice how he invokes a politically less emotive superordinate category (Europe) to include both Ireland and, by implication, the troublesome division of Catholic and Protestant.

To test this model, Gaertner and his colleagues conducted several experiments in which they first created two artificial groups and then, by varying the seating arrangements in a subsequent intergroup encounter and by providing different interdependencies between the groups, manipulated the extent to which the subjects perceived the situation as one in which there were present one single group, two groups or just separate individuals (Gaertner et al., 1989, 1990). Typically, they found least ingroup bias in the first of these three arrangements and most in the second. Nor are their findings confined to the laboratory. In a survey of a multi-ethnic high school in America, they found that students' positive attitudes towards other groups were positively correlated with responses to items stressing a superordinate identity (for example, 'Despite the different groups at school, there is frequently the sense that we are all just one group'), but negatively related to items emphasizing the existence of different groups (Gaertner et al., 1994).

One way or another, the two models I have considered so far propose a reduction in the salience of the existing group identities. Although each has a sound rationale for this, one problem that it creates for both of them is that generalization is thereby made more difficult. Suppose I interact with an outgroup person under either decategorized or recategorized conditions. To the extent that these conditions have been successful in preventing me from perceiving that person as a member of an outgroup (or, indeed, any group at all), then any change in attitudes I experience towards that person cannot easily be extrapolated to other members of his or her group whom I have not yet met. Thus, my more general intergroup attitudes may remain intact, unaffected by the contact situation. It was this consideration that led us to propose a rather different model of intergroup contact (Hewstone and Brown, 1986; Vivian et al., 1997). We suggest that rather than attempting to eliminate the existing

350

ingroup–outgroup division, there may be some virtue in keeping it at least minimally salient while simultaneously optimizing the various Allport (1954) conditions for successful contact. In this way the contact will take place at an intergroup rather than an interpersonal level, between people acting as group representatives rather than as unaffiliated individuals (see chapter 1). If this can be successfully arranged, then any positive change engendered during contact is likely to transfer readily to other members of the outgroup because one's contact partners are seen as somehow typical of that group (Rothbart and John, 1985).

In some ways this seems a somewhat paradoxical strategy. In order to reduce prejudice towards an outgroup we are suggesting that maintaining the psychological salience of the intergroup distinction can be advantageous. Nevertheless, various lines of evidence are beginning to converge to this conclusion. Wilder (1984b) varied how typical a member of a rival college was seen to be during a cooperative encounter. In addition, this outgroup member behaved pleasantly or unpleasantly. Only the pleasant encounter with a 'typical' outgrouper produced significant improvements in the evaluation of the outgroup as a whole. Unpleasant encounters or encounters with an atypical person produced little change in attitude. Using the outgroup category 'homosexual', Scarberry et al. (1997) arranged for a confederate outgroup person (allegedly a homosexual) to adopt either a personal or an impersonal linguistic style during a cooperative interaction. There was only a significant positive shift in attitudes towards homosexuals in general in the impersonal condition. Apparently the more individuated (i.e. less identity salient) condition inhibited the possibility of generalization (see also Desforges et al., 1991).

In an attempt to test our model directly we have carried out studies in which we could examine the effects of making group membership more or less salient (Brown et al., 1999). One was an experiment involving a cooperative encounter with someone of a different nationality. Our British participants arrived in the laboratory and were required to work with a German confederate for a substantial joint reward (if successful). This confederate was depicted as someone who possessed some characteristics that were either stereotypical for how British people viewed Germans or rather atypical. In addition, we provided some bogus information about how homogeneous or heterogeneous

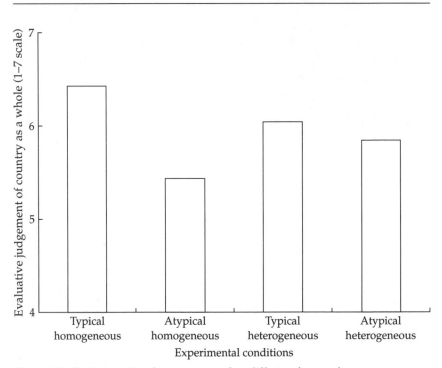

Figure 8.6 Positive national stereotypes after different forms of outgroup contact (from Brown et al., 1999, derived from table 1)

German people were on various attributes. Our reasoning was that the situation would be seen in the most 'intergroup' terms when typicality was combined with homogeneity, and that there the link between the target person and the group as a whole would be strongest. Conversely, if they met atypical members of the outgroup, the encounter would be more 'interpersonal' and the chances of generalization correspondingly lower. Our primary interest was in our participants' subsequent perceptions of German people as a whole. As expected, we observed more favourable perceptions after interaction with a 'typical' rather than an 'atypical' partner, and on one of the measures this was particularly pronounced in the 'homogeneous' conditions (see figure 8.6).

In the Netherlands, using a different method of invoking category salience, Van Oudenhouven et al. (1996) have obtained similar results. The ethnicity of a Turkish confederate was either kept quite implicit by the experimenter never making reference to it (low salience), or was drawn to people's attention only at the end of the interaction (moderate salience), or was emphasized throughout (high salience). After two hours of working cooperatively with this confederate, Dutch participants evaluated both him and Turks in general. The general attitudes towards Turks were reliably more favourable in the two conditions where his ethnicity had been made salient than in the low-salience condition.

We followed up these experiments with a survey conducted in six different European countries (Brown et al., 1999). One of the sections of the survey questionnaire asked respondents to think of someone from another country with whom they had had some contact. There then followed a series of questions exploring the nature of this contact – how frequent was it, was it competitive or cooperative, how typical of the country did they regard the person, and how salient was nationality in their conversations with this person? The final and crucial question asked how much they would like to live in the country concerned. This was our index of a favourable and generalized intergroup attitude. Consistent with the traditional contact hypothesis, more frequent contact of a cooperative nature was positively correlated with positive attitudes. However, this was especially true if the contact person was seen as typical of the country (again, we selected Germany so as to be consistent with the laboratory study) *and* if their respective nationalities featured regularly in their interactions (that is, were salient).

Although the Hewstone and Brown model seems to offer a promising way of tackling the generalization problem, it is an approach fraught with difficulties. One of these follows directly from the very same argument which provided the original rationale for the model. If identity-salient contact permits greater generalization of the attitudes promoted by the encounter then, in principle, both positive *and* negative attitudes can be generalized. Indeed, if the cooperative interaction goes wrong, perhaps in failing to achieve the common goal or because it turns competitive, then structuring the interaction at the intergroup level could well make matters worse. Not only might one's fellow interactant(s) be derogated but there is a risk of reinforcing negative stereotypes of the outgroup precisely because those people are seen as typical of it. This danger is heightened by a second problem.

This is that intergroup encounters may be more anxiety-provoking than interpersonal ones and anxiety is usually not conducive to harmonious social relations (Stephan and Stephan, 1985). Studying Muslim–Hindu contact in Bangladesh, Islam and Hewstone (1993) found that features indicative of intergroup relationships tended to be correlated with increased anxiety, which, in turn, was correlated with less favourable attitudes towards the outgroups. Greenland and Brown (1999) also observed an associated between intergroup anxiety and more salient group identities, this time in the context of contact between British and Japanese people.

Identity assimilation or pluralism

So, what should we conclude from the above analyses in thinking about interventions designed to alleviate intergroup tensions and to promote greater tolerance? Should those working in real-world multicultural settings adopt a 'colour-blind' policy, avoiding at all costs any reference to existing group divisions? Or should they, alternatively, seek to create new common group identities, redrawing the group boundaries to create more inclusive superordinate categories? Or should they accept the social reality of ethnic, religious and class distinctions and seek to capitalize on these in programmes that explicitly recognize group diversity? Or, as Pettigrew (1998) has advised, should all three approaches be adopted, but in a specific temporal order so as to exploit the benefits and minimize the risks with each taken separately?

At first sight, the decategorization approach seems the better bet. It fits well with the liberal ethos of many of those committed to integration in applied settings that one should treat each student (or worker or resident) as an individual without regard to their group affiliation. Moreover, it would seem to avoid some of the problems that seem to arise in more openly intergroup situations, namely the possibility of increased anxiety with its adverse consequences for acceptance and cooperation. There is also evidence, as we saw, that decategorization is compatible with a measure of attitude generalization.

However, despite all these advantages, I fear that this apparently progressive approach may run into difficulties. To begin with, we should note that the experiments that have supported the decategorization

model have mostly employed ad hoc laboratory groups, which typically have little significance for their members. This may have made it
easy for the participants to shed these identities when encouraged to
engage in 'personalized' interaction. In real intergroup contexts it
may not be so simple to distract people's attention from their group
memberships. A second problem is that to ignore group differences
can sometimes mean that existing intergroup inequalities persist by
default. Schofield (1986) has made this point in the context of desegregated schools in the USA. Given that many of these schools still
practise some form of ability streaming, a 'colour-blind' policy can
result in the re-establishment of ethnic desegregation as socially and
educationally deprived minority-group students end up in the lower
ability streams and the majority group dominates the academically
more prestigious streams. In occupational settings, too, 'colour-blind'
or 'gender-blind' or handicap-blind' approaches can easily mean the
continued exclusion of disadvantaged groups from the higher ech-
elons of organizations, or, indeed, from the world of work altogether
(Blanchard and Crosby, 1989; Glasser, 1988). In fact, there is evidence
that a denial of categorical information in connection with performance evaluations can actually result in less favourable judgements.
Ferdman (1989) presented a videotape of a Hispanic manager to some
white non-Hispanic managers. In some conditions they received only
individuating information about the target person (for example, his
hobbies), in others they learned also about how important his ethnicity was to him and about his involvement with Hispanic organizations,
and in others both individuating and categorical information was
presented. On a series of measures the latter condition elicited the most
favourable evaluations, especially when compared to the individuating
information-only conditions.

What of the second approach, the one which advocates the recategorization of the multi-ethnic school or workplace so that the school or
company as a whole becomes the main source of people's social identity rather than the subgroups within it? This strategy, too, has much
to recommend it. It seeks to harness the potential of social identity
processes for positive ends rather than to eschew them altogether.
Furthermore, it is based on some impressively consistent empirical
evidence, mostly, it is true, from laboratory experiments with artificial
groups, but not all (e.g. Gaertner et al., 1994). However, there may be

problems here too. It is not clear how the recategorization strategy, if implemented fully, will facilitate generalization. To the extent that one is successful in dissolving subgroups in favour of a superordinate category, then the social benefits may not transfer to other subgroup members outside the immediate setting. It is notable in this respect that one of the few experiments in the Gaertner group's programme of research to test generalization found relatively weak (nonsignificant) effects on a measure of helpfulness towards an unknown outgroup member (Dovidio et al., 1997). A second difficulty is that a recategorization approach runs the risk of being 'assimilationist', whereby members of minority groups are expected to conform to the norms and values of the dominant group (Berry, 1984). Such an outcome, which implies that minority-group members give up their distinctive social identities, can have deleterious consequences. On the one hand, it can be associated with a greater incidence of health problems in the minority groups (Berry et al., 1987). But, perhaps more seriously from the point of view of the goals of any intervention programme, such a surrendering of linguistic or cultural identity may be strenuously resisted by those minority groups, with corresponding negative implications for the final outcome of the programme itself. An important modification of the common ingroup identity model offers the prospect of avoiding these difficulties (Dovidio et al., 1998). In this development it is proposed that there can be advantages in maintaining some degree of subgroup distinctiveness *within a strong superordinate identity*. Here is Luigi di Palo, owner of a New York delicatessen, expressing exactly these sentiments:

I am proud to be an American, but I am proud of my Italian heritage also. (The *Independent*, 14 March 1999)

This dual identity approach exploits the possibilities of generalization offered by group salience, as noted by Hewstone and Brown (1986), and also permits the retention of what may be psychologically significant identities to the subgroups concerned. Dovidio et al. (1998) found that cooperating equal-status groups that had distinctive areas of expertise showed less ingroup bias than those which were very similar and hence had little opportunity to obtain recognition for their unique group input to the common product. This echoes the findings from some other research that I presented in an earlier chapter (Brown and Wade, 1987; Deschamps and Brown, 1983; see chapter 6).

Extending such an approach to a societal level is what Berry (1984) calls 'pluralism'. In a pluralist policy, cultural diversity is recognized and different value systems are acknowledged. The aim is to develop programmes – in schools, workplaces and community projects – which capitalize on group differences for the mutual benefit of both majority and minority group members. To give a concrete example, consider the cooperative learning groups that I discussed in chapter 2 and that are consistently found to facilitate educational achievement and to improve intergroup attitudes (Slavin, 1983, 1985). In multi-ethnic schools it should be possible to devise group projects in which students are assigned different subtasks, which would allow them to contribute something unique to the overall group goal *because of* the knowledge or experience that derives specifically from their religion or ethnicity (see Aronson et al., 1978). Of course, such a pluralist approach, based as it is on making some group distinctions more salient, must tread a very delicate path between fostering positive mutual differentiation between groups and avoiding the regression into familiar and destructive patterns of negative stereotyping which so often accompany salient category divisions. Nevertheless, as Tajfel (1981) concludes in his discussion of minority groups:

It may be useful to see in each intergroup situation whether and how it might be possible for each group to achieve, preserve, or defend its vital interests ... in such a way that the self respect of other groups is not adversely affected at the same time. (Tajfel, 1981, p. 343)

A Few Last Words

Before concluding this chapter – and this book – a few last comments are necessary. It will probably not have escaped your attention that I have liberally sprinkled this book with examples of group phenomena from the real world. Some of these, particularly in the last three chapters, have concerned quite large groups or wide-scale social change. I have done this in the belief that the processes I have been discussing are not mere theoretical abstractions but have real and very concrete social implications. However, in providing these illustrations, I do not want for one moment to imply that social psychology – even a thoroughgoing group psychology – can provide all, or even most, of the explanation for these phenomena. Such an explanation will never be complete without a proper understanding and analysis of the historical, political and economic factors at work in each context, and I believe that social psychologists would do well to be more modest about the extent and explanatory power of their theories.

Nevertheless, it must also be recognized that, in the last analysis, group behaviour does still involve the actions of individuals. It was individual citizens and policemen involved in that Bristol 'riot' which I described in chapter 1; it was individual shop stewards who talked of their concern over eroded differentials in the aircraft engine factory in this final chapter. Thus, however important socio-structural forces undoubtedly were in all the situations described in these pages, it is still important to know how these forces were perceived by, reacted to and reshaped by the groups of individuals concerned. This, for me, is ultimately what the social psychology of group processes is all about.

Summary

1   Social identity theory provides an explanation for a wide variety of ingroup-favouring biases, particularly in settings where there is no obvious material basis for such favouritism. In this theory, people's sense of self-worth partly derives from their group memberships and the evaluation of those groups compared to other groups. It is assumed that people prefer a positive self concept, which then leads them to seek out some positive distinctiveness for their ingroup(s) in the form of biased judgements and discriminatory behaviour.

2   Most intergroup situations involve status and power differences, which complicates the search for positive distinctiveness, especially for members of 'inferior' groups. Dominant groups generally show more ingroup favouritism than subordinate groups, particularly if the status quo is seen to be legitimate and stable.

358

Members of subordinate groups may seek to obtain positivity by leaving the group. When this is difficult or impossible because group boundaries are impermeable, they may resort to choosing a less threatening comparison outgroup, or to changing the dimensions along which 'favourability' is judged. In circumstances where the situation is highly unstable and the dominant group's position is perceived to be illegitimate, they may engage in attempts to change the status quo directly.

3　The acquisition or maintenance of self-esteem may not be the sole or main reason for social identification. Recent research suggests that other motives – for example, the search for meaning, the desire for social interaction or self-insight – may also be associated with social identity. This may help to explain why the correlation between strength of group identification and ingroup bias is not always strongly positive.

4　Intergroup prejudice can be reduced by bringing groups into contact with one another in conditions that involve cooperation between equal-status participants and where social norms actively support a change in attitudes. Through such means, attitudes towards outgroup members that one has encountered will usually become more positive. It may be harder to get those positive attitudes to generalize to the outgroup as a whole.

5　When category memberships overlap, the possibility of shared group identities exists, which may reduce intergroup discrimination in terms of any one category dimension singly. However, in many situations one group identity will dominate to the exclusion of others, thus lowering the potential of crossed-category memberships to eliminate bias. Moreover, individuals who are perceived to be outgroup members on two or more dimensions may be doubly discriminated against.

6　Changing the salience of group identities in contact situations offers the promise of achieving generalized attitude change. Three different strategies exist: decategorization, in which all group identities are de-emphasized; recategorization, in which a superordinate identity is made salient, thus subsuming the problematic subgroup divisions; and categorization, in which it is attempted to engineer cooperation while retaining the distinctive identity of the participating groups. Each approach has advantages and disadvantages, and some combination of them may provide the basis for genuine intergroup harmony and mutual tolerance.

Notes

1   This is not a universal or necessary consequence of minority group membership. Studies in different historical and cultural contexts have failed to find such misidentification (Brown, 1995).
2   There was also a third intermediate illegitimate condition where some justification for the status assignment was given. To simplify matters, I have omitted this condition. The means from that condition were always approximately mid-way between the other two conditions.
3   Note that the vertical axis shows standardized factor scores and these do not correspond literally to positive and negative identification levels.
4   Of course, in a properly designed experiment the order of phases 3 and 4 is counterbalanced.

Further Reading

Abrams, D. and Hogg, M. (1990) *Social Identity Theory: Constructive and Critical Advances*, chs 3, 4, 10–12. Hemel Hempstead: Harvester Wheatsheaf.
Brewer, M.B. and Miller, N. (1996) *Intergroup Relations*, chs 1, 2, 4, 5. Milton Keynes: Open University Press.
Brown, R. (1995) *Prejudice: Its Social Psychology*, ch. 8. Oxford: Blackwell.
Stroebe, W. and Hewstone, M. (1993) (eds) *European Review of Social Psychology*, vol. 4, chs 1–3. Chichester: Wiley.
Tajfel, H. (1981) *Human Groups and Social Categories*, chs 11–13, 15. Cambridge: Cambridge University Press.

REFERENCES

Abeles, R.P. (1976) Relative deprivation, rising expectations and black militancy. *Journal of Social Issues*, 32, 119–37.

Aboud, F. (1988) *Children and Prejudice*. Oxford: Basil Blackwell.

Abrams, D. (1990) Political identity: relative deprivation, social identity and the case of Scottish Nationalism. *ESRC 16–19 Initiative Occasional Papers*. London: Economic and Social Research Council.

Abrams, D. and Hogg, M. (1988) Comments on the motivational status of self-esteem in social identity and intergroup discrimination. *European Journal of Social Psychology*, 18, 317–34.

Abrams, D. and Hogg, M.A. (1990) *Social Identity Theory: Constructive and Critical Advances*. Hemel Hempstead: Harvester Wheatsheaf.

Abrams, D., Wetherell, M., Cochrane, S., Hogg, M.A. and Turner, J.C. (1990) Knowing what to think by knowing who you are: self-categorization and the nature of norm formation, conformity and group polarization. *British Journal of Social Psychology*, 29, 97–119.

Abrams, D., Ando, K. and Hinkle, S.W. (1998) Psychological attachment to the group: cross-cultural differences in organizational identification and subjective norms as predictors of worker's intentions. *Personality and Social Psychology Bulletin*, 24, 1027–39.

Aharpour, S. and Brown, R. (1997) Functions of social identification. Paper presented to British Psychological Society Social Psychology Section Conference, Brighton.

Albert, S. (1977) Temporal comparison theory. *Psychological Review*, 84, 485–503.

Alexander, C. and Sagatun, I. (1973) An attributional analysis of experimental norms. *Sociometry*, 36, 127–42.

Allen, V.L. (1965) Situational factors in conformity, in Berkowitz, L. (ed.) *Advances in Experimental Social Psychology*, vol. 2. New York: Academic Press.

Allen, V.L. (1975) Social support for nonconformity, in Berkowitz, L. (ed.) *Advances in Experimental Social Psychology*, vol. 8. New York: Academic Press.

Allen, V.L. and Wilder, D.A. (1980) Impact of group consensus and social support on stimulus meaning: mediation of conformity by cognitive restructuring. *Journal of Personality and Social Psychology*, 39, 1116–24.

Allport, F.H. (1924) *Social Psychology*. New York: Houghton Mifflin.

Allport, F.H. (1962) A structuronomic conception of behaviour: individual and collective. *Journal of Abnormal and Social Psychology*, 64, 3–30.

Allport, G.W. (1954) *The Nature of Prejudice*. Reading, MA: Addison-Wesley.

Allport, G.W. and Kramer, B.B. (1946) Some roots of prejudice. *Journal of Psychology*, 22, 9–39.

Alvaro, E.M. and Crano, W.D. (1997) Indirect minority influence: evidence for leniency in source evaluation and counter argumentation. *Journal of Personality and Social Psychology*, 72, 949–64.

Amir, Y. (1976) The role of intergroup contact in change of prejudice and ethnic relations, in Katz, P.A. (ed.) *Towards the Elimination of Racism*. New York: Pergamon.

Anderson, A.B. (1975) Combined effects of interpersonal attraction and goal path clarity on the cohesiveness of task-oriented groups. *Journal of Personality and Social Psychology*, 31, 68–75.

Appelgryn, A.E.M. and Bornmann, E. (1996) Relative deprivation in contemporary South Africa. *Journal of Social Psychology*, 136, 381–97.

Appelgryn, A.E.M. and Niemwoudt, J.M. (1988) Relative deprivation and the ethnic attitudes of Blacks and Afrikaans-speaking Whites in South Africa. *Journal of Social Psychology*, 128, 311–23.

Armstrong, B., Johnson, D.W. and Balour, B. (1981) Effects of co-operative versus individualistic learning experiences on interpersonal attraction between learning disabled and normal progress elementary school students. *Contemporary Educational Psychology*, 15, 604–16.

Aronson, E. and Mills, J. (1959) The effect of severity of initiation on liking for a group. *Journal of Abnormal and Social Psychology*, 59, 177–81.

Aronson, E., Blaney, N., Stephan, C., Sikes, J. and Snapp, M. (1978) *The Jig-Saw Classroom*. London: Sage.

Asch, S.E. (1951) Effects of group pressure upon the modification and distortion of judgements, in Guetzkow, M. (ed.) *Groups, Leadership, and Men*. Pittsburgh, PA: Carnegie Press.

Asch, S.E. (1952) *Social Psychology*. Englewood Cliffs, NJ: Prentice Hall.

Asch, S.E. (1955) Opinions and social pressure. *Scientific American*, 193, 31–55.

Asch, S.E. (1956) Studies of independence and conformity: I. A minority of one against a unanimous majority. *Psychological Monographs*, 70(a), 1–70.

Aschenbrenner, K.M. and Schaefer, R.E. (1980) Minimal group situations: comments on a mathematical model and on the research paradigm. *European Journal of Social Psychology*, 10, 389–98.

Association of University Teachers (1985) *Rules of the Association*. London: Centurion Press.

Bakeman, R. and Helmreich, R. (1975) Cohesion and performance: covariation and causality in an undersea environment. *Journal of Experimental Social Psychology*, 11, 478–89.

Bales, R.F. (1950) *Interaction Process Analysis: A Method for the Study of Small Groups*. Chicago, IL: University of Chicago Press.

Bales, R.F. (1953) The equilibrium problem in small groups, in Parsons, T., Bales, R.F. and Shils, E.A. (eds) *Working Papers in the Theory of Action*. New York: Free Press.

Bales, R.F. (1970) *Personality and Interpersonal Behaviour*. New York: Holt, Rinehart and Winston.

Bales, R.F. (1984) The integration of social psychology. *Social Psychology Quarterly*, 47, 98–101.

Bales, R.F. and Cohen, S.P. (1979) SYMLOG: A *System for the Multiple Level Observation of Groups*. New York: Free Press.

Bandura, A. (1973) *Aggression: A Social Learning Analysis*. Englewood Cliffs, NJ: Prentice Hall.

Baron, R.A. and Ransberger, V.M. (1978) Ambient temperature and the occurrence of collective violence: the 'long, hot summer' revisited. *Journal of Personality and Social Psychology*, 36, 351–60.

Baron, R.S. (1986) Distraction–conflict theory: progress and problems, in Berkowitz, L. (ed.) *Advances in Experimental Social Psychology*, vol. 19, pp. 1–40. New York: Academic Press.

Baron, R.S. and Roper, G. (1976) Reaffirmation of social comparison views of choice shifts: averaging and extremity effects in an autokinetic situation. *Journal of Personality and Social Psychology*, 33, 521–30.

Baron, R.S., Vandello, J.A. and Brunsman, B. (1996) The forgotten variable in conformity research: impact of task importance on social influence. *Journal of Personality and Social Psychology*, 71, 915–27.

Bartlett, J. (1962) *Familiar Quotations*. London: Macmillan.

Bartsch, R. A. and Judd, C. M. (1993) Majority–minority status and perceived ingroup variability revisited. *European Journal of Social Psychology*, 23, 471–83.

Bass, B.M. (1985) *Leadership and Performance beyond Expectations*. New York: Free Press.

Bass, B.M. (1990) From transactional to transformational leadership: learning to share the vision. *Organizational Dynamics*, 18, 19–31.

363

Bavelas, A. (1969) Communications patterns in task-oriented groups, in Cartwright, D. and Zander, A. (eds) *Group Dynamics: Research and Theory*, 3rd edn. New York: Harper & Row.

Bennett, M., Dewberry, C. and Yeeles, C. (1991) A reassessment of the role of ethnicity in children's social perception. *Journal of Child Psychology and Psychiatry*, 32, 969–82.

Berger, J. and Zelditch, M. (1985) (eds) *Status, Rewards and Influence*. San Francisco, CA: Jossey-Bass.

Berger, J., Cohen, B.P. and Zelditch, M. (1972) Status characteristics and social interaction. *American Sociological Review*, 37, 241–55.

Berkowitz, L. (1954) Group standards, cohesiveness and productivity. *Human Relations*, 7, 509–19.

Berkowitz, L. (1962) *Aggression: A Social Psychological Analysis*. New York: McGraw-Hill.

Berkowitz, L. (1974) Some determinants of impulsive aggression: role of mediated associations with reinforcements for aggression. *Psychological Review*, 81, 165–76.

Berkowitz, L. (1989) Frustration–aggression hypothesis: examination and reformulation. *Psychological Bulletin*, 106, 59–73.

Berndt, T.J. (1979) Developmental changes in conformity to peers and parents. *Developmental Psychology*, 15, 608–16.

Bernstein, M. and Crosby, F. (1980) An empirical examination of relative deprivation theory. *Journal of Experimental Social Psychology*, 16, 442–56.

Berry, J.W. (1967) Independence and conformity in subsistence level societies. *Journal of Personality and Social Psychology*, 7, 415–18.

Berry, J.W. (1984) Cultural relations in plural societies: alternatives to segregation and their sociopsychological implications, in Miller, N. and Brewer, M.B. (eds) *Groups in Contact: The Psychology of Desegregation*. New York: Academic Press.

Berry, J.W., Kim, V., Minde, T. and Mok, D. (1987) Comparative studies of aculturative stress. *International Migration Review*, 21, 491–511.

Berteotti, C.R. and Seibold, D.R. (1994) Coordination and role-definition problems in health-care teams: a hospice case study, in Frey, L.R. (ed.) *Group Communication in Context: Studies of Natural Groups*. Hillsdale, NJ: Lawrence Erlbaum.

Bettencourt, B.A., Brewer, M.B., Croak, M.R. and Miller, N. (1992) Cooperation and the reduction of intergroup bias: the role of reward structure and social orientation. *Journal of Experimental Social Psychology*, 28, 301–9.

Bettencourt, A., Charlton, K. and Kernaham, C. (1997) Numerical representation of groups in co-operative settings: social orientation effects on ingroup bias. *Journal of Experimental Social Psychology*, 33, 630–59.

Biernat, M. and Vescio, T.K. (1993) Categorization and stereotyping: effects of group context on memory and social judgement. *Journal of Experimental Social Psychology*, 29, 166–202.

Biernat, M. and Vescio, T.K. (1994) Still another look at the effects of fit and novelty on the salience of social categories. *Journal of Experimental Social Psychology*, 30, 399–406.

Biernat, M. and Wortman, C.B. (1991) Sharing of home responsibilities between professionally employed women and their husbands. *Journal of Personality and Social Psychology*, 60, 844–60.

Billig, M.G. (1976) *Social Psychology and Intergroup Relations*. London: Academic Press.

Blake, R.R. and Mouton, J.S. (1962) Overevaluation of own group's product in intergroup competition. *Journal of Abnormal and Social Psychology*, 64, 237–8.

Blake, R.R., Shepard, H.A. and Mouton, J.S. (1964) *Managing Intergroup Conflict in Industry*. Texas: Gulf Publishing Company.

Blanchard, F.A. and Crosby, F.J. (1989) *Affirmative Action in Perspective*. New York: Springer-Verlag.

Blanchard, P.A., Weigel, R.H. and Cook, S.W. (1975) The effect of relative competence of group members upon interpersonal attraction in cooperating interracial groups. *Journal of Personality and Social Psychology*, 32, 519–30.

Blank, W., Weitzel, J.R. and Green, S.G. (1990) A test of the situational leadership theory. *Personnel Psychology*, 43, 579–97.

Blanz, M., Mummendey, A. and Otten, S. (1997) Normative evaluations and frequency expectations regarding positive versus negative outcome allocations between groups. *European Journal of Social Psychology*, 27, 165–76.

Blanz, M., Mummendey, A., Mielke, R. and Klink, A. (1998) Responding to negative social identity: a taxonomy of identity management strategies. *European Journal of Social Psychology*, 28, 697–730.

Blascovich, J., Veach, T.L. and Ginsburg, G.P. (1973) Blackjack and the risky shift. *Sociometry*, 36, 42–55.

Blascovich, J., Ginsburg, G.P. and Howe, R.C. (1975) Blackjack and the risky shift. II: monetary stakes. *Journal of Experimental Social Psychology*, 11, 224–32.

Blascovich, J., Ginsburg, G.P. and Howe, R.C. (1976) Blackjack, choice shifts in the field. *Sociometry*, 39, 274–6.

Bohner, G., Moskowitz, G.B. and Chaiken, S. (1995) The interplay of heuristic and systematic processing of social information, in Stroebe, W. and Hewstone, M. (eds) *European Review of Social Psychology*, vol. 6. Chichester: Wiley.

Bond, C.F. and Titus, L.J. (1983) Social facilitation: a meta-analysis of 241 studies. *Psychological Bulletin*, 94, 265–92.

Bond, R. (1998) Group size and conformity. Paper presented to East–West meeting of EAESP, Gommern, Germany. April, 1998.

Bond, R. and Smith, P.B. (1996) Culture and conformity: a meta-analysis of studies using Asch's (1952b, 1956) line judgement task. *Psychological Bulletin*, 119, 111–37.

Borgatta, E.F. and Bales, R.F. (1953) The consistency of subject behaviour and the reliability of scoring in interaction process analysis. *American Sociological Review*, 18, 566–9.

Bornstein, F., Crum, L., Wittenbraker, J., Harring, K., Insko, C.A. and Thibaut, J. (1983a) On the measurement of social orientations in the Minimal Group Paradigm. *European Journal of Social Psychology*, 13, 321–50.

Bornstein, F., Crum, L., Wittenbraker, J., Harring, K., Insko, C.A. and Thibaut, J. (1983b) Reply to Turner's comments. *European Journal of Social Psychology*, 13, 369–81.

Bourhis, R.Y. and Giles, K. (1977) The language of intergroup distinctiveness, in Giles, H. (ed.) *Language, Ethnicity and Intergroup Relations*. London: Academic Press.

Bourhis, R.Y., Giles, H., Leyens, J.P. and Tajfel, H. (1978) Psycholinguistic distinctiveness: language divergence in Belgium, in Giles, H. and St Clair, R. (eds) *Language and Social Psychology*. Oxford: Blackwell.

Brandstatter, H., Davis, J.H. and Stocher-Kreichganer, G. (eds) (1982) *Contemporary Problems in Group Decision Making*. New York: Academic Press.

Branthwaite, A., Doyle, S. and Lightbown, N. (1979) The balance between fairness and discrimination. *European Journal of Social Psychology*, 9, 149–63.

Brewer, M.B. (1979) In-group bias in the minimal intergroup situation: a cognitive–motivational analysis. *Psychological Bulletin*, 86, 307–24.

Brewer, M.B. (1999) Superordinate goals versus superordinate identity as bases for intergroup cooperation, in Capozza, D. and Brown, R. (eds) *Social Identity Processes: Trends in Theory and Research*. London: Sage.

Brewer, M.B. and Brown, R.J. (1998) Intergroup relations, in Gilbert, D.T., Fiske, S.T. and Lindzey, G. (eds) *The Handbook of Social Psychology*, 4th edn. New York: McGraw-Hill.

Brewer, M.B. and Campbell, D.T. (1976) *Ethnocentrism and Intergroup Attitudes: East African Evidence*. New York: Sage.

Brickner, M.A., Harkins, S.G. and Ostrom, T.M. (1986) Effects of personal involvement: thought provoking implications for social loafing. *Journal of Personality and Social Psychology*, 51, 763–9.

Brinthaupt, T.M., Moreland, R.L. and Levine, J.M. (1991) Sources of optimism among prospective group members. *Personality and Social Psychology Bulletin*, 17, 36–43.

Brockner, J. and Weisenfeld, B.M. (1996) The interactive impact of procedural and outcome fairness on reactions to a decision: the effects of what you do depend on how you do it. *Psychological Bulletin*, 120, 189–208.

Brown, B.B., Clasen, D.R. and Eicher, S.A. (1986) Perceptions of peer pressure, peer conformity dispositions, and self-reported behavior among adolescents. *Developmental Psychology*, 22, 521–30.

Brown, Roger (1965) *Social Psychology*. New York: Macmillan.

Brown, R.J. (1978) Divided we fall: an analysis of relations between sections of a factory work-force, in Tajfel, H. (ed.) *Differentiation between Social Groups: Studies in the Social Psychology of Intergroup Relations*. London: Academic Press.

Brown, R.J. (1984a) The effects of intergroup similarity and cooperative vs. competitive orientation on intergroup discrimination. *British Journal of Social Psychology*, 23, 21–33.

Brown, R.J. (1984b) The role of similarity in intergroup relations, in Tajfel, H. (ed.) *The Social Dimension: European Developments in Social Psychology*. Cambridge: Cambridge University Press.

Brown, R. (1995) *Prejudice: Its Social Psychology*. Oxford: Blackwell.

Brown, R.J. and Abrams, D. (1986) The effects of intergroup similarity and goal interdependence on intergroup attitudes and task performance. *Journal of Experimental Social Psychology*, 22, 78–92.

Brown, R. and Capozza, D. (1999) Social Identity Theory in prospect and retrospect, in Capozza, D. and Brown, R. (eds) *Social Identity Processes: Trends in Theory and Research*. London: Sage.

Brown, R. and Haeger, G. (1999) 'Compared to what?': comparison choice in an international context. *European Journal of Social Psychology*, 29, 31–42.

Brown, R. and Middendorf, J. (1996) The underestimated role of temporal comparison: a test of the life-span model. *Journal of Social Psychology*, 136, 325–31.

Brown, R.J. and Ross, G.F. (1982) The battle for acceptance: an exploration into the dynamics of intergroup behaviour, in Tajfel, H. (ed.) *Social Identity and Intergroup Relations*. Cambridge: Cambridge University Press.

Brown, R. and Smith, A. (1989) Perceptions of and by minority groups: the case of women in academia. *European Journal of Social Psychology*, 19, 61–75.

Brown, R. and Torres, A. (1996) Recognising group diversity. Paper presented to the International Congress of Psychology, Montreal, August.

Brown, R.J. and Turner, J.C. (1979) The criss-cross categorization effect in intergroup discrimination. *British Journal of Social and Clinical Psychology*, 18, 371–83.

Brown, R.J. and Turner, J.C. (1981) Interpersonal and intergroup behaviour, in Turner, J.C. and Giles, H. (eds) *Intergroup Behaviour*. Oxford: Blackwell.

Brown, R.J. and Wade, G.S. (1987) Superordinate goals and intergroup behaviour: the effects of role ambiguity and status on intergroup attitudes and
task performance. *European Journal of Social Psychology*, 17, 131–42.

Brown, R. and Wootton-Millward, L. (1993) Perceptions of group homogeneity during group formation and change. *Social Cognition*, 11, 126–49.

Brown, R.J., Tajfel, H. and Turner, J.C. (1980) Minimal group situations and
intergroup discrimination: comments on the paper by Aschenbrenner and
Schaefer. *European Journal of Social Psychology*, 10, 399–414.

Brown, R.J., Condor, S., Mathews, A., Wade, G. and Williams, J.A. (1986)
Explaining intergroup differentiation in an industrial organisation. *Journal
of Occupational Psychology*, 59, 273–86.

Brown, R., Hinkle, S., Ely, P.G., Fox-Cardamone, L., Maras, P. and Taylor,
L.A. (1992) Recognising group diversity: individualist–collectivist and
autonomous–relational social orientations and their implications for intergroup process. *British Journal of Social Psychology*, 31, 327–42.

Brown, R.J., Vivian J. and Hewstone, M. (1999) Changing attitudes through
intergroup contract: the effects of group membership salience. *European
Journal of Social Psychology*, 29, 741–64.

Bruner, J.S. (1957) On perceptual readiness. *Psychological Review*, 64, 123–51.

Bryman, A. (1992) *Charisma and Leadership in Organisations*. London: Sage.

Burns, J.M. (1978) *Leadership*. New York: Harper.

Burnstein, E. and McRae, A.V. (1962) Some effects of shared threat and prejudice in racially mixed groups. *Journal of Abnormal and Social Psychology*,
64, 257–63.

Burnstein, E. and Vinokur, A. (1973) Testing two classes of theories about
group-induced shifts in individual choice. *Journal of Experimental Social
Psychology*, 9, 123–37.

Burnstein, E. and Vinokur, A. (1977) Persuasive argumentation and social
comparison as determinants of attitude polarization. *Journal of Experimental
Social Psychology*, 13, 315–32.

Buunk, B.P., Collins, R.L., Taylor, S.E., VanYperen, N.W. and Dakof, G.A.
(1990) The affective consequences of social comparison: either direction
has its ups and downs. *Journal of Personality and Social Psychology*, 59, 1238–
49.

Buys, C.J. (1978) Humans would do better without groups. *Personality and
Social Psychology Bulletin*, 4, 123–5.

Byrne, D. (1971) *The Attraction Paradigm*. New York: Academic Press.

Campbell, D.T. (1956) Enhancement of contrast as a composite habit. *Journal
of Abnormal and Social Psychology*, 53, 350–5.

Campbell, D.T. (1958) Common fate, similarity, and other indices of the status
of aggregates of persons as social entities. *Behavioural Science*, 3, 14–25.

Campbell, D.T. (1965) Ethnocentric and other altruistic motives, in Levine, D. (ed.) *Nebraska Symposium on Motivation*, pp. 283–311. Lincoln, NB: University of Nebraska Press.

Campbell, D.T. and Stanley, J.C. (1963) Experimental and quasi-experimental designs for research, in Gage, N.L. (ed.) *Handbook of Research on Teaching*. Chicago, IL: Rand McNally.

Cantril, H. (1965) *The Pattern of Human Concerns*. New York: Rutgers University Press.

Caplan, N. (1970) The new ghetto man: a review of recent empirical studies. *Journal of Social Issues*, 26, 59–73.

Capozza, D. and Brown, R. (1999) *Social Identity Processes: Trends in Theory and Research*. London: Sage.

Carli, L.L. (1989) Gender differences in interaction style and influence. *Journal of Personality and Social Psychology*, 56, 565–76.

Carlsmith, J.M. and Anderson, C.A. (1979) Ambient temperature and the occurrence of collective violence: a new analysis. *Journal of Personality and Social Psychology*, 37, 337–44.

Carlyle, T. (1841) *On Heroes, Hero-worship, and the Heroic*. London: Fraser.

Carter, L.F. and Nixon, M. (1949) An investigation of the relationship between four criteria of leadership ability for three different tasks. *Journal of Psychology*, 27, 245–61.

Cartwright, D. and Zander, A. (eds) (1969) *Group Dynamics: Research and Theory*, 3rd edn. New York: Harper & Row.

Chafel, J.A. (1986) A naturalistic investigation of the use of social comparison by young children. *Journal of Research and Development in Education*, 19, 51–61.

Chen, M. and Bargh, J.A. (1997) Nonconscious behavioral confirmation processes: the self-fulfilling consequences of automatic stereotype activation. *Journal of Experimental Social Psychology*, 33, 541–60.

Cialdini, R.B., Borden, R.J., Thorne, A., Walker, M.R., Freeman, S. and Sloan, L.R. (1976) Basking in reflected glory: three (football) field studies. *Journal of Personality and Social Psychology*, 34, 366–74.

Cini, M., Moreland, R.L. and Levine, J.M. (1993) Group staffing levels and responses to prospective and new members. *Journal of Personality and Social Psychology*, 65, 723–34.

Clark, K.B. and Clark, M.P. (1947) Racial identification and preference in Negro children, in Newcomb, T.M. and Hartley, E.L. (eds) *Readings in Social Psychology*. New York: Holt, Rinehart and Winston.

Clark, R.D. and Maass, A. (1988) Social categorization in minority influence: the case of homosexuality. *European Journal of Social Psychology*, 18, 347–64.

Clark, R.D. and Maass, A. (1990) The effects of majority size on minority influence. *European Journal of Social Psychology*, 20, 99–117.

369

Clement, D.E. and Sullivan, D.W. (1970) No risky shift effect with real groups and real risks. *Psychonomic Science*, 18, 243–5.

Clore, G.L., Bray, R.M., Itkin, S.M. and O'Murphy, P. (1978) Inter-racial attitudes and behaviour at a summer camp. *Journal of Personality and Social Psychology*, 36, 107–16.

Coch, L. and French, J.R.P. (1948) Overcoming resistance to change. *Human Relations*, 11, 512–32.

Codol, J.-P. (1975) On the so called 'superior conformity of the self' behaviour: twenty experimental investigations. *European Journal of Social Psychology*, 5, 457–501.

Cohen, E.F. (1972) Interracial interaction disability. *Human Relations*, 25, 9–24.

Cook, S.W. (1978) Interpersonal and attitudinal outcomes in cooperating interracial groups. *Journal of Research and Development in Education*, 12, 97–113.

Cook, S.W. (1979) Social science and school desegregation: did we mislead the Supreme Court? *Personality and Social Psychology Bulletin*, 5, 420–37.

Costanzo, P.R. and Shaw, M.E. (1966) Conformity as a function of age level. *Child Development*, 37, 967–75.

Cottrell, N. (1972) Social facilitation, in McClintock, C. (ed.) *Experimental Social Psychology*. New York: Holt, Rinehart and Winston.

Courtright, J.A. (1978) A laboratory investigation of groupthink. *Communication Monographs*, 45, 229–46.

Cowen, E.L., Landes, J. and Schaet, D.E. (1958) The effects of mild frustration on the expression of prejudiced attitudes. *Journal of Abnormal and Social Psychology*, 58, 33–8.

Crandall, C. (1988) Social contagion of binge eating. *Journal of Personality and Social Psychology*, 25, 588–98.

Crano, W.D. and Mellon, P.M. (1978) Causal influence of teachers' expectations on children's academic performance: a cross-lagged panel analysis. *Journal of Educational Psychology*, 79, 39–49.

Crawford, T.J. and Naditch, M. (1970) Relative deprivation, powerlessness, and militancy: the psychology of social protest. *Psychiatry*, 33, 208–23.

Crosby, F. (1979) Relative deprivation revisited: a response to Miller, Bolce, and Halligan. *American Political Science Review*, 73, 103–12.

Crosby, F. (1982) *Relative Deprivation and Working Women*. New York: Oxford University Press.

Darley, J.M. and Fazio, R.H. (1980) Expectancy confirmation processes arising in the social interaction sequence. *American Psychologist*, 35, 867–81.

Darley, J.M. and Gross, P.H. (1983) A hypothesis-confirming bias in labelling effects. *Journal of Personality and Social Psychology*, 44, 20–33.

Darwin, C. (1859) *On the Origin of Species by Natural Selection*. London: Murray.

Dashiell, J.E. (1930) An experimental analysis of some group effects. *Journal of Abnormal Social Psychology*, 25, 190–9.

Davey, A. (1983) *Learning to be Prejudiced*. London: Edward Arnold.

David, B. and Turner, J.C. (1996) Studies in self-categorization and minority conversion: is being a member of the outgroup an advantage? *British Journal of Social Psychology*, 35, 179–99.

Davies, J. (1978) Communication. *American Political Science Review*, 72, 1357–8.

Davies, J. (1979) Comment. *American Political Science Review*, 73, 825–6.

Davies, J.C. (1969) The J-curve of rising and declining satisfactions as a cause of some great revolutions and a contained rebellion, in Graham, H.D. and Gurr, T.R. (eds) *The History of Violence in America: Historical and Comparative Perspectives*. New York: Praeger.

Davis, J.H. (1973) Group decision and social interaction: a theory of social decision schemes. *Psychological Review*, 80, 97–125.

Davis, J.H. (1992) Some compelling intuitions about group consensus decisions and internal aggregation phenomena: selected examples, 1950–1990. *Organizational Behavior and Human Decision Processes*, 52, 3–38.

Davis, J.H. and Restle, F. (1963) The analysis of problems and prediction of group problem solving. *Journal of Abnormal and Social Psychology*, 66, 103–16.

Davis, J.H., Kerr, N.L., Sussman, M. and Rissman, A.K. (1974) Social decision schemes under risk. *Journal of Personality and Social Psychology*, 30, 248–71.

Davis, J.H., Kerr, N.L., Atkin, R.S., Holt, R. and Meek, D. (1975) The decision process of 6- and 12-person juries assigned unanimous and two-thirds majority rules. *Journal of Personality and Social Psychology*, 32, 1–14.

de Dreu, C.K.W. and de Vries, N.K. (1993) Numerical support, information processing and attitude change. *European Journal of Social Psychology*, 23, 647–62.

de La Rey, C. and Raju, P. (1996) Group relative deprivation: cognitive versus affective components and protest orientation among Indian South Africans. *Journal of Social Psychology*, 136, 579–88.

de Vries, N.K., de Dreu, C.K.W., Gordijn, E. and Schuurman, M. (1996) Majority and minority influence: a dual role interpretation, in Stroebe, W. and Hewstone, M. (eds) *European Review of Social Psychology*, vol. 7. Chichester: Wiley.

Deaux, K., Reid, A., Misrahi, K. and Ethier, K.A. (1995) Parameters of social identity. *Journal of Personality and Social Psychology*, 68, 280–91.

Deaux, K., Reid, A., Mizrahi, K. and Cotting, D. (in press) Connecting the person to the social: the functions of social identification, in Tyler, T.R., Kramer, R. and John, O. (eds) *The Psychology of the Social Self*. New York: Lawrence Erlbaum.

Deschamps, J.-C. and Brown, R.J. (1983) Superordinate goals and intergroup conflict. *British Journal of Social Psychology*, 22, 189–95.

Deschamps, J.-C. and Doise, W. (1978) Crossed category membership in intergroup relations, in Tajfel, H. (ed.) *Differentiation between Social Groups. Studies in the Social Psychology of Intergroup Relations*. London: Academic Press.

Desforges, D.M., Lord, C.G., Ramsey, S.L., Mason, J.A., van Leeuwen, M.D., West, S.C. and Lepper, M.R. (1991) Effects of structured cooperative contract on changing negative attitudes towards stigmatized groups, *Journal of Personality and Social Psychology*, 60, 531–44.

Desmond, A. and Moore, J. (1991) *Darwin*. Harmondsworth: Penguin.

Deutsch, M. (1949a) A theory of cooperation and competition. *Human Relations*, 2, 129–52.

Deutsch, M. (1949b) An experimental study of the effects of cooperation and competition upon group process. *Human Relations*, 2, 199–231.

Deutsch, M. and Gerard, H.B. (1955) A study of normative and informational social influence upon individual judgement. *Journal of Abnormal and Social Psychology*, 51, 629–36.

Devine, P. (1989) Stereotypes and prejudice: their automatic and controlled components. *Journal of Personality and Social Psychology*, 56, 5–18.

Devos, T., Comby, L. and Deschamps, J.C. (1996) Asymmetries in judgements of ingroup and outgroup variability, pp. 95–144 in Stroebe, W. and Hewstone, M. (eds) *European Review of Social Psychology*, vol. 7. Chichester: Wiley.

Di Pietro, J.A. (1981) Rough and tumble play: a function of gender. *Developmental Psychology*, 17, 50–8.

Diehl, M. (1988) Social identity and minimal groups: the effects of interpersonal and intergroup attitudinal similarity on intergroup discrimination. *British Journal of Social Psychology*, 27, 289–300.

Diehl, M. (1989) Justice and discrimination between minimal groups: the limits of equity. *British Journal of Social Psychology*, 28, 227–38.

Diehl, M. (1990) The minimal group paradigm: theoretical explanations and empirical findings, pp. 263–392 in Stroebe, W. and Hewstone, M. (eds) *European Review of Social Psychology*, vol. 1. Chichester: Wiley.

Diehl, M. and Stroebe, W. (1987) Productivity loss in brainstorming groups: toward the solution of a riddle. *Journal of Personality and Social Psychology*, 53, 497–509.

Diener, E. (1976) Effects of prior destructive behavior, anonymity, and group presence on deindividuation and aggression. *Journal of Personality and Social Psychology*, 33, 497–507.

Diener, E. (1979) Deindividuation, self-awareness and disinhibition. *Journal of Personality and Social Psychology*, 37, 1160–71.

Diener, E. (1980) Deindividuation: the absence of self-awareness and self-regulation in group members, in Paulus, P. (ed.) *The Psychology of Group Influence*. Hillsdale, NJ: Lawrence Erlbaum.

Doise, W. (1969) Intergroup relations and polarization of individual and collective judgements. *Journal of Personality and Social Psychology*, 12, 136–43.

Doise, W. (1976) *L'articulation psychosociologique et les relations entre groupes*. Brussels: A. de Boeck. English translation: *Groups and Individuals*. Cambridge: Cambridge University Press, 1978.

Doise, W., Deschamps, J.-C. and Meyer, G. (1978) The accentuation of intra-category similarities, in Tajfel, H. (ed.) *Differentiation between Social Groups: Studies in the Social Psychology of Intergroup Relations*. London: Academic Press.

Dollard, J., Doob, L.W., Miller, N.E., Mowrer, O.H. and Sears, R.R. (1939) *Frustration and Aggression*. New Haven, CT: Yale University Press.

Doms, M. and van Avermaet, E. (1980) Majority influence, minority influence, and conversion behaviour: a replication. *Journal of Experimental Social Psychology*, 16, 283–92.

Dornbusch, S.M. (1955) The military academy as an assimilating institution. *Social Forces*, 33, 316–21.

Dovidio, D.L., Evans, N. and Tyler, R.B. (1986) Racial stereotypes: the contents of their cognitive representations. *Journal of Experimental Social Psychology*, 22, 22–37.

Dovidio, J.F and Fazio, R.H. (1992) New technologies for the direct and indirect assessment of attitudes, in J.M. Tanur (ed.) *Questions about Questions: Inquiries into the Cognitive Bases of Surveys*. New York: Russell Sage.

Dovidio, J., Gaertner, S.L., Validzic, A., Matoka, K., Johnson, B. and Frazier, S. (1997) Extending the benefits of recategorization: evaluations, self-disclosure and helping. *Journal of Experimental Social Psychology*, 33, 401–20.

Dovidio, J. Gaertner, S.L. and Validzic, A. (1998) Intergroup bias: status differentiation and a common ingroup identity. *Journal of Personality and Social Psychology*, 75, 109–20.

Durkin, K. (1995) *Developmental Social Psychology*. Oxford: Blackwell.

Duval, S. and Wicklund, R.A. (1972) *A Theory of Objective Self Awareness*. New York: Academic Press.

Duveen, G. and Lloyd, B. (1986) The significance of social identities. *British Journal of Social Psychology*, 25, 219–30.

Eagly, A.H. and Chaiken, S. (1993) *The Psychology of Attitudes*. San Diego, CA: Harcourt Brace Jovanovich.

Eagly, A.H. and Steffen, V.J. (1984) Gender stereotypes stem from the distribution of women and men into social roles. *Journal of Personality and Social Psychology*, 46, 735–54.

Earley, P.C. (1989) Social loafing and collectivism: a comparison of the United States and the People's Republic of China. *Administrative Science Quarterly*, 34, 565–81.

Earley, P.C. (1993) East meets West meets Mid East: further explorations of collectivistic and individualistic work groups. *Academy of Management Journal*, 36, 319–48.

Easterbrook, J.A. (1959) The effect of emotion on cue utilization and organization of behavior. *Psychological Review*, 66, 183–201.

Ebbesen, E.B. and Bowers, R.J. (1974) Proportion of risky to conservative arguments in a group discussion and choice shifts. *Journal of Personality and Social Psychology*, 29, 316–27.

Ebbesen, E.E., Kjos, G.L. and Konecni, V.J. (1976) Spatial ecology: its effects on the choice of friends and enemies. *Journal of Experimental Social Psychology*, 12, 505–18.

Egerbladh, T. (1981) A social decision scheme approach on group size, task difficulty and ability level. *European Journal of Social Psychology*, 11, 161–71.

Eiser, J.R. (1971) Enhancement of contrast in the absolute judgement of attitude statements. *Journal of Personality and Social Psychology*, 17, 1–10.

Eisman, B. (1959) Some operational measures of cohesiveness and their interrelations. *Human Relations*, 12, 183–9.

Ellemers, N., van Knippenberg, A., de Vries, N. and Wilke, H. (1988) Social identification and permeability of group boundaries. *European Journal of Social Psychology*, 18, 497–513.

Ellemers, N., Wilke, H. and van Knippenburg, A. (1993) Effects of the legitimacy of the low group or individual status as individual and collective status-enhancement strategies. *Journal of Personality and Social Psychology*, 64, 766–78.

Ellemers, N., Spears, R. and Doosje, B. (1997) Sticking together or falling apart: ingroup identification as a psychological determinant of group commitment. *Journal of Personality and Social Psychology*, 72, 617–26.

Ellemers, N., Kortekaas, P. and Ouwerkerk, J.W. (1999) Self categorization, commitment to the group and group self-esteem as related but distinct aspects of social identity. *European Journal of Social Psychology*, 29, 371–90.

Epstein, J.L. (1985) After the bus arrives: resegregation in desegregated schools. *Journal of Social Issues*, 41, 23–43.

Erb, H.-P., Bohner, G., Schmälzle, K. and Rank, S. (1998) Beyond conflict and discrepancy: cognitive bias in minority and majority influence. *Personality and Social Psychology Bulletin*, 124, 620–33.

Estrada, M., Brown, J. and Lee, F. (1995) Who gets the credit? Perceptions of idiosyncrasy credit in work groups. *Small Group Research*, 26, 56–76.

Fagan, J.F. and Singer, L.T. (1979) The role of simple feature differences in infants' recognition of faces. *Infant Behaviour and Development*, 2, 39–44.

Farnham, S.D., Greenwald, A.G. and Banaji, M.R. (1999) Implicit self esteem, in Abrams, D. and Hogg, M. (eds) *Social Identity and Social Cognition*. Oxford: Blackwell.

Faust, W.L. (1959) Group versus individual problem solving. *Journal of Abnormal and Social Psychology*, 59, 68–72.

Feldbaum, C.L., Christenson, T.E. and O'Neal, E.C. (1980) An observational study of the assimilation of the newcomer to the preschool. *Child Development*, 51, 497–507.

Ferdman, B.M. (1989) Affirmative action and the challenge of the color-blind perspective, in Blanchard, F.A. and Crosby, F.J. (eds) *Affirmative Action in Perspective*. New York: Springer-Verlag.

Festinger, L. (1950) Informal social communication. *Psychological Review*, 57, 271–82.

Festinger, L. (1953) An analysis of compliant behaviour, in Sherif, M. and Wilson, M.O. (eds) *Group Relations at the Crossroads*. New York: Harper & Row.

Festinger, L. (1954) A theory of social comparison processes. *Human Relations*, 7, 117–40.

Festinger, L. (1957) *A Theory of Cognitive Dissonance*. Evanston, IL: Row, Peterson and Co.

Festinger, L., Schachter, S. and Back, K. (1950) *Social Pressures in Informal Groups*. New York: Harper.

Fiedler, F.E. (1965) A contingency model of leadership effectiveness, in Berkowitz, L. (ed.) *Advances in Experimental Social Psychology*, vol. 1. New York: Academic Press. Reprinted 1978 in Berkowitz, L. (ed.) *Group Processes*. New York: Academic Press.

Fiedler, F.E. (1978) Recent developments in research on the contingency model, in Berkowitz, L. (ed.) *Group Processes*. New York: Academic Press.

Fiedler, F.E. and Chemers, M.M. (1984) *Improving Leadership Effectiveness: The Leader-Match Concept*. New York: Wiley.

Field, R.F. (1982) A test of the Vroom–Yetton normative model of leadership. *Journal of Applied Psychology*, 67, 523–32.

Field, R.F., Read, P.G. and Louviere, J.J. (1990) The effect of situation attributes on decision method choice in the Vroom–Jago model of participation in decision making. *Leadership Quarterly*, 1, 65–176.

Fischhoff, B. and Beyth-Marom, R. (1976) Failure has many fathers. *Policy Sciences*, 7, 388–93.

Fishbein, M. and Ajzen, I. (1975) *Beliefs, Attitudes, Intention and Behaviour: An Introduction to Theory and Research*. Reading, MA: Addison-Wesley.

Fiske, S.T. (1998) Stereotyping, prejudice and discrimination, in Gilbert, D.T., Fiske, S.T. and Lindzey, G. (eds) *The Handbook of Social Psychology*, 4th edn. New York: McGraw-Hill.

Fleishman, E.A. (1973) Twenty years of consideration and structure, in Fleishman, E.A. and Hunt, J.F. (eds) *Current Developments in the Study of Leadership*. Carbondale, IL: Southern Illinois University Press.

Flowers, M.L. (1977) A laboratory test of some implications of Janis' groupthink hypothesis. *Journal of Personality and Social Psychology*, 35, 888–96.

Fodor, E.M. and Smith, T. (1982) The power motive as an influence on group decision making. *Journal of Personality and Social Psychology*, 42, 178–85.

Fogelson, R.M. (1970) Violence and grievances: reflections on the 1960s riots. *Journal of Social Issues*, 26, 141–63.

Foster, M.D. and Matheson, K. (1995) Double relative deprivation: combining the personal and political. *Personality and Social Psychology Bulletin*, 21, 1167–77.

France-Kaatrude, A.C. and Smith, W.P. (1985) Social comparison, task motivation and the development of self evaluative standards in children. *Developmental Psychology*, 21, 1080–9.

Fraser, C., Gouge, C. and Billig, M. (1971) Risky shifts, cautious shifts, and group polarization. *European Journal of Social Psychology*, 1, 7–30.

Frey, K.S. and Ruble, D.N. (1985) What children say when the teacher is not around: conflicting goals in social comparison and performance assessment in the classroom. *Journal of Personality and Social Psychology*, 48, 550–62.

Gabrenya, W.K., Latané, B. and Wang, T.E. (1983) Social loafing in cross-cultural perspective: Chinese in Taiwan. *Journal of Cross-Cultural Psychology*, 14, 368–84.

Gabrenya, W.K., Wang, T.E. and Latané, B. (1985) Social loafing on an optimizing task: cross-cultural differences among Chinese and Americans. *Journal of Cross-Cultural Psychology*, 16, 223–42.

Gaertner, S.L. and McLaughlin, J.P. (1983) Racial stereotypes: associations and ascriptions of positive and negative characteristics. *Social Psychology Quarterly*, 46, 23–30.

Gaertner, S.L., Mann, J., Murrell, A. and Dovidio, J.F. (1989) Reducing intergroup bias: the benefits of recategorization. *Journal of Personality and Social Psychology*, 57, 239–49.

Gaertner, S., Dovidio, J.F., Anastasio, P.A., Bachevan, B.A. and Rust, M.C. (1993) The common ingroup identity model: recategorization and the reduction of intergroup bias, in Stroebe, W. and Hewstone, M. (eds) *European Review of Social Psychology*, vol. 4. Chichester: Wiley.

Gaertner, S.L., Rust, M., Dovidio, J.F., Bachman, B. and Anastasio, P. (1994) The contact hypothesis: the role of a common ingroup identity on reducing intergroup bias. *Small Group Research*, 25, 224–49.

Gagnon, A. and Bourhis, R. (1996) Discrimination in the minimal group paradigm: social identity of self interest. *Personality and Social Psychology Bulletin*, 22, 1289–1303.

Gardham, K. and Brown, R. (in press) Two forms of intergroup discrimination with positive and negative outcomes: explaining the positive–negative asymmetry effect. *British Journal of Social Psychology*.

Gerard, H.B. and Hoyt, M.F. (1974) Distinctiveness of social categorization and attitude toward ingroup members. *Journal of Personality and Social Psychology*, 29, 836–42.

Gerard, H.B. and Mathewson, G.C. (1966) The effects of severity of initiation on liking for a group: a replication. *Journal of Experimental Social Psychology*, 2, 278–87.

Gerard, H.B., Wilhelmy, R.A. and Conolley, E.S. (1968) Conformity and group size. *Journal of Personality and Social Psychology*, 8, 79–82.

Gersick, C.J. and Hackman, J.R. (1990) Habitual routines in task performing groups. *Organizational Behavior and Human Decision Processes*, 47, 65–97.

Gibbons, F.X.A. and Buunk, B.P. (1999) Individual differences in social comparison: development of a scale of social comparison orientation. *Journal of Personality and Social Psychology*, 76, 129–42.

Gibbons, F.X., Benbow, C.P. and Gerard, M. (1994) From top dog to bottom half: social comparison strategies in response to poor performance. *Journal of Personality and Social Psychology*, 67, 638–52.

Gibson, J.J. (1966) *The Senses Considered as Perceptual Systems*. Boston, MA: Houghton Mifflin.

Gilbert, D.T., Giesler, R.B. and Morris, K.A. (1995) When comparisons arise. *Journal of Personality and Social Psychology*, 69, 227–36.

Giles, H. (ed.) (1977) *Language, Ethnicity and Intergroup Relations*. London: Academic Press.

Giles, H. and Johnson, P. (1981) Language in ethnic group relations, in Turner, J.C. and Giles, H. (eds) *Intergroup Behaviour*. Oxford: Blackwell.

Giles, H. and Powesland, P.F. (1975) *Speech Style and Social Evaluation*. London: Academic Press.

Glasser, I. (1988) Affirmative action and the legacy of racial injustice, in Katz, P.A. and Taylor, D.A. (eds) *Eliminating Racism* New York: Plenum.

Glick, P., Zion, C. and Nelson, C. (1988) What mediates sex discrimination in hiring decisions? *Journal of Personality and Social Psychology*, 55, 178–86.

377

Gluckman, M. (1956) *Custom and Conflict in Africa*. Oxford: Basil Blackwell.

Goethals, G.R. and Darley, J.M. (1977) Social comparison theory: an attributional approach, in Suls, J. and Miller, R.L. (eds) *Social Comparison Processes: Theoretical and Empirical Perspectives*. Washington: Hemisphere.

Grant, P.R. and Brown, R. (1995) From ethnocentrism to collective protest: responses to relative deprivation and threats to social identity. *Social Psychology Quarterly*, 58, 195–211.

Green, R.G. and Gange, J.J. (1977) Drive theory of social facilitation: twelve years of theory and research. *Psychological Bulletin*, 84, 1267–88.

Greenland, K. and Brown, R. (1999) Categorization and intergroup anxiety in contact between British and Japanese nationals. *European Journal of Social Psychology*, 29, 503–22.

Greenwald, A.G., McGhee, D.E. and Schwartz, J.L.K. (1998) Measuring individual differences in implicit cognition: the implicit association test. *Journal of Personality and Social Psychology*, 74, 1464–80.

Gross, N. and Martin, W.E. (1952) On group cohesiveness. *American Journal of Sociology*, 57, 546–64.

Grubb, W.N. and Wilson, R.H. (1992) Trends in wage and salary inequality, 1967–1988. *Monthly Labor Review*, 115(b), 23–39.

Guerin, B. (1986) Mere presence effects in humans: a review. *Journal of Experimental Social Psychology*, 22, 38–77.

Guerin, B. and Innes, J.M. (1982) Social facilitation and social monitoring: a new look at Zajonc's mere presence hypothesis. *British Journal of Social Psychology*, 21, 7–18.

Guimond, S. and Dubé-Simard, L. (1983) Relative deprivation theory and the Quebec Nationalist Movement: the cognition–emotion distinction and the personal–group deprivation issue. *Journal of Personality and Social Psychology*, 44, 526–35.

Gurin, P. and Townsend, A. (1986) Properties of gender identity and their implications for gender consciousness. *British Journal of Social Psychology*, 25, 139–48.

Gurr, T.R. (1970) *Why Men Rebel*. Princeton, NJ: Princeton University Press.

Hackman, J.R. and Morris, C.G. (1975) Group tasks, group interaction process, and group performance effectiveness: a review and proposed integration, in Berkowitz, L. (ed.) *Advances in Experimental Social Psychology*, vol. 8. New York: Academic Press.

Hackman, J.R. and Morris, C.G. (1978) Group process and group effectiveness: a reappraisal, in Berkowitz, L. (ed.) *Group Processes*. New York: Academic Press.

Hafer, C.L. and Olson, J.M. (1993) Beliefs in a just world and assertive actions by working women. *Personality and Social Psychology Bulletin*, 19, 30–8.

Hagendoorn, L. and Henke, R. (1991) The effect of multiple category membership on intergroup evaluations in a North-Indian context: class, caste, and religion. *British Journal of Social Psychology*, 30, 247–60.

Hains, S.S., Hogg, M.A.R. and Duck, J.M. (1997) Self categorization and leadership: effects of group prototypicality and leader stereotypicality. *Personality and Social Psychology Bulletin*, 23, 1087–99.

Hakmiller, K.L. (1966) Threat as a determinant of downward comparison. *Journal of Experimental Social Psychology, Supplement*, 1, 32–9.

Hamilton, D.L. and Rose, T.L. (1980) Illusory correlation and the maintenance of stereotypic beliefs. *Journal of Personality and Social Psychology*, 39, 832–45.

Hare, A.P. (1976) *Handbook of Small Group Research*, 2nd edn. New York: Free Press.

Harkins, S.G. and Petty, R.E. (1982) Effects of task difficulty and task uniqueness on social loafing. *Journal of Personality and Social Psychology*, 43, 1214–29.

Harkins, W.G. and Szymanski, K. (1989) Social loafing and group evaluation. *Journal of Personality and Social Psychology*, 56, 934–41.

Harkness, S. and Super, C.M. (1985) The cultural context of gender segregation in children's peer groups. *Child Development*, 56, 219–24.

Harris, J.R. (1995) Where is the child's environment? A group socialization theory of development. *Psychological Review*, 102, 458–89.

Hart, P. (1990) *Groupthink in Government: A Study of Small Groups and Policy Failure*. Amsterdam: Swets and Zeitlinger.

Hartley, J., Kelly, J. and Nicholson, N. (1983) *Steel Strike: A Case Study in Industrial Relations*. London: Batsford.

Harvey, O.J. (1953) An experimental approach to the study of status relations in informal groups. *American Sociological Review*, 18, 357–67.

Haslam. S.A., Turner, J.C., Oakes, P.J. and McGarty, C. (1992) Context-dependent variation in social stereotyping. I: The effects of intergroup relations as mediated by social change and frame of reference. *European Journal of Social Psychology*, 22, 3–20.

Haslam, S.A., Oakes, P.J., Turner, J.C. and McGarty, C. (1996) Social identity, self categorization, and the perceived homogeneity of ingroups and outgroups: the interaction between social motivation and cognition, in Sorrentino, R.M. and Higgins, E.T. (eds) *Handbook of Motivation and Cognition*, vol. 3. New York: Guildford.

Heinicke, C. and Bales, R.F. (1953) Developmental trends in the structure of small groups. *Sociometry*, 16, 7–38.

Hennessy, P. (1986) *Cabinet*. Oxford: Blackwell.

Henshel, R.C. (1980) The purposes of laboratory experimentation and the virtues of deliberate artificiality. *Journal of Experimental Social Psychology*, 16, 466–78.

Hepworth, J.T. and West, S.G. (1988) Lynchings and the economy: a time-series reanalysis of Hoyland and Sears (1940). *Journal of Personality and Social Psychology*, 55, 239–47.

Hersey, P.A. and Blanchard, K.H. (1993) *Management of Organizational Behavior.* Englewood Cliffs, NJ: Prentice Hall.

Hewstone, M.R.C. and Brown, R.J. (1986) Contact is not enough: an intergroup perspective on the contact hypothesis, in Hewstone, M.R.C. and Brown, R.J. (eds) *Contact and Conflict in Intergroup Encounters.* Oxford: Blackwell.

Hewstone, M., Fincham, F. and Jaspers, J. (1981) Social categorization and similarity in intergroup behaviour: a replication with 'penalties'. *European Journal of Social Psychology*, 11, 101–7.

Hewstone, M.R.C., Jaspers, J. and Lalljee, M. (1982) Social representations, social attribution and social identity: the intergroup images of 'public' and 'comprehensive' schoolboys. *European Journal of Social Psychology*, 12, 241–69

Hewstone, M., Islam, M.R. and Judd, C.M. (1993) Models of crossed categorization and intergroup relations. *Journal of Personality and Social Psychology*, 64, 779–93.

Higgins, E.T. (1989) Knowledge accessibility and activation: subjectivity and suffering from unconscious sources, in Uleman, J.S. and Bargh, J.A. (eds) *Unintended Thought.* New York: Guildford.

Hill, G.W. (1982) Group versus individual performance: are n + 1 heads better than one? *Psychological Bulletin*, 91, 517–39.

Hinkle, S. and Brown, R. (1990) Intergroup comparisons and social identity: some links and lacunae, in Abrams, D. and Hogg, M. (eds) *Social Identity Theory: Constructive and Critical Advances.* Hemel Hempstead: Harvester Wheatsheaf.

Hoffman, C. and Hurst, N. (1990) Gender stereotypes: perception or rationalization? *Journal of Personality and Social Psychology*, 58, 197–208.

Hofstede, G. (1980) *Culture's Consequences: International Differences in Work-Related Values.* Beverly Hills, CA: Sage.

Hogan, R., Curphy, G.J. and Hogan, J. (1994) What we know about leadership: effectiveness and personality. *American Psychologist*, 49, 493–504.

Hogg, M.A. (1992) *The Social Psychology of Group Cohesiveness: From Attraction to Social Identity.* London: Harvester Wheatsheaf.

Hogg, M.A. (1996) Intragroup processes: group structure and social identity, in Robinson, W.P (ed.) *Social Groups and Identities: Developing the Legacy of Henri Tajfel.* Oxford: Butterworth.

Hogg, M. and Abrams, D. (1990) Social motivation, self–esteem and social identity, pp. 28–47, in Abrams, D. and Hogg, M. (eds) *Social Identity Theory: Constructive and Critical Advances.* Hemel Hemstead: Harvester Wheatsheaf.

Hogg, M.A. and Hains, S.C. (1996) Intergroup relations and group solidarity: effects of group identification and social beliefs on depersonalized attractions. *Journal of Personality and Social Psychology,* 70, 295–309.

Hogg, M.A. and Hardie, E.A. (1992) Prototypicality, conformity and depersonalized attraction: a self-categorization analysis of group cohesiveness. *British Journal of Social Psychology,* 31, 41–56.

Hogg, M.A. and Mullin, B.A. (1999) Joining groups to reduce uncertainty: subjective uncertainty reduction and group identification, in Abrams, D. and Hogg, M.A. (eds) *Social Identity and Social Cognition.* Oxford: Blackwell.

Hogg, M.A. and Sunderland, J. (1991) Self-esteem and intergroup discrimination in the minimal group paradigm. *Journal of Social Psychology,* 30, 51–62.

Hogg, M.A. and Turner, J.C. (1985) Interpersonal attraction, social identification and psychological group formation. *European Journal of Social Psychology,* 15, 51–66

Hogg, M.A. and Turner, J.C. (1987) Intergroup behaviour, self stereotyping and the salience of social categories. *British Journal of Social Psychology,* 26, 325–40.

Hogg, M.A., Cooper-Shaw, L. and Holzworth, D.W (1993) Group prototypicality and depersonalized attraction in small interactive groups. *Personality and Social Psychology Bulletin,* 19, 452–65.

Hollander, E.P. (1958) Conformity, status, and idiosyncrasy credit. *Psychological Review,* 65, 117–27.

Hollander, E.P. (1960) Competence and conformity in the acceptance of influence. *Journal of Abnormal and Social Psychology,* 61, 361–5.

Hollander, E.P. (1978) *Leadership Dynamics: A Practical Guide to Effective Relationships.* New York: Free Press.

Hollander, E.P. and Julian, J.W. (1970) Studies in leader legitimacy, influence, and innovation, in Berkowitz, L. (ed.) *Advances in Experimental Social Psychology,* vol. 5. New York: Academic Press.

Homans, G.C. (1950) *The Human Group.* New York: Harcourt, Brace and World.

Hoppe, R.A. (1962) Memorizing by individuals and groups: a test of the pooling-of-ability model. *Journal of Abnormal and Social Psychology,* 65, 64–7.

Horowitz, D.L. (1973) Direct, displaced and cumulative ethnic aggression. *Comparative Politics,* 6, 1–16.

Horowitz, E.L. and Horowitz, R.E. (1938) Development of social attitudes in children. *Sociometry,* 1, 301–38.

Horwitz, M. and Rabbie, J.M. (1982) Individuality and membership in the intergroup system, in Tajfel, H. (ed.) *Social Identity and Intergroup Relations.* Cambridge: Cambridge University Press.

House, R.J. (1977) A theory of charismatic leadership, in Hunt, J.G. and Larson, L.L. (eds) *Leadership: The Cutting Edge*. Carbondale, IL: Southern Illinois University Press.

House, R.J., Spangler, W.D. and Woycke, J. (1991) Personality and charisma in the US Presidency: a psychological theory of leader effectiveness. *Administrative Science Quarterly*, 36, 364–96.

Hovland, C. and Sears, R.R. (1940) Minor studies in aggression: VI. Correlation of lynchings with economic indices. *Journal of Psychology*, 9, 301–10.

Howard, J.W. and Rothbart, M. (1980) Social categorization and memory for ingroup and outgroup behaviour. *Journal of Personality and Social Psychology*, 38, 301–10.

Howell, J.M. and Avolio, B.J. (1993) Transformational leadership, transactional leadership, locus of control, and support for innovation: key predictors of consolidated business unit performance. *Journal of Applied Psychology*, 78, 891–902.

Howell, J.M. and Frost, P.J. (1989) A laboratory study of charismatic leadership. *Organizational Behavior and Human Decision Processes*, 43, 243–69.

Ingham, A.G., Levinger, G., Graves, J. and Peckham, V. (1974) The Ringelmann effect: studies of group size and group performance. *Journal of Experimental Social Psychology*, 10, 371–84.

Institute for Social Research (1991–2) *Newsletter*, 17(2), 5.

Isenberg, D.J. (1986) Group polarization: a critical review and meta-analysis. *Journal of Personality and Social Psychology*, 50, 1141–51.

Islam, M.R. and Hewstone, M. (1993) Dimensions of contract as predictors of intergroup anxiety, perceived outgroup variability and outgroup attitude: an integrative model. *Personality and Social Psychology Bulletin*, 19, 700–10.

Jackson, L.A., Sullivan, L.A., Harmish, R. and Hodge, C.N. (1996) Achieving positive social identity: social mobility, social creativity, and permeability of group boundaries. *Journal of Personality and Social Psychology*, 70, 241–54.

Jackson, S.F. and Schuler, R.S. (1985) A meta-analysis and conceptual critique of research on role ambiguity and role conflict in work settings. *Organizational Behavior and Human Decision Processes*, 36, 16–78.

Jacobson, S.R. (1973) Individual and group responses to confinement in a skyjacked plane. *American Journal of Orthopsychiatry*, 43, 459–69.

Jaffe, Y. and Yinon, Y. (1979) Retaliatory aggression in individuals and groups. *European Journal of Social Psychology*, 9, 177–86.

James, K. and Greenberg, J. (1989) In-group salience, intergroup comparison, and individual performance and self-esteem. *Personality and Social Psychology Bulletin*, 15, 604–16.

Janis, I.L. (1982) *Victims of Groupthink*, 2nd edn. Boston, MA: Houghton Mifflin.

Janis, I.L. and Mann, L. (1977) *Decision Making*. New York: Free Press.

Johnson, D.W., Maruyama, G., Johnson, R., Nelson, D. and Skon, L. (1981) Effects of cooperative, competitive, and individualistic goal structures on achievement: a meta-analysis. *Psychological Bulletin*, 89, 47–62.

Johnson, D.W., Johnson, R. and Maruyana, G. (1984) Group interdependence and interpersonal attraction in heterogeneous classrooms: a meta-analysis, in Miller, N. and Brewer, M.B. (eds) *Group in Contact: The Psychology of Desegregation*. Orlando, FL: Academic Press.

Johnson, R.D. and Downing, L.L. (1979) Deindividuation and valence of cues: effects on prosocial and antisocial behaviour. *Journal of Personality and Social Psychology*, 37, 1532–8.

Jones, E.E., Wood, G.C. and Quattrone, G.A. (1981) Perceived variability of personal characteristics in ingroups and outgroups: the role of knowledge and evaluation. *Personality and Social Psychology Bulletin*, 7, 523–8.

Jost, J.T. and Banaji, M.R. (1994) The role of stereotyping in system justification and the production of false consciousness. *British Journal of Social Psychology*, 33, 1–27.

Julian, J.W. and Perry, F.A. (1967) Cooperation contrasted with intragroup and intergroup competition. *Sociometry*, 30, 79–90.

Julian, J.W., Bishop, D.W. and Fiedler, F.E. (1966) Quasi-therapeutic effects of intergroup competition. *Journal of Personality and Social Psychology*, 3, 321–7.

Jussim, L. (1989) Teacher expectations: self-fulfilling prophecies, perceptual biases, and accuracy. *Journal of Personality and Social Psychology*, 57, 469–80.

Kahn, A. and Ryen, A.H. (1972) Factors influencing the bias towards one's own group. *International Journal of Group Tensions*, 2, 33–50.

Kanter, R.M. (1977) Some effects of proportions on group life: skewed sex ratios and responses to token women. *American Journal of Sociology*, 82, 965–90.

Karau, S.J. and Hart, J.W. (1998) Group cohesiveness and social loafing: effects of a social interaction manipulation on individual motivation within groups. *Group Dynamics*, 2, 185–91.

Karau, S.J. and Williams, K.D. (1993) Social loafing: a meta-analytic review and theoretical integration. *Journal of Personality and Social Psychology*, 65, 681–706.

Karlins, M., Coffman, T.L. and Walters, G. (1969) On the fading of social stereotypes: studies in three generations of college students. *Journal of Personality and Social Psychology*, 13, 1–16.

Katz, D. and Braly, K. (1993) Racial stereotypes of one hundred college students. *Journal of Abnormal and Social Psychology*, 28, 280–90.

Kelly, C. (1989) Political identity and perceived intragroup homogeneity. *British Journal of Social Psychology*, 28, 239–250.

383

Kelly, C. (1990) Social identity and levels of influence: when a political minority fails. *British Journal of Social Psychology*, 29, 289–301.

Kelly, C. and Breinlinger, S. (1996) *The Social Psychology of Collective Action*. London: Taylor & Francis.

Kennedy, J. (1982) Middle LPC leaders and the contingency model of leader effectiveness. *Organizational Behavior and Human Performance*, 30, 1–14.

Kenny, D. (1975) Cross-lagged panel correlation: a test for spuriousness. *Psychological Bulletin*, 82, 887–903.

Kerr, N.L. (1983) Motivation losses in small groups: a social dilemma analysis. *Journal of Personality and Social Psychology*, 45, 819–28.

Kerr, N. and Bruun, S. (1981) Ringlemann revisited: alternative explanations for the social loafing effect. *Personality and Social Psychology Bulletin*, 7, 224–31.

Kerr, N.L., Davis, J.H., Meek, D. and Rissman, A.K. (1975) Group position as a function of member attitudes: choice shift effects from the perspective of social decision scheme theory. *Journal of Personality and Social Psychology*, 31, 574–93.

Kirchler, E.A., Davis, J.H. (1986) The influence of member status differences and taste type on group consensus and member position change. *Journal of Personality and Social Psychology*, 51, 83–91.

Kirchler, E., Pombeni, M.L. and Palmonari, A. (1991) Sweet sixteen . . . adolescents' problems and the peer group as source of support. *European Journal of Psychology of Education*, 6, 393–410.

Kirkhart, R.O. (1963) Minority group identification and group leadership. *Journal of Social Psychology*, 59, 111–17.

Klandermans, B. (1997) *The Social Psychology of Protest*. Oxford: Blackwell.

Köhler, O. (1926) Kraftleistungen bei Einzel-und Gruppenarbeit. *Industrielle Psychotechnik*, 3, 274–82.

Köhler, O. (1927) Über den Gruppencrirkungsgrad der menschlichen Körperarbeit und die Bedingung optimaler kollektivkraftreaktion. *Industrielle Psychotechnik*, 4, 209–26.

Koomen, W. and Fränkel, E.G. (1992) Effects of experienced discrimination and different forms of relative deprivation among Surinamese, a Dutch ethnic minority group. *Journal of Community and Applied Social Psychology*, 2, 63–71.

Kramer, R.M. (1998) Revisiting the Bay of Pigs and Vietnam decisions 25 years later: how well has the groupthink hypothesis stood the test of time? *Organizational Behavior and Human Decision Processes*, 73, 236–71.

Kravitz, D.A. and Martin, B. (1986) Ringlemann rediscovered: the original article. *Journal of Personality and Social Psychology*, 50, 936–41.

Krueger, J. and Clement, R.W. (1994) Memory-based judgements about multiple categories: a revision and extension of Tajfel's Accentuation Theory. *Journal of Personality and Social Psychology*, 67, 35–47.

Kruglanski, A.W. and Mackie, D.M. (1990) Majority and minority influence: a judgmental process analysis, in Stroebe, W. and Hewstone, M. (eds) *European Review of Social Psychology*, vol. 1. Chichester: Wiley.

Kuhn, M.H. and McPartland, T.S. (1954) An empirical investigation of self attitudes. *American Sociological Review*, 19, 68–76.

La Freniere, P., Strayer, F.F. and Gauthier, R. (1984) The emergence of same-sex affiliative preferences among pre-school peers: a developmental/ethological perspective. *Child Development*, 55, 1958–65.

Lamm, H. and Trommsdorff, G. (1973) Group versus individual performance on tasks requiring ideational proficiency: a review. *European Journal of Social Psychology*, 3, 361–88.

Langer, E.J., Fiske, S., Taylor, S.E. and Chanowitz, B. (1976) Stigma, staring, and discomfort: a novel-stimulus hypothesis. *Journal of Experimental Social Psychology*, 12, 451–63.

Langlois, J.H., Roggman, L.A., Casey, R.J., Ritter, J.M., Rieser-Donner, L.A. and Jenkins, V.Y. (1987) Infant preferences for attractive faces: rudiments of a stereotype. *Developmental Psychology*, 23, 363–9.

Langlois, J.H., Ritter, J.M., Roggman, L.A. and Vaugh, L.S. (1991) Facial diversity and infant preference for attractive faces. *Developmental Psychology*, 27, 79–84.

Larson, J.R., Foster-Fishman, P.G. and Keys, C.B. (1994) Discussion of shared and unshared information in decision-making groups. *Journal of Personality and Social Psychology*, 69, 446–61.

Latané, B. (1981) The psychology of social impact. *American Psychologist*, 36, 343–56.

Latané, B. and Wolf, S. (1981) The social impact of majorities and minorities. *Psychological Review*, 88, 438–53.

Latané, B., Williams, K. and Harkins, S. (1979) Many hands make light the work: the causes and consequences of social loafing. *Journal of Personality and Social Psychology*, 37, 822–32.

Laughlin, P.R. (1980) Social combination processes of cooperative problem-solving groups on verbal intellective tasks, in Fishbein, M. (ed.) *Progress in Social Psychology*, vol. 1. Hillsdale, NJ: Lawrence Erlbaum.

Laughlin, P.R. (1996) Group decision making and collective induction, pp. 61–80 in Witte, E.H. and Davis, J.H. (eds) *Understanding Group Behavior*, vol. 1, *Consensual Action by Small Groups*. Mahwah, NJ: Lawrence Erlbaum.

Le Bon, G. (1896) *The Crowd: A Study of the Popular Mind*. London: T. Fisher Unwin.

Lea, M. and Spears, R. (1991) Computer mediated communication, deindividuation and group decision-making. *International Journal of Man–Machine Studies*, 34, 283–301.

Leavitt, H.J. (1951) Some effects of certain communication patterns on group performance. *Journal of Abnormal and Social Psychology*, 46, 38–50.

Lemaine, G. (1966) Inegalité, comparaison et incomparabilité: esquisse d'une théorie de l'originalité sociale. *Bulletin de Psychologie*, 20, 1–9.

Lemyre, L. and Smith, P.M. (1985) Intergroup discrimination and self esteem in the Minimal Group Paradigm. *Journal of Personality and Social Psychology*, 49, 660–70.

Lepore, L. and Brown, R. (1997) Category activation and stereotype accessibility: is prejudice inevitable? *Journal of Personality and Social Psychology*, 72, 275–87.

Lerner, M.J. (1980) *The Belief in a Just World: A Fundamental Delusion*. New York: Plenum.

Levine, J.M. and Green, S.M. (1984) Acquisition of relative performance information: the roles of intrapersonal and interpersonal comparison. *Personality and Social Psychology Bulletin*, 10, 385–93.

Levine, J.M. and Moreland, R. (1994) Group socialization: theory and research, pp. 305–36 in Stroebe, W. and Hewstone, M. (eds) *European Review of Social Psychology*, vol. 5. Chichester: Wiley.

Lewicki, R.D. (1981) Organizational seduction: building commitment to organizations. *Organizational Dynamics*, 10, 5–21.

Lewin, K. (1948) *Resolving Social Conflicts*. New York: Harper & Row.

Lewin, K. (1952) *Field Theory in Social Science*. New York: Harper & Row.

Lewin, K. (1965) Group decision and social change, in Proshansky, H. and Seidenberg, B. (eds) *Basic Studies in Social Psychology*. New York: Holt, Rinehart and Winston.

Leyens, J.-P., Yzerbyt, V.Y. and Schadron, G. (1994) *Stereotypes and Social Cognition*. London: Sage.

Liebkind, K. and McAlister, A. (1999) Extended contact through peer modelling to promote tolerance in Finland. *European Journal of Social Psychology*, 29, 765–800.

Lind, E.A., Kulik, C.A., Ambrose, M. and de Vera Park, M.V. (1993) Individual and corporate dispute resolution: using procedural fairness as a decision heuristic. *Administrative Science Quarterly*, 38, 224–51.

Linville, P.W., Fischer, F.W. and Salovey, P. (1989) Perceived distributions of characteristics of ingroup and outgroup members: empirical evidence and a computer simulation. *Journal of Personality and Social Psychology*, 42, 193–211.

Lippitt, R. and White, R. (1943) The 'social climate' of children's groups, in Barker, R.G., Kounin, J. and Wright, H. (eds) *Child Behaviour and Development*. New York: McGraw-Hill.

Lippman, W. (1922) *Public Opinion*. New York: Harcourt Brace.

Locke, V., Macleod, C. and Walker, I. (1994) Automatic and controlled activation of stereotypes: individual differences associated with prejudice. *British Journal of Social Psychology*, 33, 29–46.

Lockheed, M.E. (1985) Sex and social influence: a meta-analysis guided by theory, in Berger, J. and Zelditch, M. (eds) *Status, Rewards and Influence*. San Francisco, CA: Jossey-Bass.

Locksley, A., Hepburn, C. and Ortiz, V. (1982) On the effects of social stereotypes on judgments of individuals: a comment on Grant and Holmes' 'The integration of implicit personality theory schemes and stereotypic images'. *Social Psychology Quarterly*, 45, 270–3.

Long, K.M., Spears, R. and Manstead, A.S.R. (1994) The influence of personal and collective self-esteem on strategies of social differentiation. *British Journal of Social Psychology*, 33, 313–29.

Lorge, I. and Solomon, H. (1955) Two models of group behaviour in the solution of eureka-type problems. *Psychometrika*, 20, 139–48.

Lorge, I., Fox, D., Davitz, J. and Brenner, M. (1958) A survey of studies contrasting the quality of group performance and individual performance. *Psychological Bulletin*, 55, 337–72.

Lott, A.J. and Lott, B.E. (1961) Group cohesiveness, communication level, and conformity. *Journal of Abnormal and Social Psychology*, 62, 408–12.

Lott, A.J. and Lott, B.E. (1965) Group cohesiveness as interpersonal attraction. *Psychological Bulletin*, 64, 259–309.

Maass, A. (1999) Linguistic intergroup bias: stereotype-perpetuation through language, pp. 79–121 in Zanna, M.P. (ed.) *Advances in Experimental Social Psychology*, vol. 31. San Diego, CA: Academic Press.

Maass, A. and Clark, R.D. (1983) Internalization versus compliance: differential processes underlying minority influence and conformity. *European Journal of Social Psychology*, 13, 197–215.

Maass, A. and Clark, R.D. (1984) Hidden impact of minorities: fifteen years of minority influence research. *Psychological Bulletin*, 95, 428–50.

Maass, A. and Clark, R.D. (1986) Conversion theory and simultaneous majority/minority influence: can reactance offer an alternative explanation? *European Journal of Social Psychology*, 16, 305–9.

Maass, A., Clark, R.D. and Haberkorn, G. (1982) The effects of differential ascribed category membership and norms on minority influence. *European Journal of Social Psychology*, 12, 89–104.

Maass, A., Salvi, D., Arcuri, L. and Swim, G.R. (1989) Language use in intergroup contexts: the linguistic intergroup bias. *Journal of Personality and Social Psychology*, 57, 981–93.

Maass, A., Corvino, P. and Arcuri, L. (1994) Linguistic intergroup bias and the mass media. *Revue de Psychologie Sociale*, 1, 31–43.

387

Maass, A., Milesi, A., Zabbini, S. and Stahlberg, D. (1995) Linguistic intergroup bias: differential expectancies or ingroup protection. *Journal of Personality and Social Psychology*, 68, 116–26.

Maass, A., Ceccarelli, R. and Rudin, S. (1996) Linguistic intergroup bias: evidence for ingroup protective motivation. *Journal of Personality and Social Psychology*, 71, 512–26.

Maccoby, E. and Jacklin, C. (1987) Gender segregation in childhood. *Advances in Child Development and Behaviour*, 20, 239–87.

Mackie, D.M. (1986) Social identification effects in group polarization. *Journal of Personality and Social Psychology*, 50, 720–8.

Mackie, D.M. (1987) Systematic and non systematic processing of majority and minority persuasive communications. *Journal of Personality and Social Psychology*, 53, 41–52.

Mackie, D. and Cooper, J. (1984) Attitude polarization: effects of group membership. *Journal of Personality and Social Psychology*, 46, 575–85.

Macpherson, W. (1999) *The Stephen Lawrence Inquiry*. London: The Stationery Office.

Macrae, N., Stangor, C. and Hewstone, M. (1996) (eds) *Stereotypes and Stereotyping*. London: Guildford Press.

Major, B. (1994) From social inequality to personal entitlement; the role of social comparisons, legitimacy appraisals and group membership, pp. 293–355 in Zanna, M.P. (ed.) *Advances in Experimental Social Psychology*, vol. 26. San Diego, CA: Academic Press.

Major, B. and Forcey, B. (1985) Social comparisons and pay evaluations: preferences for same-sex and same-job wage comparisons. *Journal of Experimental Social Psychology*, 21, 393–405.

Mann, L. (1980) Cross-cultural studies of small groups, in Triandis, H.C. and Brislin, R.W. (eds) *Handbook of Cross-Cultural Psychology*, vol. 5. New York: Allyn & Bacon.

Mann, R.D. (1961) Dimensions of individual performance in small groups under task and social-emotional conditions. *Journal of Abnormal and Social Psychology*, 62, 674–82.

Maras, P. and Brown, R. (1996) Effects of contact on children's attitudes toward disability: a longitudinal study. *Journal of Applied Social Psychology*, 26, 2113–34.

Marcus-Newhall, A., Miller, N., Holtz, R. and Brewer, M.B. (1993) Crosscutting category membership with role assignment: a means of reducing intergroup bias. *British Journal of Social Psychology*, 32, 125–46.

Marquart, D.I. (1955) Group problem solving. *Journal of Social Psychology*, 41, 102–13.

Martin, J., Brickman, P. and Murray, A. (1984) Moral outrage and pragmatism: explanations for collective action. *Journal of Experimental Social Psychology*, 20, 484–96.

Martin, R. (1988) Ingroup and outgroup minorities: differential impact upon public and private responses. *European Journal of Social Psychology*, 18, 39–52.

Martin, R. (1998) Majority and minority influence using the after image paradigm: a series of attempted replications. *Journal of Experimental Social Psychology*, 34, 1–26.

Matsui, T., Kakuyama, T. and Onglatco, M.U. (1987) Effects of goals and feedback on performance in groups. *Journal of Applied Psychology*, 72, 407–15.

McDougall, W. (1920) *The Group Mind*. Cambridge: Cambridge University Press.

McGarty, C. and Penny, R.E.C. (1988) Categorization, accentuation and social judgement. *British Journal of Social Psychology*, 27, 147–57.

McGrath, J.E. (1984) *Groups: Interaction and Performance*. New York: Prentice Hall.

McGrew, W.J. (1972) Aspects of social development in nursery school children, with emphasis on introduction to the group, in Blurton-Jones, N. (ed.) *Ethological Studies of Child Development*. London: Cambridge University Press.

Mead, G.H. (1934) *On Social Psychology*. Chicago, IL: University of Chicago Press.

Mead, M. (1935) *Sex and Temperament in Three Primitive Societies*. New York: Morrow.

Merei, F. (1949) Group leadership and institutionalization. *Human Relations*, 2, 23–39.

Merton, R.K. (1957) *Social Theory and Social Structure*. New York: Free Press.

Milgram, S. (1963) Behavioral study of obedience. *Journal of Abnormal Social Psychology*, 67, 371–8.

Milgram, S. (1964) Group pressure and action against a person. *Journal of Abnormal Social Psychology*, 69, 137–43.

Milgram, S. (1965) Liberating effects of group pressure. *Journal of Personality and Social Psychology*, 1, 127–34.

Milgram, S. and Toch, H. (1969) Collective behaviour: crowds and social movements, in Lindzey, G. and Aronson, E. (eds) *Handbook of Social Psychology*, 2nd edn, vol. 4. Reading, MA: Addison-Wesley.

Milgram, S., Bickman, L. and Berkowitz, L. (1969) Note on the drawing power of crowds of different size. *Journal of Personality and Social Psychology*, 13, 79–82.

Miller, A. and Bolce, L. (1979) Reply to Crosby. *American Political Science Review*, 73, 818–22.

Miller, A., Bolce, L. and Halligan, M. (1977) The J-curve theory and the Black urban riots: an empirical test of progressive relative deprivation theory. *American Political Science Review*, 71, 964–82.

Miller, N. and Brewer, M.B. (eds) (1984) *Groups in Contact: The Psychology of Desegregation*. New York: Academic Press.

Miller, N. and Davidson-Podgorny, F. (1987) Theoretical models of intergroup relations and the use of co-operative teams as an intervention for desegregated settings, in Hendrick, C. (ed.) *Group Process and Intergroup Relations: Review of Personality and Social Psychology*, vol. 9.

Miller, N., Brewer, M.B. and Edwards, K. (1985) Cooperative interaction in desegregated settings: a laboratory analogue. *Journal of Social Issues*, 41, 63–79.

Miller, N.E. (1948) Theory and experiment relating psychoanalytic displacement to stimulus-response generalization. *Journal of Abnormal and Social Psychology*, 43, 155–78.

Miller, N.E. and Bugelski, R. (1948) Minor studies in aggression: the influence of frustrations imposed by the ingroup on attitudes toward out-groups. *Journal of Psychology*, 25, 437–42.

Milner, D. (1975) *Children and Race*. Harmondsworth: Penguin.

Minard, R.D. (1952) Race relationships in the Pocahontas coal field. *Journal of Social Issues*, 8, 29–44.

Minuchin, S. (1974) *Families and Family Therapy*. Cambridge, MA: Harvard University Press.

Mischel, W. (1968) *Personality and Assessment*. New York: Wiley.

Moede, W. (1920–21) Einzel und Gruppenarbeit. *Praktische Psychologie*, 2, 71–81.

Monteil, J.-M., and Huguet, P. (1999) *Social Context and Cognitive Performance*. Hove: Psychology Press.

Moorhead, G. and Montanari, J.R. (1986) An empirical investigation of the groupthink phenomenon. *Human Relations*, 39, 399–410.

Moreland, R.L. (1985) Social categorization and the assimilation of 'new' group members. *Journal of Personality and Social Psychology*, 48, 1173–90.

Moreland, R.L. and Levine, J.M. (1982) Socialization in small groups: temporal changes in individual–group relations, in Berkowitz, L. (ed.) *Advances in Experimental Social Psychology*, vol. 15. New York: Academic Press.

Morland, J.K. (1969) Race awareness among American and Hong Kong Chinese children. *American Journal of Sociology*, 75, 360–74.

Moscovici, S. (1976) *Social Influence and Social Change*. London: Academic Press.

Moscovici, S. (1979) A rejoinder. *British Journal of Social Psychology*, 18, 181.

Moscovici, S. (1980) Towards a theory of conversion behavior, in Berkowitz, L. (ed.) *Advances in Experimental Social Psychology*, vol. 13. San Diego, CA: Academic Press.

Moscovici, S. and Lage, E. (1976) Studies in social influence: III. Majority vs minority influence in a group. *European Journal of Social Psychology*, 6, 149–74.

Moscovici, S. and Personnaz, B. (1980) Studies in social influence: V. Minority influence and conversion behaviour in a perceptual task. *Journal of Experimental Social Psychology*, 16, 270–82.

Moscovici, S. and Personnaz, B. (1986) Studies on latent influence by the spectrometer method: I. The impact of psychologization in the case of conversion by a minority or a majority. *European Journal of Social Psychology*, 16, 345–60.

Moscovici, S. and Personnaz, B. (1991) Studies in social influence VI: is Lenin orange or red? Imagery and social influence. *European Journal of Social Psychology*, 21, 101–18.

Moscovici, S. and Zavalloni, M. (1969) The group as a polarizer of attitudes. *Journal of Personality and Social Psychology*, 12, 125–35.

Moscovici, S., Lage, E. and Naffrechoux, M. (1969) Influence of a consistent minority on the responses of a majority in a colour perception task. *Sociometry*, 32, 365–79.

Mucchi-Faina, A., Maass, A. and Volpato, C. (1991) Social influence: the role of originality. *European Journal of Social Psychology*, 21, 183–98.

Mugny, G. (1982) *The Power of Minorities*. London: Academic Press.

Mullen, B. (1986) Atrocity as a function of lynch mob composition: a self-attention perspective. *Personality and Social Psychology Bulletin*, 12, 187–97.

Mullen, B. and Copper, C. (1994) The relation between group cohesiveness and performance: an integration. *Psychological Bulletin*, 115, 210–27.

Mullen, B., Johnson, C. and Salas, E. (1991) Productivity loss in brainstorming groups: a meta-analytic integration. *Basic and Applied Social Psychology*, 12, 3–23.

Mullen, B., Brown, R. and Smith, C. (1992) Ingroup bias as a function of salience, relevance, and status: an integration. *European Journal of Social Psychology*, 22, 103–22.

Mummendey, A. and Otten, S. (1998) Positive–negative asymmetry in social discrimination, in Stroebe, W. and Hewstone, M. (eds) *European Review of Social Psychology*, vol. 8. Chichester: Wiley.

Mummendey, A. and Schreiber, H.-J. (1984) 'Different' just means 'better': some obvious and some hidden pathways to in-group favouritism. *British Journal of Social Psychology*, 23, 363–7.

Mummendey, A., Simon, B., Dietzw, C., Grünert, M., Haeger, G., Kessler, S., Lettgen, S. and Schäferhoff, S. (1992) Categorization is not enough:

intergroup discrimination in negative outcome allocations. *Journals of Experimental Social Psychology*, 28, 125–44.

Mummendey, A., Kessler, T., Klink, A., and Mielke, R. (1999) Strategies to cope with negative social identity: predictions by social identity theory and relative deprivation theory. *Journal of Personality and Social Psychology*, 76, 229–45.

Myers, A. (1962) Team competition, success, and the adjustment of group members. *Journal of Abnormal and Social Psychology*, 65, 325–32.

Myers, D.G. (1978) Polarizing effects of social comparison. *Journal of Experimental Social Psychology*, 14, 554–63.

Myers, D.G. and Lamm, H. (1976) The group polarization phenomenon. *Psychological Bulletin*, 83, 602–27.

Nelson, T.E., Beiernat, M. and Manis, M. (1990) Everyday base rates (sex stereotypes): potent and resilient. *Journal of Personality and Social Psychology*, 59, 664–75.

Nemeth, C. (1986) Differential contributions of majority and minority influence. *Psychological Review*, 93, 23–32.

Nemeth, C.J. and Kwan, J.L. (1985) Originality of word associations as a function of majority vs minority influence. *Social Psychology Quarterly*, 48, 277–82.

Nemeth, C.J. and Wachtler, J. (1983) Creative problem solving as a result of majority vs minority influence. *European Journal of Social Psychology*, 13, 45–55.

Nemeth, C., Mayseless, O., Sherman, J. and Brown, Y. (1990) Exposure to dissent and recall of information. *Journal of Personality and Social Psychology*, 58, 429–37.

New Earnings Survey (1998) London: Office of National Statistics.

Newcomb, T.M. (1961) *The Acquaintance Process*. New York: Holt, Rinehart and Winston.

Newcomb, T.M., Koenig, K.E., Flacks, R. and Warwick, D.P. (1967) *Persistence and Change: Bennington College and its Students after 25 Years*. New York: Wiley.

Ng, S.H. and Cram, F. (1988) Intergroup bias by defensive and offensive groups in majority and minority conditions. *Journal of Personality and Social Psychology*, 55, 749–57.

Niedenthal, P.M., Cantor, N. and Kihlstrom, J.F. (1985) Prototype matching: a strategy for social decision making. *Journal of Personality and Social Psychology*, 48, 575–84.

Nosanchuk, T.A. and Erickson, B.H. (1985) How high is up? Calibrating social comparison in the real world. *Journal of Personality and Social Psychology*, 48, 624–34.

Nowak, A., Szamrej, J.A., and Latané, B. (1990) From private attitude to public opinion: a dynamic theory of social impact. *Psychological Review*, 97, 362–76.

O'Reilly, C.A. and Caldwell, D.F. (1985) The impact of normative social influence and cohesiveness on task perceptions and attitudes: a social information processing approach. *Journal of Occupational Psychology*, 58, 193–206.

Oakes, P.J. (1994) The effects of fit versus novelty on the salience of social categories: a response to Biernat and Vescio (1993). *Journal of Experimental Social Psychology*, 30, 390–8.

Oakes, P.J. and Turner, J.C. (1980) Social categorization and intergroup behaviour: does minimal intergroup discrimination make social identity more positive? *European Journal of Social Psychology*, 10, 295–302.

Oakes, P.J. and Turner, J.C. (1986) Distinctiveness and the salience of social category membership: is there an automatic perceptual bias towards novelty? *European Journal of Social Psychology*, 16, 325–44.

Oakes, P.J., Haslam, A. and Turner, J.C. (1994) *Stereotyping and Social Reality*. Oxford: Blackwell.

Oakes, P.J., Haslam, S.A., Morrison, B. and Grace, D. (1995) Becoming an ingroup: re-examining the impact of familiarity on perceptions of group homogeneity. *Social Psychology Quarterly*, 58, 52–61.

Olson, J.M., Roese, N.J., Meen, J. and Robertson, D.J. (1995) The preconditions and consequences of relative deprivation: two field studies. *Journal of Applied Social Psychology*, 25, 944–64.

Orwell, G. (1962) *The Road to Wigan Pier*. Harmondsworth: Penguin.

Osborn, A.F. (1957) *Applied Imagination*. New York: Scribner.

Ostrom, T.M. and Sedikides, C. (1992) Outgroup homogeneity effects in natural and minimal groups. *Psychological Bulletin*, 112, 536–52.

Otten, S., Mummendey, A., and Blanz, M. (1996) Intergroup discrimination in positive and negative outcome allocations. *Personality and Social Psychology Bulletin*, 22, 568–81.

Park, B., Judd, C.M. and Ryan, C.S. (1991) Social categorization and the representation of variability information, in Stroebe, W. and Hewstone, M. (eds) *European Review of Social Psychology*, vol. 2. Chichester: Wiley.

Parsons, T. and Bales, R.F. (1956) *Family: Socialization and Interaction Process*. Glencoe, MN: Free Press.

Parsons, T., Bales, R.F. and Shils, E.A. (eds) (1953) *Working Papers in the Theory of Action*. New York: Free Press.

Pastore, N. (1952) The role of arbitrariness in the frustration–aggression hypothesis. *Journal of Abnormal and Social Psychology*, 47, 728–31.

Paulus, P.B. and Dzindolet, M.J. (1993) Social influence processes in group brainstorming. *Journal of Personality and Social Psychology*, 64, 575–86.

Pavelchak, M.A., Moreland, R.L. and Levine, J.M. (1986) Effects of prior group memberships on subsequent reconnaissance activities. *Journal of Personality and Social Psychology*, 50, 56–66.

Pendry, L.F. and Macrae, N. (1996) What the disinterested perceiver overlooks: goal-directed social categorization. *Personality and Social Psychology Bulletin*, 22, 249–56.

Perdue, C.W. and Gurtman, M.B. (1990) Evidence for the automaticity of ageism. *Journal of Experimental Social Psychology*, 26, 199–216.

Perdue, C.W., Dovidio, J.F., Gurtman, M.B. and Tyler, R.B. (1990) 'Us' and 'Them': social categorization and the process of intergroup bias. *Journal of Personality and Social Psychology*, 59, 475–86.

Perez, J.A., Mugny, G. and Moscovici, S. (1986) Les effets pardoxaux du deni dans l'influence sociale. *Cahiers de Psychologie Sociale*, 32, 1–14.

Perlmutter, H.V. and de Montmollin, G. (1952) Group learning of nonsense syllables. *Journal of Abnormal and Social Psychology*, 47, 762–9.

Personnaz, B. (1981) Study in social influence using the spectrometer method: dynamics of the phenomena of conversion and covertness in perceptual responses. *European Journal of Social Psychology*, 11, 431–8.

Peterson, R.S. (1997) A directive leadership style in group decision making can be both virtue and vice: evidence from elite and experimental groups. *Journal of Personality and Social Psychology*, 72, 1107–21.

Peterson, R.S., Owens, P.D., Tetlock, P.E., Fan, E.T. and Martorana, P. (1998) Group dynamics in top management teams: groupthink, vigilance, and alternative models of organizational failure and success. *Organizational Behavior and Human Decision Processes*, 73, 272–305.

Pettigrew, T.F. (1971) *Racially Separate or Together?* New York: McGraw-Hill.

Pettigrew, T.F. (1998) Intergroup contact theory. *Annual Review of Psychology*, 49, 65–85.

Phillips, E.L., Shenker, S. and Revitz, P. (1951) The assimilation of the new child into the group. *Psychiatry*, 14, 319–25.

Platow, M.J., Hoar, S., Reid, S., Harley, K. and Morrison, D. (1997) Endorsement of distributively fair and unfair leaders in interpersonal and intergroup situations. *European Journal of Social Psychology*, 27, 465–94.

Pratkanis, A.R., Greenwald, A.G., Leippe, M.R. and Baumgardner, M.H. (1988) In search of reliable persuasion effects: III. The sleeper effect is dead. Long live the sleeper effect. *Journal of Personality and Social Psychology*, 54, 203–18.

Putallaz, M. and Gottman, J.M. (1981) An interactional model of children's entry into peer groups. *Child Development*, 52, 986–94.

Pyszczynski, T., Greenberg, J. and LaPrelle, J. (1985) Social comparisons after success and failure: biased search for information consistent with

394

a self serving conclusion. *Journal of Experimental Social Psychology*, 21, 195–211.

Quattrone, G.A. (1986) On the perception of a group's variability, in Worchel, S. and Austin, W. (eds) *Social Psychology of Intergroup Relations*. Chicago, IL: Nelson.

Rabbie, J.M. and Bekkers, F. (1978) Threatened leadership and intergroup competition. *European Journal of Social Psychology*, 8, 9–20.

Rabbie, J.M. and Horwitz, M. (1969) Arousal of ingroup–outgroup bias by a chance win or loss. *Journal of Personality and Social Psychology*, 13, 269–77.

Rabbie, J.M. and Horwitz, M. (1988) Categories versus groups as explanatory concepts in intergroup relations. *European Journal of Social Psychology*, 18, 117–23.

Rabbie, J.M., Schot, J.C. and Visser, L. (1989) Social identity theory: a conceptual and empirical critique from the perspective of a behavioural interaction model. *European Journal of Social Psychology*, 19, 171–202.

Radloff, R. (1966) Social comparison and ability evaluation. *Journal of Experimental Social Psychology, Supplement*, 1, 6–26.

Reicher, S.D. (1984a) The St Pauls riot: an explanation of the limits of crowd action in terms of a social identity model. *European Journal of Social Psychology*, 14, 1–21.

Reicher, S.D. (1984b) Social influence in the crowd: attitudinal and behavioural effects of deindividuation in conditions of high and low group salience. *British Journal of Social Psychology*, 23, 341–50.

Reicher, S.D. (1986) Contact, action and racialization: some British evidence, in Hewstone, M. and Brown, R.J. (eds) *Groups in Contract and Conflict*. London: Basil Blackwell.

Reicher, S. and Potter, J. (1985) Psychological theory as intergroup perspective: a comparative analysis of 'scientific' and 'lay' accounts of crowd events. *Human Relations*, 38, 167–89.

Reid, F.J.M. and Sumiga, L. (1984) Attitudinal politics in intergroup behaviour: interpersonal vs. intergroup determinants of attitude change. *British Journal of Social Psychology*, 23, 335–40.

Rice, R.W. (1978) Construct validity of the least preferred co-worker score. *Psychological Bulletin*, 85, 1199–237.

Ringelmann, M. (1913) Recherches sur les moteurs animés: travail de l'homme. *Annales de l'Institut National Agronomique*, 2nd series, 12, 1–40.

Rizzo, J.R., House, R.J. and Lirtzmam, S.I. (1970) Role conflict and ambiguity in complex organizations. *Administrative Science Quarterly*, 15, 150–63.

Roccas, R. and Schwartz, S.H. (1993) Effects of intergroup similarity on intergroup relations. *European Journal of Social Psychology*, 23, 581–95.

Rosenbaum, M.E. (1986) The repulsion hypothesis: on the nondevelopment of relationships. *Journal of Personality and Social Psychology*, 51, 1156–66.

Rosenbaum, M.E., Moore, D.L., Cotton, J.L., Cook, M.S., Hieser, R.A., Shover, M.N. and Gray, M.J. (1980) Group productivity and process: pure and mixed reward structures and task interdependence. *Journal of Personality and Social Psychology*, 39, 626–42.

Rosenberg, M. and Simmons, R.G. (1972) *Black and White Self-Esteem: The Urban School Child*. Washington, DC: American Sociological Association.

Rosenthal, R. and Jacobson, L. (1968) *Pygmalion in the Classroom: Teacher Expectations and Student Intellectual Development*. New York: Holt, Rinehart and Winston.

Rothbart, M. and John, O.P. (1985) Social categorization and behavioural episodes: a cognitive analysis of the effects of intergroup contact. *Journal of Social Issues*, 41, 81–104.

Rubin, M. and Hewstone, M. (1998) Social Identity Theory's self-esteem hypothesis: a review and some suggestions for clarification. *Review of Personality and Social Psychology*, 2, 40–62.

Runciman, W.G. (1966) *Relative Deprivation and Social Justice*. London: Routledge and Kegan Paul.

Rutter, D.R. (1987) *Communicating by Telephone*. Oxford: Pergamon.

Ryan, C.S. and Bogart, L.M. (1997) Development of new group members' ingroup and outgroup stereotypes: changes in perceived group variability and ethnocentrism. *Journal of Personality and Social Psychology*, 73, 719–32.

Ryen, A.H. and Kahn, A. (1975) Effects of intergroup orientation on group attitudes and proxemic behaviour. *Journal of Personal and Social Psychology*, 31, 302–10.

Sachdev, I. and Bourhis, R.Y. (1985) Social categorization and power differentials in group relations. *European Journal of Social Psychology*, 15, 415–34.

Sachdev, I. and Bourhis, R.Y. (1987) Status differentials and intergroup behaviour. *European Journal of Social Psychology*, 17, 277–93.

Sanders, G.S. and Baron, R.S. (1977) Is social comparison irrelevant for producing choice shifts? *Journal of Experimental Social Psychology*, 13, 303–14.

Sanna, L.J. (1992) Self-efficacy theory: implications for social facilitation and social loafing. *Journal of Personality and Social Psychology*, 62, 774–86.

Scarberry, N.C., Ratcliff, C.D., Lord, C.G., Lanicek, D.L. and Desforges, D.M. (1997) Effects of individuating information on the generalization part of Allport's Contact Hypothesis. *Personality and Social Psychology Bulletin*, 23, 1291–9.

Schachter, S. (1951) Deviation, rejection and communication. *Journal of Abnormal and Social Psychology*, 46, 190–207.

Schachter, S., Ellertson, N., McBride, D. and Gregory, D. (1951) An experimental study of cohesiveness and productivity. *Human Relations*, 4, 229–38.

Schachter, S., Nuttin, J., de Monchaux, C., Maucorps, D.H., Osmer, D., Duijker, J., Rommetveit, R. and Israel, J. (1954) Cross-cultural experiments on threat and rejection. *Human Relations*, 7, 403–39.

Schlenker, B.R. (1975) Liking for a group following an initiation: impression management or dissonance reduction. *Sociometry*, 38, 99–118.

Schofield, J.W. (1986) Black–white contact in desegregated schools, in Hewstone, M.R.C. and Brown, R.J. (eds) *Contact and Conflict in Intergroup Encounters*. Oxford: Blackwell.

Schriesheim, C.A., Tepper, B.J. and Tetrault, L.A. (1994) Least preferred co-worker score, situational control, and leadership effectiveness: a meta-analysis of contingency model performance predictions. *Journal of Applied Psychology*, 79, 561–73.

Schulz, R. and Decker, S. (1985) Long-term adjustment to physical disability. *Journal of Personality and Social Psychology*, 48, 1162–72.

Schwartz, S.H. (1994) Cultural dimensions of values: towards an understanding of national differences, in Kim, U., Triandis, H.C., Kagitcibasi, C., Choi, S.C. and Yoon, G. (eds) *Individualism and Collectivism Theory, Method and Applications*. Thousand Oaks, CA: Sage.

Scott, W.A. and Scott, R. (1981) Intercorrelations among structural properties of primary groups. *Journal of Personality and Social Psychology*, 41, 279–92.

Seago, D.W. (1947) Stereotypes: before Pearl Harbor and after. *Journal of Social Psychology*, 23, 55–63.

Semin, G. and Glendon, A.I. (1973) Polarization and the established group. *British Journal of Social and Clinical Psychology*, 12, 113–21.

Seta, J.J. (1982) The impact of comparison process on coactors' task performance. *Journal of Personality and Social Psychology*, 42, 281–91.

Sharan, S. (1990) *Cooperative Learning: Theory and Research*. New York: Praeger.

Shaw, Marjorie E. (1932) A comparison of individuals and small groups in the rational solution of complex problems. *American Journal of Psychology*, 44, 491–504.

Shaw, Marvin E. (1964) Communication networks, in Berkowitz, L. (ed.) *Advances in Experimental Social Psychology*, vol. 1. New York: Academic Press.

Shaw, Marvin E. (1976) *Group Dynamics*, 2nd edn. New York: McGraw-Hill.

Shaw, Marvin E. and Ashton, N. (1976) Do assembly bonus effects occur on disjunctive tasks? A test of Steiner's theory. *Bulletin of the Psychonomic Society*, 8, 469–71.

Shepperd, J.A. (1993) Productivity loss in performance groups: a motivation analysis. *Psychological Bulletin*, 113, 67–81.

Sherif, C.W., Kelly, M., Rodgers, H.L., Sarup, G. and Tittler, B.I. (1973) Personal involvement, social judgement and action. *Journal of Personality and Social Psychology*, 27, 311–28.

Sherif, M. (1936) *The Psychology of Social Norms*. New York: Harper & Row.

Sherif, M. (1966) *Group Conflict and Cooperation*. London: Routledge and Kegan Paul. Originally published as *In Common Predicament*. Boston, MA: Houghton Miffin.

Sherif, M. and Sherif, C.W. (1953) *Groups in Harmony and Tension: An Integration of Studies on Intergroup Relations*. New York: Octagon Books.

Sherif, M. and Sherif, C.W. (1964) *Reference Groups*. New York: Harper & Row.

Sherif, M. and Sherif, C.W. (1967) The adolescent in his group in its setting, in Sherif, M. (ed.) *Social Interaction*. Chicago, IL: Aldine.

Sherif, M. and Sherif, C.W. (1969) *Social Psychology*. New York: Harper & Row.

Sherif, M., White, B.J. and Harvey, O.J. (1955) Status in experimentally produced groups. *American Journal of Sociology*, 60, 370–9.

Sherif, M., Harvey, O.J., White, B.J., Hood, W.R. and Sherif, C.W. (1961) *Intergroup Conflict and Cooperation. The Robber's Cave Experiment*. Norman, OK: University of Oklahoma.

Siegel, A.E. and Siegel, S. (1957) Reference groups, membership groups, and attitude change. *Journal of Abnormal and Social Psychology*, 55, 360–4.

Siegel, J., Dubrovsky,V., Kiesler, S. and McGuire, T.W. (1986) Group process in computer mediated communication. *Organizational Behavior and Human Decision Processes*, 37, 157–87.

Simon, B. (1992) The perception of ingroup and outgroup homogeneity: reintroducing the intergroup context, in Stroebe, W. and Hewstone, M. (eds) *European Review of Social Psychology*, vol. 3. Chichester: Wiley.

Simon, B. and Brown, R.J. (1987) Perceived intragroup homogeneity in minority–majority contexts. *Journal of Personality and Social Psychology*, 53, 703–11.

Simon, B. and Pettigrew, T.F. (1990) Social identity and perceived group homogeneity. *European Journal of Social Psychology*, 20, 269–86.

Simon, B., Glässner-Bayerl, B. and Stratenwerth, I. (1991) Stereotyping and self stereotyping in a natural intergroup context: the case of heterosexual and homosexual men. *Social Psychology Quarterly*, 54, 252–66.

Simon, B., Loewy, M., Stürmer, S., Weber, U., Freytag, P., Habig, C., Kampmeier, C. (1998) Collective identification and social movement participation. *Journal of Personality and Social Psychology*, 74, 646–58.

Singh, R., Bohra, K.A. and Dalal, A.K. (1979) Favourableness of leadership situations studies with information integration theory. *European Journal of Social Psychology*, 9, 253–64.

Skowronski, J.J., Carlston, D.E. and Isham, J.T. (1993) Implicit versus explicit impression formation: the differing effects of overt labelling and covert priming on memory and impressions. *Journal of Experimental Social Psychology*, 29, 17–41.

Slaby, R.G. and Frey, K.S. (1975) Development of gender constancy and selective attention to same-sex models. *Child Development*, 46, 849–56.

Slater, P.E. (1955) Role differentiation in small groups. *American Sociological Review*, 20, 300–10.

Slater, P.E. (1961) Parental role differentiation. *American Journal of Sociology*, 67, 296–311.

Slavin, R.E. (1983) When does cooperative learning increase student achievement? *Psychological Bulletin*, 94, 429–45.

Slavin, R.E. (1985) Cooperative learning: applying contact theory in desegregated schools. *Journal of Social Issues*, 41, 45–62.

Smith, H.J., Spears, R. and Oyen, M. (1994) 'People like us': the influence of personal deprivation and group membership salience on justice evaluations. *Journal of Experimental Social Psychology*, 30, 277–99.

Smith, P.B. and Bond, M.H. (1993) *Social Psychology Across Cultures: Analysis and Perspectives*. New York: Harvester Wheatsheaf.

Smith, P.B., Misumi, J., Tayels, M., Peterson, M. and Bond, M. (1989) On the generality of leadership style measures across cultures. *Journal of Occupational Psychology*, 62, 97–109.

Smith, W.P., Davidson, E.S. and France, A.C. (1987) Social comparison and achievement orientation in children, in Masters, J.C. and Smith, W.P. (eds) *Social Comparison, Social Justice, and Relative Deprivation: Theoretical, Empirical and Policy Perspectives*. Hillsdale, NJ: Lawrence Erlbaum.

Snyder, C.R., Lassegard, M.A. and Ford, C.E. (1986) Distancing after group success and failure: basking in reflected glory and cutting off reflected failure. *Journal of Personality and Social Psychology*, 51, 382–8.

Snyder, M. (1981) On the self-perpetuating nature of social stereotypes, in Hamilton, D.L. (ed.) *Cognitive Processes in Stereotyping and Intergroup Behaviour*. New York: Lawrence Erlbaum.

Snyder, M. and Swann, W.B. (1978) Hypothesis-testing processes in social interaction. *Journal of Personality and Social Psychology*, 36, 1202–12.

Snyder, M., Tanke, E.D. and Berscheid, E. (1997) Social perception and interpersonal behavior: on the self-fulfilling nature of social stereotypes. *Journal of Personality and Social Psychology*, 35, 656–66.

Sorrentino, R.M. and Field, N. (1986) Emergent leadership over time: the functional value of positive motivation. *Journal of Personality and Social Psychology*, 50, 1091–9.

Sorrentino, R.M., King, G. and Leo, G. (1980) The influence of the minority on perception: a note on a possible alternative explanation. *Journal of Experimental Social Psychology*, 16, 293–301.

Spears, R., Lea, M. and Lee, S. (1990) Deindividuation and group polarization in computer-mediated communication. *British Journal of Social Psychology*, 29, 121–34.

Spence, J.T. and Helmreich, R.L. (1978) *Masculinity and Femininity: Their Psychological Dimensions, Correlates and Antecedents*. Austin, TX: University of Texas Press.

Spence, K.W. (1956) *Behavior Theory and Conditioning*. New Haven, CT: Yale University Press.

Stagner, R. and Congdon, C.S. (1955) Another failure to demonstrate displacement of aggression. *Journal of Abnormal and Social Psychology*, 51, 695–6.

Stangor, C. and Ford, T.E. (1992) Accuracy and expectancy-confirming processing orientations and the development of stereotypes and prejudice, pp. 57–89 in Stroebe, W. and Hewstone, M. (eds) *European Review of Social Psychology*, vol. 3. Chichester: Wiley.

Stasser, G. and Stewart, D. (1992) Discovery of hidden profiles by decision-making groups: solving a problem versus making a judgement. *Journal of Personality and Social Psychology*, 63, 426–34.

Stasser, G. and Titus, W. (1985) Pooling of unshared information in group decision making: biased information sampling during group discussion. *Journal of Personality and Social Psychology*, 48, 1467–78.

Stasser, G., Kerr, N.L. and Davis, J.H. (1989a) Influence processes and consensus models in decision-making groups, in Paulus, P. (ed.) *Psychology of Group Influence*, 2nd edn. Hillsdale, NJ: Lawrence Erlbaum.

Stasser, G., Taylor, L.A. and Hanna, C. (1989b) Information sampling in structured and unstructured discussions of three- and six-person groups. *Journal of Personality and Social Psychology*, 157, 67–78.

Stasser, G., Stewart, D.D. and Wittenbaum, G.M. (1995) Expert roles and information exchange during discussion: the importance of knowing who knows what. *Journal of Experimental Social Psychology*, 31, 244–65.

Steele, C.M. and Aronson, J. (1995) Stereotype threat and the intellectual test performance of African Americans. *Journal of Personality and Social Psychology*, 69, 797–811.

Steiner, I.D. (1972) *Group Process and Productivity*. New York: Academic Press.

Steiner, I.D. (1982) Heuristic models of groupthink, in Brandstatter, H., Davis, J.H. and Stocher-Kreichganer, G. (eds) *Contemporary Problems in Group Decision Making*. New York: Academic Press.

Steiner, I.D. (1986) Paradigms and groups, in Berkowitz, L. (ed.) *Advances in Experimental Social Psychology*, vol. 19. London: Academic Press.

400

Stephan, W.G. and Stephan, C.W. (1984) The role of ignorance in intergroup relations, in Miller, N. and Brewer, M.B. (eds) *Groups in Contact: The Psychology of Desegregation.* New York: Academic Press.

Stephan, W. and Stephan, C.W. (1985) Intergroup anxiety. *Journal of Social Issues,* 41, 157–75.

Stephenson, G.M. and Brotherton, C.J. (1975) Social progression and polarization: a study of discussion and negotiation in groups of mining supervisors. *British Journal of Social and Clinical Psychology,* 14, 241–52.

Stephenson, G.M., Clark, N.K. and Wade, G.S. (1986) Meetings make evidence? An experimental study of collaborative and individual recall of a simulated police interrogation. *Journal of Personality and Social Psychology,* 50, 1113–22.

Stevens, S.S. (1957) On the psychophysical law. *Psychological Review,* 64, 153–81.

Stewart, J.K., Yee, M.D. and Brown, R. (1990) Changing social work roles in family centres: a social psychological analysis. *British Journal of Social Work,* 20, 45–64.

Stiles, W.B., Lyall, L.M., Knight, A.P., Ickes, W., Waung, M., Hall, C.L. and Primeau, B.E. (1997) Gender differences in verbal presumptuousness and attentiveness. *Personality and Social Psychology Bulletin,* 23, 759–72.

Stogdill, R.M. (1974) *Handbook of Leadership.* New York: Free Press.

Stoner, J.A.F. (1961) A comparison of individual and group decisions including risk. Unpublished thesis, Massachusetts Institute of Technology, School of Management.

Stoner, J.A.F. (1968) Risky and cautious shifts in group decisions: the influence of widely held values. *Journal of Experimental Social Psychology,* 4, 442–59.

Stroebe, W., Diehl, M. and Abakoumkin, G. (1996) Social compensation and the Köhler effect: towards an explanation of motivation gains in group productivity, pp. 37–65 in Witte, E.H. and Davis, J.H. (eds) *Understanding Group Behaviour,* vol. 2, *Small Group Processes and Interpersonal Relations.* Mahwah, NJ: Lawrence Erlbaum.

Stroop, J.R. (1935) Studies of interference in serial verbal reactions. *Journal of Experimental Psychology,* 18, 643–62.

Strube, M.J. and Garcia, J.E. (1981) A meta-analytic investigation of Fiedler's contingency model of leadership effectiveness. *Psychological Bulletin,* 90, 307–21.

Struch, N. and Schwartz, S.H. (1989) Intergroup aggression: its predictors and distinctness from in-group bias. *Journal of Personality and Social Psychology,* 56, 364–73.

Suls, J. (1986) Comparison processes in relation deprivation: a life-span analysis, in Olson, J.M., Herman, C.P. and Zanna, M.P. (eds) *Relative Deprivation and Social Comparison.* Hillsdale, NJ: Lawrence Erlbaum.

Suls, J.A. and Mullen, B. (1982) From the cradle to the grave: comparison and self-evaluation across the life-span, in Suls, J. (ed.) *Psychological Perspectives on the Self*, vol. 1. London: Lawrence Erlbaum.

Suls, J. and Sanders, G.S. (1982) Self-evaluation through social comparison: a developmental analysis, in Wheeler, L. (ed.) *Review of Personality and Social Psychology*, vol. 3. Beverly Hills, CA: Sage.

Sumner, W.G. (1906) *Folkways*. New York: Ginn.

Szymanski, K. and Harkins, S.G. (1987) Social loafing and self-evaluation with a social standard. *Journal of Personality and Social Psychology*, 53, 891–7.

Tajfel, H. (1959) The anchoring effects of value in a scale of judgements. *British Journal of Psychology*, 50, 294–304.

Tajfel, H. (1969) Social and cultural factors in perception, in Lindzey, G. and Aronson, E. (eds) *Handbook of Social Psychology*, vol. III. Reading, MA: Addison-Wesley.

Tajfel, H. (1972) Experiments in a vacuum, in Israel, J. and Tajfel, H. (eds) *The Context of Social Psychology*. London: Academic Press.

Tajfel, H. (ed.) (1978) *Differentiation between Social Groups: Studies in the Social Psychology of Intergroup Relations*. London: Academic Press.

Tajfel, H. (1981) *Human Groups and Social Categories*. Cambridge: Cambridge University Press.

Tajfel, H. (ed.) (1982a) *Social Identity and Intergroup Relations*. Cambridge: Cambridge University Press.

Tajfel, H. (1982b) Social psychology of intergroup relations. *Annual Review of Psychology*, 33, 1–30.

Tajfel, H. and Turner, J.C. (1986) An integrative theory of social conflict, in Worchel, S. and Austin. W. (eds) *Psychology of Intergroup Relations*. Chicago, IL: Nelson Hall.

Tajfel, H. and Wilkes, A.L. (1963) Classification and quantitative judgement. *British Journal of Psychology*, 54, 101–14.

Tajfel, H., Billig, M.G., Bundy, R.P. and Flament, C. (1971) Social categorization and intergroup behaviour. *European Journal of Social Psychology*, 1, 149–78.

Tanford, S. and Penrod, S. (1984) Social influence model: a formal integration of research on majority and minority influence processes. *Psychological Bulletin*, 95, 189–225.

Taylor, D.W., Berry, P.C. and Block, C.H. (1958) Does group participation when using brainstorming facilitate or inhibit creative thinking? *Administrative Science Quarterly*, 3, 23–47.

Taylor, D.M., Doria, J. and Tyler, J.K. (1983) Group performance and cohesiveness: an attributional analysis. *Journal of Social Psychology*, 119, 187–98.

Taylor, S.E. (1981) A categorization approach for stereotyping, in Hamilton, D.L. (ed.) *Cognitive Processes in Stereotyping and Intergroup Behaviour*. New York: Lawrence Erlbaum.

Taylor, S.E. and Lobel, M. (1989) Social comparison activity under threat: downward evaluation and upward contacts. *Psychological Review*, 96, 569–75.

Taylor, S.E., Fiske, S.T., Etcoff, N.L. and Ruderman, A.J. (1978) Categorical and contextual bases of person memory and stereotyping. *Journal of Personality and Social Psychology*, 36, 778–93.

Teger, A.I. and Pruitt, D.G. (1967) Components of group risk taking. *Journal of Experimental Social Psychology*, 3, 189–205.

Tetlock, P.E., Peterson, R.S., McGuire, C., Chang, S. and Feld, P. (1992) Assessing political group dynamics: a test of the groupthink model. *Journal of Personality and Social Psychology*, 63, 403–25.

Thompson, S.K. (1975) Gender labels and early sex-role development. *Child Development*, 46, 339–47.

Tougas, F. and Veilleux, F. (1988) The influence of identification, collective relative deprivation, and procedure of implementation on women's response to affirmative action: a causal modelling approach. *Canadian Journal of Behavioural Science*, 20, 15–28.

Tougas, F., Beaton, A.M. and Veilleux, F. (1991) Why women approve of affirmative action: the study of a predictive model. *International Journal of Psychology*, 26, 761–76.

Treiman. D.J. and Hartman, H.I. (1981) *Women, Work, and Wages: Equal Pay for Jobs of Equal Value*. Washington, DC: National Academy Press.

Triandis, H.C. (1989) The self and social behavior in different cultural contexts. *Psychological Review*, 96, 506–20.

Tripathi, R.C. and Srivastava, R. (1981) Relative deprivation and intergroup attitudes. *European Journal of Social Psychology*, 11, 313–18.

Triplett, N. (1898) The dynamogenic factors in pacemaking and competition. *American Journal of Psychology*, 9, 507–33.

Trost, M.R., Maass, A. and Kenrick, D.T. (1992) Minority influence: personal relevance biases cognitive processes and reverses private acceptance. *Journal of Experimental Social Psychology*, 28, 234–54.

Turner, J.C. (1978) Social categorization and social discrimination in the minimal group paradigm, in Tajfel, H. (ed.) *Differentiation between Social Groups: Studies in the Social Psychology of Intergroup Relations*. London: Academic Press.

Turner, J.C. (1980) Fairness or discrimination in intergroup behaviour? A reply to Branthwaite, Doyle and Lightbown. *European Journal of Social Psychology*, 10, 131–47.

Turner, J.C. (1981) The experimental social psychology of intergroup behaviour, in Turner, J.C. and Giles, H. (eds) *Intergroup Behaviour*. Oxford: Blackwell.

Turner, J.C. (1982) Towards a cognitive redefinition of the social group, in Tajfel, H. (ed.) *Social Identity and Intergroup Relations*. Cambridge: Cambridge University Press.

Turner, J.C. (1983a) Some comments on . . . 'the measurement of social orientations in the minimal group paradigm'. *European Journal of Social Psychology*, 13, 351–67.

Turner, J.C. (1983b) A second reply to Bornstein, Crum, Wittenbraker, Harring, Insko and Thibaut on the measurement of social orientations. *European Journal of Social Psychology*, 13, 383–7.

Turner, J.C. (1987) The analysis of social influence, in Turner, J.C., Hogg, M.A., Oakes, P.J., Reicher, S.D. and Wetherell, M.S. *Rediscovering the Social Group: A Self-Categorization Theory*. Oxford: Blackwell.

Turner, J.C. (1991) *Social Influence*. Milton Keynes: Open University Press.

Turner, J.C. and Bourhis, R. (1996) Social identity, interdependence, and the social group: a reply, in Robinson, W.P. (ed.) *Social Groups and Identities*. Oxford: Butterworth.

Turner, J.C. and Brown, R.J. (1978) Social status, cognitive alternatives, and intergroup relations, in Tajfel, H. (ed.) *Differentiation between Social Groups: Studies in the Social Psychology of Intergroup Relations*. London: Academic Press.

Turner, J.C. and Giles, H. (eds) (1981) *Intergroup Behaviour*. Oxford: Blackwell.

Turner, J.C., Hogg, M.A., Turner, P.J. and Smith, P.M. (1984) Failure and defeat as determinants of group cohesiveness. *British Journal of Social Psychology*, 23, 97–111.

Turner, J.C., Hogg, M.A., Oakes, P.J., Reicher, S.D. and Wetherell, M.S. (1987) *Rediscovering the Social Group: A Self-Categorization Theory*. Oxford: Blackwell.

Turner, J.C., Wetherell, M.S. and Hogg, M.A. (1989) Referent informational influence and group polarization. *British Journal of Social Psychology*, 28, 135–47.

Turner, M.E., Pratkanis, A.R., Probasco, P. and Leve, C. (1992) Threat cohesion and group effectiveness: testing a social identity maintenance perspective on groupthink. *Journal of Personality and Social Psychology*, 63, 781–96.

Turner, R.H. and Killian, L. (1957) *Collective Behaviour*. Englewood Cliffs, NJ: Prentice Hall.

Tyler, T.R. and Lind, E.A. (1992) A relational model of authority in groups, in Zanna, M. (ed.) *Advances in Experimental Social Psychology*, vol. 25. New York: Academic Press.

Tyler, T.R. and Smith, H.J. (1998) Social justice and social movements, in Gilbert, D.T., Fiske, S.T. and Lindzey, G. (eds) *The Handbook of Social Psychology*, 4th edn. New York: McGraw-Hill.

Urban, L.M. and Miller, N. (1998) A theoretical analysis of crossed categorization effects: a meta-analysis. *Journal of Personality and Social Psychology*, 74, 894–908.

van der Zee, K., Oldersma, F., Buncuk, B.P. and Bos, D.M. (1998) Social comparison preferences among cancer patients as related to neuroticism and social comparison orientation. *Journal of Personality and Social Psychology*, 75, 801–10.

van Gennep, A. (1960) *The Rites of Passage*. Chicago, IL: University of Chicago Press.

van Knippenberg, A. and van Oers, H. (1984) Social identity and equity concerns in intergroup perceptions. *British Journal of Social Psychology*, 23, 351–61.

van Knippenberg, A. and Wilke, H. (1988) Social categorization and attitude change. *European Journal of Social Psychology*, 18, 395–406.

van Maanen, J. (1976) Breaking in: socialization to work, in Dubin, R. (ed.) *Handbook of Work, Organization and Society*. Chicago, IL: Rand McNally.

van Oudenhouven, J.P., Groenewoud, J.T. and Hewstone, M. (1996) Co-operation, ethnic salience and generalization of inter ethnic attitudes. *European Journal of Social Psychology*, 26, 649–62.

Vanbeselaere, N. (1991) The different effects of simple and crossed categorizations; a result of the category differentiation process or differential category salience, in Stroebe, W. and Hewstone, M. (eds) *European Review of Social Psychology*, vol. 2. Chichester: Wiley.

Vanneman, R.D. and Pettigrew, T.F. (1972) Race and relative deprivation in the urban United States. *Race*, 13, 461–86.

Vaughan, G.M. (1964) Ethnic awareness in relation to minority-group membership. *Journal of Genetic Psychology*, 105, 119–30.

Vaught, C. and Smith, D.L. (1980) Incorporation and mechanical solidarity in an underground coal mine. *Sociology of Work and Occupations*, 7, 159–87.

Vecchio, R.P. (1987) Situational leadership theory: an examination of a prescriptive theory. *Journal of Applied Psychology*, 72, 444–51.

Verkuyten, M., Masson, K. and Elffers, H. (1995) Racial categorization and preference among older children in The Netherlands. *European Journal of Social Psychology*, 25, 637–56.

Vinokur, A. and Burnstein, E. (1974) Effects of partially shared persuasive arguments on group-induced shifts: a group problem solving approach. *Journal of Personality and Social Psychology*, 29, 305–15.

Vinokur, A., Burnstein, E., Sechrest, L. and Wortman, P.M. (1985) Group decision making by experts: field study of panels evaluating medical technologies. *Journal of Personality and Social Psychology*, 49, 70–84.

Vivian, J., Hewstone, M. and Brown, R. (1997) Intergroup contact: theoretical and empirical developments, in Ben-Ari, R. and Rich, Y. (eds) *Understanding and Enhancing Education for Diverse Students: An International Perspective.* Ramat Gan: University of Bar Ilan Press.

Vollebergh, W. (1991) *The Limits of Tolerance.* Utrecht: Rigksuniversitait te Utrecht.

Volpato, C., Maass, A., Mucchi-Faina, A. and Vitti, E. (1990) Minority influence and social categorization. *European Journal of Social Psychology*, 20, 119–32.

Vroom, V.H. and Jago, A.G. (1978) On the validity of the Vroom/Yetton model. *Journal of Applied Psychology*, 63, 151–62.

Vroom, V.H. and Jago, A.G. (1988) *The New Leadership: Managing Participation in Organizations.* Englewood Cliffs, NJ: Prentice Hall.

Vroom, V.H. and Yetton, P.W. (1973) *Leadership and Decision Making.* Pittsburgh, PA: University of Pittsburgh Press.

Walker, I. and Mann, L. (1987) Unemployment, relative deprivation, and social protest. *Personality and Social Psychology Bulletin*, 13, 275–83.

Walker, T.G. and Main, E.C. (1973) Choice shifts in political decision making: federal judges and civil liberties cases. *Journal of Applied Social Psychology*, 3, 39–48.

Wallach, M.A., Kogan, N. and Bem, D.J. (1962) Group influence on individual risk taking. *Journal of Abnormal and Social Psychology*, 65, 75–86.

Wanous, J.P. (1977) Organizational entry: newcomers moving from outside to inside. *Psychological Bulletin*, 84, 601–18.

Watson, R.I. (1973) Investigation in deindividuation using a cross-cultural survey technique. *Journal of Personality and Social Psychology*, 25, 342–5.

Welsh Campaign for Civil Liberties (1984) *Striking Back.* Cardiff: Welsh Campaign for Civil Liberties.

West, M.A. and Wallace, M. (1991) Innovation in health care teams. *European Journal of Social Psychology*, 21, 303–15.

Wetherell, M. (1987) Social identity and group polarization, in Turner, J.C., Hogg, M.A., Oakes, P.J., Reicher, S.D. and Wetherell, M.S. *Rediscovering the Social Group: A Self-Categorization Theory.* Oxford: Blackwell.

Wheeler, L. (1966) Motivation as a determinant of upward comparison. *Journal of Experimental Social Psychology*, 1, 27–31.

Wheeler, L., Shaver, K.G., Jones, R.A., Goethals, G.R. and Cooper, J. (1969) Factors determining choice of a comparison other. *Journal of Experimental Social Psychology*, 5, 219–32.

Wheeler, L., Koestner, R. and Diver, R.E. (1982) Related attributes in the choice of comparison others: it's there, but it isn't all there is. *Journal of Experimental Social Psychology*, 18, 489–500.

Whyte, W.F. (1943) *Street Corner Society*, 2nd edn. Chicago, IL: University of Chicago Press.

Whyte, W.H. (1956) *The Organization Man*. New York: Simon & Schuster.

Wilder, D.A. (1984a) Predictions of belief homogeneity and similarity following social categorization. *British Journal of Social Psychology*, 23, 323–33.

Wilder, D.A. (1984b) Intergroup contact: the typical member and the exception to the rule. *Journal of Experimental Social Psychology*, 20, 177–94.

Wilder, D.A. (1990) Some determinants of the persuasive power of ingroups and outgroups: organization of information and attribution of independence. *Journal of Personality and Social Psychology*, 59, 1202–13.

Williams, J.E. and Best, D.L. (1982) *Measuring Sex Stereotypes: A Thirty Nation Study*. Newbury Park, CA: Sage.

Williams, J.E. and Morland, J.K. (1976) *Race, Color and the Young Child*. Chapel Hill, NC: University of North Carolina Press.

Williams, K.D. and Karau, S.J. (1991) Social loafing and social compensation: the effects of expectations of co-worker performance. *Journal of Personality and Social Psychology*, 61, 570–81.

Williams, K.D., Harkins, S. and Latané, B. (1981) Identifiability as a deterrent to social loafing: two cheering experiments. *Journal of Personality and Social Psychology*, 40, 303–11.

Williams, P. (1997) *The Genealogy of Race . . . Towards a Theory of Grace*. London: BBC Publications.

Wills, T.A. (1991) Similarity and self-esteem in downward comparison, in Suls, J. and Wills, T.A. (eds) *Social Comparison: Contemporary Theory and Research*. New York: Hillsdale.

Witte, E. (1989) Köhler rediscovered: the anti-Ringelmann effect. *European Journal of Social Psychology*, 19, 147–54.

Wittenbrink, B., Judd, C.M. and Park, B. (1997) Evidence for racial prejudice at the implicit level and its relationship with questionnaire measures. *Journal of Personality and Social Psychology*, 72, 262–74.

Wolf, S. (1979) Behavioural style and group cohesiveness as sources of minority influence. *European Journal of Social Psychology*, 9, 381–95.

Wolf, S. (1985) Manifest and latent influence of majorities and minorities. *Journal of Personality and Social Psychology*, 48, 899–908.

Wood, J.V., Taylor, S.E. and Lichtman, R.R. (1985) Social comparison in adjustment to breast cancer. *Journal of Personality and Social Psychology*, 49, 1169–83.

407

Wood, W., Lundgren, S., Ouellette, J.A., Busceme, S. and Blackstone, T. (1994) Minority influence: a meta-analytic review of social influence processes. *Psychological Bulletin*, 115, 323–45.

Worchel, S. and Austin, W. (eds) (1986) *The Social Psychology of Intergroup Relations*, 2nd edn. Chicago, IL: Nelson Hall.

Worchel, S. and Norvell, N. (1980) Effect of perceived environmental conditions during cooperation on intergroup attraction. *Journal of Personality and Social Psychology*, 38, 764–72.

Worchel, S., Lind, E.A. and Kaufman, K.H. (1975) Evaluations of group products as a function of expectations of group longevity, outcome of competition and publicity of evaluations. *Journal of Personality and Social Psychology*, 31, 1089–97.

Worchel, S., Andreoli, V.A. and Folger, R. (1977) Intergroup cooperation and intergroup attraction: the effect of previous interaction and outcome of combined effort. *Journal of Experimental Social Psychology*, 13, 131–40.

Worchel, S., Rothgerber, H., Day, E.A., Hart, D. and Butemeyer, J. (1998) Social identity and individual productivity within groups. *British Journal of Social Psychology*, 37, 389–413.

Word, C.O., Zanna, M.P. and Cooper, J. (1974) The non-verbal mediation of self-fulfilling prophecies in interracial interaction. *Journal of Experimental Social Psychology*, 10, 109–20.

Wright, S.C., Taylor, D.M. and Moghaddam, F.M. (1990) Responding to membership in a disadvantaged group: from acceptance to collective protest. *Journal of Personality and Social Psychology*, 58, 994–1003.

Wright, S.C., Aron, A., McLaughlin-Volpe, T. and Ropp, S.H. (1997) The extended contact effect: knowledge of cross-group friendships and prejudice. *Journal of Personality and Social Psychology*, 73, 73–90.

Yee, M.D. and Brown, R. (1992) Self evaluations and intergroup attitudes in children aged three to nine. *Child Development*, 63, 619–29.

Yee, M.D. and Brown, R. (1994) The development of gender differentiation in young children. *British Journal of Social Psychology*, 33, 183–96.

Yuker, H.E. (1955) Group atmosphere and memory. *Journal of Abnormal Social Psychology*, 51, 17–23.

Zaccaro, S.J., Foti, R.J. and Kenny, D.A. (1991) Self-monitoring and trait-based variance in leadership: an investigation of lender flexibility across multiple group situations. *Journal of Applied Psychology*, 76, 308–15.

Zajonc, R.B. (1965) Social facilitation. *Science*, 149, 269–74.

Zajonc, R.B. (1980) Compresence, in Paulus, P.B. (ed.) *Psychology of Group Influence*. New York: Lawrence Erlbaum.

Zander, A. (1972) The purposes of national associations. *Journal of Voluntary Associations*, 1, 20–9.

Zander, A., Stotland, E. and Wolfe, D. (1960) Unity of group, identification with group, and self esteem of members. *Journal of Personality*, 28, 463–78.

Zanna, M.P., Goethals, G.R. and Hill, J.F. (1975) Evaluating a sex related ability: social comparison with similar others and standard setters. *Journal of Experimental Social Psychology*, 11, 86–93.

Zelditch, M. (1956) Role differentiation in the nuclear family, in Parsons, T. and Bales, R.F. (eds) *Family: Socialization and Interaction Process*. Glencoe, MN: Free Press.

Zimbardo, P. (1969) The human choice: individuation, reason and order versus deindividuation, impulse and chaos, in Arnold, W.J. and Levine, D. (eds) *Nebraska Symposium on Motivation*, vol. 17. Lincoln, NB: University of Nebraska Press.

Zuber, J.A., Crott, H.W. and Werner, J. (1992) Choice shift and group polarization: an analysis of the status of arguments and social decision schemes. *Journal of Personality and Social Psychology*, 62, 50–61.

NAME INDEX

410

SUBJECT INDEX